THE
MADMAN
AND THE
BUTCHER

TIM COOK

THE
MADMAN
AND THE
BUTCHER

THE SENSATIONAL
WARS OF
SAM HUGHES AND
GENERAL ARTHUR CURRIE

ALLEN LANE
CANADA

ALLEN LANE CANADA

Published by the Penguin Group

Penguin Group (Canada), 90 Eglinton Avenue East, Suite 700,
Toronto, Ontario, Canada M4P 2Y3 (a division of Pearson Canada Inc.)

Penguin Group (USA) Inc., 375 Hudson Street, New York, New York 10014, U.S.A.
Penguin Books Ltd, 80 Strand, London WC2R 0RL, England
Penguin Ireland, 25 St Stephen's Green, Dublin 2, Ireland (a division of Penguin Books Ltd)
Penguin Group (Australia), 250 Camberwell Road, Camberwell, Victoria 3124, Australia
(a division of Pearson Australia Group Pty Ltd)
Penguin Books India Pvt Ltd, 11 Community Centre, Panchsheel Park, New Delhi – 110 017, India
Penguin Group (NZ), 67 Apollo Drive, Rosedale, North Shore 0745, Auckland, New Zealand
(a division of Pearson New Zealand Ltd)
Penguin Books (South Africa) (Pty) Ltd, 24 Sturdee Avenue, Rosebank, Johannesburg 2196,
South Africa

Penguin Books Ltd, Registered Offices: 80 Strand, London WC2R 0RL, England

First published 2010

1 2 3 4 5 6 7 8 9 10 (RRD)

Manufactured in Canada.

LIBRARY AND ARCHIVES CANADA CATALOGUING IN PUBLICATION

Cook, Tim, 1971–
The madman and the butcher : the sensational wars of Sam Hughes
and General Arthur Currie / Tim Cook.

Includes bibliographical references.
ISBN 978-0-670-06403-8

1. Hughes, Sam, Sir, 1853–1921. 2. Currie, Arthur, Sir, 1875–1933.
3. Currie, Arthur, Sir, 1875–1933—Trials, litigation, etc. 4. Canada.
Canadian Army. Canadian Corps—History. 5. World War, 1914–1918—
Canada. I. Title.

FC556.H84C66 2010   940.400922   C2010-904343-X

Visit the Penguin Group (Canada) website at **www.penguin.ca**

Special and corporate bulk purchase rates available; please see **www.penguin.ca/corporatesales** or call
1-800-810-3104, ext. 2477 or 2474

For Paige, Emma, Chloe,
and Sarah

CONTENTS

CONTENTS

INTRODUCTION

Soldiers of Battle, Men of History

There would be blood. Sir Sam Hughes, the ex-minister of militia and defence, the man who had run Canada's war effort for the first two and a half years of the Great War, was looking to settle old scores and to repay those who he believed had stabbed him in the back.

Sir Sam pulled himself to his feet behind his little wooden desk in the temporary House of Commons, which was now sitting in the castle-like Victoria Museum. Members of Parliament had been meeting in the museum for three years, since the fire of February 1916 had left the magnificent Gothic Revival–style Commons buildings in charred ruins. Now, on March 4, 1919, in the two-storey, semi-circular salon on the third floor of the museum, with an enormous Union Jack reminding all parliamentarians of Canada's enduring allegiance to Crown and Empire, Sir Sam addressed his colleagues and the nation. This was a new session of Parliament, and a time to heal the terrible wounds the country suffered during the Great War that had lurched to a close five months earlier, on November 11, 1918, after four long years of mind-numbing slaughter.

The European powers had been bled white, and Canada had left behind more than 60,000 of its sons and daughters in shallow graves. Another 173,000 Canadians had been wounded. The country was still reeling from these losses and struggling to integrate the waves of returning veterans, including those with broken bodies and shattered minds, back into the fabric of society. But Sir Sam was not a healer; he was not a man to reconcile the nation. He was a warrior, and rumours had abounded for weeks that he would be launching a fierce attack in the House of Commons. But what would he say and whom would he target?

Hughes was one of the most experienced members of the House, having won his first election in 1892. He had never lost since, winning seven elections in three decades. This seasoned politician was also one of the most feared members of Parliament, a scrapper who laid into his opponents pitilessly, employing ruthless tactics, exploiting weaknesses, and stretching the truth to fit his particular needs. Dangerous to friend and foe, he had survived a career of attacking his lifelong enemies, the Liberals, as well as, on occasion, his own party in a seemingly maverick-driven madness. Such was his fame and infamy that, next to Prime Minister Sir Robert Borden and the recently deceased Sir Wilfrid Laurier, Sir Sam Hughes was probably the best-known member of Parliament of his day.

"The man is five feet, eight inches tall, of a square sturdy build, a thick neck, strong jaw and firm lipless mouth. His features suggest the Roman Caesars. His eyes are grey beneath beetling brows and his hair, which is cropped close, silver white. His voice is rough and imperious; when he smiles he shows small regular teeth. And with the smile, his expression undergoes a marked change, he grows benignant, even humorous, but at the same time more vulgar. His attitudes are ungainly and heavy."[1] So wrote man of letters Beckles Willson of Sir Sam during the Great War, then in his early sixties, and known throughout the land and in Britain as Canada's warlord.

Hughes had led Canada's war effort in August 1914 and earned a reputation as a whirlwind of activity for raising an enormous army and putting the nation on a war footing. But after two and a half years of uninterrupted service, Hughes's erratic behaviour, his inability to delegate authority, and his failure to evolve with Canada's expanding war effort—which demanded careful planning instead of improvisation, experts instead of amateurs, and professionals instead of political hacks—had resulted in his removal as minister of militia and defence in November 1916.

He would lead no more. It was a blow to a man who revelled in the spotlight, believed fervently in his own abilities, and sniffed that no one could replace him. Despite his absurd ego, he cared deeply for the soldiers overseas, who he believed were ill-used by his many political enemies and by the British. Hughes had a long hatred for British generals, which stretched back to the late nineteenth century and was cultivated by running feuds with imperial professional soldiers who had occupied the highest military appointments in the Dominion. And while he railed against the imperials, both politicians and generals, he had also made many enemies among Canadian officers, especially those who he felt had turned their backs on him after his removal from office.

One of the worst offenders, in his mind, was Lieutenant-General Sir Arthur Currie, who had been Canada's senior battlefield commander since June 1917. Currie was celebrated overseas by Canadian and British senior officers for his careful attention to detail in planning operations, his moral bravery in arguing freely with his superiors, and his demands that overwhelming shellfire support his soldiers at the sharp end. Sir Sam knew little of this. He had no way of gauging how effective Currie had been on the battlefield, aware only that he'd been the commanding general responsible when countless Canadians were killed and wounded at battles like Hill 70, Passchendaele, and during the war-ending Hundred Days campaign. Currie's Canadian Corps had achieved victory after victory, but the cost of success had been high. Who was to blame? demanded Hughes. Who had killed off his boys? Sir Sam planned to answer these

3

festering questions on March 4, 1919, almost five months after the end of the Great War.

At sixty-six, the once robust and bull-like Sir Sam was showing the effects of prolonged illness. He had given his best years to the war and, like so many Canadians, had been consumed by it. Yet Hughes was in his element in the fierce battleground of the House. He began his tirade on March 4 by condemning the government of the day, a coalition headed by Sir Robert Borden but now known as Unionists, the Conservative Party having poached nearly two dozen Liberal members who had supported conscription in the 1917 election to form a "win-the-war" party. As usual, Hughes attacked the cost of the war and some of his long-standing enemies, but on that day Sir Sam Hughes had a new target: Sir Arthur Currie.

Hughes began by picking at lightly healed scabs, bringing the House's attention to the terrible casualties of the Hundred Days campaign, in which the Canadian Corps had won a series of important victories in the last ninety-six days of the war, but at the cost of nearly 46,000 killed and maimed Canadians. The House shifted uncomfortably. Where was the ex-minister going with this? And then Hughes attacked, his voice rising sharply as it sometimes did when he was excited. He focused on the last day of the war, November 11, lashing out at the commander of the Canadian forces, Arthur Currie, unnamed by Hughes but known to all. Currie was, Hughes declared, guilty of "needlessly sacrificing the lives of Canadian soldiers." Any general who ordered an attack on Mons on the last day of the war should be "tried summarily by court martial and punished so far as the law would allow." Hughes finished by twisting the dagger, telling his fellow MPs, "You cannot find one Canadian soldier returning from France who will not curse the name of the officer who ordered the attack on Mons."[2]

The House of Commons was shocked into silence. Here was one of the most knowledgeable politicians in the land, who had been a soldier in one form or another for fifty years, who wore the lieutenant general's uniform, and who had virtually run Canada's war effort during the first two and a half years of the war, calling the Dominion's victorious battle-field commander a wanton butcher. There were no cheers for Hughes. But nor were there cries of opposition. The silence was broken only by muffled coughs and chairs scraping on the wood. It would be two weeks before a member of Parliament stood up to respond to the ex-minister's claims. By then, the accusations had filtered across the country. Veterans and newspapers condemned Hughes, but for those Canadians who had lost a loved one or who had simply wondered how the war overseas could have gone on for almost five years in a blood fury of killing, perhaps here was an answer. Was not Sir Arthur Currie, as commander, responsible for his soldiers? Did he not share some of the blame for the grave losses? Victory, yes, but at what cost?

The Canadians had played a key part in that triumph on the Western Front, from the first major battle of April 1915, when the Canadians withstood the Germans' lung-searing chlorine gas, to the titanic 1916 battles of Mount Sorrel and the Somme, the April 1917 capture of the seemingly impregnable Vimy Ridge, the victories at Hill 70 and Passchendaele that same year, and, finally, the Hundred Days campaign of 1918. During these hard battles the Canadians had lived up to and reinforced their reputation as shock troops.[3] Thrown against the most heavily fortified enemy positions, the Corps had proven to be an elite fighting formation that distinguished itself time and time again. While much of the nation was firmly committed to victory through performing war work, producing food for the Allied armies, and engaging in stag-gering levels of volunteer, unpaid patriotic contributions, it was the Canadian Corps that was the most recognized symbol of the nation's war effort. The Corps had allowed the young Dominion to step out onto the world stage, and Prime Minister Borden would use the sacrifice of his soldiers to demand greater autonomy from Britain for Canada—then still

5

a colony of the British Empire, with London controlling foreign policy and even having the right to disavow Canadian legislation.

Entwined with the excellent reputation of the Canadian Corps was that of its third and final commander, Sir Arthur Currie. Currie was a commanding figure who stood six foot three, wore his hair short, and had a smooth, roundish face. One of Currie's close friends observed that he was always "struck with his fine blue eyes and direct demeanour … but when a man made any attempt to overstep the bounds with him there would be a warning droop to the lids and his eyes would become narrow, and cold grey steel in colour."[4] The general was not a talker by nature, and did not feel the need to own the room by telling stories and anecdotes. He was more comfortable simply sitting back and observing. Sir Arthur followed conversations rather than leading them, laughing freely at dirty jokes and dry witticisms when he was at ease in the company of his fellow officers.[5]

His height let him look down on most men, although since his bean-pole youth he had fleshed out considerably, and many described him as fat during the war years, when he put on weight from stress and inactivity. He gave the impression, wrote one British general, of "great physical strength; physically a 'strong man' rather than an athlete, with massive sloping shoulders and rather awkward legs, slow in movement."[6] Though Currie slimmed down after the war, during his service on the Western Front he was well over 250 pounds. His pear-shaped body worked against him: his uniform never seemed to fit him and rode up considerably on his rotund belly, giving him an unattractive, blimpish appearance. His long, fleshy jowls left an impression on those who met him, partly because they did not seem to fit a man in his early forties or in his position. Currie looked like a corpulent civilian banker stuffed into a general's breeches and jacket.

Minister of Militia Sam Hughes had given Currie one of the prestigious brigade commands in August 1914, but Currie was rightly unsure of himself in such a role, having never commanded more than 400 men in peacetime and now being asked to lead ten times that number. But he soon distinguished himself. Currie was widely regarded as Canada's best infantry brigadier, and then its best divisional commander. He was not brilliant, but brilliance had little place on the stalemated Western Front, where firepower drove soldiers into the trenches and most operations were reduced to frontal assaults. The hard-working Currie listened intently, questioned deeply, and encouraged discussion and dissent among his junior officers. Unlike many British generals, Currie never stood on his rank, and as brigadier, then divisional commander, and finally, in June 1917, corps commander, he ran his headquarters less as an autocratic ruler than as the leader of a large company.

Currie was a contradiction: he had little or no rapport with the common man, but was loved by his officers. He fought hard to reduce casualties by ensuring overwhelming artillery or logistical support for his troops, but he was willing to accept casualties in exchange for battlefield success. Like all good generals, Currie gambled in the search for victory, but only when he had ensured that the odds were, as much as possible, in his favour. He usually succeeded, but as a result of thorough planning and hard work, which was not always apparent to outsiders or to his soldiers. He was a militia man who rose to nearly the top of the military profession in the British army, where backing, lineage, and bearing, all of which Currie lacked, were virtually prerequisites for the senior ranks. Currie was also morally brave, willing to stare down his superiors and argue forcefully on behalf of his troops at the front. He was one of the finest generals of the war, although he neither looked the part nor had the devotion of the rank and file. No wonder he was an open target for his critics, who painted him in black-and-white strokes, focusing on his apparent limitations rather than his proven abilities.

Both Currie and Hughes were strong, self-made men who had found success in the ranks of Canada's non-professional army, the militia. They came from poor backgrounds in rural communities, and were able to carve out better lives. They believed in themselves even though they endured agonizing failures before the war. Imperialists at heart, both men found during the course of the war that they increasingly embraced an emerging sense of Canadian nationalism. While neither man sought to break from the British Empire, both had witnessed Britain's heavy reliance on its dominions for victory. After passing through four years of war, these knights of the Empire, Sir Sam and Sir Arthur, believed that Canada needed to embrace its destiny as a full-fledged nation.

Few would have predicted such fame and success for either man, and if not for the Great War, history might remember Sam Hughes for little other than his achievements as minister of militia and defence from 1911 to 1914, and possibly for his wild antics. By 1914 the Conservative Party seemed to be doing its best to hand back the reins of power to the Liberals after three short years of undistinguished government. Without the war, Laurier's Liberals would likely have soon returned to power, and Hughes would have become an amusing footnote to history. And if Hughes would have been remembered as little more than a bit player, Arthur Currie would surely have been forgotten. In 1914 his career was in turmoil and his finances in ruin, and he was looking for a way out of the militia. All of that changed with the outbreak of war. While Hughes and Currie had known each other in the first decade of the twentieth century, and had respected each other, their lives would intersect more frequently during the war, and their relationship would soon deteriorate into one of open conflict. The Great War shaped their lives, made or broke their reputations, and ultimately sent each to an early grave.

When the last shots of the Great War were fired on November 11, 1918, a new war of reputations erupted, with the embers of the shooting war igniting the flames of this new conflict. By war's end, both Currie and Hughes knew they were destined to become men of history, whose actions and deeds would be recorded, studied, and dissected for centuries to come. While Canadians are generally wary of labelling their own as heroes or villains, leaving them instead in some kind of historical purgatory shaped by indifference or amnesia, over time Currie has indeed come to be viewed as a national hero, while Hughes has been reduced to a buffoon-like clown at best, a sociopath at worst.

"A corpse is open to all comers," remarked Jean-Paul Sartre on the work of biographers.[7] We can do justice to the dead only by telling the truth, and this book aims to place these two Canadians within the context of their time, avoiding hagiography or caricature, which fall short of representing the complexity of these two accomplished and flawed men. *The Madman and the Butcher* follows the lives of Sir Sam and Sir Arthur, but it is less a womb-to-tombstone analysis than one that emphasizes the intersections and conflicts that formed their war of reputations. Both Hughes and Currie seem not to have relied heavily on their families; or perhaps they did, but they were not the type of men to commit such feelings to paper, and little correspondence has survived that sheds light on their familial relations. Hughes was more than twenty years Currie's senior, and so the first chapters that follow are devoted more to him, as his personal history, triumphs, and defeats before the war shaped his wartime actions and outlook. Currie was a prewar nobody, but he would become one of the nation's best-known figures, although not one who escaped with his reputation untarnished. Their fierce engagements after 1914—the central focus of this book—would culminate in 1928 in one of Canada's most famous trials, when Sir Arthur Currie sought to permanently exorcise the ghost of Sir Sam Hughes.

Throughout history, wars have been fought on the battlefields, over the oceans, and in the air. Because war is so intense, differences among leaders and populations over war's aims, policies, implementations, outcomes, and possible alternatives are highly charged and very emotional. With the stakes so high, praise is sought, blame ascribed, and justification—of self or others—rendered, during and especially after the war. The war of reputations is the fighting and refighting of the war, but with new weapons and champions. It occurs in speeches, newspapers, public opinion, and memorials, and more privately in letters, diaries, and shared conversations, and can be almost as vicious as the actual armed conflict.

This war is not just a curious sideshow after the main event. Through the lens of this postwar battle we can discern a fresh perspective on the war itself and on those who took part in it. No less a war leader than Winston Churchill wrote, "History will be kind on me for I propose to write it."[8] The battle for control of the past, and for the protection or destruction of reputations, is at the heart of this book, and of the clash between the madman and the butcher over the memory of Canada's Great War.

CHAPTER 1

A Fighter

SAM HUGHES, 1853–1900

The burly Sam Hughes liked to fight. And he generally gave as good as he got. In January 1894, already a Conservative member of Parliament for over two years and a militia officer for longer than two decades, he was involved in one of his multiple battles with Liberal opponents. While he was usually engaged in a series of protracted arguments through his paper, the *Warder*, of which he was owner and publishing editor in Lindsay, Ontario, this one had heated up. His political rival, a man named Richard Kylie, a forty-three-year-old Roman Catholic blacksmith in Lindsay, needled Hughes mercilessly to the point where he challenged Kylie to a fist fight. They took it to the middle of Lindsay's main street in the dead of winter, snow covering the rough road while a crowd of onlookers cheered and jeered to see their MP raise his fists. The brawl did not last long. The blacksmith smashed Hughes in the face, driving him to the ground, and then pummelled him with sledgehammer blows while Hughes scuttled, rolled, and turtled in the mush to avoid the worst of the beating. When the blacksmith was pulled off the bloodied Hughes, some hooted their approval, while Sam's supporters slunk away.

To add insult to considerable injury, Kylie had Hughes arrested for assault, and he was charged and convicted. A mortified Hughes had to pay a fine and live with the infamy. His enemies hounded him. The local newspapers chortled away, with the Grit-supporting *Canadian Post* taunting: "Major Hughes after first insulting and then striking a civilian several pounds lighter than himself, showed the white feather so conspicuously that if he were in the regular army he would probably be cashiered for conduct unbecoming an officer or a gentleman."[1] Hughes used his own paper to defend himself, noting lamely that he had just recovered from the flu and that he had been constrained by his overcoat during the battle royal. The fight did not fade from public memory, but it was remarkable that Hughes, humiliated and beaten, continued his antagonistic ways, almost as if nothing had happened. Rural Lindsay, Ontario, at the turn of the century was the rough frontier still, and a place where political opponents attacked and counterattacked with words, and sometimes fists.[2] It was where Sam Hughes was bred, and where he learned to fight any and all who stood in his way.

He was Sam Hughes, not Samuel and certainly not Sammy. Somehow "Sam" seemed right for the man. Sam Hughes was born on January 8, 1853, in Durham County, then known as Canada West (now Ontario). He remained deeply associated with the province all his life. Raised in a farming community, he was the third of four boys and had seven sisters. As in so many small Canadian towns, the men and women of these rural areas carved out a hardscrabble living from the harsh winters and sweltering summers.

Old country immigrants had settled Durham County: English, French, Scots, and Irish, as well as some French Canadians. Sam's family was fiercely Protestant and linked to the Orange Order. Like much of rural Ontario, the community was often split by sectarian and religious bigotry. Young Sam was a product of his environment, and took to his intolerances of Roman Catholics and French Canadians with vigour. But he was not simply a country hick. While neither of Sam's parents—Caroline or John—was a book-learner, the Hughes clan were encouraged to reach beyond their frontier existence. Both parents impressed on their children the value of a formal education. Important, too, was imagination, and young Sam's fertile mind drew him back to his martial ancestry. Both of his grandfathers had fought in the empire-changing Battle of Waterloo in 1815, one on each side with Wellington and Napoleon.[3] Hughes admitted toward the end of his life, "Among my earliest memories were the stories repeated by my parents and others of those two old veterans, and let me frankly confess, they gave not only an inspiration but an education throughout my whole life."[4]

It probably surprised few that Hughes entered the militia at the age of twelve, serving with the local 45th Battalion. The militia was the backbone of Canada's defence. Although permanent British troops were the thin red line that had historically held back the American Republican hordes, and that would garrison Canada until most were pulled out in 1871, it was the citizen-soldiers of the country who banded together in communities across the Dominion to form militia units that acted as the secondary but weightier line of defence. Opponents of the militia derided the local units as little more than a social club for men (and boys): a chance to get away, march, and target shoot before washing away their thirst and roughhousing in a laddish, even loutish manner. Few denied that the militia allowed for some excitement compared to the ordinarily drab days in rural Canada. Supporters rightly noted that although the militia might have been impoverished, it played an important role not only in defence but also as an aid to the civil power—usually in putting down strikes—and that it fostered a martial spirit in young men and a positive sense of Empire and country.

Even before Sam had sprouted his first facial hair, officers could see that he would grow into a robust man. Years of work on the farm, combined with a life spent outdoors and engaged in any sport he could play, had already transformed him into a burly lad. Sam had brains, too. His sharp wit, friendly nature, and book smarts had impressed his instructors in the drill halls and the classroom. But his first militia camp revealed that the mixing of boys and men was not always easy. Sam came from an uncompromising temperance family and never drank alcohol, but his sergeant called all the men forward the first night to initiate them with a bottle of whisky. "I saw his eye rested on me and learned afterwards that he boasted how he would comb my feathers," recounted Sam Hughes. "When the bottle reached me, I simply passed it on. He let out a yell and ordered me to drink. I thanked him, stating I never drank. He then attempted to force it down my throat, cut my face and lips and half choked me. I struggled free, grabbed his own short sergeant's rifle and struck him along by the ear. When he recovered there was no more talk of forcing me to drink. I had meantime fixed the bayonet and warned him."[5] Sam was a fighter and remained a lifelong opponent of alcohol—an oddity in the militia, where drink greased most actions and events.

In 1866, at the age of thirteen, the young Hughes defended his country against Fenian raids from Irish-American Civil War veterans. The Fenians raided north in the absurd hope of overrunning what would become the Dominion of Canada in the next year, and then ransoming it back to Great Britain in order to free Ireland.[6] These nineteenth-century terrorists scored one significant victory against Canadian militia units, but were soon shattered as a force, defeated in several battles, and largely destroyed when American authorities arrested their leaders as they crossed the border back to the United States. Although Hughes did not fire a shot in anger, he believed rightly that he had done his duty, as he had mustered out with his father and brothers, and could feel superior to those townsfolk who were furiously burying their silverware and making obsequious plans to greet their new occupiers.

Sam would join the ranks of teachers at age sixteen, an age not as shocking then as it might be today. Still, the job required a firm belief in oneself and an ability to master multiple tasks, since teachers were required to juggle students from half a dozen or more grade levels and instruct in all or most subjects. Sam was restless, though, and for several years he bounced between schools in the region and worked on the railway. At age twenty he married one of his former students, Caroline Preston, but was widowed within a year. For a man of energy and drive, there seemed to be no way forward out of the dullness of small-town Ontario. Another marriage soon followed, this one to Mary Burk, who came from a good farming family and whose father was a Liberal member of Parliament. It was clearly a strong relationship, and had to be, considering Sam's unrestrained hatred for anything Liberal. The couple went to big-city Toronto to find their fortune. More uncertainty followed as Hughes articled for a year and then dropped it, not finding the legal profession to his liking or temperament.[7]

The dispirited Sam went back to teaching, and, assisted by his older brother Dr. James L. Hughes, who was a well-regarded school principal, he eventually found a job at the prestigious Toronto Collegiate Institute (now Jarvis Collegiate). "His classes were a blessed relief after the humdrum of orthodox classrooms," remembered one former student.[8] Original and erratic, and with an odd habit of chewing chalk during his classes, Hughes often sought controversy among his students, goading them on with absurd or inflammatory statements in the hope that they would contradict him, thereby finding their own voice. He cultivated creative thinking. "My bearing towards the student was always that of an equal, a companion," wrote Hughes. "I participated in their games, taught them military drill and callisthenics outside of school hours.... There was never any trouble about discipline."[9] He also took part-time courses in history and modern languages at the University of Toronto, and earned a provincial school-inspector's certificate.[10]

While he was comfortable in the classroom, Sam's heart seemed to be out on the pitch. Despite periodic flare-ups of a childhood knee injury that had almost required amputation of his leg, the square-jawed and broad-shouldered Hughes was a champion runner and a terror on the lacrosse field. He played on a Toronto championship lacrosse team and was known for delivering devastating checks against his opponents, occasionally sending them through the wooded boards and fences that cordoned off the field.[11] Sam played to win.

At age thirty-three Hughes quit being a teacher. He pulled together his meagre resources and bought the *Warder*, the local Conservative paper in Victoria County, which had Lindsay at its centre. Victoria County was divided electorally into North and South Victoria, and although Sam lived in the south, it was in the north where, according to his grandson, "he preached his political beliefs and became a familiar figure on platforms and at social gatherings."[12]

Small and large papers across the country were rigorously partisan for either the Conservatives or Liberals, the two leading parties. Hughes was publisher, editor, and lead writer of the *Warder*. He used his paper as a weapon and attacked all who crossed his path: Catholics first, Liberals and anti-militia opponents next, and anyone or anything else that angered or concerned him after that. In one opinion piece from October 4, 1889, on the perceived Roman Catholic conspiracy in Lindsay and Victoria, Hughes wrote that the "Romanists," as he called them, had a "systematic organization for lying and deception"; their "soul-saving gang" seemed "neither more or less than a disloyal murder-planning society."[13] Future premier of Ontario Leslie Frost, who would also eventually represent many of the constituents of Hughes's former riding at the provincial level, observed that Hughes "used editorial invective hardly believable" to modern readers.[14]

Hughes used his paper to slash and parry, and his bigoted comments were often more fodder in the centuries-long battle between the ultra-Protestant Orange Order, of which he was a member, and Roman Catholics. In the year he bought the paper, he wrote that the deadly smallpox epidemic in Montreal that was laying waste to thousands was caused by a nefarious plot by the Roman Catholic Church. It was shocking stuff, although other members of the Orange Order had said far worse in the past. Perhaps to soften the blow, Hughes recorded that he felt bad for the dying French, who were "very little better than brutes. The poor creatures have for ages been kept in darkness, ignorance and superstitions till now; they are so dulled and blinded as to be insensible to the ordinary feelings of humanity."[15] As an increasingly powerful figure in the Orange community, Sam was no doubt driven by his religious comrades to express intolerant feelings against French Canadians and Catholics, and while some of his inflammatory opinions may have been exaggerated to sell copy, he truly believed there was a backwardness to Quebec. "I neither asked for nor gave any quarter in dealing with Rome [Catholics and Quebec]," snarled an obstinate Hughes toward the end of his life.[16]

Hughes was sued for slander; someone tried to burn down his printing press; and anonymous assassins shot at him on occasion.[17] Hughes's sentiments were not too shocking for late-nineteenth-century rural Ontario, but the burning and assassination attempts reveal that he was a figure who, to say the least, excited opposition and polarized debate beyond the normal level. Admired by his supporters, who rallied behind him with each attack and lawsuit—during one of which he defended himself brilliantly—Hughes was just as firmly despised by his enemies.[18] Throughout the turmoil, Hughes embraced his role as pundit. In these hard years, Sam drew his battle lines between French and English, Roman Catholics and Orangeism, Liberals and Tories, temperance and abstinence, and duty and cowardice. For Hughes, there was never any middle ground.

By 1891 Hughes was ready to run for a federal seat in Parliament after the local incumbent had died in harness. Sir John A. Macdonald, who had been prime minister for all of Canada's existence except from 1873 to 1878, was now old and in declining health. He was taking his party into his last election. Hughes saw his chance with the Old Chief leading the party. While he had little money for an elaborate campaign, Sam had his newspaper, his Tory grassroots connections, and the support of the influential Orange Lodge.[19]

Hughes was a product of the late nineteenth century. He espoused the values of hard work, strength, and manliness. Sam was not simply an editor; he founded the Victoria County Rifle Association and became a member of the Lindsay Board of Trade, the Freemasons, the Oddfellows, and of course the Orange Order. Here was a man who was profoundly Canadian, but also an imperialist. He was a champion of imperial federation, which in his particular version—and that of many other Canadians—saw the Dominion contributing soldiers to support the Empire, and in return emerging with a stronger sense of Canadian identity and a chance for the young nation to be recognized internationally. Imperialism was a way for Canadians like Hughes to promote nationalism.[20] Sam Hughes would doubtless have agreed with the great Canadian humorist Stephen Leacock, who thundered in the first decade of the twentieth century, "I am an Imperialist because I will not be a Colonial."[21]

Good-looking Sam remained a bull-like figure throughout his life. Like most men of the late nineteenth century, he wore a thick moustache, and with his close-cropped army hair, square jaw, and fierce blue eyes tinged with grey, he made a striking impact. He laughed freely and loudly, and was good company, telling jokes and offering acerbic accounts and barbs. Sam was a man of his own convictions, and seems to have found or sought little counsel in others. He was regarded widely as witty and intelligent, and had even invented a contraption for ventilating railway cars. Like the successful politicians of his time (and since), he had a prodigious memory, and could meet a man for a few minutes and recall the event years later. It was an impressive mind trick, although he was no doubt able to bluff his way sometimes by relying on his gruff manner. Hughes's memory was not clouded by drink or tobacco: he remained a clean-living temperance advocate. No demon alcohol for him, but he had more than a little of the devil in him without any assistance. Sam, his face ruddy from the force of his words, gave powerful stump speeches, of which, during elections, he could cram a dozen or more over the course of a day in multiple sites. His talks reverberated with confidence, were delivered in a booming voice, with no little profanity, and were always littered with local stories, rumours, and gossip. Sam had the common touch and he campaigned on the strength of his character, promises to workers of better times under the Conservatives' National Policy, and loyalty to the Empire. He was smart, but no intellectual, and cared not for the nuances of arguments. When he started talking, he crashed forward, attacking, jostling, and always hammering away, accusations flying during the frothing fray. Sam was a man of action. Modern politicians would note how he stayed "on message"; but in fact he lived by his message, refusing to compromise or shape it to meet the needs of others.

In the 1891 election, Hughes ran a strong campaign. He had been challenged hard for the Tory nomination and won, but he lost the election in a tight race to the incumbent Liberal holding the Victoria North seat. The margin of victory was only 202 votes.[22] It was a hard-fought defeat and it left Sam with heavy debts. But Hughes refused to quit. He never accepted defeat gracefully or graciously. In fact, almost immediately after his electoral defeat, he began to compile evidence of corruption in his Liberal opponent's campaign. It is generally accepted that most campaigns in the late nineteenth century were corrupt, with candidates engaging in vote-buying and a host of black-bag dirty tricks. But Jack Barron, the victorious Grit, seemed especially egregious in this regard, and was less successful than many in hiding the proof. Backed by Tory supporters, Hughes gathered evidence and presented it before two justices of the Queen's Bench who had come to Lindsay to hear the case. To the surprise of almost everyone—except Hughes—he won.

A new run-off election was called, and the reinvigorated Hughes worked his way through back roads to reach the isolated settlements where he roared and ranted, pledged support and offered patronage-laden gifts, and then moved on to the next site. He was often a solitary figure on a horse, passing the night in settlers' houses or cabins, more than once on the floor in front of a stove or near the dying embers of a fire. Through his energy and his volunteers, he added several hundred names to the voters' lists as he travelled across his ward over and over again. His opponents tried to bribe him to quit the campaign, but he refused—twice—lustily using the story for fodder about his corrupt opponent. On election night, February 11, 1892, the challenger was crowned the victor.

Hughes joined a creaky ship in Ottawa. Its great leader, Sir John A. Macdonald, had died in June 1891, within months of his last victory—a blow to the Conservatives and the country. The survivors stumbled on in a daze, with four caretaker prime ministers stepping in over the next six years in the hope of recapturing Sir John A.'s magic. But the dispirited and decrepit Conservatives had the appearance and tenor of a party shuffling off to a funeral.

As a junior member—the most junior member of the entire House— Hughes might have been expected to sit quietly on his backbench seat and learn the parliamentary process. But he remained bombastic, and while he had few official duties, he spoke freely in the House and in special committees to which he was appointed, or that he simply attended. Within a few years, one gushy account in a Toronto newspaper described him: "Sam Hughes is not only nice looking but one of the nicest members of the Commons. He is looked upon in the House as a clever young politician."[23] Clever he was, as well as persuasive. His passions in the House were similar to those in his private life: imperial federation and the militia.

Hughes was a fervent champion of the British Empire, and he lost no opportunity to preach to the converted and agnostic. Several times over the years, Sam raised the possibility of an imperial federation with his fellow parliamentarians, although it rarely went anywhere for fear of alienating Quebec or other resistant Canadians.[24] While Hughes would later be characterized by many as the quintessential Canadian nationalist, he remained fiercely proud of being a British citizen all his life. There was no United Nations or NATO at this time, and Hughes and many Canadians believed that it was the British Empire that stood for justice and fairness in the world, enforcing a broad *Pax Britannica* since 1815 and spreading civilization, Christianity, and good work across the largest empire in world history. While many of Hughes's ideas were impractical—as were those of most of the Canadian imperialists of the time—he pushed for greater integration of British, Canadian, and other Dominion defence forces and even of Parliaments.[25] Imperial unity was an idea that Hughes fully supported and from which he rarely wavered.

Sam's other passion was the militia. "Canada wants no standing army," he had railed while an editor, and he endlessly repeated the message to any and all who would listen.[26] In the House of Commons, Hughes was a member of an informal group known as "the colonels," a "cantankerous lobby" formed of militiamen and parliamentarians (even though Hughes had not yet held the rank of colonel, and would continue as a major until he took over the 45th Battalion, the Victoria Rifles, in 1897). These colonels demanded more money for the militia, and usually at the expense of the permanent force, and they were not above intimidating other members of Parliament.[27] It was hard to oppose a bump in spending when Sam Hughes was glaring at you, along with a few dozen other colonels situated around the House. Having said that, there was not a great amount spent on any kind of defence, but what there was went largely to the militia. For those who supported the notion of the self-made Dominion man, Hughes and his ilk held nationalistic appeal; for those who worried about diverting money away from more important capital projects, such as railways or bridges, or immigration, the militia was a way to have an army on the cheap—and one, if they believed Hughes and his friends, that was better than Canada's weak professional army (which had been established in the early 1870s), more independent in thought, tougher, and more effective in combat.

When the Conservatives were defeated in 1896 by Wilfrid Laurier's Liberals, Hughes kept his seat. He was a formidable foe in opposition, and one who was knowledgeable about matters related to the militia. Although Sam was a deeply partisan player, he often agreed with the government, and was especially supportive of the Liberal minister of militia and defence, Frederick Borden. The minister, a doctor from Nova Scotia and a cousin to the future Conservative leader Robert Borden, sought to reform the military in Canada, and in supporting Minister Borden, Hughes put militia before his party. Over his fifteen years as minister, Borden oversaw the war effort in South Africa, instigated important military reforms, established new organizations such as the service, signals, engineers, and medical corps, and tried to find more funds for the militia. He did it at his own pace and fought battles with successive senior British officers, who commanded the Canadian militia from 1874 to 1904. He often chose patronage and pork-barrel politics over military efficiency, but he was one of Canada's most successful defence ministers.[28]

Borden had a strange ally in Sam Hughes, who generally hated Liberals. The supposedly erratic and irrational Hughes had a cold logic to him. From his days in the rural militia, he knew it needed more money. Hughes offered to work with Borden to improve the militia, much to the dismay of his Tory colleagues, who saw his actions as somewhere between treasonous and insane. Hughes was increasingly called upon and given opportunities by the wily Borden, who could see the advantage of keeping Hughes happy and the Tories off balance, with their chief military critic often siding with the government. Most backbenchers would have been ostracized, maybe even forced out of the party for this type of action; but Hughes was a force among the Tories, especially after the 1896 election decimated their ranks.

Despite Hughes's elevation in status, he was still in financial trouble. His salary as a member of Parliament barely kept him afloat, and he had to rent lodgings in Ottawa while his family kept the home in Lindsay. He sat on a few boards, but he was so desperate for money that in 1899 he sold his beloved *Warder*, which had bled red over the years even as it had remained an influential local voice. But Hughes no longer needed his paper. War was soon to thrust him on the Canadian stage, making him a man recognized across the country, both respected and ridiculed.

In the last year of the nineteenth century, it seemed increasingly certain that the British Empire would be at war: not against its traditional European rival of France, or the new growing power in Germany, but against two small Boer republics in South Africa. Despite a propaganda battle that focused on the repressive regime of the Boers in denying political rights to British settlers, and other alleged abuses, this was a war of imperial design, with the British Empire manipulated—some thought willingly—by powerful British financiers in South Africa, who wanted access to the rich gold and diamond deposits recently discovered in the Boer territories. Few expected the ragged, nondescript Boer farmers to be much of an obstacle for the most powerful empire in the world.

The dignified, urbane, and cautious Prime Minister Sir Wilfrid Laurier, who was knighted in 1897, was opposed to committing Canada to involvement in the war, writing privately to his minister of militia: "We have too much to do in this country to go into Military expenditure."[29] Finances aside, Sir Wilfrid was always aware of the delicate balance involved in governing a country of multiple regions and peoples, and he knew that while the war would be popular among the imperial-minded, it would be abhorred by others, including French Canadians who formed his power base in Quebec. It was not Canada's war, and Laurier hoped to avoid an official commitment of forces by doing little other than publicly murmuring his approval of the righteousness of the Empire's cause.

Sam Hughes, however, desperately wanted this war. He believed in the need for imperial unity and he felt it was time for Canada to flex its martial might. Hughes raged at the country's inertia, fuming that delay was damaging the nation's reputation. On July 13, 1899, he argued in the

House of Commons that the senior Dominion had to send a force of 5,000 men to uphold its honour, and he helpfully offered to command it.[30] Some of the patriotic cheered him on, while others guffawed, questioning how he would raise such a force. However, Sam's hyperbolic talk and imperial gestures attracted the attention of the powerful, too. And they were not amused.

The governor general, Lord Minto, and the British general officer commanding of the Canadian militia (GOC), the prickly General E.T.H. Hutton, wanted Canada to support the Empire, but neither of them wanted Sam Hughes to lead an unofficial expedition.[31] Instead of envisioning a privately raised force, from which the Canadian government could distance itself, the governor general and GOC preferred that Laurier make an official commitment that would set a useful precedent and reinforce the bonds of imperial unity. A private army offered to the cause would have no such significance. Both Minto and Hutton also knew Hughes well, and thought him an irritating, unstable individual. This type of colonial blowhard would only be a hindrance to their delicate manoeuvres to push Laurier to support the war officially. No, the blustering braggart Hughes was not one for delicacy, and would have to be stopped.

Hutton, who seemed cut from the same cloth as Hughes, was intelligent and abrasive, and set on forcing the government's hand in sending an official contingent. He secretly leaked information to sympathetic journalists and officers that Canada could and should offer a military contingent, and that this would be very welcomed by Britain, hoping thereby to embarrass Laurier into action. While Minister of Militia Frederick Borden was an ardent imperialist, he had seen British officers try this in the past and was outraged by the clumsy subterfuge. Hughes did not see himself as a similar intriguer, and his offer revealed no more than a loyalty to Empire, the hope that his militia comrades could live up to his ideals of the Warrior-Canadian, and the opportunity to show off his own military expertise.

Hutton dropped the hammer. The GOC verbally thrashed Hughes for his insubordination and for failing to go through the proper channels of the military hierarchy. The vainglorious Hughes counterattacked fiercely, this time with his MP hat on, accusing Hutton of stifling his support of the Empire in this time of need and his "freedom as a citizen, [his] rights as a soldier and [his] self-respect as a man."[32] The war of words escalated quickly to nearly unprecedented levels of abuse. Governor General Minto would later write of Hughes, "I could not have conceived that any human being would write such vulgar conceited stuff."[33]

Hughes was not used to being reprimanded, and certainly not by British generals of whom he thought little as military commanders and less as men. Hughes unwisely pursued the course of spreading ill will and poisonous words about the GOC, and soon the governor general for good measure, as Minto had now turned on him as well. In one unhinged letter to Hutton, Hughes thundered that the British general represented the worst of British militarism and that the dull-minded imperial regular soldiers were incompetent, and would likely be defeated without the assistance of the Dominion irregular soldiers. For good measure, he finished: "I am desirous of learning where any British officer of note has been promoted to high command on his own merits alone."[34] Even for a man who had already made a career of outbursts and intemperate attacks in writing, this was as close to a career suicide note as has ever been penned in Canadian military history.

Even as Hughes and Hutton took their battle public, much to the detriment of both their reputations, pressure was mounting on the Liberal government to send an official contingent, especially after Great Britain declared war against the Boers on October 11, 1899. Laurier finally folded under the strain of dealing with his party's pro-war supporters, who threatened to bring down his government if he did not relent, and he eventually compromised by offering a volunteer contingent, but one with official status. Hutton intentionally left Sam Hughes off the list of potential officers. The indelicate Sam had not helped himself by replying contemptuously to one of Hutton's letters, asking acidly why he was thought to be incapable of serving alongside British forces: "Could I not retreat or surrender quick enough to the Boers?"[35]

Despite his smugness in taking on the British establishment, the manipulative Hughes had a craven side to him. When he saw that he had lost his chance of going with the official Canadian contingent, he promptly tried to mend fences with Hutton, whom he later labelled a "madman."[36] The GOC would have nothing of it, and had already written a spiteful letter to the War Office to the effect that Hughes should not be allowed into the theatre of battle in any capacity, as his "want of judgment and insubordinate self-assertion would seriously compromise success of Canadians when acting with imperial troops."[37]

Some prominent Canadians, however, thought that Hughes had stood up for Canada's dignity and imperial unity, and that he had been poorly treated by the GOC simply because of a personal grudge. They pushed overtly and covertly for Hughes's inclusion in the expeditionary force. Sympathetic newspapers accused Hutton of being a "temporary tyrant" who tried to "rob him [Hughes] of his right to fight for the Empire."[38] Even Laurier, who might have held a grudge against Sam, wrote to a powerful friend that Hughes faced the "insuperable opposition of Hutton. Hughes sadly in want of money and deserves sympathy."[39] When Minister of Militia Frederick Borden argued for Hughes's inclusion with the force, Hutton was backed into a corner. Hughes kept up the pressure, and twice offered his sobbing contrition to Hutton. The GOC finally relented. Sam would go overseas, but not, in Hutton's words, "in any military capacity whatever, and will, accordingly, not wear uniform on board ship."[40]

This suited Hughes, who, once aboard the ship, promptly ignored the censure. His forbidden uniform was pulled from his trunk and he was soon strutting around as a Canadian militia colonel, barking orders and playing the role he so dearly loved. The indomitable Hughes—the tears long dried on his face—also continued his sniping against Hutton while onboard the ship to South Africa, firing off missives to his friends in Canada, and furthered his literary barrage while in theatre as he cheerfully condemned the British regular troops.

When Hughes arrived in South Africa, he had no place within the 2nd (Special Service) Battalion, Royal Canadian Regiment, the 1,000-strong official contingent authorized by Laurier. Hutton's advance letters to his British comrades also ensured that few wanted the Canadian in their force. But the persuasive Hughes pushed hard and spent two months engaged in a letter-writing campaign, calling in all favours he had built up over years of loyal service to the Empire. While frequently rebuffed, he was undaunted, and by mid-February he had been appointed as a supply and transport officer on the lines of communication. It was an unglamorous job, but essential. The vast, open battlefield required secure lines of communication to enable the transportation of ammunition, food, and supplies, and these were the exposed spots in the British operations, which the quick-moving, flexible Boer commando forces attacked to disrupt the imperial fighting forces.[41]

Even though Hughes had lived with war on his mind for decades, this was his first and only real taste of battle. He rose to the occasion, impressing most of the British officers with whom he interacted, especially as he defended his weak transports innovatively against the mobile Boer forces. Very soon he was promoted to the role of intelligence officer, a dangerous position that required scouting in a vulnerable position ahead of the main British forces—in this case, Lord Roberts's advance northward into Boer territory.[42] Canadian gunner Lieutenant E.W.B. Morrison wrote home in April 1900 that Hughes had "gained credit as an efficient intelligence officer."[43]

In his ranger role, Hughes was frequently involved in skirmishes, ambushes, and stand-up battles. He was audacious and fearless, often putting himself in danger's way by galloping hard to attack stronger Boer forces. In one engagement against the guerrillas, he single-handedly captured eight enemy Boers. This soldier's soldier was "one of the ablest persons I have come across out here," wrote famed journalist Lionel Curtis of Hughes.[44] At the age of forty-seven, nearly ancient among front-line soldiers, Hughes had an easy way with the younger men of his command, sharing food and stories with them as they lived hard when away from the advancing columns. Hughes's men were, according to one journalist, "ready to follow him where they would follow few other men."[45]

At the Battle of Faber's Put at the end of May 1900, Hughes saved a British force that was trapped as a result of its commander's inept decision to encamp below a higher hill that was soon occupied by Boer snipers. When the enemy opened fire, Hughes's quick action of rousing a small contingent of men—some only in underwear or without boots—and riding down the enemy helped to force the Boers to retreat from their strongpoint.[46] While Hughes's British commander—Sir Charles Warren, whose claim to fame before the war was that he served as the former London chief of metropolitan police in the 1880s and failed to catch Jack the Ripper—praised him for his bold action, Sam believed that he had been promised a Victoria Cross for his bravery.[47] He deserved it, or another high gallantry award, as his lightning charge saved dozens of lives. Hughes soaked up the praise and then promptly undermined his chance of receiving a gallantry medal by writing letters to senior British commanders and Canadian friends back home, condemning the incompetence of Warren—the same general whom Hughes needed to recommend to the British War Office that he be recognized with an award. Sam often bit the hand that fed him, and then complained loudly that he was being discriminated against.

Hughes fought two wars at the end of the nineteenth century: one against the Boers, the other against the British. His ammunition included both bullets and broadside letters. Many of the latter contained intemperate and downright offensive remarks about the British. Hughes's letters included self-puffery about his adventures and battlefield successes, which he wrote about, somewhat oddly, in the third person. "It fell to the lot of Hughes to direct the British forces and in each and every instance victory fell to their lot, although the numbers and positions were invariably in favour of the Boers," wrote Hughes of his own exploits.[48] While Sam was indeed a fearless fighter, he was prone to overplaying his hand. Hughes's friends published his letters in newspapers, which brought to him equal parts acclaim and ridicule in Canada, but the letters invariably came to the attention of his enemies, who helpfully passed them along to Hughes's own British commanders in the field.[49] They were not amused. His outraged superiors sent Hughes home in July of 1900, two years before the end of the war. Yet Sam also now had real battlefield experience, which allowed him to speak with even more authority, and made him even harder to live with, as his wild claims and accusations were now fortified by his newly won military reputation.

CHAPTER 2

War Hero and Martial Madman

SAM HUGHES, 1900–1914

S am Hughes returned to Canada a war hero. He bragged and blustered, and talked non-stop about battle on the Veldt: how he had
defeated the Boers at their own type of warfare; how he had taught the
British how to fight; and how he refused to be cowed by General Hutton
and professional soldiers of his ilk. Hughes's battles with the British had
elevated him to the status of a Canadian martyr in the eyes of some
nationalists. His enviable military record stood him in good stead with
his military colleagues, even though the Liberal government had tabled
his correspondence with Hutton, in which Hughes, according to the
Toronto Telegram, "made an ass of himself."[1] Sam's posturing read badly,
but he had always outfought his opponents, refusing to accept defeat,
seemingly unaffected by the relentless blows against his character and the
inquiring questions into his sanity. Normal men would have folded
under such pressure. But not Sam. His was the long-game. And when
Hughes returned from South Africa and surveyed the political landscape

in the late summer of 1900, Hutton was gone, dispatched by a Laurier government tired of his bullying transgressions and transparent machinations. He would not be the last enemy whom Hughes buried.

The vigorous, handsome, and now battle-tested forty-seven-year-old was always at his worst when his prejudices were confirmed. Sam continued to preach the value of the militia, but more of his countrymen were now willing to listen, as something had indeed gone very wrong for the Empire in South Africa, where the outnumbered, unconventional Boer guerrilla force of 60,000, riding ponies and equipped with modern rifles (although often lacking stockpiles of ammunition), had held off British armies almost ten times as large over three long years of battle.[2] The fact that Hughes had done well on the battlefield did not, however, mean that all Canadians, or their units, had succeeded equally. And sometimes Hughes did too well in his stories, with one writer observing that the growing legend of Sam was "a mixture of fact and apocrypha. Hughes was responsible for both."[3]

While engaging in his normal parliamentary duties and easily winning re-election in 1900, Sam Hughes kept up a steady barrage of complaints to the British War Office for more recognition for his wartime service, including a war gratuity. It was rightly owed to him, even if he was not an official soldier. The British War Office denied him the claim, and its unfair action seemed to Hughes another indication of a conspiracy. Hughes's requests for recognition, spurred by his growing frustration and continuing financial woes, turned increasingly hysterical. By 1903, he was demanding a Victoria Cross—the Empire's most coveted and rarely granted gallantry award—for his service against the Boers. A few years later, while the British continued to ignore his missives, he escalated his claim to two Victoria Crosses, which even his friends must have viewed as somewhere to the right of brazen, and coming close to bizarre.[4] Assessments of Hughes by the War Office noted that he was a "little bit mad."[5] That was fairly generous: many felt he was a raving lunatic.

* * *

While Hughes kept up his letter campaign to the British, he still had more than enough invective to direct toward Laurier's Liberals. As the Tory military critic, he probed and cajoled the Liberals to make meaningful reforms and inject more funds into the militia. Laurier might have been joking when he advised one of the British GOCs that he "must not take the militia seriously," as he himself clearly did not, but Hughes would not stand for the disparagement of his life's work.[6] He was a strange critic, however. Sam continued at times to side with the minister of militia, Frederick Borden, who was making significant reforms, adding new service arms such as nurses and the medical corps, and all the while gradually raising funding for the militia. His Tory colleagues could scarcely believe their ears when the fiery Sam Hughes, long a hater of all things Liberal, would compliment the minister on his support of the militia. The Liberals, no less stunned, curried Hughes's favour, while occasionally using his words against the Tories.[7] Hughes seemed unperturbed. Politics, he was sure, would not interfere with the much-needed improvements to the militia.

Hughes may have held back from attacking Minister Borden, who occasionally offered the Tory critic military sinecures, but he showed no restraint in unleashing his venom against the rest of the Liberals. At one point, over a minor incident involving the militia, Hughes accused fisheries minister Sydney Fisher of being an "effeminate ... sissy" who "doesn't know the butt of a gun from its muzzle."[8] In turn, Liberal MPs attacked Hughes and even derided his record in South Africa, with one Liberal smear pamphlet lampooning his exploits: "He captured some Boers and said the South African War was over. But the Boers backed out and the war went on."[9] Others compared him facetiously to Julius Caesar or meanly remarked on his propensity to puff up his own reputation. Such attacks were biting and more than a little ungenerous, especially since Hughes had put himself in harm's way as no other member of Parliament had done. But the House was a hard place with hard men. The already coarsened Hughes thickened his hide under these Liberal blows.

Hughes won his fourth election in 1904, in a bitter contest in his amalgamated riding of North and South Victoria and Haliburton (thereafter known as Victoria County), even as Laurier's Liberals again ran roughshod over the Tories across the nation. The Liberals seemed unstoppable, and even Hughes's party leader, Robert Borden, the staid lawyer from Halifax, had been defeated. It was a humiliating blow for the leader, and while he later won a safe seat, Hughes had been so supportive as to offer his own seat up to the leader. This Borden did not forget, writing to Hughes that it was a "kindness I will always value and appreciate."[10] Hughes was a political survivor and a loyal supporter. In a party of inexperienced and pedestrian MPs, Hughes was, at the very least, better than most, and always, always, unforgettable.

The relationship between Hughes and Borden would be important to both men, especially after the Conservatives took power in 1911. From 1904 to 1911 Borden used Hughes as one of his enforcers in the House. His knowledge of politics and his skill in the attack made him a useful weapon. Hughes became a stronger speaker, and he could ramble on for a half hour or more with only a few notes scribbled on a scrap of paper. His ability to unleash fury at the drop of a hat kept many of the Liberals from interrupting him, and he always had a hidden reserve of statistics or figures that he could toss into the mix, most of which sounded convincing, and few of which could be discounted easily by his opposition. "Sam never talked—he shouted!" wrote one admiring journalist, and that type of aggressiveness, combined with over a decade of experience, made him a force in the House.[11]

In the spring of 1909 a new bugbear emerged in relations between Canada and Britain and between English and French Canadians. The naval debate had started as a low murmur in 1906 when the Royal Navy unveiled a new, powerful battleship, HMS *Dreadnought*. It outclassed all of its opponents in speed and armaments, and most naval experts believed that no other ship in the world could face it. The Royal Navy had pulled off a coup, but it had also started an arms race, primarily with England's new rival, Germany—a race that Britain alone might have trouble winning. The central power of Europe had displaced Britain's traditional enemy, France, with whom Britain had formed agreements and later alliances of mutual military support in 1904 and 1907. Under its unstable yet envious Kaiser Wilhelm II, who had visions of grandeur for himself and his country, Germany wanted to rule the waves and carve out a colonial empire. With the naval arms race soon in full swing, and with the fear that Britain's Royal Navy would be unable to meet its traditional claim of being as strong as its next two rivals combined, panic set in in London. It spread to Ottawa, and many imperially minded Canadians were quick to point out that Canada owed its safety to the Royal Navy. As in South Africa, the Empire was in need. What would the Dominion do?

Hughes was a champion for the imperial cause, demanding that the Dominion support Britain with a cash donation of millions of dollars to help build three new *Dreadnought*-class battleships.[12] Like many Canadian imperialists, Hughes easily squared his ardent support for the Empire with his belief in Canada's growing stature as a nation. The debates rose to hysterical proportions in 1909 and spilled into the next year, with the two parties coming at each other in unrestrained fury, but often split along language, cultural, and regional fault lines.[13]

Canada was a difficult country to govern: if the prime minister gave money to Britain, he would alienate Quebec and some like-minded anti-imperial thinkers in English Canada; if he did not, imperially minded Canadians would crucify him. Laurier tried a middle road: he created a Canadian navy in 1910, rather than contribute cash to Britain or ignore the entire matter. While the new navy would include a plan for a respectable five cruisers and six destroyers, few were satisfied with the compromise. Many French Canadians and other concerned citizens thought it would be so closely linked to the Royal Navy that in the event of any international conflict Canada's warships would be committed to battle, with the Dominion forced to follow. These critics pointed to Laurier's own words: "When England is at war we are at war and liable to attack."[14] In contrast, imperialists derided Laurier's unbuilt fleet, one of them coming up with the sneering phrase that it was little more than "a tin-pot navy."[15] The Empire needed and deserved more; the Conservatives would see to it that Canadians responded with honour. The naval debates would become a divisive issue in the 1911 election, especially in Quebec, where nationalists under Henri Bourassa, a former Liberal member of Parliament and influential editor of *Le Devoir*, railed against Laurier, his one-time mentor and leader. In seeking to bring down the Liberals, Bourassa threw his influence behind the Conservatives. It was a bizarrely short-sighted goal that ultimately delivered Bourassa and his supporters into the arms of a far more imperially minded party, and one that had little under-standing of Quebec. It would not be the last time that Canadian politics made strange bedfellows.

The country was tired of the Liberals by 1911. The party had ruled for a decade and a half, winning four straight national elections, and while Sir Wilfrid remained the shining knight, his colleagues had lost their lustre. The naval question shook Laurier's foundation of support in his home province of Quebec, and in many traditional Liberal strongholds in imperial Ontario. Far more damaging were the Liberal negotiations to open free trade with the United States, which would have potentially enriched many parts of the country, including the newly settled prairies, where Liberals hoped to consolidate their appeal to recent immigrants. The Conservatives would have none of it and fought the Liberals on the issue of loyalty to Empire. "No truck or trade with the Yankees" was the battle cry of Borden's Tories.

Robert Borden had impressed few people when he had been made party leader of the Conservatives in 1901. He did not want the position, and many wondered how the dapper, white-haired lawyer, in whose speeches journalists and party members looked long and hard for any sort of emotion, could oust the elegant, graceful, and much-loved Laurier.

After years of discouragement and defeat, the resolute Borden finally found a wedge issue in the Liberals' sensible plan for a Canadian navy and in free trade with the United States. The Conservatives wrapped themselves in the Union Jack, as Sir John A. Macdonald had done in 1891, and it was the Liberals again who were forced to defend their economic policies, as they had twenty years earlier, against the nefarious charge of treason against the Empire. With protectionist Liberals defecting to the Tory cause, Ontario turned against the Liberals, and much of the rest of the country went with it. After a decade of being a perennial loser, Borden led his Conservatives to victory; they formed the ruling party with 134 seats to the Liberals' 87, and with a strong mandate from the people.

Hughes had easily won his seat again in 1911, and had played a key part in building alliances in Ontario to help defeat the Liberals over the reciprocity issue. He was a Tory veteran who had fought well for the party for almost twenty years. But he was also a maverick who carried considerable political liabilities, especially now that the Conservatives had the added burden of meeting the demands of influential French-Canadian nationalists in a potentially divided caucus. Because of Hughes's links to the Orange Order and his previous anti-Catholic attacks, he was viewed as a harmful, even cancerous, force by most of the Conservative French Canadians. Hughes's frequent outbursts and inability to control his tongue in the House often led to embarrassing exchanges. There were countless examples of such behaviour, but in 1907, in a heated exchange with Laurier, Hughes had accused the government of tailoring immigration to bring in more Catholics at the expense of the honest, English-speaking British and, revealing his true colours, had declared that French priests were a "curse to Canada."[16] Hughes was condemned in Quebec, in the House, and even by his own party leader; he was soon branded in Quebec—not without significant justification—as the "champion of race hatred."[17]

But Hughes had his supporters, and the most important of these was the prime minister. The relationship between Hughes and Borden was a complex one. While they sometimes fell out over issues, especially Borden's plan for reforming patronage, which Hughes believed was the lifeblood of a party wanting to stay in power, the two men had been together for over a decade. And while Borden surrounded himself with more influential men such as A.E. Kemp, George Perley, F.D. Monk, Thomas White, and, later, the powerful, if cutting, orator Arthur Meighen, Hughes brought important rural Ontario support to the cabinet, as well as an influential voice for the Orange Order. The question remained: was he stable enough for a cabinet position? If not, what would happen if the bitter Hughes was left out of the cabinet? The saying "Keep your friends close, but your enemies closer" no doubt came to mind. But was there a similar pithy saying for an unstable megalomaniac, who also happened to be a twenty-year veteran of the House, a war hero, and powerful voice for the militia, rural Ontario, and the Orange Order? If there was, Borden did not know it, and so he worried and consulted colleagues about Sam's suitability, holding off his decision.

Hughes knew that he would have to work to get the portfolio he had long dreamed of—the Department of Militia and Defence. His enemies were strong, but Hughes turned his considerable skills toward rounding up support, even from those who quite literally despised him. He wrote letter after letter to powerful men, asking them to argue on his behalf. In his shotgun approach, he even targeted long-time enemies. Sir James Whitney, the premier of Ontario, could barely stand to be in the same room as the blustery Hughes, writing that he was a man "so filled with abuse and falsehood you would hardly believe it possible that any man of common sense could think as he does."[18] It is doubtful that Hughes got his recommendation, but the request sheds light on Hughes's incredible ability to delude himself into thinking that he was better-liked than he actually was. Hughes continued to plead with Borden and with those to whom the prime minister listened for advice. In his most forceful statement to the prime minister, a petitioning Hughes laid forth his case of long party service, loyalty to Borden, expertise on military matters, and, surprisingly, "tact, firmness and judgement."[19] He was right on most of these counts, although his good judgment might have related more to political issues than to social graces.

In late September 1911, as the new prime minister appointed his cabinet with great deliberation, one minister after another, Hughes waited on tenterhooks. With each man, Borden chewed over possible portfolios, pondering strengths and weaknesses as well as favours owed and promised over the past decade. His last choice was Sam Hughes. In early October, Borden summoned Hughes to Ottawa, where the prime minister interrogated him in a face-to-face meeting about his "erratic temperament and immense vanity."[20] Borden recounted in his memoirs that he lectured Hughes on "his lack of tact and his foolish actions and words on many occasions. He frankly admitted his faults and told me that he realized his impulsiveness but that he would be more discreet in the future." Upon reflection in later years, Borden noted that "discretion did not thereafter prove to be a prominent characteristic."[21] In between sobs of contrition, Hughes must have said the right things, for the prime minister decided that the militia portfolio, which was a second-tier ministry at best, could go to the old stalwart. Sworn in as minister of militia and defence on October 10, the fifty-eight-year-old Hughes had achieved the prize he had sought during nearly a lifetime of work.

Most of Sam's opponents would be surprised to find that he was a very good minister. While he was coarse—often using "violent, profane language," wrote one critic—he needed almost no time to master his portfolio.[22] He had, of course, been studying it for decades, both in Canada and abroad. When Hughes had been one of the select few to represent Canada at Queen Victoria's Diamond Jubilee ceremonies in London in 1897, he had returned home by way of Australia, New Zealand, and Fiji, where he had studied military matters. He was far better travelled and read than almost any other military thinker in Canada, even if he occasionally offered such homilies as "Real civilisation was gained by the

British Bible and the British bayonet."[23] The minister's goal, as he high-lighted in the department's 1911 annual report, was "preparedness for war."[24] Liberal opponents scoffed at the phrase, and wondered with whom Hughes planned to march as to war. The minister would not be deterred.

Hughes stayed true to his ideals, especially in strengthening the militia across the country at the expense of the permanent force. While the militia would be augmented by volunteer citizen-soldiers in times of conflict, in peacetime it would add to the nation's moral fibre and character, while serving members would also be strengthened in body and mind. Hughes had been preaching this for years, and often to the con-verted, who urged him onward in his mission. Sam was never short on military rhetoric, claiming, for example, that "the Canadian militia upbuilds manhood, defends homes and loved ones ... upbuilds youth—mentally, morally, physically; instils the spirit of obedience, discipline, patriotism, veneration and love for principle; preserves the spirit for lib-erty and independence and keeps the old flag flying in the breezes and trains boys to be an asset to the nation."[25] While his beliefs sound curi-ously outdated today, they were in tune with those held by many Canadians at the time. Hughes championed a democratic, voluntary military that would forge strong moral character, especially for young students in the cadet programs.[26] Hughes was no misogynist either, advo-cating military training for women too. The minister remained popular with those across the Dominion who cared about matters of defence.

Sam had a seemingly never-ending well of energy, which he drew upon in public speeches across the country. And whenever he toured, dressed in his militia uniform, he travelled with an entourage of journalists, many of whom wrote breathless accounts of the minister, gleefully capturing his bombastic statements. Hughes was fond of musing about an enor-mous army of Canadian snipers: "Give me one million men who can hit a target at 500 yards and we would not have a foe who could invade our country."[27] He may have been right, but since the militia had never risen above 70,000, he was simply plucking fanciful numbers from his imagination. Furthermore, his idea of an army of snipers was deeply flawed. What of the artillery, the engineers, the medical and logistical units? Hughes's attention was almost always focused on his rifle-firing militiamen; he would leave others to worry about how to feed, clothe, or care for such a force. This was the unglamorous part of war that kept professionally trained staff officers up at night. Sam slept soundly.

It goes without saying that not everyone agreed with Hughes's obsession with building the militia. "Whether as a politician or soldier, Militia advocate or Militia Minister," wrote contemporary journalist and social commentator J. Castell Hopkins, "he had frequently been denounced by political opponents as a militarist and jingoist. His encouragement of the Cadet movement since becoming Minister, his construction of dozens of armouries and drill-halls across the country—which earned him the moniker of 'Drill Hall Sam'—his avowed desire to increase and improve the Militia even if it cost more and more money, had been unpopular with a not inconsiderable school of Canadian thought and with many members of Parliament."[28] The Toronto Weekly Sun warned of Hughes's "military madness." Most Canadians, claimed the paper's editors, "realize that, with no enemy in sight, it is folly to waste time and money in a manner that could be justified only by the existence of a real emergency."[29] Moreover, if soldiers were encouraged to prepare for war, went the fear, such martial actions could actually drag the nation into war.

Hughes thought this perspective was nonsense, as did a not insignificant number of other soldiers and militiamen. Watchers of international affairs studied the naval and land arms races, the increasingly bellicose statements, and the small wars in the Balkan states and rightly predicted that conflict was coming. Even if it was averted, all nations had begun to prepare for the worst scenario. Hughes predicted that within a few years Britain and Germany would be at war, and an unprepared Canada would be vulnerable, or reveal itself to be a Dominion unworthy of nation status if it were unable to support the British Empire in a time of crisis. He was fond of quoting British prime minister William Pitt: "War with all its evils is better than a Peace in which there is nothing but usurpation and wrong."[30] While Hughes took his message across the country, he did not fail to represent himself or his constituents in the House of Commons. His personal railway car transported him back to Ottawa, where he was often forced to vigorously defend his statements against probing Liberal questions. One of the controversial issues discussed in such sessions was the Canadian-made Ross rifle, of which Hughes was the most vocal champion.

The Ross rifle had its origins in the South African War. The Canadian military could not acquire the British-made Lee-Enfield rifle for its troops, as the British army demanded priority of supply. The delays in equipping Canada's military forces were frustrating and embarrassing. The Dominion needed its own rifle. The Liberal government of the day turned to Charles Ross, a Scottish inventor and businessman, and the ninth baronet of Balnagown. But the savvy minister of militia and defence, Frederick Borden, also brought Sam Hughes on board to help secure Conservative endorsement of the Ross. Hughes was an ardent shooting expert and already a leader among the militia, and his career soon became deeply entwined with the rifle that he supported without reservation, even as an increasing number of critics highlighted its flaws. For example, the Ross required constant modifications to account for its many deficiencies, and even then the rifle jammed after rapid fire.

Despite these problems, Hughes was always there to defend "his" rifle in the House and in public, even when militiamen and members of the Royal North West Mounted Police condemned it. Hughes's vigorous and always technically informed assaults on his critics, whether members of the opposition or his own party, were delivered with the authority of a long-time military expert. Using later and much-improved models of the rifle, several Canadian shooting teams won international shooting prizes. So, what, Hughes demanded, was the problem? He was generally met with silence. Whether in opposition or later as minister of militia and defence, Hughes perceived criticisms of the rifle as attacks against his own judgment; in his words, when his enemies condemned the rifle they were in fact really trying to "kill Sam Hughes politically."[31] How the Ross would fare in rough campaigning was unknown, but for many, including its ardent champion, Hughes, the rifle epitomized an emerging industrial maturity and a rising Canadian military nation.

Hughes was deeply partisan in his actions, but he was a product of his times. He had been weaned in the hard House of Commons, where little mercy was extended to the enemy. He was, in the words of historian Desmond Morton, "perhaps the most uninhibited battler the Canadian parliament has ever seen."[32] Forceful, hard-hitting, and reckless—at times, his behaviour was so over the top as to appear clownish. William Lyon Mackenzie King saw him speak on January 27, 1911, and described him as an absurd "opera-bouffe."[33] Sam did not seem to care. He was Tory through and through, once quipping that he would offer a patronage appointment to a Liberal as soon as every last Tory was taken care of. In matters of patronage, his friends and supporters were given little bumps in militia rank or minor scraps from the minister's table. But Hughes was no different from most of his colleagues or the ministers before him.

Even as Hughes drew Liberal fire for his public predictions of coming war and the need to rearm, his influence in cabinet allowed him to double spending on the militia in the years before the war. He used this money to build more than fifty armouries across the country for the ever-expanding cadet and militia units.[34] These armouries were important, in Hughes's mind, for raising the profile of the militia in the surrounding communities, and for reminding Canadians of their important role as citizen-soldiers. It was more than a branding or marketing exercise; "Drill Hall Sam" and like-minded citizens believed that by making the militia a widely visible symbol of loyalty, manhood, and community, units would be fed and sustained by the locals. With some 40,000 cadets and about 60,000 militiamen, Hughes purchased new land for military camps and firing ranges, and large tracts of territory in Gagetown, New Brunswick, and Valcartier, Quebec, both of which remain military training centres for the Canadian forces today. While some of the Tory members felt that Hughes was pushing too hard, most of his colleagues did not object to his efforts to prepare the country for war, many of which were lauded in the papers. And by offering patronage contracts to Conservative-supporting companies, Hughes kept the rank and file of the party happy.

Most of Hughes's actions were popular with the militiamen, although the citizen-soldiers chafed against his temperance stand in the summer training camps. Hughes had long been a champion in the fight against alcohol, and a popular story circulated that when Hughes was commanding officer of the 45th Victoria Regiment, he forced a private who turned up rip-roaring drunk at a 1906 summer training camp to hand in his uniform on the spot and leave the camp only in his underwear.[35] His anti-drink stance had not softened in the intervening years. Concerned officers argued that the removal of wet canteens that served beer would only lead to the smuggling of harder alcohol and to overindulgence. Hughes refused to bend, and did not want the militiamen to emulate the professional soldiers, whom he described as "bar-room loafers."[36] On this subject he was out of step with the militia, and was continually fending off end-runs by officers who tried to find ways to bend the ban. "The Foe of Booze," the militiamen sang about him in a parodied song spun from the English hunting song "John Peel," putting Hughes in the same camp as the Women's Christian Temperance Union. No wonder most soldiers, politicians, and the public could only scratch their heads at the enigma that was Sam.

During his entire tenure as minister, Sam Hughes remained a larger-than-life figure among Canadians. While he attracted admirers from across the country, he was more often a polarizing figure. He had an amazing ability to cultivate enemies, and was despised by the governor general, the Duke of Connaught, who had actively sought to dissuade Borden from appointing Hughes as a minister. The imperious Connaught had risen to the highest military rank in the British army, that of field marshal, and was the third son of Queen Victoria, a godson of the Iron Duke, Lord Wellington, and a stickler for proper etiquette and soldierly discipline. That the pompous field marshal despised the pompous politician comes as no surprise. Connaught undermined Hughes when he could, going so far as to describe him to others as "an impossible fellow … eaten up with conceits and … very ignorant in military matters."[37] Another time, he pulled no punches, calling Hughes a "conceited lunatic."[38] Hughes did nothing to ease Connaught's abrasiveness; in fact, he seemed to do his utmost to get under the old field marshal's skin whenever he could. At one white-tie performance at Ottawa's Russell Theatre in honour of the governor general, Hughes arrived late, made his presence known by talking loudly above others, and, for good measure, flaunted a dark blue suit with a shocking red tie. Sam and the governor general would not be friends.

The British took notice of the cantankerous Canadian minister, lauding his insatiable desire for raising the profile of the militia, while condemning his role in the seemingly slow strangulation of the professionals. When one of the Empire's leading soldiers, Inspector General of Overseas Forces Sir Ian Hamilton, arrived in Canada in the summer of 1913 to assess Canadian military capabilities, a proud Hughes took him on a whirlwind tour across the Dominion. The two men and their entourages, which of course included Sam's customary gaggle of newspapermen, travelled an astounding 22,500 kilometres by rail and inspected 112 militia units, many engaged in training in the summer camps. It was a frenzied pace and even an experienced soldier like Hamilton couldn't help but be impressed. Hughes was on his best behaviour, no doubt proud of his boys. Hamilton privately recorded that Sam Hughes was a "prickly sort of personage to handle," but that he was a "very able man whose ideas on the whole are very sound."[39]

Despite Canada's place in the British Empire and its reliance on Britain for many things military, Sam Hughes told the House of Commons, "I am boss.... So long as I am Minister of Militia, no officer, British or Canadian, is going to arrogate to himself the function of the Minister of the Crown.... I am going to supervise the department and every branch of it."[40] When war broke out the next year, it came as no surprise that Sam Hughes would be the "boss" of the Canadian war effort.

CHAPTER 3

Civilian-Soldier
ARTHUR CURRIE, 1875–1914

Arthur was ordinary in every way, except perhaps for his height of six foot three. He also had a burning desire to escape life in rural Ontario. While he enjoyed basic cadet training in school, no one would have predicted that Arthur, coming from a family with no links to the military, would become one of Canada's most famous soldiers.

Young Arthur Curry (as the family name was then spelled) was born on December 5, 1875, and grew up in Middlesex County, in the farming community of Adelaide near the small town of Strathroy, about 50 kilometres west of London, Ontario. The Curry family believed in discipline and the Lord's word. Arthur was shaped deeply by his upbringing and remained religious throughout his life, writing after having converted from his family's Methodism to Anglicanism, "If I obey the commandments of our Lord and fashion my life after the teachings of Christ, I feel that my life will not be altogether useless."[1]

The Curry farm was 300 acres, with a simple house fronted by a white two-level veranda and apple trees. Arthur went to a small rural schoolhouse near his home, sometimes in bare feet. At age fourteen, he began to travel 10 kilometres a day to Strathroy Collegiate. "It took us such a long time getting there that when we had arrived we were quite content to make the most of our time," joked Arthur later in life.[2]

The lanky Arthur was a recognized leader among his mates, with an outgoing and gregarious attitude, revealing a prodigious memory, a fondness for literature, and convincing oratorical prowess.[3] A strong student, the young Curry seemed destined for a professional career as a lawyer or doctor, but his father, William, died in 1891, when Arthur was sixteen. It was a blow to the family. The Currys needed money, so Arthur trained as a teacher. He graduated with a third-class certificate, but could find no job, so he went back to high school to continue his studies and find a way into a university.

Perhaps reacting to the death of his father, Arthur suffered from dark mood swings, and he questioned and prodded his teachers, often not to their liking. He never graduated with the necessary senior matriculation, after falling out with one of his teachers only a month before he was to write his final examination. Refusing to return to teaching and now unable to attend university, the nineteen-year-old Arthur left his family in May 1894 to go West to find his fortune.

As Arthur and a few friends crossed the country on a six-day voyage, his eyes were opened to the vastness of the land and the regions he had only read about in books. All across the nation, Canadians were working hard to prosper, and there was money to be made for entrepreneurs. Curry went all the way to the west coast, and soon set up in Victoria, which was booming with excitement, vibrancy, and prospects.

The bracing Pacific air and the foreignness of a city bursting at almost 20,000 souls must have been exhilarating for the young farm boys from Adelaide and Strathroy. But the ambitious Arthur could find no job that met his satisfaction, so he returned to teaching, securing a post in Sidney, some 30 kilometres north of Victoria. The town was a lot like the sleepy one he had left behind in Ontario, and the salary of sixty dollars a month meant the job was only a stopgap measure. But while in Sidney, the cheerful teacher was actively involved in society and became an avid sportsman. Even as Arthur taught thirty pupils ranging in age from six to eighteen, he was rarely challenged by the task, although his energy and knowledge impressed the school trustees, as did his deep baritone voice and his "insistence on punctuality and general discipline."[4]

As Arthur sought to find new challenges, he continued to be plagued by a recurring stomach ailment that left him bedridden for days at a time. His stomach issue flared up again in late 1899, although this time more seriously, leaving him hospitalized for a few months. The relapse may have been brought on by the stress of trying to get ahead in the world, which increasingly seemed impossible in the teaching profession. Historian Stanley Frost has suggested that Arthur's ailment may have had a "psychological rather than a physiological basis," meaning that perhaps the young teacher's desire to succeed, and his subsequent floundering, was eating away at him.[5] Arthur would be affected by similar illnesses throughout his life, often during highly stressful periods, but he learned to overcome the ailments, despite the intense pain. While in hospital and with time to reflect on his career and life, Arthur decided to break from teaching. In early 1900, he moved back to Victoria and started a new job as an insurance salesman at a local agency, Matson and Coles.

A young Arthur had an awkward quality of movement as he loped along, but his bearing had improved as he grew up, and even more so since his enlistment in the militia in 1897. There were other changes too. Around this period, Arthur, anxious to complete the break from his old life and to avoid barrack-room teasing along the lines of "Curry is hot stuff," changed the spelling of his name to Currie.[6] Though this may seem the action of an overly sensitive man, it was a time of transformations for Arthur, who also rejected his mother's fervent Methodism to embrace Anglicanism.

In the business world, Arthur found a friend and mentor in J.S.H. Matson, the owner of the insurance firm. Gregarious, well-respected in society, and widely travelled, Matson was a strong Tory supporter. Currie was in direct contrast as a sometimes lonely man, inexperienced in the ways of the world, whose political beliefs had drawn him toward supporting the Liberal Party. These two opposites found ways to overcome their differences, with the youngish Arthur gaining much from the relationship.

The men's friendship flourished and Matson developed confidence in the small-town Currie. Arthur's salary was immediately three times what he had earned as a teacher, and in 1904, Matson handed over the running of the business to Currie, who had grown into the job, at ease with new and increasing responsibilities. Arthur took much direction from his mentor, but he also had his own beliefs and opinions. When Matson tried to entice Currie to join the Conservatives, he politely declined. Currie was influenced positively by Matson, but he was not pliable material in his hands.

Arthur's circumstances were further enhanced by a happier private life after his marriage to Lucy Sophia Chaworth-Muster on August 14, 1901, who was the same age as Arthur. Lucy had been born into death, with birthing complications leading to her mother's passing. Lucy's father never overcame his grief, and every time he looked at the baby, anger and sadness flooded over him.[7] Unable to stand it, he returned to England with his other children, but left Lucy in the care of family friends, Arthur Currie's aunt and uncle, who raised her as their own daughter. Arthur had known Lucy since coming West in 1894, but it had taken him seven years of courtship to win her hand.[8] Theirs would be a happy marriage, producing two children, Marjorie and Garner, and another daughter who died in infancy. Currie's voluminous correspondence is almost barren of personal and family detail, but Lucy and the children were important pillars in his life.

In 1897, when Currie joined the militia, he exhibited little evidence of being particularly patriotic. He did, however, believe in the militia, which played many roles in Canadian society, providing a venue not only to show one's duty to nation and Empire, but also to socialize, exercise, and partake in community activities. Currie enlisted at the lowest rank of gunner, serving in the British Columbia Brigade, Canadian Garrison Artillery, more commonly known as "the Fifth" or the "Dandy Fifth." While none of Arthur's family had ever served in the military, this was a chance for him to meet other men his age, and he took pride in his white helmet and the uniform that had to be altered to fit his large frame.

In early spring of 1898 the young Arthur began musketry training and was promoted to the rank of bombardier. He was clearly pegged from early on as a man on the rise. He took to drill and instruction and was a surprisingly excellent marksman, considering that he had little previous experience with the rifle. While the rifle was important, the artillerymen were trained on the 13-pounder muzzle-loader gun, an ancient relic that had been vastly superseded by more modern, breech-loading artillery pieces. Even though Currie had little aptitude for the mechanics of the gun—with one close friend noting uncharitably that "He had not sufficient mechanical aptitude to drive in a nail"— his gun teams were always among the best in the Dandy Fifth.[9]

Arthur was offered a commission on December 19, 1900, which elevated him to the rank of lieutenant. He had wanted to go overseas and fight in the South African War, but was declared medically unfit because of his ongoing stomach ailment.[10] Over the next decade, Currie was promoted steadily, each time mastering the duties of his rank and showing strong leadership. He became more self-assured and learned to overcome his awkwardness. Even though he was a little too old for boyish pranks, he continued to play and jostle with the lads during the two weeks of summer training camp. But he could also be stern and severe when necessary. Regardless of his mood—playful or serious—he perpetually devoted himself to soldiering: "When some of my associates were playing lawn tennis or swinging golf clubs," wrote Currie, "I was at the armories or on the rifle ranges with the boys."[11] Currie enrolled in courses offered by the detachment of British and Canadian professional officers at the

Esquimalt base; he took full advantage of his superiors' knowledge and read the latest military treatises. In the words of one friend, Arthur "schooled himself sedulously for the unknown future."[12]

A valued member of the regiment, Currie had pushed himself not only to know every man in his company but to show an interest in their lives. Yet his compassion came with demands for strict discipline. He let nothing slide in his peacetime unit, even as others found it hard to enforce such discipline in the face of a non-existent enemy. Currie's hard-nosed inspections of uniforms became legendary. So, too, did his swearing. He had a "tremendous command of profanity," remembered his son; it was not uncommon for him to fire off vulgarities, machine-gun-like, for up to a minute without repetition.[13]

Arthur was ambitious, and his forceful manner, when combined with growing expertise, made him the strongest candidate to lead when the regiment's commanding officer retired in 1909. At that point, the regiment had had over two years to train with their modern 12-pounder quick-firing guns, which allowed Currie's men to compete in Dominion gunnery competitions. These gatherings were a chance for the artillery units to test their skills, work together, and show off. Currie proved himself gifted at training, a key skill in Canada's prewar militia, and he also had a commanding presence. As one fellow militia officer observed, Currie was always the range officer during the major British Columbia Range Artillery Matches, as "he seemed to be the obvious choice and could control all the militia, the civilian shots, ... [and] everyone else."[14] Currie's gunners won several national awards and competitions between 1909 and 1913. These accomplishments came through hard work on the part of Currie, the energetic commanding officer, who had to balance his family and professional life, yet still averaged 150 nights a year at the armoury, as well as every Saturday at the firing range.[15] The success and skill of his gunners brought Currie to the attention of the fiery Minister of Militia and Defence Sam Hughes, who kept a close eye on all of his leading militia officers.

Hughes was already a legendary figure who inspired trepidation, if not outright fear in most militia officers. But Currie was not easily cowed. While Victoria was far from Ottawa, the two men had met each other a few times, and though the Liberal-leaning Currie did not support the minister politically, they seem to have got on well. During one trip to Victoria, in 1912, the minister inspected Currie's unit; Hughes was pleased and the review successful. However, the relationship was strained when during Hughes's visit Currie's second-in-command gave permission to the regiment's band to play at a church parade, a common act when the formation received spiritual guidance. Currie was not aware of the order, and when he found out, he cancelled the event. It was a minor issue, but Currie was a stickler for formality. As the unit's commanding officer, he should have been the one to give the order, following a formal request from the junior officer. The matter made its way back to the minister, who directed Currie to permit the band to play. He refused.

Not many people said no to the minister. Hughes threatened Currie with repercussions, but the lieutenant colonel refused to bend to the minister's will. Did he not command his own regiment? The minister's aides held their breath, waiting for an explosion. Instead, a surprised Hughes—who had of course commanded his own infantry regiment for many years—crossed over to Currie, put his hands on his shoulders and remarked, "Well, Currie, I came out here to get your scalp but you're right."[16] It was a seemingly odd stand for Currie to take over an insignificant incident, but like the powerful minister, he knew his mind and was not easily swayed by others. It would not be the last time Currie revealed himself to be morally courageous in conditions that others might have assessed as requiring a more politic approach.

Currie showed his iron again during the difficult Nanaimo Coal Strike of 1913–14. The twelve-month strike was one of the bitterest in Canadian labour history, pitting the miners, supported by two unions, against the owners, who were backed by the provincial government. Currie was involved in the strike, as the militia had been called out to aid the civil power, in this case the owners. Bloody clashes had erupted, but on August 12, 1913, there was a pitched battle between 1,000 strikers and scabs, which soon brought in baton-wielding police who only worsened the situation.

Lieutenant-Colonel Currie and a fellow senior officer acted decisively. The 88th Victoria Fusiliers and the 5th Regiment were called out and armed. After misinformation was supplied to the strikers on the movement of the units, the infantry and artillery marched quickly to Nanaimo by a different route and occupied the town. Currie ensured that the two sides did not again come to bloody blows. Though he was a government man, Currie also paid daily visits to the imprisoned strikers in the Nanaimo jail, and ensured that their families could see them. Currie's actions helped to defuse the situation, and he was lauded in the province's papers, even the *Daily Times*, which supported the strikers: "A state of anarchy never yet and never will do a country, province or community any good; and because of this all fair-minded men must sympathize with the somewhat drastic action of ordering out the militia to quall the disturbance."[17] The operation enhanced Currie's reputation, but he had come to the end of his military career. He was set to retire from the militia at the age of thirty-eight, after more than fifteen years of service, in order to focus on his business interests.

Having risen to the rank of lieutenant colonel in the militia, become a leader in the Young Men's Liberal Association, and functioned as the Deputy Grand Master of the Victoria District of Freemasonry, Currie was a recognized and prominent member of Victoria's society. He had switched careers again in late 1908, leaving his job as a senior manager in insurance to take a partnership in the new real estate firm of Currie and Power. The usually level-headed Currie was soon caught up in the superheated speculative economy. Great profits were being made in Victoria as brokers like Currie bought and sold properties; it was easy money as prices rose and then soared. Coming as he did from a poor background,

Arthur found the large profits especially intoxicating, as there seemed no limit to the money that could be made. Within a few years, Currie had invested all his wealth in other expensive properties. "He had maps of the city on his walls," recounted Augustus Bridle, "and could solemnly point to some timid newcomer, what little house there or nice wooded lot yonder might suit her; and the price—oh yes, the price; seems high, but the location is excellent, the neighbourhood fine, the scenery superb …"[18] Currie was good at his job and achieved rapid success; in 1911, for example, Currie made $17,000 in profits from buying and selling property.[19] One journalist noted years after the war that businessmen in Victoria remarked of him: "Currie is a smart fellow, it is a pity he doesn't stick to business and not waste so much time soldiering."[20]

For the next two years, Currie devoted himself to business and soldiering, but in early 1913 the boom was coming to an end. With a national downturn in the economy, buyers were no longer willing to speculate on expensive property. The curtain was pulled away and the stark realization that property was overpriced started a panic. Creditors began to tighten purse strings. Currie was caught in the downward spiral, and from September 1913 his finances were in a critical state. While he was a rich man on paper, his equity was tied up in property that he could not sell. A desperate Currie began to shuffle money from account to account, robbing Peter to pay Paul, and all the while more and more pressed to pay creditors or his taxes. He believed that his retirement from the militia would give him more time to focus on overcoming his financial difficulties.

Despite the economic downturn, a new infantry battalion was authorized for Victoria in August 1913. The 50th Regiment would be a Highland unit, which was always popular among young recruits because of the Scottish traditions, kilts, and bagpipers. There were various officers vying for command, but Arthur's name was at the top of the list. When several of Currie's friends pressed him to take command, he scoffed at the idea, swearing and joking that he would look silly in the elaborate uniform of the Gordon Highlanders, with kilts, plaids, and feather bonnets. In reality, he could not offer the energy or resources to build a new regiment during his personal financial crisis. Commanding officers were expected to devote not only enormous time to their regiments but also significant funds, and this Currie could now ill afford. But prominent citizens pressed him to take the unit and he reluctantly let his name go forward for consideration by Minister Sam Hughes, but only after a prominent local businessman, William Coy, agreed to put up the then enormous sum of $35,000 to pay for uniforms and the eventual pipe and brass band.[21]

Sam Hughes had long been impressed by Currie's dedication and skills, and he appointed him to command the new regiment, with the minister's son, Garnet, as second-in-command. Garnet Hughes obviously had the right pedigree. His father's connections had not hurt him, to be sure, but in his own right he was a graduate of the Royal Military College, where he had received the Sword of Honour in recognition of his academic achievement and military skills. He was an engineer by trade, which no doubt pleased his father, who thought little of the professional soldier. Arthur and Garnet became close friends as they struggled to create the new regiment. They must have talked frequently of Currie's financial problems, as the strain weighed heavily on the lieutenant colonel and could be seen in his face and in his short temper. Although stretched to the limit, Currie did not neglect the regiment; he continually upgraded his skills, which included taking the demanding three-month staff course. Currie did well in the class, even though he had little time to devote to it, often working late into the night to complete the various staff solution assignments.[22]

Despite facing financial ruin, Currie continued to do his duty for the militia. In April 1914 Currie had 300 men in uniform, and a second order of impressive Highland uniforms was being made in Scotland. His infantry thronged to the firing range each weekend, and were led by their lieutenant colonel, who remained an excellent shot. "With such a spirit in the regiment," Currie noted to one journalist, "its future success seemed assured."[23] But Currie was fighting a private battle with the regiment's benefactor and honorary colonel, William Coy, who was becoming increasingly problematic to deal with. Coy was no doubt suffering in the deepening financial catastrophe that had hit the nation, and he was withholding his cash gift to the regiment, which in today's terms would be worth several hundred thousand dollars. Currie lamented to a friend, "He has been as sulky as a man could be. We all had to toady to him always to get him to do anything."[24]

Currie, too, was feeling the strain of the worsening economic crisis. His financial situation kept him up at night as he sat anxiously in his study, poring over his crippling financial records, devising means by which to raise capital. The stress reduced his attention span, as he tried to make deals, raise funds, and fend off creditors. Nothing worked. He tried to quit the regiment on several occasions. Each time, however, his junior officers convinced him to keep at it, as his experienced hand was needed to guide the Highlanders to maturity. Currie relented, although he was a man torn between his duty to the regiment and the need to provide for his family.

In the midst of Currie's financial crisis, the assassination of the Austrian Archduke Franz Ferdinand in July 1914 led to a month of heated rhetoric and escalating threats. The Austro-Hungarian Empire blamed Serbia for funding the political assassins, and the Empire's heavy-handed response involved threats of occupying the country with a paramilitary force. The regional conflict threatened to escalate into Europe-wide war, as Germany backed Austria and Russia supported the Serbs. If Britain was dragged into that maelstrom, Canada would find itself at war. Good soldiers like Currie would be needed to defend country, King, and Empire. And such an event would bring Currie and the indomitable Sam Hughes into close, and possibly more violent, situations.

CHAPTER 4

Canada's Warlord

SAM HUGHES, 1914

The sixty-one-year-old Sam Hughes was livid at the thought that Canada might somehow miss the war that was brewing in Europe in early August 1914. Throughout the day on August 4, as German forces were already marching into Belgium, he paced back and forth in his office, fuming at his assistants. "They're going to skunk it," he roared. "By God, I don't want to be a Britisher under such conditions." Hughes was apoplectic about missing the war if Britain's government were somehow to avoid its treaty commitments or find a diplomatic solution. The minister had been putting the Dominion on a war footing since 1911. In the process, he had suffered harsh condemnation in the House of Commons and the media, with his opponents questioning his motives and sanity. Who would Canada fight, they taunted? Sam had always pointed to Imperial Germany. And now the time was near, and it was indeed Germany that threatened the old European order and, more importantly, the continued supremacy of the British Empire as the world's leading power.

In a shocking display of adolescent petulance, Hughes ordered that the Union Jack be lowered outside militia headquarters. His embarrassed staff tried to reason with him, but he swore so loudly and violently that they followed his orders and brought down the flag. Experienced heads finally talked down the frothing Hughes, and the Union Jack went back up the pole.[1] Later that night, Britain's declaration of war arrived. Canada was at war.

The immediate concern for Sir Robert Borden's government was not an issue of manpower but a fear that war would create a serious run on the banks, as panicking Canadians withdrew money. Calming announcements and the freezing of funds ensured there would be no collapse. Indeed, Canadians had not panicked. Tens of thousands had greeted the war by rushing into the streets, cheering and singing.

But others had more sober thoughts, especially the parents and wives and sisters who wondered if their son or husband or brother would march to war and never return. Sir Edmund Walker, president of the Canadian Bank of Commerce, wrote on August 4, the day Canada went to war as part of the British Empire: "It is as yet nearly impossible to realize that the 'Universal European War' about which so much has been said and regarding which those who feared it were called 'alarmists' and 'jingoes,' is now a positive reality and our Empire literally depends on the success or failure of Britain, Russia, France, and Belgium against Germany and Austria. Let us hope it will be quickly over."[2] It would not be.

Prime Minister Borden should have been the leading figure in Canada's war effort, but it was not yet in his retiring nature to assume such a visibly dynamic persona. And so, the last man picked for the cabinet would now be the first citizen in leading the country to war. A war needed a warlord, someone to galvanize the nation to arms and to action. Dedicated to the cause, enthusiastic to the point of crusading, and possessed of seemingly boundless energy, in those heady days of August 1914, Sam Hughes was the politician most closely identified with the Canadian war effort.

As the German land forces pushed back retreating French, Belgian, and British forces on the continent that fateful August, there was a growing sense of alarm. The War Office in London was in particular need of men, as its professional force was dwarfed by the enormous land armies of the Continental powers. It gratefully accepted Canada's offer of an infantry formation, 25,000 strong. Hughes and his departmental officers would be responsible for creating the force from across the country. An optimistic Hughes boasted on August 6, "We could raise 100,000 men if needed."[3]

The long-suffering professional soldiers at the Department of Militia and Defence had prepared for war with a detailed mobilization plan that would ensure proper representation from across the country, moving men quickly to a centralized training area, so that they could be efficiently equipped. The decentralized scheme was in the hands of some of the local district commanders in August 1914, but not all. Many of the details, moreover, had not been worked out.[4] But by giving local commanders the role of coordinating the enlistment, the plan took the pressure off an Ottawa headquarters that was too small to organize such a complicated event through telegraph messages and the incomplete phone lines.

Colonel Hughes threw the plans away. He would raise Canada's army almost single-handedly. "There was really a call to arms like the fiery cross passing through the Highlands of Scotland or the mountains of Ireland in former days" was how Hughes described the mobilization.[5] Urgent action was required, felt Hughes, and the preapproved plan was too slow for his liking. It would also put the authority in the hands of regional commanders. No, Sam would lead Canada to war like the chieftains of old. He famously sent out 226 night telegrams to unit commanders of the Active Militia, asking them to forward names of potential volunteers to his headquarters. It appeared that the minister wanted to personally vet the 25,000 or more Canadians who would be stepping forward. He was saved from this lunacy on August 10, when the district commanders mobilized units and companies for overseas service. But first they had to be grouped together for training and transportation. In Hughes's most audacious move, he changed the mobilization camp from Petawawa, located on the Ottawa River some 130 kilometres from Ottawa, to Valcartier, near Quebec City. That way the troops, once trained, would be able to sail overseas from Quebec as quickly as possible. More than a few officers must have double-checked their orders since they had never heard of Valcartier. Do we have a camp there? asked the perplexed commanders. The answer was no. But Hughes was going to build it.

Hughes succeeded in raising the First Contingent—as the force was known—while others fretted, debated, and struck committees. Hughes was a man of action, albeit impromptu action, and he always had an eye for theatrics. Moreover, it did not really matter what the minister did in August 1914: the men around whom he had so deeply created a romanticized vision of citizen-warriors rose to the occasion and flocked to the colours. Canadians wanted war.

For a short period in August, the government turned to the governor general for advice, as he was a field marshal in the British army. But this was bound to create tension, as Governor General Connaught ached to take over the mobilization of Canadian forces. He and Hughes despised each other, and Sam was quick to remind the cabinet that under Canada's constitution it was he, the minister, who oversaw the militia. Borden supported Hughes and was forced to push back hard against the unbending Connaught, eventually writing to his secretary, "The Duke takes up too much of our time and he has a false impression as to his status and powers as Commander-in-Chief."[6] Borden, the cabinet, and especially Hughes would support the Empire to the hilt, but they were already showing a desire to exert Canada's own independence in the war effort. Hughes first, and later Borden, was convinced that if Canadians were going to pay and die, then Canadians should be in control. The path to achieving that control over the next few years would not be clear or easy, and the bloody experience would test who among the Canadians would do it, and how.

Sam returned to mobilizing his army. Revelling in the limelight, the minister held daily press conferences, which journalists swarmed, since Hughes was unguarded in his statements and claims.[7] During these "séances," as journalists called them, the papers received the inside scoop and printed it as delivered. Sam lapped the attention up, especially since the stories made it seem as though he was running the war. One observer of this circus was George Nasmith, a diminutive chemist who pleaded with the minister to be sent overseas with the First Contingent. He wrote this of his experience at the Department of Militia and Defence headquarters: "The greeting of the Minister of Militia, Sam Hughes, as he turned from the desk where he sat in shirt-sleeves, with typewriters on all sides of him, was a cordial handshake and a slap on the back." As Nasmith described it, Hughes's office was a hive of activity:

> Officers of all ranks, from Generals to Majors, hurried in one after another to obtain permission to do this or that; prominent men anxious to do anything they might to assist in the great crisis, crowded the office. Telephone conversations, telegrams, cables, interview, dictation of letters, reading letters aloud—to watch or listen to the incessant commingling of all these, with the Minister of Militia as the centre of energy, was a unique experience for me. Sir Sam cracked jokes, dictated letters, swore at the telephone operator, and carried on conversations with a number of persons—all at the same time. It was a marvellous demonstration of what a man could do in an emergency, if he happened to be the right man—the man who not only knew what needed to be done but had sufficient force of character and driving power to convert his decisions into practical achievements.[8]

Hughes was the right man for the time, and few others seemed able or willing to step up. Borden agreed but was not without his concerns, noting, "Hughes [is] doing well but gives too many interviews."[9] There were other, more serious problems beginning to emerge. Hughes kept power to himself, and was most comfortable appointing friends and loyal supporters to run major military establishments. He thought little of and cared less for the small number of staff-trained officers, who knew how to train, equip, and move an army. Shaped by his experience in South Africa and his own sense of self-importance, Hughes felt he understood the soldiers better than anyone. Despite his attempts to ensure the care of his "boys," as he often referred to the men who would form his army, Hughes's truculent, impetuous, and bullying nature made him enemies at every turn.

Sam Hughes battled to control his passion throughout his life, oscillating between unstable emotions while showing an uncomfortable tendency to break down in weeping fits. There was an unhinged quality to Hughes that was evident before the war and that escalated as he acquired more influence. It is likely that his behaviour would today be diagnosed as a form of mania. Sir Robert Borden was later to write of Hughes that "his intense vanity and a rather vindictive temper," which worsened with the stress of the war, were exacerbated by his "absurd inclination to fill not only the role of Minister of Militia [but also] that of Military Commander."[10]

As Hughes raised a new army, he appointed William Price to build it a Canadian home. In 1912 the Department of Militia and Defence had purchased land at Valcartier, where the Jacques Cartier River meets the St. Lawrence above Quebec City, as it would make a good embarkation point. But there was nothing on this site in August 1914. Price was a wealthy and loyal Tory who had raised money for the party over the years, and was also a very successful lumber baron. He would need all of that experience to pull off the feat required of him. For appointing Price, Hughes was immediately accused of putting party before nation, but as he was working within a patronage-driven system, and was in charge of a militia whose structure mirrored it, the minister ran the war much like he did an election or the regular business of government. Neither Borden nor his colleagues objected to this, as most expected the war to be short and Canada's contribution to it limited.

With an army of carpenters, labourers, and lumberjacks, Price went to work in the area. Amazingly, within days there were roads and vast cleared areas. Water mains, sewers, chlorinating plants, rail lines, and multiple bridges were erected in record time. At peak capacity, some 500,000 gallons of water a day could be pumped from the river to the camp. Hughes claimed the rifle ranges were the longest in the world. There was even a permanent house for Hughes, which looked distinctly like a castle. The king was pleased.

When Sam's new army started to arrive at the end of August, the camp was a sea of dust and wood chips, but it was there. Few could deny Hughes's energy and accomplishment, with Borden gushing that "no other man could have accomplished during a similar period what he did achieve."[11] Hughes was living up to his own considerable billing, yet in succeeding in getting Valcartier operational, he was unable or unwilling to delegate authority. Instead of allowing the soldiers at Valcartier to carry out their duties, the minister travelled to the camp frequently in his private railway car, "Rolleen" (the name drawn from an amalgamation of his two daughters Roby and Aileen). These trips, in turn, led to delays in Ottawa, where his long-suffering departmental employees could not meet the daily demands of the burgeoning war effort because nothing could happen without the customary "OK, S.H." annotating a form or report.[12] This centralization of control under the minister had begun to break down in the prewar years, but with the massive expansion of the forces during the first months of the war, the system ground to a halt. Long-time militiaman and friend of Sam Hughes, William Griesbach, wrote candidly: "How the wretched staff at National Defence Headquarters carried on, I do not know. I suspect that they did not carry on at all."[13]

Hughes roared through the camp like a whirlwind, shouting inspirational things like: "We are determined that the tyrant's heel shall never grind down upon the people of Canada."[14] Dressed in his colonel's uniform, occasionally augmented by sword and feathered hat, he barked out orders and corralled the men for impromptu speeches. "Sam spoke yet other homilies to the officers, and his address, delivered from a mound on which he and his staff were drawn up, was irreverently referred to around camp as the 'Sermon on the Mount,'" wrote W.W. Murray of the 2nd Battalion. "A story is also told that one of his aides suggested that all could not hear him. 'That's all right,' he is credited with replying; 'they can all see me!'"[15]

A delegation of officers and journalists trailed the minister, the latter jotting down his words, the former hoping that everyone would forget them. For it was the officers who had to fix the mess that Hughes left behind him, be they promises that could not be kept or morale-affecting changes or charges. Hughes would appoint men at the drop of a hat. There was mounting evidence that the minister would run the war effort by his own rules. One eyewitness, for example, described an instance when Hughes addressed a small group of soldiers: "'A fine unit you have here, major,' remarked Hughes. "'Pardon me, sir,' the officer remarked, 'I'm only a captain.' 'You're a major now.'"[16] Such actions left many officers more worried about pleasing Hughes than about discharging their duties. "He is cursing and swearing at the Officers, and making everybody sore," wrote Sam Sharpe, an experienced major who had already had his run-ins with Hughes. The overbearing minister, recalled a horrified Sharpe, "said to one officer, a captain, yesterday, 'Pipe up you little bugger, or get out of the service.' To another decorated officer, he told him it would be a 'crime to allow him to take men to the front.'" In a plea to Borden, Sharpe appealed to his guardianship of the Conservative Party: "The Minister is doing the craziest things in the world, and he is setting up everybody in arms against our party, and unless he is checked, there will be the very devil to pay."[17] Those soldiers who had less of a stake in fighting over the limited command positions viewed it more with bemusement: eighteen-year-old Horace Brown of Carleton Place heard one of Hughes's speeches, calling him the "awfull [sic] old blusterer."[18]

Liberal-supporting papers accused the boisterous bully of forcing Liberal opponents out of the camp and unsettling the training, and demanded that Hughes either be fired or "recede into the background of a resignation from office or a permanent withdrawal from the specialties of his performance as the war lord of Valcartier."[19] Sam took no heed. He had developed a thick skin as a result of repeated Liberal attacks he had endured throughout his life. For good measure, he blustered to Borden: "I have before me today hundred upon hundreds of letters offering, each, anyone from one man to fifteen hundred men. I can enroll two hundred thousand as easily as I enrolled forty three thousand men."[20]

Borden continued to back his minister, despite a growing number of complaints, and he duly forwarded all the angry letters to Hughes. The minister, as was his way, penned replies to any and all, in which he made no apology for his actions. In one letter he asserted quite rightly that "no man ever organized anything of the kind in as short a time, with less friction, dealing with thousands upon thousands of cranks, contractors, grafters, self-seekers and interlopers, as well as the tens of thousands of decent men." Borden must have agreed with his rough minister, despite being uncomfortable with his foul language and aggressive tactics. But he may have been less certain of his position when Hughes made claims such as, "I know I am loved by millions; but—thank goodness—I am hated by some people. I have, all my lifetime, let my slanderers fire ahead, and, unless they get directly in my way, I do not even cuff them. Perhaps it is the best way to continue."[21] Hughes would not stop to listen to the criticism. He was too busy raising an army.

"It is necessary that we secure competent officers," Sam Hughes noted as he addressed his soldiers on August 31 at Valcartier. "Many have applied to me for commands, but I have refused even some of my personal friends. I want men for action. Action—that is the word."[22] Despite Hughes's heady words, however, the army was ultimately born out of political appointments and patronage positions. Hughes was largely responsible, but there was much in-fighting between officers clamouring for more prestigious roles and using whatever Tory or militia connections they had to further their own careers.

But not all appointments were destined for card-carrying Tories. To fill the three positions of infantry brigadier—the key senior officers, as no divisional commander had yet been appointed—the minister not surprisingly turned to militia officers. Sam knew every officer of quality in the country, and his first choice for command was Richard Turner, a strong Tory supporter, grocery business owner, former president of the Canadian Cavalry Association, and Victoria Cross winner during the South African War. He was one of Canada's most celebrated heroes. Hughes's second selection was equally strong: Colonel Malcolm Mercer, a fifty-five-year-old former commander of the Queen's Own Rifles of Canada, from Toronto. Mercer was a long-time friend of the minister, and looked every inch the soldier with his ramrod straight back, bushy moustache, and stern appearance. Hughes and Mercer had crossed the Atlantic together before the war to study European armies. The least known of the three was Arthur Currie, partially because he was on the west coast but also because he had never commanded one of the nation's historic militia infantry regiments. But while Currie lacked experience as a war leader, he was not out of place: none of the brigadiers had ever commanded any unit larger than a battalion.

"I was determined to get the best man I could to take a hold of this thing and drive it through," declared Hughes.[23] Experience would prove that Hughes had made some good choices for the brigadiers, and even the battalion commanders, but there were countless rumours, some supported by hard facts, of Hughes turning down officers who had displeased him or who were known to be Liberals.[24] Sam wielded the power and he was settling old scores. Few positions were allotted to regular force officers, such as the gifted François-Louis Lessard, a well-respected professional soldier who had sided against the minister in the past. The vindictive Hughes disliked Lessard and denied him a brigade, a command that he merited, and did not even have the good grace to give him a battalion, actions nothing short of ruinous to Lessard's chances of going overseas. With no French-Canadian battalion commanders in the First Contingent, Hughes all but guaranteed that no French Canadians would have the chance to achieve a senior rank in the Canadian Expeditionary Force.[25] This situation compounded the historic weakness of the militia in Quebec in the decades before the war, where there were far fewer militia units and therefore fewer experienced officers to draw upon for the new overseas force.[26]

Although Hughes could be malicious, as he was with Lessard, Lieutenant-Colonel Arthur Currie, then commanding four battalions as brigadier of the 2nd Provisional (Western) Brigade, noted the awesome pressure on Hughes, especially by the officers vying for the limited positions in the First Contingent. "The Minister's life must have been a misery for days on end ... every squirt of a politician in the country and especially those in camp were trying to arrange things to their own selfish ends. Everyone was at everyone else's throat."[27] While Hughes was not the type to try to please everyone, he did his best. He had his prejudices, but so did everyone else. Powerful militia commanders argued forcefully that their battalion, regiment, or battery should be sent overseas. Who would be selected? Which units would get to add the honours of battle to their regimental colours? Hughes agonized over the decision. Realizing that any selection of one of the dozens of representative militia units would alienate others, he devised a new system of creating numbered battalions. The famous regional units with a history stretching back decades, such as the Queen's Own Rifles and the 5th Royal Highlanders, were now subsumed by blandly numbered battalions, from the 1st to 17th infantry battalions. The move was highly unpopular, and more than a few militia officers felt betrayed by their militia champion, but it was the only course of action open to Hughes. Cynics might note that such a new organization further strengthened the minister's control over appointments.

Having created an entirely new force, Hughes showed off his army of 30,000 in a series of parades, including one on September 20 that drew an estimated 10,000 sightseers. The crowd included the prime minister and the governor general: the former was deeply impressed while the latter could not help but grudgingly offer respect to a man whom he had recently classified as "mentally off his base."[28] But more than a few soldiers must have shared the opinion of Peter Anderson, a Danish-born officer: "A good deal of time was spent in rehearsals for numerous reviews—marching past Sam Hughes, and other dignitaries, that might have been spent to better advantage."[29]

Hughes had every reason to be proud of his new army—and indeed he was—but his pride led him into conflict with his cabinet colleagues. His bloated sense of accomplishment made him even more difficult to accept by such influential ministers as George Foster and A.E. Kemp, who were more than a little jealous of Hughes but also worried about his increased propensity to make important decisions concerning the war that should have been debated and decided in cabinet. Minister of Finance Thomas White was furious for other reasons, primarily over Hughes's blatant disregard of rules in issuing contracts. Rumours circulated that Ottawa was being defrauded, largely because of the haphazard approach of Hughes's ministry in tendering and filling war-related contracts for goods and services.[30] Foster wrote acidly of Hughes and his handling of the war effort in September 1914: "The Militia Department is lawless and Kaiserism runs mad."[31]

In cabinet, the lone-wolf style of the minister of militia and defence alienated his colleagues. It was not just a case of Hughes hogging the limelight; he also violated the basic principles of cabinet solidarity and collective responsibility. Often his independent decisions forced the government's hand, and this increasingly became an issue. Hughes responded vigorously to the complaints of his cabinet colleagues, alternating fighting like a cornered tiger with offering sincere contrition but then promptly carrying on as before. Even Hughes's staunchest supporter, Borden, found his minister's imperious methods hard to stomach. Hughes justified his actions, as he always did, by arguing, "My one aim … is the successful prosecution of this war." As had been true all his life, he felt "little inclination to waste time in fighting enemies within."[32]

While Hughes's attention was devoted to his growing army at Valcartier, he was under constant pressure by the patriotic and sycophantic who sought his favour. Hughes's already short temper had an even shorter fuse as a result of overwork and chronic insomnia. In one case, after a long day of meetings, Hughes met with the secretary of the Toronto Humane Society, who complained to the minister about the mistreatment of military horses. Hughes called him a liar. Then, thinking better of his words, he amended them. The do-gooder was instead a "damned liar." The minister grabbed the shocked man by the collar and threw him out of his office.[33]

As his soldiers learned to soldier, the question of who would assume overall command was raised. The First Contingent had enough men to produce a division in the field, with several thousand to spare for reinforcements. Many expected Sam himself to lead his boys into battle. The rumours had legs probably because Hughes often mused aloud that he should perhaps resign as minister and lead the men in the field, thereby achieving what he described to the House of Commons as "the dearest ambition of my life."[34] He thought better of the idea, however, and decided not to resign. Instead, he would do both jobs! It was the height of hubris, but then, throughout Hughes's life, there had been few actions that he'd considered too outlandish to pursue.

Borden did not object to Hughes taking command of the force, indicating that he wished to reward Hughes or to have him leave Ottawa, where he was already drawing fire, or perhaps that he simply had no concept of what was required to lead a division.[35] A combination of all three factors was likely at play. While the Canadians had already made a habit of putting mere colonels in command of forces far larger than what they had commanded in peacetime, the British remembered their experience with Hughes in South Africa, where he had been an efficient but difficult subordinate officer. Field Marshal Lord Kitchener, Britain's secretary of state for war, must have spent some time in carefully selecting his words when he cabled Borden, observing that "it would be a mistake to change the minister [of] militia at this juncture."[36] Borden did not often stand up to his volatile minister, but he now forced Hughes to choose one post or the other. Hughes opted to remain a politician—noting without the slightest trace of inhibition, although probably correctly, "My position here is much larger than it could possibly be in command of a mere division or corps at the front." Although it was in his "heart's ambition ... to go to the front," he would remain minister; nonetheless, he used his influence to have his rank of colonel raised to that of major general, leap-frogging the rank of brigadier.[37] A British general, E.A.H. Alderson, would command Hughes's "boys." Sam vowed to keep a close eye on him.

Hughes remained intensely proud of his soldiers. He was fond of proclaiming loudly, and to all, that with their Ross rifles, the Canadian citizen-soldiers could "pink the enemy every time."[38] It was a good thing they were such alleged sure-shots, as Hughes had banished Canada's only regular infantry battalion, the Royal Canadian Regiment, to Bermuda, where they relieved British soldiers who were then sent to Europe to fight. It was definitely the wrong place for Canada's experienced regulars, who would have been of value in training Canada's new army, and this decision clearly exposed Hughes's prejudices. His heart was with the citizen-soldiers of the militia, who vastly overshadowed the 3,000-strong professional force. And the militiamen who formed the new army seemed to like the minister too. The cheeky soldiers could show their respect in many ways, but one of them was through satirical song:

We are Sam Hughes's Army,
Thirty thousand men are we
We cannot fight, we cannot march
What bloody good are we?[39]

With over 30,000 of the "world's best soldiers," as the minister called them, at Valcartier, Sam agonized over the thought of having to send thousands of them home, since the War Office had only requested 25,000 men to make the trip overseas.[40] Hughes pleaded to Borden to let them all go. The prime minister concurred and Hughes, as he was wont to do in stressful or emotional situations, "broke down and sobbed."[41]

With the camp built in weeks and housing the new citizen-soldier army, Valcartier became the first symbol of Canada's eventually momentous war effort. Private Harold Peat wrote that "if the credit for it all must be given to any one man, that man is Sir Sam Hughes."[42] The improviser had raised an army, and one normally caustic journalist, Augustus Bridle, thought Hughes should have been raised to the peerage and taken the title Lord Valcartier.[43] Sam Hughes was the driving force behind the initial Canadian war effort, as cocksure in the righteousness of the cause as he was in his own abilities. J.B. Maclean, owner and publisher of numerous newspapers and magazines, wrote to Borden that he did not like Hughes, with whom he had engaged in running battles for years, but while he found his outrageous statements and utterances "contemptible," he believed that "any man who had done what he had in preparing Canada for this war and in organizing the ... Contingent should have his sins forgiven."[44]

Borden agreed. Others were less sure. Sir George Foster, the deputy prime minister, wrote in his diary, "There is only one feeling as to Sam, that he is crazy."[45] Indeed he might have been. But mad times called for mad men.

CHAPTER 5

The Brigadier

ARTHUR CURRIE,
AUGUST 1914–APRIL 1915

In August 1914 one of Sam Hughes's inspired choices for command was Arthur Currie. At the start of the war, Currie had requested a position, but had hoped it would be in Canada. Befitting his high reputation as a fine trainer and an effective leader of men, Currie was offered the prestigious post of commanding officer of the west coast military district. He would have been responsible for training and equipping the forces from British Columbia that would have gone overseas according to the mobilization plans. But even as Hughes threw those plans out, Currie's fellow officers were attempting to persuade him to turn down a position that would have kept him in Canada riding a desk. For a man reeling from a financial crisis, the position as district commanding officer would have been an appealing option, as it would have enabled him to deal more effectively with his money problems. But duty called, and upon the urging of his second-in-command, Garnet Hughes, Currie allowed the minister's son to make a case on his behalf to his father. Within a day, Hughes telegraphed again, asking if Currie would take command of one of the infantry brigades that would be forming up at the central training camp at Valcartier, Quebec.

Currie was at a crossroads and continued to agonize over the decision. Garnet Hughes stiffened his backbone, and the two talked for hours about the need for men like Arthur to lead from the front.[1] After a short delay, Currie accepted the position on August 26 and tried to straighten out his financial situation before leaving by train for Valcartier the next day. He was conflicted over leaving behind his loving family, but no doubt relieved to escape the financial shambles of his business, which he left in the hands of his partner, R.A. Power. Currie had been on the brink of bankruptcy, and in one last desperate move had taken $10,833.34 from his regiment's funds—earmarked for new uniforms—to pay off his debts.[2] He well knew the seriousness of his action, especially when the new regimental commander quite rightly asked Currie to transfer the money back to him. But a reckless Currie had already used the funds to pay his debts, and he wrote to his old friend J.S.H. Matson, imploring him to hold off the regiment by either paying them or pleading with them for time.[3] Any public revelation of his pilfering would surely require Currie to abandon his position as brigadier. While the issue weighed on him, and he told Matson that he'd left instructions that if he were killed overseas his estate should pay back the money, Currie did little to follow up on the issue.[4] This neglect would come back to haunt him. Matson did not have the money to cover the debt, but Arthur pushed the embezzlement from his mind as he travelled alone by rail to Valcartier, anxious over how he would train and command an infantry brigade in the face of Canada's greatest struggle.

Arthur Currie had studied war most of his adult life, but he had never seen the real thing. "I doubted myself. I knew that the routine would prove simple enough. One knew it already or could learn it from books. But I knew that was not all—that the rest, which was the greater part, was not to be learned from any book or at second hand from the experience of any other men. I had to find out for myself and master it if

I could."[5] Currie never claimed to have all the answers, but he was the type to seek them out, and even to learn from his own errors.

The thirty-eight-year-old lieutenant colonel arrived at Valcartier at 10 P.M. on Tuesday, September 1. Currie carried only a small bag, arrived to find neither a proper brigade staff nor even a headquarters, and initially shared a tent with his second-in-command, Garnet Hughes. Despite lacking almost everything he needed, Currie worked day and night for his soldiers in what was known as the 2nd Provisional (Western) Infantry Brigade. The real-estate developer who had never commanded more than 400 men in peacetime was now responsible for ten times that number. His days of carefree pranks were left behind, and Currie was seen as a disciplinarian, with a forceful personality and a profane tongue when he did not get his way. He left the direct training to the four battalion commanders in his brigade, and concentrated on organizing units, ensuring that proper supplies and weapons arrived, establishing training goals, and sorting out hundreds of minor, if time-consuming, problems.

"The Old Man," as Currie was known informally by his men—and to his liking, even though he was younger than some of his soldiers—soon proved an effective brigadier. He had chosen his command staff wisely, and most were experienced British officers or members of the Canadian permanent force. He oversaw a popular officer's mess and was known to joke freely with his subordinates. Outside of the mess, however, Currie was stern and unforgiving. He had no reference manual for commanding a brigade, and he turned back to his prewar disciplinarian ways. As one soldier-friend, T.V. Scudamore, wrote, "I once heard the criticism of General Currie that he had no—or a very elementary—sense of humour."[6] But he also noted that the war dampened Currie's good nature: "From 1914 onwards he took his responsibilities so seriously; he really felt the war and the losses that it entailed."[7]

Minister Hughes and Lieutenant-Colonel Currie crossed paths a few times at Valcartier, but Currie seemed to do his best to steer clear of the warlord. Hughes admired Currie, and at some level found his independence refreshing. Currie, for his part, tried to accommodate Hughes, as he "was fully conscious of what he owed to Sam Hughes and his son," but he would not, according to a friend, "go one step out of his way to pander to Hughes."[8]

Currie had earned the confidence of the minister, his soldiers, and even the prime minister, who, visiting Valcartier, wrote that he "was impressed" by Currie, who "spoke with evident emotion, with apt expression and a thorough appreciation of the duty that lay in front of him and his men. From the first he was an outstanding man among the Canadians."[9] Despite this support, Currie was pleased to see the last of Valcartier. At the beginning of October, he joined with 33,000 other Canadians who boarded 32 ocean liners and similar vessels bound for England and eventually the Western Front in Belgium and France.

In England, Arthur Currie met the new commander of the Canadian forces, Edwin Alderson. Sam Hughes had made his choice and remained the minister, but he continued to meddle in the overseas forces, making life difficult for the general of the First Contingent. Alderson, an experienced professional British soldier, had been called out of retirement but had over thirty-five years of experience and several wars under his belt. He had commanded Canadians in South Africa and was aware of their reputation for lacking soldierly discipline, but in that war he had proved adept at harnessing the colonial unruliness and channelling it into forging an effective fighting force. He would have been unsurprised to find the same behaviour here, though he would have been perplexed by the heavy English and Scottish accents that he heard among the ranks. One astute journalist observed, "Many British immigrants had been settled so long in the country that they were as much Canadians in the local sense of the word as a man born in the Dominion could be."[10] While the rank and file were largely British-born (although that changed as the war dragged on), the majority of officers were Canadians.[11] Regardless of their birthplace, the Canadians were seen as different from British formations. Alderson had dealt with colonials before, but this was a new formation and one overseen in Ottawa by a far more intrusive politician.

The elderly Alderson, with his lined face and enormous moustache, had been promoted to lieutenant general when he was given command of the Canadian Division, a rank above the normal major general who commanded divisions, but perhaps this was his reward for having to deal with the colonials and their erratic minister. Things did not go well at first. Alderson was unlucky to have to train the Canadians in the mud of Salisbury Plain, where it rained during much of the winter of 1914–1915, reducing the grounds to a quagmire. But there were imperial troops there too, suffering in solidarity.

Colonel John Carson, a successful Montreal businessman and now Hughes's special representative overseas, kicked up a storm over the conditions, demanding that the Canadians be moved. A mortified Alderson refused special treatment.[12] The Canadian soldiers did not seem to blame him for the mud and misery, with many First Contingent men sharing the sentiments of one Canadian who described their general as a "kind gentle little man." But Carson reported Alderson's refusal to a puzzled Borden and an angry Hughes, neither of whom understood why the British general would not move the Canadians from the mud.[13] Borden put it quickly from his mind, but Hughes carried the grudge longer.

The experienced Alderson could see the raw material in the Canadian force, as well as in its commanders. He thought highly of the hardworking and conscientious Arthur Currie, later remarking that, of his brigadiers, "Currie is out and out the best."[14] For his part, Currie worked well for Alderson, but never took to him in the way that he did with a later mentor, Sir Julian Byng, the corps commander who would replace Alderson in May 1916.

"I shall not spare myself, and if a good example is worth anything I shall do my best," wrote the diligent Currie.[15] In October 1914 Currie was busy trying to draw together his brigade, which consisted of four battalions, each with an infantry 1,000 men strong. Most of the men were armed with the Ross rifle and bayonet, although there were a few specialists trained to use the two (later raised to four) Colt machine guns. As one militia colonel observed, "The Brigadiers are good enough men in themselves, but all lack experience in leading and staff work."[16] Aware of his own failings, Currie was dedicated to his men, took few breaks, and pushed himself relentlessly. He was responsible for military training and ensuring overall discipline. Both were a challenge, as discipline was lacking among many of the new soldiers, who preferred to see themselves as tough battlers with little time for the inanities of saluting or polishing buttons. There were men with physical disabilities or tuberculosis who had to be returned home, as well as a small number of incorrigibles unfit for soldiering. Even for the physically fit, drinking and fighting seemed the order of the day, although the behaviour was likely engaged in by a smaller portion of the force than claimed by sensational news reporters.[17] "Crude accounts appear in English papers re: Canadians," wrote a worried Currie on October 16. The lieutenant colonel dispatched one of his staff officers to investigate and the report came back that there were indeed a "great many drunken officers and men" in London and surrounding towns.[18] Even as the Canadians were getting into trouble, they played up their colonial image. It was a way to distinguish themselves from their British countrymen, something that Australians and New Zealanders were also doing halfway around the world. British newspapers regularly referred to the Canadians as a breed apart, as men who seemed to "exhale an atmosphere of fearless dash, open-handedness, and resource.... This spirit is surely the sturdy and breezy individualism born of their own hard yet always picturesque conditions of life on the great rolling uplands of our Colonies."[19] Lieutenant-Colonel Currie—who should have held the rank of brigadier—dealt with the problem cases within his command, sending home dozens of the worst offenders.

As discipline was brought under control, Currie and his fellow senior officers also had to deal with faulty equipment. The problem lay in a lack of suitable kit for a force of this size, which dwarfed anything Canada had ever fielded for battle. Most of the Canadian-made equipment failed, and failed badly. The soldiers' leather harness, worn on the torso to store water bottles and ammunition, was inadequate in comparison to the British model. The much-derided MacAdams shovel was a small steel spade with a firing loop drilled in it. In theory the invention was not a bad idea—designed as it was to provide the soldiers with some sort of armoured protection on the battlefield—but it proved incapable of stopping a high velocity round and was impractical as a shovel.[20] That the shovel had been patented by Sam Hughes's secretary, Ena MacAdams, seemed to suggest that its adoption by the militia reeked of patronage, and although no wrongdoing was ever uncovered, that did not stop the spread of nasty rumours. In addition, boots were poorly constructed and dissolved in the mud. The soldiers derided them as "Sham shoes"—a play on Sam Hughes. Such cheerfulness in the face of misery showed that civilian-soldiers were learning to grouse and lump it; but because Hughes was perceived as the one who got all this equipment for "his boys," he suffered the scorn of his soldiers, who increasingly held a poor view of the minister.

Back in Ottawa, the Liberals, too, linked these deficiencies in equipment back to the minister or the cronies to whom he had awarded contracts. One had to expect such problems in the fledgling Canadian war industry, but Sam Hughes proved inflexible in reappraising the situation. Hughes blamed the British, arguing forcefully to Borden that there were no problems with any of the equipment and that it was an imperial conspiracy. In the letting of contracts, Hughes insinuated, "It appeared British manufacturers rather than Canadian soldiers were being considered."[21] When the minister's friends were condemned for incompetence, graft, or simply for failing, he felt it as an attack on himself. Despite his burst of energy and enthusiasm in whipping up the country, Hughes was quickly proving inadequate to deal with the complexities of the war effort.

* * *

"Sam is reported to be here!" wailed John J. Creelman, commander of the 2nd Brigade of Canadian Field Artillery, to his diary on October 18, 1914. "Surely Canada is not safe without him!"[22] Creelman, a Liberal Party supporter, was poking fun at Hughes, but actually despised him. Most Canadians did not share this feeling, but the minister was increasingly revealing his flaws. Sam did not know enough to stay clear of his boys: they no longer needed him, but the minister could not see that. He had enjoyed such a grand time at Valcartier that when his First Contingent had sailed from Quebec, the impetuous Hughes had begged Borden to let him join the forces overseas. The prime minister agreed, as he too wanted to ensure that the Canadians were well treated, and he hoped that with the minister out of the country he might soothe some of the bruised egos in his cabinet.

An excited Sam raced to New York and took a fast ship across the Atlantic. Borden had warned his minister—pleaded might be the better word—that he should keep a low profile in England, as the press had been told that an exhausted Hughes was leaving Canada for a much-needed rest. Hughes duly agreed, yet even before he left New York, the media-friendly minister had announced to gawking Americans—who were of course still neutral in the war, and would remain so until April 1917—that Canada could "send enough men to add the finishing touches to Germany without assistance from either England or France."[23] Borden was not amused. Neither was British Rear-Admiral R.E. Wemyss, who commanded the escort warships guiding the First Contingent to England. "With an ignorance that was truly sublime in its magnitude," wrote Wemyss of Hughes after a conversation, he "told me that when 'his boys' arrived in Flanders—and he thought they would land at Calais immediately—the enemy would begin to feel unhappy. The spirit was splendid but the ignorance colossal."[24]

Sam Hughes arrived in England before his boys. That suited him fine and gave him time to attend to other business, which he did in his full colonel's uniform. So much for a rest. One essential duty occurred on

October 22, when Sam was finally gazetted major general, a promotion backdated to 1912, when his appeal for the rank had first started.[25] The high rank was another sign of his blurred role as political minister and military commander, and it allowed him to bully most of the soldiers as well as his fellow politicians.

The British greeted the "holidaying" Sam as a hero. One writer described him as "Commander-in-Chief of Canada's Army," much to the minister's delight.[26] The English press showered him with praise for his patriotic and "stirring" speeches, although some Canadians were disturbed by his vanity and indiscretion.[27] Canadian Herrick Duggan, who was in England at the time on business, wrote of how Hughes's hyperbolic speeches grated on him and others, and pleaded for "somebody [to] keep him quiet."[28] Nobody could do that of course, and Hughes opened temporary offices in the Savoy Hotel in London. According to Lieutenant-Colonel George Nasmith, "men looking for contracts frequented the place and the Savoy quickly became the Canadian headquarters in London." It was close to the War Office and it "speedily became the centre of all things Canadian in London."[29] Hughes did his part, promising more men, more supplies, more of everything. There is little indication that he consulted with anyone in Ottawa.

Before Major-General Hughes left England to return to Canada in November 1914 to raise a second fighting division, the minister was shocked to hear about his soldiers getting into trouble with alcohol and displays of indiscipline. Following the orders of Hughes—the "Foe of Booze," as he was known to some of the soldiers—the Canadian training camp on Salisbury Plain was "dry," even if the ground was not.[30] After marching and training in driving rain and the ankle-deep mud, the soldiers were informed that they would have to be content with coffee and tea. That arbitrary decision was unacceptable to many of the men, who promptly made their way to nearby villages, where they converged on the taverns, got drunk, and fought. As a result of censorship in both England and Canada, scant news of this aberrant behaviour made its way back to the home front, but the Canadian commander, Edwin Alderson, heard about it from his military superiors and the local civilian authorities, who demanded that he rein in his unruly colonials.

Responding to the pressure, Alderson reversed Hughes's decision and set up canteens to sell beer, although with restricted hours.[31] "Prolonged cheers" greeted the announcement to revoke the dry policy.[32] Lieutenant Victor Tupper, grandson of former prime minister Sir Charles Tupper, noted in a letter home, Alderson "seems to be a fine fellow; he has won the hearts of all ranks by fighting Sam Hughes and establishing wet canteens."[33]

Sam was not amused, but he did not pursue the matter. In a visit to the soldiers on Salisbury Plain, he must have been informed by loyal officers that it was a lost cause. He did not raise the wet canteen issue, although his passion got the better of him during several addresses. One soldier wrote of watching cringingly as Hughes spoke to him and his comrades with "explosive language, and at times was quite hysterical and seemed to lose control of himself completely."[34] While the excitable Sam did not push the issue of drink, he harboured a grudge against Alderson, later telling the House of Commons that the British general's actions were a deliberate "slap" at himself, and that he "took this as a personal insult."[35] At the time, Hughes's distrust of Alderson was deepened; here was a professional soldier so timid that he had seemed to lack the gumption to pull the Canadians out of Salisbury mud, now also lacking the moral courage to deny soldiers body-damaging drink. Hughes and Alderson would cross swords again and again over the next eighteen months.

The commanding officer of the 15th Battalion, Colonel John Currie, who was no relation to Arthur, remarked snidely in his wartime memoirs, "It was fondly imagined that any Canadian who could shoot straight and who had a week's training could take his place in the ranks and would be just as good as a [regular] soldier."[36] These wishful thoughts were soon driven from the minds of most Canadians soldiers. Training was needed, and an awful lot of it, to prepare for trench warfare on the Western Front. Senior officers, too, were learning their craft.

Lieutenant-Colonel Arthur Currie earnestly carried out his duties, working hard and rarely leaving the camp. He wrote revealingly to his mother: "I want so to act here that you will be proud of me and even my enemies will have cause to respect me."[37] While the pear-shaped, jowly Currie looked older than his years because of his weight and awkward manner, he put his agile mind toward making his brigade battleworthy. As Currie's brigade major, the British professional Major H. Kemmis Betty, wrote of the brigadier after two months of training, "It appeared that Currie was getting a very definite 'grip' on his Brigade both in an administrative sense and what is implied in the term 'Command.'"[38]

Most of Currie's officers could see how hard he was working and sought to meet his expectations. The brigadier had a commanding presence, but not in a way that dwarfed others. As G.C.W. Gordon-Hall, one of the senior British staff officers with the Canadian Division, remarked, "He listened to the other side of the matter under discussion; he did not blindly and violently push forward his own interest and without prejudice or 'arriere' accepted the position. If he could not attain what he considered the best he was quite ready to do the best he could with what was available."[39] These were impressive qualities, and another officer observed that Currie "was direct in address and manner. Voice strong and vibrant. A good listener and when something had to be decided, expressed himself carefully."[40] He had strong powers of observation and liked to talk to his officers and men face to face. Many noted his calmness and imperturbability. T.V. Scudamore, who had known Currie in Victoria before the war, observed that the only time he saw the lieutenant colonel flustered in England was on a Brigade Church Parade, shortly after arriving at Salisbury, when he observed a man smoking. "Quite forgetting that he was standing next to the padre, he shouted in a tremendous voice of his that could be heard distinctly by everyone present, 'Put out that cigarette. Doesn't that BUGGER realize that he's in church.' He immediately realized his mistake and blushed."[41]

While Arthur was a leader among the officers with whom he interacted, he seemed cautious around his men. He had roughly 4,000 under his command, and, according to one officer, they "had no more than a passing acquaintance with him."[42] Currie was busy and he tended to focus on those directly under him rather than meeting and mixing with the rank and file. There were many ways to command troops, but this one did not endear him to the men. Tough choices were made easier for a commander when he had some distance from his troops, yet many of the men, who rarely saw Currie except when he was inspecting them or at ceremonies, had the impression that he was only "a big man in plaid breeches with a stentorian command who thought a lot of himself."[43] The usually observant Currie seemed unwilling or unable to turn a critical eye on himself, and he either did not care what his men thought or was too busy to give it much worry. This did not mean, however, that he was not proud of his soldiers; indeed, he wrote to his old friend Matson that they were a fine and fit body of men, who would fight like "Billy be damned."[44] But displaying some of this enthusiasm would have gone a long way with his soldiers. Currie's inability to communicate his warmth to the men was a flaw in his command style, and it was one that he carried with him throughout the war. It would be magnified in the closing months of the conflict, even transformed into the charge that he was guilty of wasting his own soldiers' lives.

On February 2, 1915, Currie was promoted to the rank of colonel, still a full grade below brigadier. Two days later, his brigade was reviewed by the King, as part of the entire 18,000-strong Canadian Division, which consisted of the three infantry brigades (commanded by brigadiers), each comprising four battalions (commanded by a lieutenant colonel). There were also artillery, medical, and logistical formations to support the 12,000 infantrymen. The inspection was an indication that the Canadians would soon be off to France and then to the Western Front, where the division would serve in the British Expeditionary Force (BEF) as part of a British corps (of which there would eventually be eighteen) that was grouped in one of the British armies (of which there would eventually be five) under commander-in-chief Sir John French. Currie could only wonder if his training and hard work would pay off when his soldiers met the enemy in battle.

Colonel Arthur Currie's arrival on the continent was an inauspicious event. Although he had withstood the terrible storm that beset his ship as it crossed the Channel, he had almost immediately succumbed to a grave flu, and for almost a week could barely stand. It was maddening to be confined to a bed, but he was healthy enough to be present for the inspection of the Canadian Division by Field Marshal Sir John French on February 20. Currie and his men were aching for the action of a fight, but static trench warfare had replaced the sweeping manoeuvre battles of 1914. The armies had dug into the ground and stayed there, as shallow temporary protective ditches became deep and fortified trenches. Drudgery and danger characterized the soldiers' rotation through the front lines, rather than heroic charges or gallant operations.

Currie was almost immediately sent on a trench warfare course, even as the infantry of the four battalions in his 2nd Brigade began their tours into the underground fortifications that criss-crossed the Western Front. This subterranean world of sandbags and muddy ditches would be the soldiers' home for the next four years. The stench of death filled the air. Unburied corpses lay rotting in No Man's Land, the stretch of earth that separated the enemy lines from the Allies. Rats gorged on the rotting flesh, and their revolting squeals and scurrying sounds haunted the sleep-deprived soldiers. The men were soon infested with lice that clung to the seams of their shirts and trousers, feasting on their blood, causing crazed itching. All the while, the enemy fired shells and mortars. There was little rest and a constant need for vigilance in ducking down, and walking stooped over. A man's punishment for inattentiveness could be a sniper's bullet through the head.

While Currie's men learned in the hard school at the front, the brigadier—who had finally been appointed that rank on March 4—made a good impression on the British as he studied the problems of trench warfare. "He wanted to absorb what you knew and did so," wrote one of the most impressive British soldiers of the war, William Edmund Ironside, who would later rise to become chief of the imperial general staff (CIGS).[45] Another future CIGS, Archibald Montgomery-Massingberd, was directly involved in Currie's training at this time; years later, he described his trainee as "obviously an enthusiast with a well balanced mind, who wanted to know the reason for decisions taken. He looked what he was—a lawyer and could not at the time have been described as a soldierly figure."[46] While Currie was no lawyer, he certainly seemed out of place as a brigadier, but he won over his critics quickly with his agile mind and desire to learn.

When Currie returned to the Canadian Division, he went immediately to the front lines. After studying trench warfare in the abstract, he wanted to experience the reality, and unlike in England when he seemed too busy for the men, now he was sharing some of the dangers with them. It was as grim as he had imagined, but he made it routine to visit his soldiers, even those in the firing line. Trekking through the sleet and mud, and occasionally across wooden boards that had been laid over shell craters, he examined defences, talked to his men, and stared through periscopes into the desolation of No Man's Land. During these forays to the front, Currie believed strongly in setting an example for the men, so he often refused to duck when snipers' bullets whizzed by or shells exploded in the distance. Many soldiers took courage from their brigadier, who seemed impervious to the worst that the enemy would send over.[47]

But there was no avoiding the danger at the front, and Currie's force was slowly reduced as men were killed relentlessly by bullet and shell. Currie grieved over the death of a young lieutenant, Herbie Boggs, who was the son of a neighbour in Victoria. The brigadier attended the funeral and wrote to inform Boggs's parents.[48] Many officers felt similar to Currie, revealing paternal attitudes toward their men. The death of each man under their command wore away at the officers, although the pain became more numbing as the numbers climbed.

After acclimatizing to the trenches in February and March 1915, Alderson's Canadians were moved to the fearsome Ypres salient in Belgium. Known as "Wipers" to the soldiers there, the salient was a horror show. The Allied lines jutted into the German positions in a half-circle, running 27 kilometres in total, but only 13 kilometres from the base, with the Belgian city of Ypres located to the west. The guns rumbled day and night, sending down showers of shrapnel and thundering high explosions, but the trenches could not be abandoned in favour of safer positions. The salient was important symbolic ground, as it was the last major Belgian city in Allied hands and the British had shed blood in a heroic stand, holding back German forces in the previous November and December. It was also an essential logistical hub through which to get supplies and men to the front. Ypres was not to be relinquished.

As part of the British Second Army, Alderson's Canadian Division went into the salient, with Currie's 2nd Brigade relieving French troops on April 14. The Canadians began to strengthen the trenches by shoring up the walls with sandbags or digging secondary lines of defence. There was a sense of urgency, as Currie had warned his men that intelligence indicated a possible enemy attack, which seemed all the more evident since the German bombardment had increased in intensity. Currie's headquarters also fell victim to the shelling, as the brigadier was stationed in a shattered village near Wieltje, and his advanced headquarters were even closer to the front at Pond Farm, another shattered farmhouse. That advanced headquarters still held the building's civilian occupants, who sheltered in the basement, and farm animals roamed the grounds, many of which were soon gutted by shrapnel.

The Germans ruined a fine spring day on April 22 by heavily shelling Ypres and the roads leading from the city to the front lines. Hundreds of Belgian refugees were caught in the bombardment, and soon the city was on fire. The gag-inducing smell of roasting flesh was mixed with burning possessions. At 4 P.M., the Germans unleashed a green-yellow cloud of chlorine gas, with the highest concentrations drifting through the Allied lines to the left of the Canadians.[49] One by one the guns fell silent, and those French or Algerian troops who were not immediately suffocated pulled back or fled in terror in the face of this unprecedented chemical pestilence. While some of the resilient French forces remained in pockets of resistance behind the initial front lines, the two divisions were all but destroyed as fighting formations.

Richard Turner's 3rd Brigade was on the left flank of the division, and his forces were closest to the cloud's periphery. They watched French forces stumbling to the rear as they fled the gas clouds. Hacking and coughing Canadian soldiers, eyes streaming tears, trained their Ross rifles on the German infantry units advancing tentatively behind the noxious clouds. Dozens, then hundreds, were cut down, but still the enemy pushed deep into the Allied lines. Some of those Germans were saved as many of the Ross rifles jammed in the firing frenzy of sustained combat; the straight-pull bolts were unable to extract the spent cartridges, and much of the hastily produced British ammunition was irregularly shaped. Canadians left defenceless in the heat of battle blamed their rifle. One veteran remarked angrily, "The Ross Rifle Company got the money; our brave men died for the aforesaid company's folly and greed. It was hell."[50]

On the right flank, Currie could not see the gas clouds or the retreating French troops due to the uneven terrain. But he knew that something had happened from the audible density of fire. Despite the confusion at the front, Currie's report to headquarters was a model of clarity and conciseness, and this continued throughout the battle. On the left flank, Turner was bombarded continuously, and had far less control over his forces. Within this chaos, erroneous reports emanated from the 3rd Brigade headquarters, with Currie's old friend Garnet Hughes and Brigadier Turner unable to ascertain what was happening on the front. At 7:10 P.M., the 3rd Brigade informed Alderson's divisional headquarters that they had "no troops left," and that the line was being driven in by enemy advances. The brigade's front was indeed under heavy pressure, but Turner's men were holding fast, although some platoons had been overwhelmed by enemy fire and troops.

While Currie's men had not yet faced enemy action beyond heavy shelling, he realized that the centre of gravity for the battle was on Turner's front. If the 3rd Brigade folded, the base of the salient could be cut off and some 50,000 Allied troops trapped and made prisoners of war, or worse. Currie acted decisively, sending his 10th Battalion, composed of men drawn from Calgary, to shore up Turner's crumbling defences.[51]

In the first Canadian offensive operation of the war, the 10th and 16th Battalions counterattacked the Germans at Kitcheners Wood around midnight on the 22nd. In a massed bayonet charge against a dug-in defender, the Canadians pierced the enemy's lines and drove them back. While the losses were high, with more than 1,000 casualties over the course of the night and the next day, the Canadians slowed the German advance through great bravery and personal sacrifice.

Throughout April 22 and 23, the Allied lines along the front were pushed back, but were not broken, even though seventeen British battalions—of which twelve were Canadian—were fighting off 42 German battalions.[52] Most of the pressure had been on Turner's front, but Currie had not sat on his heels, knowing that it was only a matter of time before his forces were attacked. He ordered his soldiers to strengthen the line by building new positions and sighting rifle pits to lay down a crossfire of withering bullets, and he gathered counterattacking forces. It was nearly impossible to travel over the broken terrain during the day, as the front was swept with unceasing machine-gun fire, but Currie hurried from position to position, running crouched over, finding the folds and safety in the ground. The brigadier had too few men to hold the front, so he paid special attention to the four batteries of artillery guns supporting his front-line formations, the 5th and 8th Battalions. The gunners could offer fire support to beleaguered infanteers, especially if the enemy was forced to attack over open ground. And then they waited.

At 4 A.M. on April 24, the Germans launched the second lethal gas cloud of the war. The dense, greenish cloud of chlorine rolled menacingly like a fog bank toward the apex of Turner and Currie's battalions in the front lines. While Canadians with an education in science had discerned the enemy's use of chlorine two days earlier, and passed that information along, most of the men at the front were still helpless and forced to fend for themselves against the lung-searing gas by breathing through wetted clothes. The cold vapours brought terror and death. But the Canadians held their ground. They paid the price. So too did the Germans advancing nervously behind the death cloud. While hundreds of Canadians succumbed to the gas or lay gasping through ravaged lungs, the angry survivors cut the enemy to bits. Even as their Ross rifles jammed, several hundred riflemen, supported by a few Colt machine guns and artillery fire, made a red mess of the advancing German troops who had expected to face only the chemically contorted dead.

Behind the front lines, Currie's worst fears were realized. His nose and eyes ran, and his head was pounding from the fumes, but he knew that his soldiers had taken the brunt of the gas and he could see from the fighting that they were slowly being overwhelmed. The brigadier had few reserve troops to support his wavering front lines. His 10th Battalion had been shot to bits during the counterattack against Kitcheners Wood on the night of the 22nd, but three of his companies of about 600 riflemen from the 7th Battalion had pulled back from Turner's front and dug in around the strongpoint of Locality C. It was a weak force with which to hold off a sustained enemy assault. With sandpaper eyes and throbbing head, and with shells crashing and bullets rending the air, Currie coolly studied the situation.

Panicky communiqués from Brigadier Richard Turner's 3rd Brigade headquarters had misrepresented the battlefront; these included reports that Currie's troops had broken in the face of the gas attack at 4:55 A.M., when in fact the trenches were still held. But Currie could see that the situation was going from bad to catastrophic, especially when at 6 A.M. the 15th Battalion (one of Turner's units), to the left of Currie's line, was pierced and then broke under the strain of a series of enemy advances. While pockets of the Highlanders held their ground, most were annihilated as the Germans streamed through their lines. One of the few survivors bleakly recounted of the battle: "If hell was ever let loose it was around that spot. We were gassed, we were charged, we were bayoneted and shelled most unmercifully. We were blown from out of our positions by high-explosive shells, many buried alive, many torn and wounded … many blown to eternity."[53]

Although the front trenches on the left were breached, a second line of Canadian defenders (the 7th Battalion) were containing the Germans for the moment, but not for long. While Currie had complete faith in his two excellent battalion commanders in the front lines, L.J. Lipsett and G.S. Tuxford, whose 8th and 5th Battalions had not broken but were now forced to shoot into the advancing Germans, some of whom were in their rear areas, the brigadier was cut off from Turner's headquarters. With no more reserves to stem the tide, Currie could do little but watch the battle unfold. Around 7 A.M. Currie's headquarters was hit by enemy high-explosive shells and all of its equipment destroyed. Currie moved to the 2nd Artillery Brigade and used its communication network to keep in touch with headquarters.

In the late morning Currie's second ad hoc headquarters was destroyed by shellfire, and he barely escaped death. While shells exploded around his position, he continued to try to rouse the British on the flanks and rear from their inertia with urgent telegrams. The British troops consistently refused to move forward into the line without orders from divisional headquarters.[54] An exhausted and frustrated Currie could scarcely believe the absurdity of having armed and fresh troops waiting a few thousand metres to the rear but refusing to move forward, while his force—and the British to his right for that matter—were in danger of being cut off and decapitated. In fact, with the Germans driving deep into the Canadian interior—to Locality C—by 10:30 A.M., several of his platoons had been surrounded and snuffed out, while the entire garrison holding that key position was in a desperate firefight with the enemy.

It was far worse on Currie's left. Turner's headquarters was in a panic. They had been shelled and gassed, and neither Turner nor Garnet Hughes had control of the battle. Driven from his headquarters by enemy fire, Turner had taken refuge with livestock. The farm was destroyed, soldiers killed, and cows and pigs splayed around the area. Turner was injured in the battle, too, for he recounted in his diary over the next month that his head was ringing and that he could not think clearly at times.[55] At the very least he suffered a severe concussion; he may have also succumbed to what was known as shell shock, a form of post-traumatic stress disorder.

With the British leaving Currie twisting in the wind, the Canadian brigadier believed that divisional headquarters several kilometres to the rear did not understand the gravity of the situation. Currie had received a desperate message from Turner's headquarters at 11:30 A.M. noting that there were "no substantial re-inforcements at my disposal to re-inforce your left.... My right front is being blown out of successive positions."[56] With the Germans steadily pressing in on his forces, his left flank now severed from Turner's forces, and no further reserves, Currie made the bold, if controversial, decision to leave his headquarters and go to the rear to talk sense to the British. He wanted to attack to restore the situation. He needed men for that. And he was going to get them.

Shortly after noon, the big brigadier set out under shellfire for the rear, but not before informing his subordinates, battalion commanders Lipsett and Tuxford, of his plans, and ordering them to retire to a more stable position. They refused Currie's 11:45 A.M. order, and Currie did not press the issue. Both of his battalion commanders agreed with the brigadier's decision to leave the front, especially since Currie had no more reinforcements with which to support them. While neither of the battalion commanders thought it wise to pull troops back from their entrenched position, Lipsett and Tuxford were empowered by Currie to order a retreat if they deemed the situation desperate.[57]

The brigadier passed through the once-green fields that were pitted with shell craters. Bodies lay unburied; the wounded cried out in agony. With stray bullets snapping around him, Currie frequently had to dive into craters or ditches before picking himself up again and resuming his steady movement toward Major-General Thomas D'Oyly Snow's 27th divisional headquarters at Potijze. Along the way, Currie ran into a fresh British battalion of infantry who were dug-in and awaiting orders. He implored the commanding officer to attack, but the unit had conflicting orders and refused to move. The British were relying on Alderson's divisional headquarters, several kilometres to the rear, to tell them what to do. Currie simply appeared like a panic-stricken brigadier, but he was well aware that the British and Canadian headquarters were trying to control a battle that was changing by the minute, though it took several hours for messages to be delivered by foot or horse. That the British refused to move would have been a ludicrous joke if the Canadian front was not so perilously close to being driven in and destroyed.

Alderson's headquarters was trapped in the rear, as the roads were clogged with advancing soldiers and retreating civilians, so it fell to Currie to convince General Snow of the dangerous situation at the front. Snow had a reputation for being one of the nastiest men in the British army. A red-faced Currie, uniform muddied and hair plastered with sweat to his head, arrived at Snow's headquarters around 3 P.M. Taking a minute to catch his breath and compose himself, he entered the dugout and prepared to offer a summary of events before asking for assistance. Snow had never met Currie before but seems to have harboured a prejudice against the Canadians, perhaps because he was a professional soldier and they largely amateurs. His notoriously short temper had not been helped by a fractured pelvis suffered earlier in the year, which still ailed him, and his prejudices against the Canadians seemed reinforced since their flank was folding. These events made him distrustful, even belligerent, toward the colonial standing before him, looking unsoldierly in every way.

An already upset Snow bellowed at Currie before he had opened his mouth: "Well, what now?" Despite the stress of almost three days of constant battle, poison gas, and having seen hundreds of his men killed, Currie gave Snow a calm report listing the difficulties faced by the Canadians, and even used Snow's map to illustrate his points. The incredulous British general was barely listening. What was this colonial doing in his headquarters? Why was he not fighting it out at the front? Snow snapped to attention and exploded in rage when he heard that there was a gap between Currie's 8th Battalion and Turner's forces on the left, where the poison gas had drifted through their lines. With bulging eyes and neck veins throbbing, Snow blamed Currie, demanding how he had "allowed such a thing to occur."[58] Currie explained the situation again, but when he suggested that reinforcements be sent to shore up the front, Snow exploded, "Have you come to teach me my profession and dictate to me how I shall handle my Division?"[59] A rebuked Currie later remarked that the British general "roundly abused me" and told me to "get out," shouting "give them hell, give them hell." The Canadian was not pleased, noting, "I have never heard a more stupid remark," especially since Snow refused to give him any men.[60] When an exasperated Currie asked for some paper to update Alderson with a message, Snow pounced on him again, denouncing his slowness, perhaps expecting him to lead a counter-charge back against the enemy lines by himself and his batman. To Currie, Snow was simply a fool. But maddeningly, he was a fool who controlled the reserves.[61]

A dispirited Currie left Snow's headquarters and prepared to go back to the front. E.F. Lynn, then with the Canadian Engineers, witnessed the brigadier's degrading experience with Snow, later writing admiringly to Currie that Snow was "in a very ill temper and excited, while you were cool."[62] But none of that mattered now. Currie had gambled in a last-ditch effort to find reinforcements and he had failed. It must have appeared to him that the British were willing to sacrifice his men while the imperials prepared a new line of trenches. As he pondered such grim prospects, Currie eventually stumbled across a number of stragglers from Canadian units. He ordered some to dig in, and those from his four infantry battalions—numbering around 200 men—he marched back to the front.[63] Even though he must have believed that he was facing certain death, neither he nor his men wavered as they returned to battle.

When Currie finally returned to the front, he was surprised to hear that Snow's headquarters had already issued orders to counterattack. Snow's failure to tell Currie about the attack was either some sort of malicious motivator—perhaps the Canadians would hold out more fiercely if they believed they were alone—or an indication that Snow too had lost control of the battle, and was unsure of where the Canadians or his own troops were located. Or one of Snow's more cogent staff officers may have sent some of the battalions ahead into the attack, circumventing the general's authority.[64] Whatever the case, this attack was exactly what Currie had argued for, and the British operation on the 24th halted the German advance during the course of a hard day of battle.

The British forces had been trying to close a gap between Currie and Turner's forces that had started to open up when the 15th Battalion had been annihilated and overrun at 6 A.M., an event that sent convulsions through the 3rd Brigade's headquarters. Sporadic communication from front to rear plagued the command and control of forces and left Turner reeling. After eight more hours of desperate fighting, he either misunderstood or wilfully refused to follow a divisional order to hold and strengthen his line. Instead, around 2 P.M. he ordered a retreat of his infantry to a secondary trench, the G.H.Q. Line, which was only half built and easily enfiladed by enemy fire since much of the fortifications faced the wrong direction. This order spelled disaster for Turner's men, many of whom questioned the authenticity of the order, thinking it might be a German ruse.[65] It was not, and Turner's headquarters offered no direction as to how the infantry, dug-in and exchanging fire with the enemy, were supposed to disengage in broad daylight and run rearwards the length of several football fields. They would be shot in the back. When the Canadians were finally forced to retreat from the enemy, they paid a crippling price in lives.

The night of April 24 saw the ragged, brutalized Canadians holding a series of shallow trenches and ad hoc strongpoints. Currie later wrote that, during the intense fighting, he "thought more than once that it was all over but we stuck."[66] Even in a heavy rain, exhausted soldiers slept like—and with—the dead. Leaders had been killed and units mixed up, but still the Canadians had banded together to fight onward. The various divisional commands in the rear had little reliable intelligence, and often threw forces into the breach, some of which had been destroyed as they moved over open ground. A British counterattack by the 10th Brigade at 5:30 A.M. on the 25th was shattered, but the operation forced the enemy to ground again, spoiling an advance that would have fallen on the British and Canadian lines.

Currie had been absent from his headquarters for a significant portion of the 24th, since he had been slow to return to the front after his encounter with Snow, both getting lost and taking some time to redistribute the 200 reinforcements he found in the rear. Rumours of his death had been quelled, and after Currie snatched a few hours of furtive sleep—

his first since the 22nd—he was up and organizing the defences by 3 A.M. Sick with exhaustion and the lingering cough brought on by the gas, he remained in control, and one of the senior staff officers sent from Alderson's headquarters, Lieutenant-Colonel Gordon-Hall, could scarcely believe his calm and professional attitude. As dawn was breaking on the 25th, Currie was still conducting a tour of his lines, trying to rally his men for an attack he knew would come sometime during daylight hours. "We must hang on till nightfall," he implored.[67] They did, but at the cost of hundreds of lives.

The Canadians were close to collapse by nightfall on April 25, and Currie was forced to pull back his front lines, especially the 5th and 8th Battalions, to Gravenstafel Ridge, one of the few highpoints still in Allied hands. Confusion reigned from front to rear, and the British forces on the right of Currie's brigade accused him of pulling out of the line and leaving them to their fate. It appears that Currie failed indeed to inform the British of his withdrawal, although his order to pull back from an untenable position was not crippling to the defence since it created a "bag" into which the Germans poured, allowing them to be fired at from three sides.[68] It was not until the early hours of the 26th that Currie's limping, shattered men marched to the rear, having lost almost half of their comrades to capture, maiming, or death.

Currie felt abandoned by the British, his divisional commander Alderson, Turner, and his good friend Garnet Hughes. Turner had commanded his brigade in the battle as if it were fighting alone, pulling back without regard for Currie's brigade on the right and leaving it vulnerable to a catastrophic counterattack in which his boys would take it in the neck. The British had been no better, seemingly leaving the Canadians to fight to their deaths. And that they did, with Currie's forces suffering 1,829 casualties between April 22 and May 3, the bulk of them occurring between the 22nd and 24th.[69] The other two Canadian brigades suffered just as grievously, and it was clear that Alderson had failed to exert a firm grip on the degenerating situation at the front, his headquarters remaining woefully out of touch several kilometres behind the lines.

Yet Brigadier Arthur Currie's own unorthodox actions, which took him away from the battlefront, left him open to severe criticism. Although he was trying to find a solution to a desperate situation, Currie knew that it was not the role of a brigadier to go roaming in search of reinforcements. While he empowered his battalion commanders to act as they saw fit in his absence, such an order surely could have led to greater confusion if Lipsett and Tuxford had not been working in accordance. Even worse, Currie's journey to the rear had left his own headquarters out of touch with the division's. While Currie's actions can be explained, it is perhaps not surprising that the already prejudiced Snow viewed the Canadian brigadier as a coward who had fled the front.

Turner's continuous series of failures in the battle is not easily understood, except by reiterating the chaos and confusion that plagued the front. While communication lines were constantly severed, Richard Turner and Garnet Hughes had lacked a commander's feel for the battle, and both would likely have been fired from a British division. Currie and Alderson might have got the axe too. Alderson believed that Turner's confused decision making had almost doomed the Canadians, a conclusion he was helped to reach when an angry and fatigued Turner denounced him for abandoning his forces.[70] Alderson did not like being reminded of his own impotence in the battle; however, he did nothing other than carry a grudge. Firing Canada's South African war hero Turner would have cast a shadow over the Canadians' tenacity and bravery. Moreover, Turner was a Hughes man, and Alderson was not yet certain how to manage the mercurial minister. In the end, Turner, Alderson, and Currie were saved by their own soldiers, who had fought like lions in the face of overwhelming odds and the new terror of poison gas.

CHAPTER 6

A One-Man Army

SAM HUGHES, 1915

A roaring Sam Hughes pushed his way past the military secretary and crashed through the doors to Lord Kitchener's room at the War Office. The stunned British war hero, face flushed with anger, famed moustache twitching, seemed to be confronted by a madman. The Canadian minister marched over to Kitchener, pinning him behind his desk. Hughes wagged his finger as he verbally dressed down the Hero of Khartoum—the face on ubiquitous recruitment posters that had convinced tens of thousands to enlist.

Hughes's tongue-lashing was over "his army." Kitchener, it was rumoured, had decided to break up the Canadian formations and spread the soldiers among British units at the front. An indignant Hughes barked, "Sir, do I understand you to say that you are going to break up these Canadian regiments that came over? Why, it will kill recruiting in Canada." A ruffled Kitchener dismissed the minister with a curt reply:

"You have your orders, carry them out." Hughes turned on his heels, but not before cussing, "I'll be damned if I will."[1]

The nationalistic Hughes had thus saved the Canadian forces from being broken up and used as cannon fodder among British formations. Without the minister, there would have been no Canadian Corps, and thus no Vimy Ridge and other famous Canadian victories in 1917–1918. Canada's independence from Britain was won on these battlefields, partly because the Canadians were an identifiable force. Without Sam Hughes, the road to autonomy would have been far longer.

Perhaps. And certainly the story of Sam Hughes dressing down a quivering field marshal has appealed to Canadian nationalists. The only problem is that the incident seems never to have happened. Hughes's action was published in the Canadian official history of 1938, and repeated periodically ever since. But there is no corroborating evidence other than that of an unnamed supposed eyewitness. Kitchener never wrote of such a shocking event, although he was not shy in portraying Hughes unfavourably in both official and unofficial correspondence. And, even more damning to the anecdote's probability, Hughes never told it in public or private.[2] Sam was not one to keep a story of this magnitude a secret, especially one that featured him putting a British field marshal in his place.

No, the story of Sam cowing the British into keeping the Canadians as a coherent force was a myth, one of many surrounding the astonishing Sam Hughes. Hughes was larger than life. And he was certainly larger than the pesky problem of the truth. But his armour of invincibility, his ability to deflect, block, or absorb the blows of his opponents, was increasingly cracking from unceasing assaults. By mid-1915, the minister found himself under almost constant attack.

The casualties from the Battle of Second Ypres in April 1915 shocked Canadians. "This baptism of blood will arouse amongst us a deeper consciousness of national duty," preached a fiery Reverend W.D. Herridge of

Ottawa.[3] He was not alone in his belief that Canada's blood sacrifice demanded even greater exertions on the part of all Canadians, in the form of committing money and men to the overseas war effort. The division had fought well in the battle and been feted throughout the Empire, but the long lists of casualties revealed the deep extent of the carnage. There was no cover-up, no attempt to hide the human cost of the war.[4] With the British Empire threatened, and Canada already having suffered several thousand casualties, many Canadians believed they were in a fight for their very survival against a skilled and resilient enemy. Hughes was also shaken by the casualties to his "boys," and his response was to scathingly attack British strategy by observing, not so innocently, "It is more congenial to bury the dead of the enemy than have the enemy bury ours."[5]

Despite the high casualty rate, Canadians were not deterred from enlisting; in fact, more men, women, and children were galvanized behind the war effort, with tens of thousands of men stepping forward to join the colours. Hughes's return from England in November 1914 had coincided with the raising of a second overseas contingent, which was accomplished in a more organized fashion this time, with divisional and district commanders across the country responsible for finding, training, and quartering the new recruits. Perhaps Hughes realized how the war effort had expanded or that he was too busy to repeat his personal feat in recreating the "miracle at Valcartier," as the newspapers were wont to call it (much to Hughes's satisfaction). Whatever the case, the minister had little involvement in raising the second contingent, and he did not push for centralization again at Valcartier, largely because the camp was not equipped to house men over the harsh winter months. This time, there was no "fiery cross" to follow—the image Hughes had used early in the war in an attempt to hearken back to the raising of armies in Scotland centuries earlier—but instead a measured plan for regional representation, which included a French-Canadian battalion, the 22nd.

Hughes remained the most identified face of the Canadian war effort. As one political observer noted presciently, "The pivot upon which turned Canada's share in the War and Canada's organization for war, enlistment and training in 1915, was the Department of Militia and Defence; the pivot of that Department, the driving-wheel of the Government in this connection, was the Minister in charge."[6] Sir Sam travelled the country in his private rail car, delivering patriotic speeches in the aggressive style of a man possessed. In November, in London, Ontario, he told a crowd that he supported the shooting of dishonest contractors and the "rawhiding" of anyone who questioned the fighting capacity of the Canadian soldiers.[7] The assembled crowd cheered him on; his fellow ministers could only shake their heads at the unstable force sweeping across the nation. "His is the name, nowadays, on every Canadian tongue," wrote a journalist of Sam. "Some roll it like a delicious morsel, some like a quinine capsule; only everybody's rolling it."[8]

The war was becoming a crusade. This was a war for civilization, as some called it, against an evil, barbaric, militaristic German *Kultur* that needed to be opposed to the last man and the last dollar. Hughes increasingly saw himself as an avenging angel. But his staff at militia headquarters barely saw him at all. Hughes's military secretary, Charles Winter, wrote that the minister's many forays overseas or across the country meant "the departmental files awaiting his decisions would accumulate to alarming piles."[9] In fact, from August 1914 to November 1916 Hughes was out of the country about one-third of the time, and much of the rest he spent criss-crossing the Dominion.[10] In early January 1915 Borden had to go to the hospital where Hughes was kept for two weeks while suffering from illness and exhaustion, because no one in the minister's department could do anything in his absence. Hughes was almost pathological in refusing to delegate authority or share information with his staff, even the long-suffering militia chief of staff, Willoughby Gwatkin. A frustrated Borden would only mutter, "On matters which touch his insane egotism he is quite unbalanced. On all other matters able and sometimes brilliant."[11]

Hughes did not deliberately aim to sow confusion in his own department. He had enormous energy but lacked a structured mind to carry out

the work. With throngs of officers seeking his decision on some important question or another, Hughes instead diverted them with tales of his
adventures. P.D. Ross and a delegation of journalists met with Hughes to
discuss whether the government could spend more advertising money in
their newspapers, which were suffering financially as paper became
scarcer and more expensive. About fifteen journalists met Hughes in his
office. They barely got a word in. Sam charmed them with stories of his
days as a rural editor and reporter, broke into poetic verse, referenced
literary figures, and talked without pause while the journalists looked on
helplessly. After half an hour, Sam called the meeting to a close, and said
he would look into the matter, even though the journalists had not had a
chance to raise it.[12] Much like his counterpart in England, Lord Kitchener,
Hughes was simply not cut out for the extensive office hours needed to
coordinate the ballooning war effort, and he seemed to treat his wartime
work like an extended election campaign. He was best when he was on
the hustings, selling the war and recruiting, his radiating energy, powerful voice, and enormous stamina both inspiring and cajoling Canadians.
He was an engaging recruiting sergeant, but what the nation needed was
a CEO-like general.

Without an adequate bureaucratic structure to administer the burgeoning war effort, ministers like Hughes were left to fend for themselves
as they encountered new duties and challenges.[13] Sam complicated things
further with his fierce partisan views, which resulted in the appointment
of close friends or party cronies to positions of influence. His choices
were sometimes inspired, as he found industrious businessmen to help
run the war effort. But, increasingly, his appointees let him down badly,
even when he gave them honorary ranks in the hope of controlling them
through military channels. Indeed, this practice became a joke, gener-
ating apocryphal stories such as the one in which Hughes had been well
served by a railway waiter, whom he'd then rewarded with a large tip and
a commission![14]

Hughes was easy to caricature, and the opposition went after him relentlessly. They charged rightly that Hughes's issuing of war-related contracts and handing out of important appointments were such obviously partisan acts that they were an embarrassment to the government and to a war effort that demanded selfless sacrifice. "Contracts are sent to a great extent to those firms who have political pull," wrote John Bassett, a former newspaperman who worked closely with Hughes at his headquarters. But even good Tories needed to win the favour of the minister, as Bassett noted: "The only way to get anything is by coming to Ottawa, securing an interview with the minister, and if he thinks it worthwhile, keeping in touch with the contracts branch."[15] Hughes saw little contradiction here in the pursuit of victory, and he was often pushed by the Tory faithful to be even more blatant in his rewarding of friends, although he found some contracts for Liberals—"I know you would not willingly give business to Grits," wrote one bristling political hack upon hearing that a Liberal hat company had secured a contract. While the Tory rank and file wanted their just rewards, Borden and some members of the cabinet worried that such obvious enriching of friends would hurt the party when it sought re-election.[16] Despite Hughes's limitations as an administrator, however, Borden remained a defender, whether as a result of intimidation, loyalty, or the minister's continuing indispensability to the war effort. But Borden can almost be heard moaning to himself in his description of Hughes's "erratic temperament, countless indiscretions, absurd vanities and lack of systematic administrative capacity" and his opinion that the minister's "judgement was unbalanced and his temperament constantly led him into difficulty and controversy."[17]

In addition to overseeing Canada's primary contribution to the army, Sam Hughes also took on the role of urging industry to meet the insatiable demands of the overseas forces for artillery shells. The war on the Western Front chewed up men and munitions more quickly than anyone could imagine. If the Allies were to break through the German lines and drive the enemy from their occupation of France and Belgium, they had to attack. And to clear the razor-sharp barbed wire and hammer the enemy's entrenched positions, high explosive artillery shells especially were needed. Britain turned to Canada to supply shells or to act as a purchasing agent to secure American munitions. The latter would have been easier, but the nationalist Hughes—ever desirous to show that Canada could stand on its own—had responded to the call that arrived from his British counterpart, Lord Kitchener, on August 24, 1914, by promising that Canada would take up the slack and supply shells.

The only problem was that Canada had almost no armament industry and no organization through which to coordinate an operation on such a large scale. The one prewar government munitions company that existed, Dominion Arsenal, working to its 1914 full capacity, would have taken twelve years to fill the first order of 200,000 shells![18] But Hughes was not deterred. Borden supported him, as he saw the lucrative British contracts as a means of pulling the country out of its economic depression. With characteristic energy, Hughes entered the fray in late August 1914, driven to a frenzy when American munitions agents scoffed at the possibility of the Dominion producing enough shells. A furious Hughes, who was always at his best when battling those who impugned Canada's honour, barked, "By God, the work shall be done in our own country."[19] The Yankees scurried back across the border.

"For action, S.H.," was the curt message from Sam written on his ministerial correspondence from Valcartier on September 7. As David Carnegie, a British munitions expert attached to the Canadians to help guide the fledgling industry, then noted, Sam's signature "carried with it all the authority of any Government seal."[20] In the previous week, Hughes had rounded up industrialists and party friends, and with the above note, he established the Shell Committee. While the committee of businessmen had no clear official status, working neither for the Canadian nor the British government, it began to secure contracts for Canadian manufacturers in the lucrative and patriotic market of munitions. The committee accepted contracts, promised the price per unit of shell manufactured, and then distributed the contracts.

Despite Hughes's dynamic ways, the wartime industry began slowly and cautiously, as most Canadians expected a short war. To retool machines and plants, to hire new staff and experts, would mean financial ruin if the war ended in a few months.[21] Hughes cajoled and pleaded with the financiers and manufacturers to meet Britain's demands—even resorting to the occasional threat—and they slowly did so, but only after he was liberal in handing out contracts. It is hard to imagine how anyone else could have been more effective, and certainly more timid men would have done far worse. In order to entice manufacturers, bids were accepted and signed off on, with the promise of large profits. But the committee maintained almost no transparency in its decisions, and kept few records, which allowed the Liberals to accuse Hughes of gouging the British and favouring his friends. "Rumours of the grossest graft and scandal were in circulation everywhere," noted one Liberal propaganda pamphlet.[22] No one knew for certain what was happening, but the stink of patronage seemed so ripe that even loyal Tories complained that Hughes was too obvious in helping out his friends and exposing the party to unnecessary accusations of selfish partisanship.[23] The *Ottawa Citizen* blasted Hughes and his patronage system as a "maggot eating at the heart of Canadian national life."[24]

Britain faced similar munitions problems in the first year of the war: the need to create an almost entirely new industry from nothing. It responded only marginally faster than Canada to the enormous demands of producing shells, no doubt because the war was on its doorstep, because the country had a much deeper industrial infrastructure than Canada's, and because the aggressive, dynamic, and highly capable David Lloyd George was brought in as minister of munitions in May 1915. By the time Lloyd George sorted out the imperial mess, the vast majority of the Canadian shell contracts were still unfilled, despite Hughes and his committee having been on the case since August 1914.[25] Hughes has often been condemned for the slow output of the Canadian war munitions industry, but he was not responsible for actually manufacturing shells; nor did he have much of a hammer with which to punish those companies that were slow to fill their orders. Munitions production was fraught with difficulties: even after the armies of workers and inspectors were trained, the plants refitted, the equipment purchased—everything from securing the properly tempered steel to finding the right presses to forge the shells—was new and exceedingly complicated. The chemical composition, heating, and cooling of shells needed to be perfect or the shells would be damaged, possibly exploding in the Allied artillery barrels overseas and killing the gun crews. The creation of intricate fuses was even more complicated, and took over two years to master, requiring the Shell Committee to turn initially to American firms. Again, it is worth noting that the enormously complicated act of manufacturing shells by the hundreds of thousands came from nearly nothing, with no precedents, no expertise, and almost no instructions from the British.

There was almost no bureaucratic apparatus in place to administer the new functions imposed on the government, such as dealing with the manufacture of shells and all other wartime contracts. Hughes turned to friends and political cronies to help him secure raw materials from the United States, often bypassing his own department. "I have to do things in a summary way. I have done so all my life and I will go on doing so until the end," Hughes stated publicly when questioned about his ad hoc system. Indeed, the minister got things done; but with no oversight and few auditors or experts, Hughes's system lent itself over time to inefficiency at best, and graft and corruption at worst.[26] He was praised by some of the manufacturers and condemned by others, especially those who arrived late to the industry and did not receive as many lucrative contracts. Sam did not help matters by openly sneering at the whiners: "The trouble is that Canadian firms are all trying to get in on this shell making now when they discover that there is money in it, but they wouldn't touch it at first." Here, Sam was entirely correct, and even his long-time enemy in the cabinet, Minister of Finance Sir Thomas White, recounted the difficulty of enticing manufacturers to turn to munitions.[27] Hughes spoke the hard truth, but he did not know when to back away, and in one justifying letter to the prime minister he was on the attack, questioning the complaining manufacturers' patriotism, insinuating that they were only in it for the profit. Borden would not stand for it, observing coldly, "You were never more completely mistaken in your life."[28]

With increasing problems in doling out contracts and in getting results from the various shell manufacturers, Hughes offered more honorary military titles to leading businessmen in the hope that they might feel bound by duty. Many did, but more than a few scoundrels would soon embarrass the government and leave Hughes hanging in the wind. The worst of these political bagmen was John Wesley Allison, a Tory supporter from Morrisburg, Ontario. Hughes entrusted him to make purchases of tooling machines and other key equipment in the United States, and to dispense contracts there for the intricate shell fuses that could not be manufactured in Canada. Rumours were soon circulating that Allison was lining his pockets by siphoning off large amounts of money through finding fees and, it was whispered, bribes.[29] Profiteering was a serious charge in the patriotic atmosphere of the day, and one that Hughes later described as easily solvable by firing squad. Yet through a misplaced sense of loyalty, Hughes stuck by Allison, even though his Tory colleagues implored him to distance himself as the charges piled up. Even after Allison was discredited, Hughes defended him, calling him "the friend of every honest man."[30] A supporter of Sam remarked on his tendency to see things "in either black or white," noting that "once he had his mind made up, he was virtually immoveable and undoubtedly some of his accomplishments were affected by his mistaken judgements."[31] It was a quality that gave him the strength to fight through almost any form of opposition, but it also meant that when he was wrong, he entrenched, often digging deeper and deeper until he had made a grave for himself.

The Canadian munitions industry had responded slowly with the necessary shells, despite the fact that within nine months an astounding 250 munitions firms were functioning in Canada, where before the war there had been only one. The Shell Committee was damned by its own figures—manufacturers accepted $170 million in contract orders for shells, but delivered only $5.5 million worth by May 1915.[32] Historians have been unkind, comparing the successful production of the last two years of the war to the output in 1915. For example, the Canadian Cartridge Company of Hamilton produced one million shells in October 1917 alone, the largest single-month output in the entire war.[33] That same year, Canada was supplying one-quarter of all shells to the British armies, which were consumed in the prodigious battles on the Western Front, where armies might fire off several hundred thousand shells a day. But foundation for this exceptional productivity had been laid by Sam Hughes.

Borden understood the difficulties facing the Canadian industry in 1915 and had enormous sympathy for Hughes, especially since he had seen the British flail almost as incoherently at the start of the war. The prime minister also understood the value of patronage in the Canadian political system for buying loyalty, but he was increasingly uncomfortable with accusations regarding Hughes's rampant abuse of the process. There were problems with the Shell Committee, but also dozens of scandals relating to the procurement of equipment, with the Liberals seemingly uncovering new ones almost every day. Hughes's critics were legion, but it is worth remembering that in the first three weeks of August 1914 alone, the small Militia Department that numbered a mere 919 employees spread across the entire country was swamped with contract seekers. More than 3,000 contracts were awarded during this time, for all manner of war equipment.[34] No department could have handled such a tidal wave of demand without difficulty, although Hughes devoted far less energy and time to his department than was required. Borden worriedly confided to his diary in April, "Hughes [is treating] scandals affecting his Department very casually and does not seem to realize the situation."[35]

In May 1915, responding to the escalating chorus against the mounting scandals, Borden established a War Purchasing Commission (WPC), headed by Sir Edward Kemp, a Toronto business magnate and close confidant of the prime minister. The WPC would oversee and centralize the purchase of war materiel, including everything from boots to razors. For the moment, the acquisition of shells remained with Hughes and his committee. The wounded Hughes howled that his reputation would be tarnished, and he hated the idea of being blocked from rewarding friends with war contracts. Fed up with Hughes's whining, Borden lost his temper and dismissed him forcefully. The minister took it hard: "As was not unusual, his eyes filled up."[36] One had to be rough with Hughes, something that Borden had learned over the years. As a contemporary observed of attempts to get Sam Hughes to agree to anything against his will, "It was like getting a bull into a box and shutting the door on him before he knew where he was."[37] In this case, Sam slunk away, but he was hurt by having lost a prestigious role in directing the war effort, even though he continued to helm the Shell Committee.

Despite the efficiency of the WPC, the scandals began to pile up regarding contracts awarded by Hughes in the first year of the war, the faults and failings of which were only revealed months later. The sheer number of problems was staggering: from poor Canadian-made boots that dissolved in the mud to the soldiers' webbing that was too constrictive or confining, to Canadian-made cars and wagons that broke down and had no spare parts. Most of the made-in-Canada equipment was found to be deficient, and much of it led back to Hughes or his department. Sam was unrepentant. The critics, he told a cheering crowd in London, Ontario, were "yelping like a puppy dog chasing an express train."[38] But many Canadians read about the charges or received letters from loved ones overseas complaining of faulty Canadian-made equipment, and condemned the government accordingly for its failure to support the troops.

As always, the fiery, nationalistic Hughes was slow to acknowledge that Canuck-manufactured kit could in any way be inferior to its British counterparts. While Hughes was not bothered by such a smear campaign, or simply saw it as partisan posturing, the stink of scandal had lodged itself in Liberal nostrils, and the opposition focused enormous energy in the coming months on embarrassing the minister, hoping ultimately to destroy him.[39] In writing to one supporter after fending off public attacks, Sam Hughes described himself: "My character is unique, my ways are unique, and I propose to follow the old road to the end."[40] Indeed he was unique, but soon it would no longer be possible for Hughes to simply stay on course and follow the same old road.

While Sam seemed a man of solid granite in 1914 and early 1915, cracks had begun to reveal themselves by the latter part of the year. An ongoing source of stress for the minister was the ever-growing need to recruit men for overseas service. No one had foreseen the enormous armies required to fight a major European war between the Great Powers. Canada's initial offer of a division was a significant commitment for the Dominion, especially in relation to the South African War only fifteen years earlier, when Canada had first offered a 1,000-man battalion as sufficient to the scale of its first official overseas modern war. But that scale now seemed positively miniature by comparison to the current war.

Sam had been a one-man army in 1914. As Canada's military figurehead, he had been deeply associated with raising the First Contingent. A figurehead was all that Canada had seemed to need at the time, as the government had to do very little in the first full year of the war to encourage enlistment. Patriotic Canadians responded by the thousands, driven by a sense of adventure, a desire to support the Empire, a belief in the justness of the fight for liberty and against German militarism, and a multitude of other personal reasons. In early 1915, Hughes was up to his usual boastful tricks, bragging, "Canada has sent one contingent, a second is on the way, and if necessary we will send a fifth, a sixth or a twentieth."[41]

Hughes planned for an army of volunteers. In this, he was backed by his prime minister, who, in a December 1914 address to a Halifax audience, insisted, "There has not been, there will not be, compulsion or conscription."[42] The militaristic Sam Hughes would not force Canadians to fight against their will, as shirkers were clearly not the right kind of soldierly material and, in 1915, there was no need to turn to such dregs. "Every true Canadian," believed Hughes, "demands that Canada train and send men, and if necessary, more men, and still more men."[43] For Hughes the important idea was "true Canadian," and those who did not serve deserved only contempt.

After the first 30,000 volunteers, the next 70,000 had come easily too, with over 100,000 recruits reached in early 1915. But recruiting on this scale required enormous planning, and Hughes's professional staff officers warned him of the danger of taking more and more men and grouping them into units that could not be reinforced due to a lack of reserves.[44] Hughes's ultimate dream, and one he had spoken of since the summer of 1915, was that there would be a Canadian army of two corps consisting in total of six divisions. Such a force, it should be noted, would be equal in strength to Britain's entire prewar professional force in England. The goal may have been possible for Canada in terms of raising the roughly 120,000 to 130,000 men needed to fill these formations, but Hughes revealed no understanding of how to keep the divisions up to strength as death, injuries, and illness from battle continually thinned out the fighting formations.

When enlistment numbers dipped a little at the beginning of 1915, Hughes changed the focus of the recruitment drive from local and already established militia units to communities. It was an inspired move. Community leaders—politicians, businessmen, sports stars, celebrities, and other notables—stepped forward to corral their neighbours into service.[45] The war had come home. Loyal citizens were given the opportunity to serve with their pals, neighbours, or co-workers, and they responded in droves, many no doubt fearful of being singled out as not having done their bit by their fellow community members. Hughes also criss-crossed the country in late January and early February 1915, travelling some 7,000 miles in two weeks and delivering at least twenty-five barn-burning recruiting speeches—maybe they were closer to war sermons—as he demanded of his fellow Canadians that they serve the Empire and Canada in their time of need.[46] Many flocked to enlist in Hughes's crusade. Dozens of new battalions were raised in this way, and Hughes beamed with pride. Yet the problem remained of how to keep the formations up to strength when they arrived overseas and were sent to the Western Front. A 1,000-man battalion would last only a few months in the cauldron of battle—and then what? How would it be reinforced? Hughes had no answers and simply authorized the creation of more and more battalions, even though it was apparent by mid-1915 that these newly formed units were being sent overseas and broken up for reinforcements for the existing fighting units on the Western Front. This created great outrage among the soldiers who were shuffled into new units, often without their comrades, and it was viewed widely as a betrayal of the local communities in Canada that lost their hometown battalions or units. Hughes's method attracted soldiers for overseas service, but it was unsustainable and left a bitter legacy.

Back in Ottawa, Hughes's staff worked on establishing coherent plans for enlisting Canadians, asking questions such as how many males there were between eighteen and forty-five, and how many could be enlisted before their absence began to hurt the economy by leaving insufficient numbers to build munitions or bring in the crops? Hughes was not alone in thinking that the human resources for this field force remained untapped, and the prime minister clearly held the same conviction since he raised the target number of men to send overseas to 150,000 in July and then, three months later, to 250,000. These new figures made the recruitment effort incredibly large and complex. Captain Harold Daly recounted how Hughes continued to drive the process and urge new men to join the colours, especially after Borden raised the number of recruits to half a million through a heady decision implemented on January 1, 1916. Although Borden had tied the country to the half-million mark after scant consultation with professional soldiers, his cabinet, or even Canadians, Hughes was fully supportive, and he took on the challenge of raising as big an army as possible. When Borden had second thoughts about his impetuous move, he justified it as "a token of Canada's unflinchable resolve to crown the justice of our cause with victory and with an abiding peace."[47] In the days after the announcement, Borden and Hughes met and talked about how to raise the men. Daly described the scene in which the two men stood over an atlas of Canada, Hughes "showing the different [political] constituencies [across the country]." The minister then "dictated about a hundred telegrams to different people, one in each constituency and out of that I think we got 60,000–70,000 men. He knew everybody all over the country who was popular and who could raise men."[48]

Hughes believed that the success of his personal appeals vindicated him, and that he had no reason to change his approach. With some 218,000 Canadians having enlisted by the end of 1915, no one could have imagined this sort of response at the start of the war, and it far outstripped that of Canada's previous war effort in 1899.[49] When it came to recruiting, Hughes was certainly not the bumbling fool he is often made out to be.

This is not to suggest, however, that there were no problems. Hughes saw the Canadian war effort in terms of raising a national army not only to defend the Empire but also to carve out a place for Canadians on the world stage. Yet, influenced by his fierce partisan beliefs and intolerant religious background, he never understood the need to build consensus within Canada, especially with French Canadians.

Hughes's national crusade did not play well in Quebec. While Canada's largest city, Montreal, had contributed thousands of soldiers to the overseas forces, most were Anglo-Canadians. French-speaking Canadians from Quebec, Acadia, Ontario, and the West served in almost all units, but only the 22nd Battalion went to Europe as an all-French infantry formation. Part of the problem was Sam Hughes. His bigoted words and actions of the past were well remembered in Quebec, the province that had the least significant ties historically to Great Britain and that had recently felt under attack by restrictive anti-French language laws for schools in Ontario and Manitoba. Even appeals to support "mother France" in her hour of need often fell on deaf ears, since many French Canadians felt that secular France was no model for conservative and Catholic Quebec. Furthermore, young men who came from French-speaking rural society, often with large families to support, were less inclined to enlist for overseas service, especially in an English-speaking army.[50] With all these factors working against recruitment, Hughes chose not to devote any extra attention to Quebec, and by the time he needed men from that province in 1916, irreparable damage had already been done to the cause. Hughes was not the only guilty party here, as surely Borden and his Quebec ministers were far too silent on the issue, but Sam has remained an easy target for criticism throughout the years.

Across the country, other prominent Canadians stepped forward and lent their voices to the war effort. Local politicians, patriotic clergy, influential businessmen, women's groups, and many others demanded that Canadians "fight or pay."[51] There was growing pressure, especially in the large cities, on young, white males who were not in uniform. The casualties overseas, especially those from Second Ypres, appeared not to dissuade the patriotic; rather, it impelled them to greater heights of fervour. They must not break faith with those who had fallen. And neither would Sam.

Sam Hughes held almost total control over which units were allowed to go overseas, and his word extended across the country. His partisan ways kept some good Liberal soldiers from commanding units and elevated other Tories who were not fit for command. Hughes also maintained a network of snoops who passed on information as to who was loyal and who could not be trusted. Even long-time Tories such as William Griesbach feared the minister. Griesbach, the former mayor of Edmonton who had served in South Africa, had raised a regiment from Edmonton and it was set to go overseas after months of training. But on May 13, 1915, he received a startling telegram from Hughes, reading, "Have you made the statement that you and your regiment are going overseas in spite of Sam Hughes? You will please give me details of this matter. Meanwhile I am postponing the movement of your regiment that I had previously arranged for."[52] A humbled Griesbach responded quickly: "If an engineer stopped to throw coal at every cur that yelled at his locomotive, he would never bring his train to its destination." No, he had said no such thing, he pleaded. Having quelled the minister, and sufficiently kowtowed to him in the process, he and his regiment were able to proceed overseas. But each man, from chaplain to infantryman, from senior officer to medical doctor, owed their war to Sam Hughes. He was not above reminding them of this obligation when he saw fit.

Sam was resistant to loosening his control even after his forces went overseas. Believing in his own skills, Hughes saw no need to draw a distinction between his civilian ministry and the overseas fighting forces, and he continued to meddle in the army in England and Europe. His previous run-ins with the British high command and his pervasive disdain for professional officers drove him to take a strong role in his soldiers' overseas service. Hughes also framed this interaction as part of a desire to see Canada receive proper recognition for its service and sacrifice, and he had an ongoing worry that the Dominion's war effort would be subsumed within the British worldwide operations and campaigns. Colonel A.F. Duguid, a decorated artillery officer and future official war historian, observed that Hughes was "a tireless advocate of the principle that the colonies should assist the Mother Country in time of war," but he was also a Canadian nationalist who wanted to see Canada rewarded with more autonomy.[53]

Hughes was not alone in demanding that the Canadians fight together as an identifiable unit, but there were other prominent voices, such as Canada's acting high commissioner to London, George Perley, and even the senior military officer in Canada, the chief of staff, Colonel Willoughby Gwatkin, who argued that the Canadians should simply fight as "British regular troops."[54] Hughes might have admitted in 1914 that "Canada had no say whatever" with regard to its place in the war, but that had begun to change, and Sam was far too proud a Canadian nationalist to allow Gwatkin's or Perley's opinions to prevail.[55] While Hughes may not have roughed up Lord Kitchener, as the apocryphal story suggests, he did put his argument multiple times to the British War Office.[56] As Hughes bluntly told Kitchener in 1915, Canada would have "supreme control of her troops," especially since Hughes believed that, as a result of the South African War, the "halos [had] been knocked off the heads" of a lot of British professional soldiers.[57] Under Hughes's watchful eye, the Canadians would serve as part of the British Expeditionary Force—the name given to the largest combined British, Dominion, and colonial forces serving around the world, although largely on the Western Front—and would even be commanded by a British general, but they would keep their own identity.

While Hughes was wary of the British controlling Canadian interests, he seemed equally wary about giving too much power of influence to his generals who were training soldiers in England. His was a policy of divide and confuse, which he put into practice by encouraging senior officers and political appointees to fight for control of the Canadian army. "Everybody hates everybody else like the very devil," wrote veteran soldier Agar Adamson, commenting on the rivalries within the Canadian high command in England.[58] The overseas command was utterly chaotic, and became increasingly so as thousands of Canadians disembarked monthly from the steady stream of ships that carried them across the Atlantic.

The system in place overseas reflected the amateur approach of the wartime government in the first year of the conflict. The Victorian ideal of a largely passive or laissez-faire state, with a small-scale administrative apparatus, was firmly entrenched, even as the war demanded more of citizens and governments. While in 1915 few could anticipate that more than 420,000 Canadians would eventually cross the Atlantic, Hughes exerted little strategic or administrative vision in determining how to deal with the increasing flood. Even worse, Hughes established his own appointees overseas, who often clashed with the proper military and civilian authorities, especially Perley, whom Hughes hated.

But Perley was no political neophyte. The Harvard-educated lumber baron was a long-time supporter of Borden, and had helped him several times during his rocky leadership to put down party insurrections. While Perley was sometimes written off as an English dandy, with his expensive clothes, social graces, and perfectly trimmed beard, he was a political survivor and not easily bullied. As acting high commissioner overseas, he was the eyes, ears, and occasionally the voice for the Canadian government. Defending Canadian interests—and his own position—he wrote pointedly to the prime minister in May of 1915 that few in the British War Office or government could decipher who was in charge of the Canadian forces in England, as there appeared to be at least two conflicting groups: Perley himself, as an official government representative, and a second group "represented here by various people sent out by Hughes and not under the control of the other."[59] The unperturbed Borden ignored Perley's warning, no doubt soothed by Hughes's constant assurances that all was well in England.

The situation steadily degenerated as vicious power struggles ensued. Hughes had his henchmen, in particular Colonel John Carson, a chubby Montreal mining executive and former commander of the Canadian Grenadier Guards, who had the unlucky job of acting as the minister's key administrator in England. Yet the cautious and cryptic Hughes never quite told anyone what Carson was to do, other than to liaise with the British. This was not very helpful, especially since there were other Canadian representatives, the most prominent being Perley, who were to do such liaising officially on behalf of the Canadian government. But because Carson took his job seriously, he soon found himself doing everything, from procuring equipment to dealing with the British, but never with the full confidence that he would be backed by the minister should troubles arise. Carson wrote frequently to Hughes for guidance or clarification, but the minister often ignored his pleading missives or did not get back in a timely manner. When Hughes did reply, it was sometimes in the form of bizarre encoded messages to which Carson did not always have the cipher. Even after the cabinet created a formal position for Carson in February 1915, he continued to be smeared by Hughes's enemies as the minister's toadie.[60] Carson's voluminous correspondence indicates that he was trying to do his best for Canada, with little support from the minister, the Canadian government, or the mystified British, who could not understand his role in the Dominion organization. Neither could anyone else.

Most of the senior officers overseas owed fealty to the minister, however, and few were willing to rock the boat. Since Hughes rarely put any of the competing generals' duties in writing, they often encroached upon one another's domain, fighting for scraps from the minister's table. The arrival of new formations—especially the 2nd Division, commanded by the legendary Major-General Sam Steele, hero of the Royal North West Mounted Police and of the Klondike—added more leaders and egos to the mix. Steele represented Hughes's ideal: a model citizen-soldier with a larger-than-life reputation for having pacified the West and North (almost single-handedly, by some accounts). But Kitchener felt that he could not allow the sixty-six-year-old Steele to command the division at the front because he was too old and too inexperienced. His fame and reputation would be smashed on the Western Front. When an enraged Hughes heard of Kitchener's decision, he fired off a nasty telegram on April 7, 1915:

I know many of your Major Generals; some good and capable but many absolute reverse, far inferior for administration in office, or capability in the field to Steele or a dozen other of my Officers. Have calmly and loyally remained aloof from interference with Salisbury horror and disintegration of First Canadians, but please do not ask that too much be borne. Claim no authority to manage force in field, but under Army Act, Canada has absolute authority in respect to appointments. Further, offensiveness and contemptuousness of some Army Officers in First Division became almost intolerable. I look to you to see that courtesy, even-handed justice and fair play are accorded to all my deserving officers.[61]

Hughes did not press the matter beyond insulting Kitchener and the professional soldiers, although the incident revealed his propensity to fight for the right of Canadians to be given commands, even if they were unsuitable. For Hughes, obtaining command positions for Canadians was an important step toward the Dominion's receiving due respect for its service; the imperials, however, thought his obsession little more than small-minded, colonial madness. It is worth noting that Hughes was backed by Borden and much of the cabinet in this deliberate policy of Canadianizing command. Nonetheless, Ottawa journalist Augustus Bridle hit the nail on the head when he sniped, "Indiscretion was always the better part of Hughes' valour."[62]

Steele was left behind in England to fight for his piece of the pie, which was increasingly hoarded by regional commands. Canadians training in one camp received different instructions and directions than another, because the generals refused to share information, or even talk. It seemed that each time Hughes authorized a new camp, he appointed a new commander, often affording them independent powers. No one in England had the overall authority to sort out the mess, and Hughes refused to intervene, perhaps willing to let the forces be fragmented to ensure his own overriding influence as the only person who could see the whole picture. Moreover, the minister was never comfortable with delegating authority, and the more important the decision, the more at a loss he was as to what to do. All of this squabbling among the Canadian generals in England was embarrassing and detrimental to fighting efficiency, as the newly arriving reinforcements were often trained to different standards.

Out of the infighting and turf wars, Sir Max Aitken elbowed his way to greater influence. Like Carson, he was Hughes's friend and confidant, although a far more powerful and influential figure because of his political connections in Britain, his media empire, and his vast fortune. The grinning gnome, in his top hat and expensive suits, was dismissed by more than a few as "simply a little Canadian adventurer on the make," but those who underestimated Sir Max tended to come out on the losing end of any bargain with him.[63] Aitken had made an enormous fortune in Canada before the war, but had been pressured to leave the country in 1910 under a cloud of suspicion, especially when many of his business partners cried foul at the enormous profits he'd pocketed, often at their expense. Sir Max had never been convicted of any wrongdoing, but he had been condemned in the court of public opinion. Small, wiry, and bearing an enormous grin—"in spite of its ugliness, his face [was] attractive, and his laugh and manner frank and boyish," according to one contemporary—he was a charmer, a deal-maker, and always remained a Canadian at heart.[64] Whereas Sam had few business smarts, Max was a financial wizard. Both men could be vindictive, but Sir Max had a more friendly and convivial way about him as he plunged the dagger in.

Max Aitken was knighted in 1911, but he maintained his connections to Canada and the Conservatives, even contributing some of his immense fortune to Sam Hughes's 1911 election campaign. At the start of the war, Sir Max had hoped for a position in Prime Minister Herbert Asquith's Liberal government, but he had received nothing. Bitterly disappointed, the thirty-five-year-old Aitken was desperate to serve; he called upon his old Tory friends, Borden and Hughes, for a role. Sam offered Sir Max the job of Canadian eyewitness in the war, an ambiguous function that allowed Aitken leeway to travel to the front to gather information for the Canadian government. It was needed, since the imperials often left the Canadian cabinet in the dark about overseas actions, which upset Hughes and Borden in particular, and fuelled both men's nationalism. Sir Max soon augmented his role by becoming the Canadian forces' wartime publicist and the country's first overseas war archivist.[65] While Aitken would forge a historical legacy of official photographs, art, and film for all Canadians, it was his role as eyewitness that was paramount to Hughes. Paranoid, and anxious to pre-empt any strikes against him or his boys by the British, Hughes relied heavily on Sir Max to keep him informed. In turn, having the ear of Canada's most influential politician gave Aitken unique leverage with the British. Beckles Willson, a man of letters who would run afoul of Aitken, wrote that Sir Max was "never troubled about official authority; it was his influence with the all-powerful Sir Sam which carried him triumphantly along."[66]

The imperials were quite unsure of what to make of Sir Max, but they liked dealing with him more than with Hughes. Sir Max was a skilled schemer, but at least he was rational. He travelled in elevated political circles that included Winston Churchill and the Conservative party elite, and while he was viewed by many as a conspirator, he understood how the "game" was played, unlike the volatile Canadian minister. Hughes "interfered at all points," wrote an incredulous Perley. "He wrote long letters to Kitchener advising him as to how the war should be run."[67] Hughes's loose-cannon ways scared even seasoned soldiers. In one missive, Hughes accused the British of incompetence in failing to get the proper number of shells to the front and wondered if the British would like him to raise regiments of "Texas steers to rush the wire instead of sending men."[68] Kitchener was apoplectic. It is reported that when the field marshal heard of one of Hughes's forthcoming trips to England in 1915, he groaned in despair: "Good heavens! Can't we choke him off?"[69]

Hughes "clanked about, patronizing people in a loud voice, behaving as if trying to maintain some popular image of himself," wrote Sir Max Aitken's daughter, Janet.[70] This was an accurate portrait of Hughes, except that he did not try to maintain his image; he *was* the image—firm in his conviction that he could do no wrong. Hughes was quite unlike anyone the British had ever met. Aitken used the imperials' wariness of setting off Hughes's short fuse to demand concessions from the British (such as getting official photographers and painters to the front), but he also manoeuvred and managed the Canadian minister to his own advantage. As the mediator, Aitken wrote to Prime Minister Borden—who was also a supporter—that he did not always send Hughes's telegrams along to the British because they frequently contained "unsatisfactory confessions," noting further that he considered it his duty "to suppress anything which conflicts with harmonious relations now existing between" the minister and the British War Office.[71] Borden no doubt appreciated anyone who could soften Hughes's aggressive messages, as he too frequently had to offer "sharp reproof" to Sam. After the second such condemnation over a short period, Borden wrote in his diary about his minister, who had been reduced to tears both times, describing him as "most mercurial."[72] The British would have agreed, but would perhaps have added "maniacal," "unfathomable," and "shamefully rude" to a growing list of negative descriptors that suited Hughes.

While Aitken often mediated between Hughes and the British, few other than the Canadian prime minister and the War Office found Hughes and Aitken's relationship a positive force, since at their worst the two men conspired to affect command appointments and interfered in a host of other military issues. Aitken established the Canadian War Records Office (CWRO) in January 1916 to gather Canadian war records and disseminate positive publicity about the Canadians fighting in the field, but Sir Max was always one to expand his role, and soon the CWRO became another competing headquarters. Sir Max's shadowy organization was described by one contemporary:

It was as if Aitken had clandestinely—save for his powerful friend's good-will, built up a simulacrum of Sir Sam Hughes's office in Ottawa, where place-hunters, contractors, official, politicians, and pressmen came and went all day.... It was, in effect, the real centre and immediate source of authority of the Canadian Corps in Europe. The same audacity and arrogance which made Sam Hughes supreme and omnipotent in military affairs in Canada was exercised here by his representative and lieutenant in London.[73]

Hughes and Aitken worked in conjunction, although occasionally at cross-purposes, to push their friends and supporters into senior command positions. This conspiracy to influence the appointment of officers was absolutely shocking to the British commanders, although they stayed clear of Aitken, likely for fear of angering Hughes, who demanded control in the name of Canadian nationalism. With the War Office refusing to put up much of a struggle against the duo's string-pulling, and content to let the Canadians muddle along within their own isolated national force, Aitken and Hughes continued to intrigue. In early October 1915, Aitken informed Hughes that Robert Rennie was to get the 1st Brigade, but boasted that "if you prefer Loomis have no doubt my influence is sufficiently strong to secure appointment."[74] The War Office, rightly horrified, accused Sir Max of "attempting to introduce political considerations into a purely military affair."[75] He denied having engaged in such practice, and then did just that. The Canadian Corps was riddled with politically motivated appointments at the highest levels.

General Alderson tried to put a stop to this political jobbery. In late October 1915, Sam Hughes instructed Aitken to have his son, Garnet Hughes, appointed to command the 4th Brigade in the newly established 2nd Division. Alderson refused, despite Aitken's pressing the case "vigorously."[76] Sir Max considered orchestrating the fall of the existing brigadier, Lord Brooke, and after he and Garnet met for manoeuvres, Aitken cabled Hughes senior, saying that Garnet would now command the 1st Brigade and that Rennie would get the 4th.[77] Even a year later, Aitken was pushing for appointments to senior command positions; on June 5, 1916, a few days after the 3rd Division's commander had been killed during the Battle of Mount Sorrel, Sir Max wrote revealingly to Hughes: "Will ask War Office [to] appoint Lipsett to command 3rd Division. Recommend you give Lipsett's Brigade to Loomis and Victor Williams' Brigade to Embury." The next day Hughes replied, "Your suggestions regarding command of fourth brigade alright."[78] Hughes had no problem with treating the CEF as an extended arena for political patronage, writing— no doubt honestly in his own mind—"I know all these officers better than anyone else knows them and have not yet made a mistake."[79] He indeed knew the officers in a prewar militia context, but overseas events were changing rapidly: some officers had excelled under fire in the first six months of combat, while others had been found wanting. His own son Garnet fell into the latter category after the fiasco at Second Ypres, when he had failed to grasp where his units were during the battle, and had sent inaccurate and panicky messages that left higher commands equally confused and vulnerable.

Another favourite of Sam's was David Watson, managing editor of the *Quebec Chronicle* and long-time militia officer, who had proven himself a brave and adept battalion commander at Second Ypres. His short career as brigadier had been spotty, but he was wildly ambitious and wanted a divisional command. He sidled up to Aitken, writing in October 1915, "I am continually in your debt in one way or another."[80] Watson endeared himself shamelessly to Aitken and Hughes, buttering them up, supplying them with information, using his newspaper to support Hughes in Quebec, and easing in their appointments to his brigade when he could, including accommodating Sir Max's brother in a staff position. They in turn cleared his way of competitors, and Watson was eventually given the 4th Division, with Sir Max writing when his friend took command to France in August of 1916, "Goodbye to you my dear Dave and in your great adventure my hopes go with you. I am as anxious for your success as a fond father who looks forward to the achievements of his favourite son."[81] It is interesting to note that the paternalistic Aitken was in fact almost two decades younger than his "son." Watson would be the weakest of all the Canadian divisional commanders, yet perhaps the wiliest. He turned his back on Hughes later in the war, attaching himself to new patrons, and would ultimately rank as the longest-serving Canadian divisional commander.

Hughes kept up his fervent desire to see Canadians take over the command positions in the CEF, which was perhaps not an unreasonable goal for a Canadian minister to have. But there were few of his countrymen who possessed the necessary command experience. To make room at the top, Hughes pressured Kitchener after the Battle of Second Ypres to remove Alderson and promote Turner, arguing that "it would solve a problem and satisfy Canada." Kitchener rebuffed the minister, writing curtly that "General Alderson did extremely well" during the battle and would retain his command.[82] Hughes was not dissuaded and continued to seek ways to edge out British professionals. Such actions were part of Sam's long game to Canadianize the Dominion land forces, although his beliefs also dovetailed nicely with his desire to promote his friends, supporters, and cronies.[83]

Although the British generally tried to support the Canadians, it must have been more than a little trying for them to receive Hughes's rantings, such as the following one dated December 1, 1915. The letter must rank as one of Sam's most outrageous statements—no small feat for a man who made a career of sticking not only his feet, but the lower portion of his body, routinely into his mouth.

> It is discreditable to have British officers run the army corps and [Canadian] divisional positions. It would be insulting to have them brought into the Brigades. The men who fought so well at St. Julien and Festubert require no staff college theorists to direct them [;] on the contrary it is the general opinion that scores of our officers can teach the British officers for many moons to come. You must stand firm. There is altogether too much staff college paternalism and

espionage abroad. If the feeling of returned soldiers were known another Boston tea party might be looked for. Surely they can find position for the pets among the British but I will not submit to our force being burdened with them.[84]

Putting aside the inflammatory absurdity that Canadians might carry out a 1776-style revolution during a patriotic war effort, the irony of Hughes's attacks was that the British had selflessly sent many of their best staff officers to the Dominion force to groom Canadian officers for their complicated roles in command and staff work. Even nationalistic commanders such as Turner and Currie believed that Canadians should not take over until they were ready. "No Imperial in this division could at present be replaced by a Canadian officer now serving and available without great loss of efficiency," wrote Currie. "It is not a question of whether a man is a Canadian or otherwise, it is one of the best man for the job."[85] At the front, the British placed Canadians in junior roles to study under the professionals, and then over time to move up in ranks. Hughes backed down after the objections from his front-line officers, but would continue to snipe at the imperials who were helping his boys throughout 1915 and the next year. Currie and his comrades were right, but Hughes did not like to feel wrong.

Colonel William Wood, a contemporary military historian, judged that Sam Hughes "simply personified civilian interference at its worst."[86] Soldier-friends of Hughes, such as Richard Turner, David Watson, and his son, Garnet Hughes, received or kept their commands largely because of the actions of Sam and Sir Max.[87] Turner and Watson were not complete failures, but both stumbled badly as divisional commanders at times, with Turner faring poorly in his first major battle at St. Eloi in April 1916 and Watson's senior staff officer, the very effective Brigadier William Edmund Ironside, writing that Watson "had risen above anything that he should have done and was at a loss commanding a Division." It should be noted, too, that from 1914 to 1916, Arthur Currie also benefited from Hughes's protection. The minister's assistant and a close friend of Currie's, Harold Daly, testified after the war that Hughes "did everything possible during those years to protect Currie's interest," including burying Currie's embezzlement scandal.[88] Yet Hughes backed many losers, too, and much of this political interference was detrimental to the fighting efficiency of the Corps, as a commander's loyalty to the minister was viewed as more important than his battlefield competence.[89]

At least this is how most historians have portrayed Hughes's meddling. Sam saw it as something quite different. For him, it was about the Canadian government exerting influence over its own forces. "For the first year of the war," Hughes admitted in late 1916, "Canada had practically no control over her forces overseas." But he vowed that under his leadership, promotions and appointments, when they did not conflict with the British commander in the field, would be made by the Canadian government.[90] Hughes thus saw himself as a Canadian nationalist and a well-informed military expert who had decades of experience, not as an interfering politician aiming to promote his friends and hold back his enemies.

While Hughes made a habit of offering impertinent advice to, or making incendiary statements against, the imperials, Canadian soldiers generally did not seem to care who was commanding them—British or Canadian—as long as he was competent. But they did not want political profiteers as commanders, men whose only qualifications were that they had voted for and, more likely, contributed financially to the right party. Such "qualifications" got fighting men killed. There were enough bad officers—and rumours of many more up and down the line—that the front-line soldiers found an easy scapegoat in Sam Hughes. The minister was not responsible for all the officers who could not rise to the occasion, but he was an increasingly vulnerable target. William Mitton, an overseas gunner, wrote to his parents in December 1915, "I had a letter from Bernice the other day. They are both well. She was talking to Sam Hughes when he visited Berlin [now Kitchener, Ontario] recently and seems to think he is the greatest military genius since poor old Napoleon snuffed out. She told him that she had a brother with the 1st contingent and he asked for my name and number, so don't be surprised if you hear that I have been made a corporal or a spare general or something like that."[91] Hughes had become a joke. His good, tireless, even monumental work on behalf of Canadians before and especially during the war was frequently overshadowed by his ridiculous preening and posturing, all of which seemed too self-indulgent to those facing shells and snipers at the front.

Sir Robert Borden was not the type to interfere in his ministers' running of their departments, but he seems to have been particularly ineffective in pushing Sam to delegate authority or rethink some of his appointments.[92] And for his part, Hughes refused to accept suggestions that he change his approach. He battled everyone, and, as seen already, he had a particular hatred for Canada's governor general, the Duke of Connaught. He even spread a rumour that the governor general's wife, Duchess Louise Margaret, who was Prussian-born, was a spy, at one point suggesting to journalists that they investigate her entirely honourable Prisoner of War Fund that might—might!—be the means by which she sent messages to the enemy, perhaps by rolling traitorous messages in the socks being sent to Germany where Canadian prisoners were detained.[93]

So from mid-1915 onwards, Borden was continually forced to chastise Hughes for overstepping his bounds. His proclivity for making decisions without advising cabinet did not go over well with the other ministers, whose collective voices were forming a steady and rising chorus of disapproval that they expressed to the prime minister. "Whether it was blame or praise," wrote one journalist, "Sir Sam Hughes took it all with indifference and even seemed to enjoy it; he fought charges of corruption in the press and Parliament as he had fought the Boers in South Africa, and would have liked to fight the Germans in France, without fear or favour."[94] Hughes was increasingly the source of disharmony in Borden's government.

Sir Joseph Flavelle, like many loyal Conservatives, had faith in the prime minister, but could scarcely believe how he continued to stand by Hughes, whom he described as a "degenerate … incapable, intellectually and morally, to distinguish between truth and falsehood."[95] With most of the cabinet in open conflict with Hughes, Flavelle perceived that "The Prime Minister has not only been a good friend, and therefore reluctant to remove him, but he dislikes anything disagreeable, and shrinks from it to such an extent that he lives in a perpetual atmosphere of the disagreeable rather than deal decisively with the troublesome factor."[96]

Borden backed Hughes for many reasons, not least because he was the driving force of the Canadian war effort. Moreover, Hughes believed implicitly in Canada and was determined to give the nation pride of place in both a reborn Empire and the world. Sir Sam had justly earned his knighthood, awarded on August 24, 1915, for his enormous personal effort to create the overseas contingents and to turn an unprepared peaceable kingdom into a significant military power. The knighthood—the first civilian K.C.B. (Knight Commander, Order of the Bath) to be awarded since Sir John A. Macdonald had received it—went straight to Sir Sam's head. Shortly after he had accepted the honour, a delegation from Elgin County arrived to speak to the minister. Their spokesman began the meeting by buttering up Hughes, congratulating him and observing that the knighthood had resulted in much positive talk in Elgin County. Sir Sam interrupted the surprised speaker: "Just a minute, Dave. It has caused satisfaction not only in the county of Elgin but all across Canada. In fact, His Majesty said that there had never been an honour it had given him so much pleasure to bestow. Go ahead, Dave."[97]

Borden was certainly not blind to his minister's foibles. As it slowly dawned on him that Hughes could not handle his crushing workload, the prime minister reduced his responsibilities. Hughes saw this as a loss of faith in him rather than as assistance, and so each reduction or removal of power slowly poisoned his relationship with the prime minister. But it took time for Borden to move toward a total withdrawal of power from Hughes, as there were significant obstacles. Although it was easy to find violent assaults against Hughes in the Liberal papers, this was to be expected from the partisan press. The success of Valcartier and the First Contingent balanced these printed attacks, and resonated for a long time in the memory of Canadians. Hughes's vigour also personified the desire of his fellow citizens to prosecute the war to the fullest degree. Moreover, for Borden to remove Hughes would hand political ammunition to the Liberals in the upcoming election, and would be de facto proof of the Conservative failure to prosecute the war effectively. Hughes also had support among some of the rank and file in the party, especially in the Conservative stronghold of rural Ontario. It is also likely that at some deeper level, the somewhat reserved Borden admired Hughes for his fearlessness. But was he cowed too? Hughes's aggressive reputation doubtless gave many hard men and politicians pause so that they attacked him behind his back rather than openly confronting him. Borden's long friendship with Hughes, his feelings of indebtedness to Hughes for what he had accomplished early in the war, and his own lack of military knowledge combined to influence the prime minister, so that while Hughes's many indiscretions weighed heavily upon him, they were not enough to sink him in Borden's eyes. Not yet, at least.

CHAPTER 7

Divisional Commander
ARTHUR CURRIE, 1915–1916

In the aftermath of the Second Ypres battle, Arthur Currie could scarcely believe the slaughter that had befallen his men during four days of fighting. His eyes red and raw from the chlorine and lack of sleep, he had shaved his stubble, but the reek of cordite and sweat clung to his clothes. Worse were the images that flashed before his eyes when he tried to catch some sleep. His men had been outnumbered and outgunned, and had faced the first lethal chlorine gas attacks in the history of warfare. They had fought with the tenacity of the condemned. Time and time again the infantry had banded together, fighting to the brutal end even after their officers were killed, with new leaders rising from the ranks to take their place. But the confusion and chaos of the battlefield had clouded everything. Mistakes had been made. Currie knew that his force had nearly been annihilated when his fellow brigadier, Richard Turner, had pulled back his right flank, exposing the 3rd Brigade. But Currie too had stumbled. Who could blame him, as it seemed that the British had abandoned him on the right flank, Turner on the left, and the high command to the rear? His order to pull back his front-line forces in the late morning on the

24th, which had been ignored by his battalion commanders, Lieutenant-Colonels G.S. Tuxford and L.J. Lipsett, did not look good after the shooting had stopped, and perhaps he could be excused for omitting the order in his official report. He had tried to convince the confused or deluded British that he needed reinforcements. He knew they had soldiers quite literally sitting waiting for orders, while his men were fighting for their lives. The incident at Major-General Thomas Snow's headquarters was distressing, if only because it revealed how out of touch the erratic British general had been. In the end, the Battle of Second Ypres had not been won but, more importantly, it had not been lost.

Arthur Currie now had to rebuild his shattered brigade, which had lost about half its strength. Reinforcements arrived from England, and new men now outnumbered the veterans. Currie spent much of early May trying to procure sufficient supplies and equipment for his forces. He also spent many late nights writing letters to grieving parents and friends of the fallen. There was little rest.

With battalions still several hundred men short, the Canadian Division was moved only weeks later to the La Bassée front in support of a new British offensive. By mid-May, the Canadians were thrown into battle at the ruined French village of Festubert, which was no bigger than a Canadian hamlet. The Ypres battle had been characterized by confusion and enemy firepower raking the front, but the Canadians had exacted a terrible toll on the enemy, who had been forced to advance against them over open terrain. Although the Ross rifles had failed at times, enough had functioned properly to ensure that hundreds of German corpses littered the battlefield. At Festubert, however, the Canadians would be involved in their first large-scale offensive operation.

The Battle of Festubert, which began on May 15, did not start well for the Allies. While the German line was pushed back, the defenders shattered the British operation with massed fire, as the Allied guns were not able to deliver enough shells in support of the ground forces. In the belief that further pushes might deliver victory, the Canadians were thrown into the line on the 18th to take part in another phase of the operation.

A day later, Alderson ordered Currie's brigade to the front in preparation for an attack on May 20. Even the inexperienced Currie could see that the operation had all the makings of a disaster. His soldiers' objective was a position named K.5, but the only intelligence he had been given was a map, printed upside down. When he sent out officers to reconnoitre the battlefield, they reported back that their single, precious map was wildly inaccurate, off by hundreds of metres in many places. Enemy objectives were mixed up with Canadian jumping-off positions, key geographical features were missing, and there was no hint of where the Germans were concentrated. Upon receiving the report and again studying the British order to attack, Currie unleashed a torrent of vulgarities, raging to several of his officers that the "son of a bitch who wrote this order never saw a trench."[1] The British high command had pointed the Canadians vaguely to the east and told them to charge. It was suicide.

In the hope of finding a solution, Currie himself crawled through the mud to survey the objective of K.5. While Turner's brigade was to attack to the north against a position that would be known as Canadian Orchard—a strongpoint that could be made out against the landscape—there was nothing on the battlefield that seemed to correspond to K.5. If Currie and his officers could not find it, how in the world were the gunners further to the rear to hit any of the objectives? Currie hurriedly cabled back to divisional headquarters, arguing that the operation should be postponed until more accurate information could be gathered as to the enemy's location.

Alderson ignored the brigadier's protest. His superior, Sir Douglas Haig, was urging him to press the attack, no matter what the cost.[2] Currie wrote of the affair after the war: "This was my first difference with the High Command. I protested on the grounds of insufficient time for reconnaissance and preparations. I now know better than ever that I was right, but still I was ordered to make the attack."[3] Currie was not alone, with

Turner also complaining, and both brigadiers displayed moral courage in objecting to the operation. Indeed, such objections were rare in the British army, as they were often interpreted as timidity, and could result in a commander's firing.[4] Yet neither Currie nor Turner had enough experience or clout to do anything more than object, and without Alderson's support, they were overruled, and their forces ordered forward.

The attack predictably failed, with the infantry in the advance ripped apart by enemy rifle, machine-gun, and artillery fire. It was an unfettered slaughter as the Germans even had the advantage of firing at the Canadians in clear light, as the operation had idiotically been planned to go over the top at 7:45 P.M. Currie and Turner were ordered to attack again the next night across the quagmire of a waterlogged battlefield, now strewn with the unburied corpses of their countrymen. Through bravery and resilience, the Canadians captured parts of their objectives, although the week of fruitless battles had cost Currie's brigade another 1,200 men and officers. The brigadier had learned an important lesson. Objectives had to be clear; preparation and intelligence were essential for any hope of success; and shellfire had to be applied to properly support the attacking infantry and to suppress enemy fire. None of this had been applied at Festubert, and it was the most forlorn and useless battle fought by the Canadians in the entire course of the Great War. It was hard for Arthur Currie and his men not to be dispirited. Currie wrote to Sam Hughes after the battle, "I have wept. I have cursed but now I am numb."[5]

The only good news after the battle was that the Canadian Division would spend the rest of the summer in quieter sectors of the front, where there were no major offensive operations. Currie remained fiercely proud of his men and paid particular attention to new drafts arriving to rebuild his shattered four battalions. The brigadier was the linchpin between the battalion commanders and the division; he controlled no artillery assets and had little say in orchestrating operations, but he was responsible for training and often for revising tactics. With only a small brigade headquarters staff, Currie was often forced to spell off his staff officers from the job of keeping track of incoming and outgoing reports, equipment, the transfer of men, and the rotation of units, and from the other duties required to keep the brigade running. He also kept up a steady correspondence with well-wishers at home, many of whom wrote hero-worship letters to him. As one of the three infantry brigadiers in the division, Currie had become a national figure. And he owed much of the credit to Hughes. Later in May, the brigadier acknowledged this, writing to the minister after he had complimented Currie's work on the Western Front: "I am in more ways than one indebted to you for the privilege of being connected with the Brigade since its mobilization. I gave you my word that I would use every endeavour to make good and that promise I have worked hard to keep.... Let me express my deep and lasting gratitude to you for your kindness to me and for having given me the chance."[6]

In the aftermath of Ypres and Festubert, Alderson ordered a full investigation into the rumours he heard that the Ross rifle had failed on the battlefield, jamming repeatedly and leaving his soldiers defenceless. The results were grim. Reports condemned the rifle. While not all rifles had malfunctioned, and much of the problem could be attributed to mass-manufactured and irregular British ammunition, it was clear to the Canadian soldier that his Ross was not nearly as reliable as the British-made Lee-Enfield. Most soldiers showed their displeasure by ditching their Rosses and arming themselves with Lee-Enfields taken from fallen Tommies.

Currie quickly became involved in the Ross rifle crisis. He condemned the rifle in print, his comments being circulated up the chain of command and eventually back to Ottawa. Although Currie owed his position to Hughes, he was nonetheless courageous enough to go against the minister. Colonel C.T. Romer, a senior staff officer, wrote of Currie's "moral courage at the time of the Ross rifle controversy. Although he must have known that by taking the stand as he did on that occasion he might lose the favour of the Canadian Defence Minister, he adhered to his opinion. I always admired him for declaring himself in such a definite and manly way on that occasion."[7] Currie's stand was all the more impressive since several of Hughes's appointees, especially Turner, refused to condemn the rifle, instead citing the challenges all weapons faced on the muddy battlefields. As William Griesbach observed, "Criticism of the rifle got to mean that the critic was attacking Sam Hughes, whereas a man who praised the rifle extravagantly attracted such favourable attention from the minister that it sometimes resulted in his appointment and promotions for which the individual was not fitted."[8] The politicization of the Canadian Division made it hard for soldiers to speak truth to power, even when lives were at stake, since Hughes was the power. While Currie damned the Ross rifle, it was divisional commander Alderson who had the responsibility for taking them to the minister.[9]

Even in the face of battlefield reports that questioned the Ross's effectiveness, Hughes refused to entertain any criticism. Did expert snipers not use the Ross effectively? he bashed on. Were not the British simply trying to impose their own equipment on the Canadians because they always hated the Ross, as it was a better weapon? Were there not confirmed rumours of the Germans spreading lies about the Ross's failure in battle, because it was so effective?[10] Hughes freely turned to rumour and innuendo to save his cherished rifle. As wounded officer R.C. Coops remarked to his friend, Victor Odlum, in July 1915,

> General Sam Hughes addressed the officers here on Friday, to me it seemed that he only calls them together to abuse the Lee Enfield Rifle and advertise the Ross, the whole address only lasted 5 minutes and the only subjects mentioned were the Ross Rifles, the formation of new Brigadiers and commanders of the two Divisions. His actual words about the Ross were—"The Ross Rifle has proved itself on the field of Ypres and Festubert to be the finest Rifle in the World, the Lee Enfield does not compare to it. Any troubles that there are in the rifle are due to the fact that Company officers know nothing of the rifle." Cheerful sort of cad, is he not?[11]

While the technical failures of the rifle and the poor ammunition could be rectified, there was no chance of redeeming the soldiers' faith in their rifle, as they believed increasingly that using the Ross was akin to a death sentence. Hughes never understood this, and fought against soldiers at the front being equipped with the British rifle. Beckles Willson, then working in Sir Max Aitken's Canadian War Records Office, remarked candidly to his diary on February 19, 1916: "Sir Sam is positively hated by the soldiers; they refuse to carry his Ross rifle."[12]

On September 13, 1915, Currie visited Alderson at divisional headquarters. The British general greeted him warmly and they talked about the summer's quiet campaign. Currie was also at headquarters to attend a ceremony, at which he learned of his promotion to major general and his appointment as commander of the 1st Canadian Division.[13] "Dogged, dependable, thorough and increasingly knowledgeable," wrote army commander Sir Henry Horne of Currie, he was "unquestionably the ablest senior officer the Canadian Corps had produced."[14] Alderson took over the Canadian Corps, and Turner received the 2nd Division. Although Alderson did not think the latter was fit for command, he had been intimidated by Sam Hughes, who had made it clear that Turner should get the division. "Canadian politics have been too strong for all of us," was Alderson's sad comment through gritted teeth.[15]

The Canadian Corps included Alderson's headquarters and the two fighting divisions, with a third division arriving in a few months. While British corps often had different divisions pass through them to meet operational requirements, the Canadian Corps was more homogeneous, underpinned by an understanding that the Canadian divisions would not be dislodged and sent to fight with other imperial formations. This semi-permanent structure would later accrue operational value, as it allowed formations to serve together and to create bonds of camaraderie, and it became a focal point throughout the war as a readily identifiable symbol of Canada's sacrifice and service.

Currie took over 1st Division's headquarters on September 14. Alderson had raided many of the best officers to take them to corps headquarters, so Currie was able to promote a number of his favourites. Currie is sometimes portrayed as a selfless prince, who always put efficiency ahead of friendship, and while this was often the case, he also had an inner circle of loyal men whom he supported and turned to for support. But the 18,000-man division also required that Currie expand his circle, for he had little experience with the other arms of the combat forces—except for the artillery, with which he was intimately familiar from his prewar militia experience in Victoria.

Together, the Canadian divisions consisted of about 12,000 infantrymen, 76 field guns and heavy howitzers, and another 6,000 men in engineer, medical, machine-gun, and logistical units. There would always be rivalries between the infantry units, and between front- and rear-force echelons, but a reasonably harmonious relationship overall was needed. This would be strengthened through training and social activities behind the lines. In the front lines, these relationships were reinforced in blood.

Sir Sam was thrilled with the creation of the Canadian Corps, seeing it as an important step in elevating Canada's wartime contribution to the Empire. At the same time, he could not stop his tinkering. In October 1915, for instance, the minister told Alderson that his son, Garnet, then a divisional staff officer with the rank of lieutenant colonel, should be promoted to command an infantry brigade. Currie was caught in the crossfire since Garnet would go to either his division or Turner's. It was Arthur's first serious encounter with Sam's meddling ways. Neither Currie nor Alderson felt that Garnet was up to the task, but there was enormous pressure put on them by the elder Hughes. Alderson was already on shaky ground with the minister because of previous battles with him over Salisbury Plain, the wet canteens, the high casualties suffered in the two major battles, and the Ross rifle, and so he relented. But he refused to let Garnet serve in the same division as Turner, no doubt remembering their disastrous combination during the Battle of Second

Ypres. Instead, Alderson appointed Garnet to the 1st Brigade in Currie's division, which the junior Hughes took over on November 25. Currie was not happy. He strongly objected because of Garnet having "practically no experience whatever in military matters," but as Currie wrote disappointedly, "the Corps Commander and the Minister were against me."[16]

Minister Hughes exhibited the worst form of interference here. The appointment did no service to Garnet Hughes, who laboured under his father's shadow, with Sam's influence turning many against his son. Currie certainly had soured on Garnet, to whom he owed at least some of his opportunities. He sniped that Garnet was "the most favored of all the favored Sons of Canada, [and] had been given every kind of promotion and consideration" because of his father's influence.[17] But while Garnet may have had doors opened for him by his father, he had a much harder time striding through them.

There can be no denying Sir Sam's shameless bolstering of friends, families, and party-men, which was indeed detrimental to fighting efficiency. But what of his insistence to the British that the Canadian Corps' senior artillery officer position go to Harry Burstall, an experienced professional Canadian gunner? When the British balked, Hughes pressed forward, refusing to be turned aside, writing menacingly, "The Canadian Government will, to say the least, be very much put out if other than Canadian Officers are chosen for these posts."[18] The British folded, and Burstall proved himself an adept gunner who was later given command of the 2nd Canadian Division, where he also excelled. Hughes was a menace, but he was often right.

"The headquarters of the 1st Canadian Division was like a band of brothers," wrote one admiring staff officer, "with the divisional commander adopting the attitude of an elder brother."[19] In the senior officers' mess, Currie was friendly and his easy laugh returned to him. But his generous nature extended out from his headquarters too. According to one staff officer who worked closely with Currie, the general had the "unusual ability of remembering names and faces" and "knew practically every officer under his command and a great many of the non-commissioned officers and men."[20] His officers in turn found that loyalty to him was not forced. "The staff were not over-awed by him," wrote a senior British officer who served with Currie. "A frank interchange of opinions … is difficult to appreciate at its true value until the contrary … has been experienced."[21] Currie's men knew that their opinions mattered, and this encouraged them to continue approaching problems with agile minds.

Currie had never been gregarious, but he did see himself as a leader of his officers, and he was loyal to them. In one visit from Sam Hughes to the front, the minister took particular umbrage with one of Currie's staff officers, a known Liberal. The fearsomely partisan minister charged the man with conspiring against him and wanted to send him back to Canada. Currie leapt to his officer's rescue. As Hugh Urquhart recounts it, Currie "told General Hughes that his charges did not even make sense."[22] Hughes rarely encountered people who stood up to him, and, perhaps impressed by Currie's courage, he dropped the issue. It would have been easy to sacrifice the staff officer to Hughes, but this went against Currie's personal code of loyalty to his officers. He felt an equally strong sense of loyalty to his men. In writing to one friend in Victoria, Currie declared, "I did not care what happened to me but to my men, to their wives, their mothers, their children, and to Canada I owed a duty which I wanted to fulfill to the very best of my ability."[23]

Currie was also busy with visitors. As he was one of the only two divisional commanders in Canada's land army, dignitaries touring the front frequently stopped by his headquarters. A diary entry noted that, on one afternoon, he hosted General Alderson and someone called only "Tommy," a private he knew from Victoria. The general also visited voraciously. He often called on the headquarters of British formations behind the lines to learn how they were confronting the challenges of trench warfare. Currie understood that he had much to learn. Although he had been a prewar gunnery officer, he knew that the gunners had made significant leaps forward in their use of technology, tactics, and weapons during the last eighteen months. He spent hours each week talking to his senior staff officers, picking their brains for solutions to problems and encouraging active discussion.[24]

Though Currie relied heavily on his team of staff officers, they could not help him with the rank and file. While Currie was, in his words, "intensely proud" of the division's reputation, he had a difficult time bonding with the soldiers who formed the blood and sinew of the formation.[25] The commander's goals in tightening discipline to improve combat effectiveness in his division rarely appealed to his men. The Canadians had acquired and enjoyed a reputation as brawlers and Wild West cowboys, and Currie believed strongly that this had to change in order for the Corps to evolve into a hard-hitting force on the Western Front. He was therefore a stickler for discipline, demanding sharp salutes, polished buttons, and all the acts of discipline that most soldiers disliked. The general inspected his soldiers up and down the ranks, looking for irregularities in their uniforms or asking probing questions. This scrutiny was highly unpopular among the men, as they could not see how it made them better fighting troops and they resented the public embarrassment of being called out for tarnished buttons or other dirty kit, not to mention the later punishment meted out by the officers. Infantryman John Becker described Currie's inspections as a "lot of poppy-cock," but noted that they appeared "a necessary evil in every man's army."[26] As acerbic artilleryman Wilfred Kerr observed, Currie "did not seem to have the gift for stroking fur the right way."[27]

During these inspections, and in other interactions with the rank and file, Currie seemed stiff and unapproachable. Privates and non-commissioned officers (the corporals and sergeants who, while not officers, were essential in leading small groups of men or specializing in key weapons such as the Lewis light machine gun) were not meant to have a jovial attitude with major generals—to pass cheeky banter back and forth—but Currie seemed particularly severe. The general "had no showy qualities," observed Field Marshal Jan Smuts.[28] While Currie made up for this lack of personality with a keen mind and relentless work, some "showiness" would likely have gone over well with the rank and file. One of Currie's staff officers observed that the general did not "devote as much time to personal inquiries [of the men] as most of the Commanders did, and though no one held his soldiers' comfort and interest more at heart than did Sir Arthur, he did not take the pains to show it that some made a habit of doing."[29] The cold-fish Currie felt no need to win the approval of his men, and so rumours went around quickly that he was a no-nonsense general, perhaps more British than the British in regard to discipline, and not particularly interested in them or their well-being.

Arthur Currie continued to do what he believed was right for his division, and although there had been no major set-piece battles since Festubert, other than a limited engagement at Givenchy in June 1915, the general had encouraged his brigadiers and battalion commanders to be aggressive along the front. Patrols were conducted in No Man's Land to gather intelligence on enemy fortifications and strength. Currie's division was also the first to conduct a trench raid. These raids were nasty, dash-and-destroy affairs, in which the raiders crawled across No Man's Land and attacked the enemy in the dead of night.[30] Raids added a new level of lethality to trench warfare, while also honing the attackers' ability to plan minor operations that employed multiple arms, such as the artillery, machine-gunners, and mortar teams. When the 5th and 7th Battalions pulled off the first raid on the night of November, 17, 1915, against a German position at La Petite Douve farm, Currie was effusive in his praise. In fact, the success of the operation reverberated throughout the entire British army, with senior commanders at all levels taking note and 4,000 copies of the operational report being printed and distributed throughout the British and French armies.[31] While Currie had had little to do with putting together the plan, he had benefited from his men's success, and his active encouragement of lower formations to plan their own operations had taken hold throughout the division.

The general had begun to distinguish himself again at a new level of command, even as it came with troubling responsibilities. Of particular concern was the issue of capital punishment. The miserable weather conditions and the constant strain from enemy shelling and snipers resulted in an increase in the number of desertions from the Corps in general, and from Currie's division in particular, over the winter of 1915–1916. After a variety of punishments for the offence had been tried, Colonel Gilbert Frith, one of Currie's senior staff officers, suggested "that we would not stop these cases of desertion until an example had been made by the infliction of the supreme penalty." By this, he meant death by firing squad, which was a punishment available to commanders under the Army Act, to which all British and Empire soldiers, except for the Australians, were subject. Currie considered the matter and after reflection replied, "Yes, I agree. If we get a clear case and the court martial sentences the man to be shot I shall recommend that the sentence be carried out." Soon after this decision was made, a soldier deserted from his unit, was caught, and the court martial assigned the penalty of death by firing squad. As per military regulations, the case came up to Currie for his confirmation, which he gave before sending it up to the corps and army commanders, after which it went to Sir Douglas Haig, who had been commander-in-chief since December 1915. All confirmed the finding of the court martial.[32]

The night before the execution was scheduled to take place, Canon Frederick Scott, the division's chaplain, came to see Currie. "His influence in the Division was only second to that of the Divisional Commander himself," wrote Colonel Frith, and he had come to plead for the condemned soldier's life. Currie quietly went over the case and the "absolute necessity of maintaining the discipline of the division." Scott argued for mercy, and tried every tactic he could muster, including warning Currie that since the soldier was French Canadian, an execution could result in political problems in Quebec. They talked for three hours. As Frith and others had noted, "to send men to meet their death in an attack is one thing, to have a man shot in cold blood and in disgrace is quite another."[33] It was a severe test for Currie, but the sentence was carried out and Frith argued that desertion was checked by this example. The execution put a terrible strain on Currie, and, in the words of one close observer, it created a "great crisis" in the general, but he never wavered from what he believed to be the necessary course of action.[34]

Sir Sam Hughes was a man of countless infelicitous remarks, but one of the more revealing ones was let slip to General Louis Botha, the first prime minister of a unified South Africa. Hughes referred to the overseas forces as "my soldiers" in a letter to Botha, which was somehow leaked to the newspapers and, as an example of Hughes's hopeless hubris, was used to smear the minister.[35] Hughes truly saw the Canadian Expeditionary Forces as his own, even though he was now quite out of touch with conditions at the front. In his heart, it was his boys who formed the fighting forces, even if others commanded it.

It is not surprising that Hughes harboured a grudge against General Alderson, who was officially responsible for "his" soldiers. The relationship between the two men had begun to fester with Alderson's appointment as Canadian divisional commander—a position that Hughes wished to hold—but things worsened after the Canadians were forced to endure the miserable conditions of Salisbury Plain. As early as May 1915, Hughes had written, "I can see no hope with General Alderson in Command of our boys."[36] The relationship deteriorated further after Hughes's absurd ego was hurt as the two men travelled together on the Western Front. Throughout the short tour they both spoke to the rank and file, but Hughes's long-winded speeches were greeted with patient clapping, while Alderson was showered with enthusiastic cheers. Alderson wrote after Hughes's departure, "All things considered I think I may say that I won all along the front."[37] Indeed he did, but a wounded and seething Hughes was a dangerous political animal.

Although the kindly Alderson seemed to have little aptitude for political intrigue, he was not naive. When he and Hughes disagreed over issues affecting the soldiers, such as in the case of the wet canteens in England, the British general used the proper military channels to report through his superiors in the British Army in order to attain his goals. These tactics made it harder for Hughes to exert pressure, but they did not stop the minister and his supporters from attacking the general. This was revealed most painfully around the issue of the Canadian-made Ross rifle.

Alderson knew that Hughes would regard any public repudiation of the Ross as a personal attack, but Alderson could not knowingly saddle his men with a faulty weapon. Even after the rifles had their chambers enlarged to create fewer opportunities for uneven cartridges to jam, new surveys of the NCOs and junior officers regarding the Ross's effectiveness indicated that they were overwhelmingly against using the rifle.[38] In February 1916, Alderson wrote to Colonel Willoughby Gwatkin, the chief of staff in Canada, supplying ten reasons why the majority of soldiers in the Corps disliked the Ross, and adding, "I should not be fit for my position, if I passed over anything which endangered men's lives or the success of our arms."[39]

When the memorandum found its way to Hughes, he responded the only way he knew how—with an attack. Refusing to believe that "his boys" were condemning the weapon, Hughes sent a telegram in March to every senior officer in the Canadian forces overseas down to the rank of battalion commander—281 in total—in a blatant attempt to undermine Alderson. He dismissed all ten of the general's points against the rifle as nonsense, and for good measure, he ridiculed Alderson's three decades of military experience, noting that "some of the [charges against the Ross] are so absolutely absurd and ridiculous that no one, excepting a novice or for an excuse, would be found seriously advancing them."[40] Hughes suggested in a passing swipe that Alderson might spend his time better in directing officers to ensure that proper ammunition was issued to the Canadians, and in watching out for British Tommies who—according to hundreds of secret reports apparently seen only by the minister—had a tendency to steal the Ross and leave behind their Lee-Enfields! Hughes was either a liar or delusional, or both, but in this direct attack he had thrown down the gauntlet. The British general, to his credit, refused to be cowed, and continued to marshal his evidence, but he had little support from the Canadian military or political authorities in England or even the staff at the War Office, who seemed exceedingly wary of incurring Sir Sam's explosive wrath. They were content to let the Canadians dig their own graves if they wanted, especially since the Ross seemed more suited to being used as a shovel than as a rifle.

In March of 1916, Hughes went overseas for another of his disruptive jaunts. "There was fire in his eye and he was clearly in more of a fighting mood than ever," wrote Beckles Willson, who accompanied Sam Hughes for part of the trip.[41] Their relationship was so poisonous that each refused to meet the other. After a few days of this nonsense, Alderson appealed to Sam's right-hand man in England, Sir Max Aitken, for assistance and advice, but Sir Max was frank, averring that he was a Hughes man, from start to finish.[42] Hughes went about steadily undermining the corps commander through whisper, rumour, and outright attack. He wrote back to Borden that Alderson was trying to "ruin" Hughes's favourites, such as Garnet Hughes and Richard Turner, and that "Haig despise[d] him." While the senior Canadian officers, Hughes claimed, were all "recognised as practical soldiers and giants," Alderson was a "pigmy and an intriguer."[43] As the government's military expert, and a virtual military dictator in Canada, Hughes's charges carried weight. The cautious Borden characteristically did nothing, but he kept a concerned eye on the commander of Canadian forces in the field.

The Hughes and Alderson standoff finally came to a showdown over a bloody battle in which neither man fought. Richard Turner's 2nd

Canadian Division had been assigned part of the line to the south of the Ypres sector in early 1916. To kick off what would be known as the Battle of St. Eloi, underground high explosive mines were set off on March 27, with the subsequent blast rocking the entire sector, collapsing trenches, and killing soldiers on both sides.[44] As the blasted earth rained down in a cloud of dust and debris, German and British survivors rushed in to fill the vacuum, with the Canadians acting as reinforcements for the British. The fighting was savage and went on for a week, in brutal conditions made worse by heavy rain.

When the Germans and British fought to a standstill in the mud, the 2nd Division was forced to relieve the exhausted and depleted British formation early, before the men had a chance to dig sturdy trenches and fortify the forward lines. Turner protested the operation, which he called suicidal, because the Germans overlooked the sector from their high ground, and because the front-line trenches now consisted only of enormous shell craters filled with corpses and wounded men.[45] But his protest was overruled, and the 2nd Division men went into what passed for the Allied front line and hunkered down in the swill. The Germans observed the Canadians' weak position and bombarded them day and night, until they drove them back on April 6. Defeats of this magnitude could not go unanswered, especially considering the importance the Allies placed on retaining territory, and so the Canadians counterattacked in a rushed and rash affair through thigh-deep mud. They recaptured a number of large craters, but, lacking the benefit of accurate and up-to-date maps based on aerial photographs (as planes were grounded in the rainy weather), those at the front had no idea where they were on the battlefield. The Canadians did not know what they held, or even where the enemy was located. This meant that much of the Canadian artillery fire did no harm to the Germans, as the gunners were firing blind. It was discovered through aerial photographs on April 16 that the Canadians had never recovered the original craters, that the brigade and divisional headquarters had failed to ascertain this during the battle through their limited intelligence, and that the Germans had consolidated the front. Even though the loss of a few hundred metres of shattered trenches meant nothing to the larger direction of the war on the Western Front, there was no denying that the Canadians had been soundly beaten.[46]

In the aftermath of the St. Eloi debacle, Alderson was pressured by his army commander, Sir Herbert Plumer, who was drawing fire from Haig, to take "severe disciplinary measures."[47] Plumer wanted Major-General Richard Turner and Brigadier Huntly Ketchen, commander of the 6th Brigade, which had been driven out of the initial craters on April 6, removed for their apparent incompetence. Alderson and Turner were not friends, and had had several disagreements over the last year, but Alderson realized how difficult the fighting had been at St. Eloi. His solution was to suggest to Turner that Ketchen might be served up to meet the High Command's sacrificial demand. However, in a stormy confrontation, the morally brave Turner refused to condemn his brigadier and, for good measure, accused Alderson of widespread incompetence. An enraged Alderson was reminded of why he disliked his Victoria Cross–wearing subordinate and promptly acted to have him removed.[48] His superiors were in agreement, and with both the corps and army commanders seeking Turner's head, his days as a divisional commander seemed to be easily counted on one hand. But the Canadian Corps was not a regular British formation.

Alderson was one step behind Sir Max Aitken, who had already caught word of the corps commander's manoeuvres via his finely tuned political radar, and had fired off a telegram to Hughes on April 20. Borden and Hughes hoped that Turner could be saved, as his firing would reflect badly on the Dominion since Sir Richard had already been applauded as a national war hero by the press.[49] Aitken used his considerable influence to arrange a meeting for himself with Sir Douglas Haig on April 23, to clear the air. Face to face with the field marshal, Aitken played a strong hand, telling Haig that the Canadian government would not stand for Turner getting the axe. After he had absorbed the shock of the brazen and blatant civilian interference in military matters and the active undermining of one of Haig's own senior officers, the politically minded Haig realized that perhaps a public row was not worth the strained relations that it would engender, especially given that Sir Max claimed to be speaking "on behalf of the civil power of the Dominion."[50]

The British commander-in-chief knew little of the Canadians, but their reputation preceded them: they were good soldiers, if rough around the edges, who were caught in a politically riven fighting formation. Perhaps a change was needed. Alderson had not always performed well in past battles, and Haig had had a previous falling out with him over the Canadians' performance during the Battle of Festubert, as he believed the general had not pushed his forces hard enough, despite the crippling Canadian casualties.[51] As odious as it was for an old soldier like Haig—one who had himself fought (and would again fight) battles against politicians—to have to decide in favour of Hughes and the Canadian government, the commander-in-chief came to the conclusion that there was only one way to go, noting privately that the importance of avoiding a "serious feud between the Canadians and the British is greater than the retention of a couple of incompetent commanders."[52]

So, the "incompetents"—Turner and Ketchen, who had done their best and, in Turner's case, had made the right recommendation to his superiors to pull out of the position and let the Germans keep the shattered and useless battlefront—kept their jobs. Haig wrote to the King after being "briefed" by Aitken that because of "the difficulty under which the commander of the Canadian Corps in the field now suffered through, having so many administrative and political questions to deal with, in addition to his duties as commander in the field," he should "be alleviated."[53] By "alleviated" he meant sacked as a field commander. Alderson was pushed onto his sword. But the cunning Haig wanted a paper trail and advised Aitken, who in turn informed Hughes, that while Haig himself would deal with the enraged Plumer, who despised the civilian interference in his army, "Canada should give him the assistance he required in disposing of General Alderson."[54] Haig also used the occasion to ensure that the Canadians would be indebted to him, for within two months the Ross rifle was replaced by the Lee-Enfield.[55] The replacement of the Ross, of course, had been one of Alderson's key goals as a commander, but he had paid a heavy price for safeguarding his boys.

Hughes and Borden abandoned with haste the British general who had led their country's forces since the start of the war.[56] Currie was saddened by the callous treatment meted out to Alderson, and noted in his diary on May 28 that the general "feels his leaving keenly."[57] Alderson was parachuted into an important job as inspector general in England, on the promise that he would be responsible for clearing up the quagmire within the Canadian training system. He was given little influence, however; as he was obviously not a Hughes man, no one listened to him. The reins of power remained in Ottawa, and among Hughes's malleable appointees in England, and Alderson's role was soon the equivalent of general in command of a broom closet. After six frustrating months, the War Office allowed him to exit the position, but he was never given another command in the field. Many Canadians felt sorry for Alderson, who had clearly been done in at the political crossroads by Hughes and Aitken, but he was all but forgotten within a few months. His successor, Sir Julian Byng, who was appointed by Haig without consulting the Canadian government, would find that Hughes's political control over the army was still strong.

No one was quite sure who Sir Julian Byng was, or how he would fare in the Canadian Corps—a colonial force, and one plagued by political interference. Although he was a rising star in the British army, not a single senior Canadian officer or politician had ever met Byng. In late March 1916, when Hughes and Alderson's respect for each other was at its lowest, a meeting took place in England between the minister and fellow conspirators David Watson, Sir Max Aitken, and Beckles Willson, at which they schemed to remove Alderson from his position of command.

Byng's name was brought up as a possible replacement as corps commander, since he had deep experience and was well respected in the BEF. Beckles Willson, an honorary major, man of letters, and chronicler of the great, had known Byng before the war, and related Sir Julian's powerful charisma. All eyes turned to the scowling Hughes, who after a few seconds grunted, "He's a lord's son, ain't he?"[58]

Byng was indeed a lord's son, and an experienced soldier who came from one of Britain's recognized fighting families. Sir Julian had served with distinction in the South African War, and from the start of the Great War was commander of the Cavalry Corps; in late 1915, he had been called in to oversee the evacuation of the Allied forces from Gallipoli. He was recognized for his able handling of that difficult retreat, and his return to the Western Front in early 1916 saw him commanding a British corps. Command of the troublesome Canadians was, for him, no prize. When Byng first heard of his new position, he could only shake his head in amazement. "Why am I sent to the Canadians?," wrote Byng. "I don't know a Canadian. Why this stunt?"[59] Bungo Byng, as he was known to his friends, who included the King, must have wondered if Haig considered him a rival. Had he given him the Canadians only to see him fail? Haig could be Machiavellian, but that was not his primary focus here. He simply needed one of his best generals to rebuild morale among the Canadians after the St. Eloi debacle, and a general with a forceful personality to hold off the Canadian politicians and their meddling ways.

When Byng was appointed as the Canadian Corps commander, he was already aware of the strange situation into which he was stepping. "These men are too good to be led by politicians," he wrote to a friend. "I want to shove on the Canadians who have proved their worth and get rid of the Bumstunts."[60] Byng also knew that his new corps was different from most of the British corps on the Western Front, as it was the embodiment of the Canadian war effort. As the British general settled into his new command at the end of May, he soon found his Canadians engaged in their bitterest battle since Second Ypres more than a year earlier.

On a warm, summery June 2 with few clouds in the sky, the Germans unleashed a massive bombardment on the Canadian lines in the southern part of the Ypres salient, mounting the attack that would start the Battle of Mount Sorrel. Although the inexperienced 3rd Canadian Division—which had arrived at the Western Front only a few months earlier—had been warned of a possible attack, no one expected such fury. Those who witnessed the geysers of earth reaching for the sky in a series of volcano-like bursts said it was the heaviest bombardment on the Western Front up to that point. The carnage was terrible. The 3rd Division was decapitated, with its commanding officer, Major-General Malcolm Mercer, killed during the opening bombardment.

Byng was horrified at the setback. He had been in command for less than a week and his Canadians had suffered a severe blow. Something had to be done with this hard-luck formation. Arthur Currie met with Byng around 4:15 P.M. on June 2 and suggested that the Canadians form a new defensive line to guard against further German thrusts, and then counterattack through it after sufficient forces could be carefully marshalled. It was a safe proposal, but Byng wanted a more aggressive plan and ordered an immediate counterattack. While it might have been the wise operational move—to drive a blade into the overextended Germans before they had a chance to consolidate their gains—the 3rd Division was in no shape for a counterattack, with its headquarters shattered and communication cut from front to rear. Coordinating any attack would be almost impossible. Even worse, Canadian counterattacking forces were held kilometres behind the lines and had to march through shellfire, bullets, and poison gas, all of which took its toll. Nonetheless, Byng ordered the attack. The Canadian force, which consisted of elements of the 3rd Division and Currie's 1st Division, was torn apart as it blindly stumbled into the German guns. A second attack the next day was just as futile.[61]

Byng reeled from the failures. He had just taken over command and suffered a grave defeat, and, barely acquainted with his staff and his soldiers, didn't know whom he could rely on to restore the situation. But

Currie's 1st Division had a good reputation, and so Byng called on his young major general to organize an operation to reclaim the lost territory and restore the Canadians' reputation. While every minute counted in reversing the loss and striking while the Germans had not yet consolidated and completed their defensive system, Currie would not be rushed. He planned carefully in organizing the counterattack, which would go in behind a heavy artillery barrage in the early hours of June 13. The operation was informed by many of the lessons Currie had learned from the last year of fighting: intricate preparation, consolidation of resources, sharing of intelligence gathered through aerial photographs, and thorough training for the attacking infantry who were given time to practise in advancing over similar ground. While these factors could not win a battle on their own, they tipped the odds in the Canadians' favour.

As the attacking troops filtered into the line on June 12, Currie was there to greet them and wish them luck. Charles Cameron of the 16th Battalion, a young NCO who had enlisted from British Columbia, remembered Currie's brief speech, which he must have repeated over and over again as hundreds of infantrymen marched past: "Now boys, I have done all I can. I can do no more, the matter is entirely in your hands, and I wish you good luck and God-speed."[62] Currie had indeed planned well, with over 200 guns, more than half of them heavy howitzers, ready to inflict a massive bombardment to shatter the enemy lines.

In the early hours of the 13th, four first-wave battalions charged forward in a risky night operation intended to surprise the enemy and sow confusion in his ranks. With the enemy front pulverized, the Canadian Tommies crashed through the stunned defenders, and most of the lost ground was recaptured in vicious hand-to-hand combat. The enemy was bombed, shot, and bayoneted. Currie was proud of his men, but he also knew that success had come thorough preparation, heavy gunpower, and of course the tenaciousness of the infantry. The "brash amateur," wrote Currie, "could not get by on enthusiasm and daring alone."[63]

In the aftermath of the shocking battle that had wrought close to 9,000 casualties, Byng found himself with a decapitated 3rd Division, which had not only lost several thousand men in fighting but also a brigadier and the divisional commander. In the midst of the chaos, Sir Sam cabled the Corps headquarters: "Give Garnet 3rd Division—Sam."[64] Brigadier-General G.J. Farmar, a new senior staff officer, received the mystifying message and passed it on to Byng, assuming it was code for something. It was not. Sam did not cover his actions in code: he demanded. But Byng would not be cowed. He discarded the order and appointed as commander of the 3rd Division the much-respected Brigadier Louis Lipsett, commander of the 2nd Infantry Brigade and a professional British officer, who would prove one of the finest divisional commanders of the war.

Byng and Hughes came face to face two months later, when the minister arrived in August 1916. A raging Hughes demanded why Byng had not followed his orders and appointed his son to command. An uncowed Byng rightly responded to the ever-reddening Hughes that the "Canadians deserved and expected the best leaders available." He did not say, but he certainly implied, that Garnet did not meet this description. While the two men's staffs watched from the sidelines, Hughes threatened to fire Byng, but the general would not budge. Hughes lectured and harassed, and at one point asserted, "I am never wrong." A quick-witted Byng, who was taking the tirade in stride, quipped back to the minister, "What a damn dull life you must have had, Minister!" Hughes's stunned entourage turned to the minister, waiting for an eruption, but were greeted instead by the sight of Hughes leaning back in his chair, roaring with laughter.[65] The tension was cut. Byng was smooth, and while he stood up to the minister, he was not foolhardy. He stroked Hughes's ego when he could, and he allowed him to visit the front, to address the soldiers, and to play the role he so dearly loved. After Byng stood up to Hughes, the minister executed an "about turn" and, in the words of one staff officer, "supported Byng in every possible way."[66] Byng had won an important battle in severing the political strings from Ottawa, but he soon needed to turn his attention to fighting on the Western Front. The biggest battle to date loomed on the horizon.

The British had been preparing for their summer offensive since late 1915. The two principal Allies on the Western Front, France and Britain, of which the former was the more senior in the first half of the war, planned for a joint attack in August 1916, along the Somme River, in France. It was here that the new British divisions, having recently been stood up and trained, would drive the Germans back from their fortified ground. But the Germans upset the plans by attacking the French at Verdun on February 21, 1916, capturing several key forts. The French forces counterattacked relentlessly to reclaim their lost possessions, and the battlefield was soon reduced to a charnel house of mud, corpses, poison gas, and never-ending shellfire. The carnage sustained by both sides was terrible.

As the fighting at Verdun dragged on, the French reduced their contributions to the upcoming Somme offensive, in which they were supposed to have been the major partner. They also pressured Sir Douglas Haig to move up his attack date from August to July 1. Without an earlier date of attack drawing German forces away from Verdun, claimed the French high command, their forces there might be annihilated. Haig objected, knowing that he did not have enough shells or guns, and that many of his newly formed divisions were not yet ready for a sustained campaign, but he was constrained by coalition warfare and realized that the war would be lost if the French crumbled. He reluctantly changed the operation to July 1, and hoped that the massive pre-battle artillery bombardment would shatter the enemy lines.

The Allies fired more than 1.7 million shells during the week before the start of the Somme battle, but the Germans had spent nearly two years digging dugouts more than 50 metres deep into the solid-chalk ground. The German defenders suffered terribly, but thousands survived the relentless bombardment. When some 120,000 British infantrymen advanced on the morning of July 1, 1916, they moved straight into the waiting enemy guns. It was a historic slaughter. Close to 60,000 men were killed and wounded. The battle did not end here, however, as the British returned obstinately to the offensive again and again in the coming weeks. Byng's Canadians were lucky to miss the first two months of these punishing battles, during which artillery fire had become shockingly dense and the front-line forces had been consumed at a mind-boggling rate. But their time would come in early September, when they were called to fight on the Somme.

Currie's division arrived on the Somme in early September, and his men relieved Australian troops near the site of Mouquet Farm, an obstinate enemy position that had held out against weeks of sustained Australian attacks. The conditions were nearly unspeakable. The rear areas were blasted beyond all recognition, reduced to little more than connected shell craters. Closer to the front, the battlefield looked like something out of Dante's nightmare. Every square metre seemed churned up; scum-filled craters of water stretched as far as the eye could see; and the unceasing pounding of the artillery guns shocked the earth. The dead were continually disgorged from their shallow graves and the rotting corpses left a stench that reached for kilometres. Soldiers being relieved trudged back from the wasteland with haunted eyes, to be replaced by new men, themselves fearful of what they might find at the front.

As the 1st Division went into the line in early September, the German guns sought them out, laying down crushing fire. Although there were a few minor successful operations, 769 men were lost in less than a week, and almost all in artillery bombardments.[67] For the Canadians, the Somme would live up to its reputation as a meat grinder of men. Currie's forces were in reserve during the Canadian Corps' first major assault against Courcelette and its surrounding terrain on September 15, which was carried out by the 2nd and 3rd Divisions. Relentless artillery bombardments and the newly introduced 8-metre-long machine-gun-bristling and cannon-armed tank supported the attacking Canucks, who drove forward through the enemy lines, stabbing and shooting their way to victory. By the end of the 18th, the Canadians had captured and held Courcelette, claiming one of the few identifiable victories of the entire Somme campaign.

The next phase of the operation was launched on September 26. Currie had been training his men for the battle, but he worried about the ability of the artillery to not only clear the enemy barbed wire but also shatter strong points, many of which were on the reverse slopes of hills and ridges, making it hard for the plunging high explosive shells to hit the nearly hidden positions. Currie's fear was well founded. The attack on the 26th was a costly failure, with the infantry forced to mill around in No Man's Land exposed to enemy fire as they looked for holes in the uncut barbed wire. The artillery bombardment had also failed to destroy enemy positions, and the creeping barrage—a slow-moving wall of shell-fire that "crept" over the battlefield and was followed closely by the infantry—had been too ragged and sporadic to keep the enemy in his dugouts.

Currie studied the wreckage and interviewed surviving officers. When he heard that the Old Red Patch—his division's informal name, referring to the newly received red divisional patches sewn on the sleeve—was going in for another attack on the 8th, he carried his protest to Byng. The artillery, he implored, could not hope to cut the wire and destroy the positions in time for the operation. But Byng was under his own pressure from the Fourth Army headquarters to keep at the enemy, and the assault could not be postponed. A desperate Currie accepted this, as he had no choice, but he redoubled his efforts to get artillery officers to the front to help direct the fall of the shells. A morally brave Currie travelled to each of the attacking battalions that were going over the top one more time. He looked his men straight in the eyes, explained why the operation had to be carried out, and treated them with respect. He could not change the orders from above, but he wanted the front-line forces to know that their sacrifice would be important. After the exhausting series of talks to the men, many of whom he was condemning to death, he visited the chief artillery officer, Major Alan Brooke, who would later rise to become field marshal and chief of staff of all British forces in the Second World War. Brooke recounted the general's worry: "I remember well how Currie's solicitude for his men struck me at the time." They spent hours going over the plans, and toward the end Currie turned to Brooke and pleaded with him: "My boys haven't got the kick in them which they had; I look to the guns to put them into Regina Trench."[68] But the guns failed the infantry, and Currie's men ran into uncut wire and deep German fortifications on October 8. A little over a week later, the skeletal remains of Currie's division limped off the Somme battlefield, battered and broken.

The Somme was as frustrating as it was deadly. This was timetable warfare at its worst, and orders to advance that might succeed on one front could be suicidal on another where wire was not cut or the enemy remained alert. Divisional commanders like Currie had no control over their start time, which was set by the army commanders, or even by Haig's general headquarters (GHQ). Even when the infantry were able to cross the killing ground of No Man's Land, their success often pushed them deeper into the enemy trench systems, placing their heads further into the noose. With enemy counter-barrages coming down and isolating the weakened attackers, the survivors, already cut apart by enemy fire as they crossed No Man's Land, soon became defenders against the rising tide of German counterattackers bent on avenging their dead comrades and recapturing lost territory. Battalion, brigade, division, and corps commanders often had little idea of what was happening beyond the haze, explosions, noise, and earth thrown up by the enormous concussion of nonstop shellfire. The *Frontsoldaten* on both sides were often abandoned, left to kill or be killed.

General Currie anguished over the losses. The lessons of war had been shattering. Artillery gunpower was needed to suppress the enemy defences. The infantry required time to prepare for battle and they had to be supported with up-to-date intelligence. Currie had realized his own impotency at headquarters as he waited for word from the front—was an attack a success or had it been blown apart? While the generals were trained to exert control from the rear, Currie knew that the Somme battles, and those that would follow, could only be won if the soldiers at the front were empowered to fight their way forward. They would need the training, the leaders, and the weapons to do it. Currie turned his mind to finding new ways to help his soldiers survive on the Western Front.

CHAPTER 8

Endgame

SIR SAM HUGHES, 1916

Prime Minister Sir Robert Borden liked Sir Sam Hughes and respected his political longevity in Parliament. Hughes was the right man for the position in 1914, and no one else could have galvanized the country as he did, by leading Canadians on a crusade. But the crusade had turned into a bloodbath and the unstable Hughes had become a liability. The minister never seemed to take heed or warning, and while Borden had given him ample rope in order the run the war effort in Ottawa, it always seemed to find its way around Hughes's neck. Borden would later write, "About half of the time he was an able, reasonable and a useful colleague, working with excellent judgment and indefatigable energy; for a certain other portion of the time he was extremely excitable, impatient of control and almost impossible to work with; and during the remainder his conduct and speech were so eccentric as to justify the conclusion his mind was unbalanced."[1] Although Borden did not like to barge into his ministers' business, he had increasingly been forced to reduce Hughes's involvement in the war effort. Yet still Hughes's behaviour had gone from embarrassing to dangerous. Borden continued to protect his errant knight against the Liberal opposition and the increasingly angry Tory caucus, but he knew it was only a matter of time before Hughes went down, whether from blows to the front, knives in the back, or by his own hand.

Whereas once Sir Sam's political instincts had been well honed from years of bluster and intimidation, parry and thrust, in 1916 he seemed to make it a habit of seeking his own jugular every time he spoke. He was an easy target for the Liberals, and they took delight in flaying him. The boots, uniform, and equipment scandals had been put to rest through official inquiries and boards, but Hughes had not escaped untainted, even though he was not entirely to blame. He was revealed to be a poor organizer and, yet more troubling, seemed unaffected by all of the problems that dogged him, refusing to accept responsibility for any mistakes and instead blaming the "whispered falsehoods" of his shadowy foes.[2] Brass and bluff had carried the minister through many battles, but his champion, Sir Robert Borden, was becoming increasingly troubled by Hughes, who lacked not only good sense but also contrition for his past misdeeds.

The ever-robust Hughes, who should have collapsed long ago under various pressures, was finally feeling the strain in the third year of the war. He had the warmed-over look of a cadaver: insomnia produced his dark bags and bloodshot eyes, revealing that some sort of rest was needed. But now, in early 1916, was not the time for a break, even though he begged Borden to let him go to England to see his boys.

The Liberals had been building a case against Hughes, and their accusations about his involvement in the supposed kickback schemes and underhanded dealings of the now-defunct Shell Committee were rising to a crescendo. Sir Sam fought back against these charges, among others, but he was being worn down. The Conservatives were taking political hits from the opposition, as well as from concerned Canadians and journalists, although the British were now happy as hundreds of thousands of shells were being sent overseas in support of the war effort. The prime minister was sympathetic toward Hughes, and just as sick with exhaustion in March 1916, but his minister had to face the Liberal music, especially given the severity of charges such as that Hughes and his Tory friends had embezzled funds in pulling a "Million Dollar Rake-off."[3]

Although Sir Sam rarely ducked a fight, he was anxious to get back overseas to see his soldiers. He eventually received his leader's assent to take a holiday after he told Borden that he had met the Liberals in secret and that they had promised to curb their attacks in the name of the war effort. Hughes was granted his leave. Either the Liberals had lied or, more likely, Hughes was delusional, convincing himself of a different outcome at the end of the meeting; or perhaps he was simply twisting the truth to meet his needs. Whatever the case, the Liberals attacked the government in his absence, first with insinuations and then with outright accusations that the minister was running away from corruption charges. Hughes did not help matters by strutting around England and Europe in his uniform, enjoying himself immensely, giving impromptu speeches—hardly the behaviour of someone on vacation.

Sir Sam's absence left the Tories vulnerable; the caucus, fellow ministers, and Borden were furious. On March 28, the Liberals laid out their case against the supposed corruption in the Shell Committee. Much of the evidence was specious and contrived, but the Liberals had dug up some hard numbers and apparent evidence of profiteering. With his minister gallivanting around the battlefields, Borden was forced to order another damning inquiry, this time of the most serious and probing nature—a formal Royal Commission.

When Hughes finally returned, he went almost immediately to see Borden. The prime minister described their meeting in his diary on April 16: "Hughes came at four and was as eccentric as ever. Wept at one time and laughed at another."[4] Borden offered to run the Department of Militia to relieve the strain on the minister and let him focus on the

Liberal attacks, but the bullish Hughes refused, feeling that it would make him look weak. The next day in the House he faced his enemies, even as a chorus of Liberal newspapers called for his resignation. But Sir Sam was always at his best with his back to the wall. The wily veteran was brilliant, deflecting blows, attacking and counterattacking. At one point he lashed out, "After an absence of four or five weeks I find, on my return to Canada, that two hundred of the ablest men in this country, members of the House of Commons, instead of being out helping on the cause, are sitting here listening to piffle."[5] That one drew blood.

Hughes accused the opposition of trying to score political points while he and his comrades worked on behalf of Canadians fighting the greatest war the world had ever seen. To some degree he was correct, and his unabashed patriotism and support of the soldiers was difficult for the Liberals to counter as they badgered and brayed from the sidelines. Hughes was not a man to be cowed. But neither did he know when to keep his tongue. When the auditor general asked some hard questions during the Royal Commission into the corruption charges, and especially into the financial dealings of John Wesley Allison, one of Hughes's cronies accused of making huge profits when acting on behalf of the Canadian government, the minister rose in Parliament to attack the inquisitor, arguing, "he makes reflections on a gentleman [Allison] who has more honor in his little finger than the Auditor General has in his whole carcass."[6] It was too much, and brought boos for the minister, but Hughes showed he would fight the charges, as he had fought everything else in his life. In the end, Hughes was cleared of any wrongdoing, even though he had tried to silence opposition newspapers and deflect the blame onto other Liberals, including some who were in service at the front. Hughes had fought like a cornered rat, teeth bared, and with every means at his disposal.

While the Royal Commission had found the Shell Committee not guilty of malfeasance, the hearings had confirmed the British decision to replace the Shell Committee with the more professionally run Imperial

Munitions Board, established in late 1915. Although Hughes had initially been the driving impetus for a new Canadian industry, his committee had not been able to strong-arm manufacturers to produce shells quickly for the desperate armies in Europe. While Hughes seemed guilty of corruption or ignorance in the eyes of many, he was guilty of neither in this case. Canadian industry had simply been unable to respond to the extent and at the speed required in the short time allotted, as the manufacturers were plagued by a lack of machines, skilled workers, and proper steel. While hundreds of new companies had entered into the lucrative business, it had taken them a long time to ramp up their production. The hard-nosed British minister of munitions, David Lloyd George, had put his own country on a proper footing for wartime manufacturing, and pushed the Canadians to do the same. Borden agreed, and took action in appointing the respected Toronto meat-packing industrialist, Sir Joseph Flavelle, to head a new body that would coordinate shell production in Canada. Although Flavelle's Imperial Munitions Board eventually became the single largest employer in Canada, it remained a British organization that answered to the Ministry of Munitions in London as it sent out tenders and contracts to the hundreds of Canadian companies. This structure surely suggested a strange, colonial mindset on the part of Borden's cabinet, although it allowed the prime minister to distance himself from the scandal-plagued domain of munitions contracts. Sir Sam, however, saw little value in handing oversight to the British; he had also been furious about losing control of the Shell Committee, and over the unfair tarring of himself and his friends on the committee by journalists seeking, as Sam put it, "my downfall."[7]

It galled Hughes to turn over his powers to Flavelle, especially when the Canadian munitions industry was picking up steam and starting to manufacture an enormous number of shells, as well as other war materiel, ships, and airplanes. After Flavelle cold-shouldered Hughes a few times when the minister approached him about Tory friends whom he wanted appointed to key positions, an angry Hughes pushed back. Soon, rumours circulating in Ottawa and published in journals such as *Saturday Night* suggested that Flavelle was disliked and disruptive, and that his autocratic methods were driving away manufacturers. Aware that Britain was suffering through a credit shortage and was engaged in a fight for its very survival, Flavelle refused to allow Canadian manufacturers to reap large profits; the whispered accusations charged him with, among other things, denying hard-working Canadians their rightful money, and all in the name of the British masters he served. Flavelle knew there would be some disaffection with regard to his bottom-line ways, but the rumours were especially virulent. He used his influence to investigate, and was soon hearing that Sam Hughes and his cronies were supplying newspapers with ammunition with which to attack him. At least one journalist told Flavelle that Hughes had come to see him directly to pass on damaging information, urging him to leave no stone unturned in dredging up Flavelle's actions, past and present.[8] Sir Sam did not take lightly to being pushed to the periphery, and the born fighter had dug in, especially as he increasingly saw Flavelle's actions as a "conspiracy" to defraud him of his well-earned glory.[9]

As one contemporary observer of politics noted, "The Minister's faults were known to all men, criticism had been abundant and often bitter, his own words at times were unwise and of the wild and whirling kind."[10] And while little could be done about Hughes's propensity to get himself into trouble with each speech or impromptu talk, Borden had systematically stripped him of the responsibilities for purchasing war supplies and organizing Canada's shell output. Hughes had also been censured by various committees and commissions, and had endured a constant barrage of verbal abuse from the opposition. Sir Joseph Flavelle's condemnation of Hughes after hearing of his involvement in the Allison corruption charge was damning: "I believe him to be mentally unbalanced, with the low cunning and cleverness often associated with the insane."[11] A saddened Borden would write almost as sharply of Hughes after the war, and in April 1916 he was forced to acknowledge that, with the ongoing embarrassment and gaffes, "It is quite evident that Hughes cannot remain in the Government."[12] This may have been the case, but no one—not even the prime minister—had the courage to immediately force the issue with Hughes.

In August 1915 Hughes had authorized the printing and distribution of 100,000 posters to encourage enlistment, which was one of the few government interventions in the recruiting process. The voluntary principle reigned supreme, and toward the end of 1915, Hughes put more authority into the hands of prominent local citizens to raise troops. It was surely the right thing to do. The centralized government in Ottawa was too small and too far away from targeted centres to have much impact on recruiting. Instead, local units were formed around friends, co-workers, and men who knew each other and their leaders. In promising that "pals" would fight together, this new method of recruiting was popular and effective in getting Canadians to join the colours.

Despite this success, Hughes failed to exercise control in the creation of these new formations. For him it was about signing up more and more men, with the goal that the staggering numbers would raise Canada's profile among the imperials. But Hughes could not get the men unless they came in the form of units mobilized in the communities. So Hughes encouraged the establishment of new units, but gave little thought as to what they were to do once they went overseas. Unfortunately, what the overseas forces desperately required were men, not units. Hughes's staff warned him about this disjunction, and about the ongoing problems of keeping full battalions up to strength at the front.[13] He ignored them.

Contrary to what had been promised, when the new formations from across the country went overseas, almost every battalion numbered from 90 to 258 (170 battalions, ranging from a few hundred men to the full complement of 1,000), was broken up. Peter Anderson, a Scandinavian-born member of the CEF, was one of those whose battalion was ransacked for reinforcements: "It was an awful blow after having worked

166

with those men all winter; after what I had promised fathers, mothers, sisters and brothers, that I would look after Tommie, Jimmy, Bill and Jack, to see them parcelled off like slaves in a slave market. I was beside myself."[14] Anderson was not overplaying his hand here; the breakup of the battalions overseas was devastating, as these units were the extension of the communities that had contributed the men, money, and support. Officers were severed from their men, as their companies and platoons were sent to the front in reinforcing drafts. "Damn his soul to Hell," raged one furious officer who lost his battalion and blamed Hughes.[15] The minister would later hold the British responsible for shattering the Canadian units, calling them "fatheads, muddleheads or woodenheads," but Sir Sam's ill-planned recruiting scheme was surely to blame for the problems.[16] The widespread dismemberment of units created tremendous anger toward Hughes.

If voluntary recruitment was difficult in English Canada, it was an enormous failure in Quebec. Before the war, Quebec had a weaker militia system than the rest of Canada, and Hughes had not helped matters, as he was often petty and vindictive toward French Canadians. In June 1914, for instance, he refused to allow the French-Canadian 65th Militia Battalion to march in the Corpus Christi celebration in Montreal, whereas he almost always allowed English militia units to do so in similar parades and ceremonies.[17] This was Hughes at his worst, Orange to the core.

When the government turned to those same militia units to help raise overseas battalions during the war, Quebec thus lacked the necessary level of internal organization. But the problem went far deeper. Quebec simply did not have the same ties to Britain. With many Quebeckers more worried about the anti-Catholic and anti-French-Canada sentiments professed by the "Prussians of Ontario" than they were about the enemy across the Atlantic Ocean, it is not surprising that the per capita enlistment figures for the province were lower than all others except for Prince Edward Island. There are inaccuracies in all recruitment statistics for the Great War, as men from one region often enlisted in another, thereby throwing off the numbers, which could only be tracked by geographical place of enlistment and not place of residence. But best estimates suggest that while Quebec made up 27 percent of the population, it provided only 14.2 percent of the CEF's enlistment, and thousands of those who joined up were English-speakers from Montreal and the surrounding region.[18]

Hughes did not help the CEF's cause in Quebec. According to his military assistant, the minister's "zeal and earnestness ... for all things British had made him a *persona non grata* with a considerable section of people, who looked upon him as a fanatical Orangeman, a visionary, and a wind-bag."[19] And such visceral reactions against the minister were not limited to French-speaking Canadians, with many Canadians across the country and outside of Quebec thinking him a fanatical windbag too. Hughes did perceive some of his own limitations, and he had looked for a prominent Catholic leader to oversee recruiting in Quebec, but no one stepped forward.[20] He was therefore forced to appoint a Methodist minister to perform this role, which did not encourage Catholic French Canadians to enlist.

Hughes's dislike of the French—which was returned freely—was well known to Borden and the cabinet, so why did a more competent and better suited minister not step up? Borden claimed after the war that the details of Hughes's activities in Quebec "escaped [him] at the time," but his observations seem a little disingenuous.[21] Where were Borden's Quebec lieutenants? In truth, Borden's party had come to power in 1911 with the support of Quebec nationalists, most of whom had run on a fear-mongering ticket against Laurier, claiming that his establishment of a Canadian navy would ultimately result in conscription. Half a decade later, most of the nationalists had fled the Conservatives or showed at best lacklustre support for the war effort. But as cabinet was formed from regional representatives, it was in no small part the role of Borden's Quebec ministers to drum up the requisite number of recruits in that province, and they failed to deliver the men. While Hughes indeed made errors, he has just as significantly been made a scapegoat for the failure of recruiting in Quebec.

As Hughes's approach to recruiting was based on getting as many men as possible to enlist, even his enemies had to admit that he was wildly successful. Putting aside his hyperbolic speeches, in which he claimed that Canada could raise forty divisions, the reality was that, by the end of June 1916, an astonishing 312,000 officers and men had enlisted.[22] To put this into perspective, the equivalent today, for a Canada four times as large, would see some 1,250,000 Canadian civilians in military uniform. Hughes's success was nothing short of astounding. Moreover, if Sam's war was to be a voluntary one, then he did not much care that some parts of the country were not contributing. While he was angry about the uneven and heavy burden carried by "loyal" Canadians, this was the price paid in a country as big and segmented as the Dominion. "It is no longer a War of peoples or nations," wrote Hughes in October 1916, "it is a War of the sacred principles of human liberty against Prussian autocracy and tyranny."[23] Those Canadians who shared Hughes's belief system often enlisted, but many more were not convinced, or not convinced enough to leave family and home to serve overseas.

Where Hughes can and should be faulted was in his desire to simply raise more and more units in Canada that were then broken up overseas. It was a con game, and one that broke sacred bonds between regions in Canada and their now dismembered units overseas. But the critics of Sam's system—those at the time and most historians since—do not offer much of an alternative: a more centralized pool of recruits who hadn't been raised in local battalions could have been created, but there would have been far less pressure placed on young men to join and the links to the community would have been virtually severed. There is no indication that this would have enlisted more men, and the evidence from Hughes's successful system as well as the various failed schemes after his firing suggests such an alternative may in fact have been less efficient. As always, there were no easy answers.

*　*　*

By the summer of 1916, Borden was clearly at the end of his tether with Hughes. He had lightened the minister's burden considerably and, in June, had appointed Fleming McCurdy, a Nova Scotia MP, as parliamentary secretary of the Militia Department. McCurdy began to pull it into shape, but Hughes missed the warning here, thinking that his new parliamentary secretary simply freed up more time for him to go overseas. This was not the patient Borden's goal, however, as he manoeuvred to formally address Hughes's inability to manage his department and the larger military effort.

Sir Sam's vanities invited additional scorn. His frequent trips to England revealed him to be panting for recognition, and perhaps notoriety. In autumn 1916, he angered the British by badgering the War Office to be made a lieutenant general. They finally gave in, hoping to avoid an unseemly row with their senior Dominion.[24] But Hughes had fallen hard in the last year, and Beckles Willson, a keen if not disinterested wartime observer of Canadian and British relations, wrote that Hughes was viewed as little more than a meddling, mendacious colonial, who felt he knew more, even when across the Atlantic, than anyone at the War Office.[25]

Canadian Liberal newspapers were no kinder to Sir Sam, who seemed to elicit a special bile. The most vicious was, not surprisingly, the leading Liberal organ in English-speaking Canada, the *Toronto Globe*, which missed no opportunity to attack the minister. In a June 22 editorial, Hughes was skewered for his dangerous "swashbuckling" speeches that, according to the paper, damaged recruiting in Canada and the country's relations with the British. On August 24 the *Globe* responded to a widespread rumour that Hughes was seeking a command position in France, possibly of the Canadian Corps. "It would be a crime," spat the *Globe*'s editors, "the ghastliest and most murderous crime of the War, no matter what the excuse or what the cause, were General Sir Sam Hughes given a real command of living soldiers in a genuine engagement anywhere on the War's battle front." Despite Hughes's many failings in Canada, they would be nothing, claimed the *Globe*, compared to

> the fate of a Canadian Army on the French or Belgian front, dependent on the strategy and judgement of Sam Hughes. To acquiesce in such a crime, as a condition of his resignation from the Canadian government, would be to try to wash out the reminders of political blundering in the life-blood of Canadian regiments. It is bad enough to have to suffer his aping of Napoleon as the world's other military genius; but to allow him a chance to put his apings into practice with the flesh and blood of Canada's sons and men— No![26]

Despite the partisan attacks that were common in the papers of the day, a vitriolic editorial such as this would only have been possible in patriotic wartime with the minister's reputation in obvious and steep decline.

Not content to simply badger the British, Hughes continued to revel in his opportunities to meet and talk to Canadian soldiers, some of whom he visited in the front-line trenches. But many of Hughes's beloved boys had soured on the minister. Hughes loved to inspect the soldiers, see them march, and receive their salutes, but this was exactly the type of nonsense that the vast majority of soldiers hated. Parades required the men to wait for hours on end, often in the rain or burning sun. When Hughes had tried this at Camp Borden in Canada before going overseas in the summer of 1916, he had been greeted by booing soldiers, and forced to flee back to his train car in the face of nearly rioting men. It had shaken him badly. His bluster had lost its appeal. He was a home-front politician posing as a general, or vice versa. His patronage appointments and his support for the Ross rifle had been damaging to morale and had cost lives. Sir Sam's rough and manly behaviour might have played well with some soldiers, but one Canadian officer was so aghast at Hughes's pompous actions and excessive swearing that he wrote to Borden, pleading with him to "get rid of this objectionable cad." The minister was insulting almost everyone he came across, using the vilest language "whether leaders are present or not, indiscriminately cursing all and several."[27]

Yet Sam had always had, and would continue to have, some champions among the soldiers. Tenth Battalion infantryman George Frost captured some of Sam's strengths and weaknesses in this bit of wartime doggerel:

> You were very oft bull baited
> When a question you debated
> Honourable Hughes
> If you cannot make a speech,
> At army raising you're a peach,
> So just let your foeman preach
> Good old Hughes.[28]

Another Canadian in the field, Hal Kirkland of Princess Patricia's Canadian Light Infantry, wrote in the summer of 1915 that while he and his comrades had annoyingly been marched 9 kilometres to be reviewed by Sir Sam, and the remarks by many of the hard-bitten soldiers had been "not very complimentary to say the least," the minister gave a memorable talk and was cheered at the end. "Personally, I think he's a good man for the job. I think he's done splendid work."[29] A year later, Kirkland had soured a little on Hughes, but not by much. It was hard to imagine anyone else in the post. Leslie Frost, who had enlisted with his brother Cecil and would later rise to become a long-serving premier of Ontario, remarked that he was won over during his one meeting with Sir Sam. His battalion was being inspected in October 1916, and the men lined up. The burly yet handsome minister moved down the line shaking hands, and when he came to Frost, he looked him in the eyes, and said, "Take care of your brother."[30] It was profoundly moving for the young soldier, and just the right thing to say.

* * *

Hughes had ridden out the storm of controversies born of the first months of the war because his leader had faith in him, or had at least tolerated him because of the skills he brought to the cabinet. It is too easy to write Hughes off as a lunatic, as many at the time did, and as most historians since have done as well. Hughes was a complicated man and he had real strengths. He was both the visible public face and the essential driving force behind Canada's war in 1914 and for much of 1915. By 1916, however, Hughes had lost his grip on the ever-expanding war effort. Even with this reduction in responsibilities, Hughes had simply carried the weight for too long to remain at all effective. He was a casualty of the war.

Despite his strong work ethic and enthusiasm for taking on new projects, Hughes was steadily digging his own grave with his hyperbolic outbursts, his bad manners, and his poor judgment. He was increasingly becoming unbearable, even for his supporters. Hughes's long-time champion and patient defender, Prime Minister Borden, realized that the war was too big to be run by one man: the nation needed to come together, its politicians and soldiers needed to professionalize, and disruptive forces like Hughes had to be curtailed or removed.

Borden had changed, too. He had been toughened by the war. In fact, the relentless stress had forged Borden into a war leader. While British prime minister Herbert Asquith had been overwhelmed by the war and eventually forced out of power, Borden had soldiered on. By 1916 he was increasingly committed to the war effort at home, driving the country forward to higher recruitment rates and increasingly pushing for greater Canadian autonomy within the British war effort. Borden grew into the role of warlord, one he never accepted easily but in which he proved to be effective.

Even as he was being forged in the fire of war, Sir Robert worried constantly about Sir Sam, with the tolerant prime minister writing more often about Hughes in his personal diary than about any other minister.[31] Yet Hughes never seemed to take Borden's gentle proddings and encouragements to heart. Perhaps he still saw him as he had before the war: as "a lovely fellow, very capable, but not a very good judge of men or tactics and gentle-hearted as a girl."[32] Hughes was in a running and uneven battle with much of the cabinet, and he continued to strike back while trying to butter up Borden, as revealed in one letter sent from England: "Your road is more or less a hard one. It is generally understood that White and Foster seek to impose their influence, adverse to me, upon you. But I know you are capable of seeing through them."[33] In fact, Borden had for a long time seen through Hughes's blandishments and coy words, but it was hard to find the right way to remove Hughes after he had been elevated to national hero as the face of the government's war effort.

After Sir Sam had seemingly survived the Liberal attacks of early 1916, and that of his increasingly angry party—Borden described it as "open revolt against Hughes' continuance as Minister"—he scheduled another trip overseas to see his boys in August.[34] When the uninhibited Hughes travelled the front, he offered advice to the soldiers, who, after nodding reassuringly to his face, probably scoffed secretly at his naive comments. In a revealingly simple-minded and condescending letter to Sir Max Aitken, which he expected would be passed on to the British, Hughes blithely offered armchair generalship to solve the problems of fighting on the Western Front: "I cannot comprehend such blunders as sending troops through unbroken wire entanglements.... I showed them how to destroy wire entanglements long ago."[35] Hughes saw himself as a man with all the answers—in fact, as perhaps the only man in the Empire with all the answers—and his solution to dealing with the miles of barbed wire that could barely be cut by mountains of high explosive artillery shells had been an absurd plan of pushing explosives underneath the enemy wire and detonating them that way. This was already one of many tactical options open to the fighting men at the front, but one of the least successful, as the Germans simply put up more wire and the soldiers pushing explosives forward tended to get killed in exposed positions. Hughes was clearly out of touch with reality at the front.

The primary focus on the trip was for Hughes to sort out the overseas crisis in the training camps, and in a forceful telegram Borden criticized the "lack of system in the arrangements for direction and control in Great Britain."[36] Hughes's multiple training camps in England had been overlapping from the start of the war, with generals competing for power, and now the system was in complete chaos. Charitable critics sneered that the minister was simply incompetent, while the uncharitable accused Hughes of having built an unworkable structure to keep power in his grasp. Whichever was the case, the failed system threatened to derail the Canadian war effort, as reinforcements were not being adequately trained, nor were they crossing to France in a timely fashion. Hughes had taken a few steps to rectify the situation, but grave problems remained as the system seemed to be based on loyalty to him first, the government second, and efficiency a distant third.

Why had someone not sorted this problem out before a critical breakdown occurred? What had the British in particular been doing, in whose backyard this mess had occurred? The simple answer is that Hughes terrified the War Office. His irrational and unpredictable actions, combined with his mad missives and barking nationalistic comments, left even hardened professional soldiers shaken and bewildered. While Hughes could have and should have been more harmonious, he was exerting the right of Canadians to have a say in their own life-and-death matters. As Sam's private military secretary, Charles Winter, observed, the minister was a "Canada first" man and believed in the necessity of keeping the Canadian Corps together and commanded by Canadians, all within a pro-Empire overall policy.[37] We now generally support this type of overt Canadianism, although not, it would seem, in Hughes. Perhaps it was Hughes's ego-driven interferences, racist rhetoric, and manic actions that caused him to be perceived, then and now, as little more than a flawed caricature that not even nationalists could embrace.

In that summer of 1916, as Hughes went to England to reform the training camps, he had been instructed by Borden to give "prompt and effective considerations" to the problems, but not to make any decisions without first receiving the approval of the cabinet.[38] Hughes was willing to make changes, as he knew of the overseas problems, but he did not want to lose his control, which had waned everywhere except in the chaos of England. An effective overseas system of command would mean that Hughes would be blocked from intervening to right wrongs, as he saw it, or meddle, as most others would classify it. As he strode about the Canadian camps, promising four new divisions and barking about how he would clean up administrative breakdowns, he established a new sub-militia council made up of cronies and headed by his friend Sir Max Aitken.[39]

The establishment of this new administrative body was the last straw for Borden, who had expressly informed Hughes that no decisions were to be made without cabinet approval. Sir Robert was enraged to find out about Hughes's new council through the newspapers.[40] He lamented that Hughes was as "wrong-headed and stupid as ever."[41] Borden dispatched an angry telegram to Hughes on September 7, reprimanding him for his disobedience, and then set in motion his plan to remove Hughes from overseas influence by setting up a new ministry in London, to be headed by Borden's loyal friend Sir George Perley, who was then the acting high commissioner.

Hughes had despised Perley for years, at least as far back as 1910, when Perley had been appointed party whip instead of Hughes. Sir Sam had described his enemy in the past as "cold, tyrannical and very ego-tistic."[42] He had not mellowed with time, and continued to find new things to dislike about the Anglophile dandy. Perley in turn loathed Hughes and consistently undermined him with Borden, sending letter after letter about the chaos in England, for much of which he blamed Hughes.

Borden did not need letters from his friend to gauge the action needed regarding Hughes. There was an avalanche of evidence against the minister. Four months after his private recording in his diary, noting that Hughes had to go, he again concluded in August 1916 that "it had become essential to curtail the activities of Hughes and to place in the hands of a responsible Minister in London, the disposition of all such matters affecting the welfare of the Canadian army as were properly the subject of the civil authority."[43] Borden's ministers continued to attack Hughes, and his absence from Canada gave them more opportunities to bring him down.

A tired and hangdog Hughes arrived back in Ottawa on October 7 to meet with Borden, aware that his prime minister was angry with his overseas decisions, and that his pathetic rebuttal that all his actions were temporary until approved by cabinet had done little to quell the storm. But Sir Sam was floored when Sir Robert told him that he was taking over the reorganization. Hughes argued strenuously against an overseas ministry that would be responsible for coordinating and running the overseas war effort, rightly seeing it as a slight against his organizational skills that would further block him from influencing the war effort. He got nowhere with the stony-faced Borden. Hughes had another stormy meeting with Borden on October 19, when, according to Borden's diary, Hughes "objected strongly and argued against it, saying that there would be nothing left for him, that he would be humiliated and he would have to leave the Government. He gave a tirade against Perley and decried his ability. Said that everything he had done himself was perfect."[44] The wounded Hughes also ranted against conspiracies targeting him, but now Borden was no longer his protector, or even his confidant; he shared Hughes's hysterical outburst with his other ministers and wondered how much longer they could endure this madness.

In the meantime, Borden implored Perley to consider his request to accept the appointment as overseas minister. But despite the appeal of poking Hughes in the eye, Perley did not want the job. Comfortable in his position as acting high commissioner, he knew well the difficulties of setting up an overseas ministry responsible for hundreds of thousands of soldiers, of dealing with the prickly British and Canadian generals and politicians, and of being always open to attacks in the House of Commons, against which he could not defend himself in person. But his leader needed him.

A few days later, on October 26, Hughes girded himself for another battle against the "conspirators," and evidently believed he had enough influence with Borden to now negotiate the appointment of who would administer the overseas ministry. Hughes wrote transparently to Borden that, as overseas minister, Perley would place Canada's "gallant boys at the Front … in danger—not from the enemy but from improper manage-ment behind them."[45] If Sir Max Aitken were to receive the position instead of the hated Perley, Sam would agree to go along with the plan.[46] Borden was having none of it. Yet the prime minister still looked for a way out for Hughes, and he had inquired with loyal Conservatives at the front whether perhaps Hughes could be dumped there as a senior com-mander. That plan dissolved when one informant told Borden bluntly,

> At the present moment, the Public Opinion among the men in Uniform is certainly against Sir Sam. He is blamed for much that he has done, and no doubt a great deal that he has not done. However, the fact is there, that the men in Uniform look on him as a kind of Joke, and men on this side of the water, who have had experience at the front are very sore, and make some very nasty statements regarding what would happen to Sir Sam, if he happened to lead a Division at the Front.[47]

There would be no spot for Hughes as a battlefield commander and, increasingly, none in the cabinet, with the ministers having turned fully against their wayward colleague, sensing with great relief that perhaps Sir Sam was going down.

Sir Sam's political antenna had long withered. As a fighter against any and all who stood in his way, he was blind to his precarious position. He continued to rail, but when the still emotional Hughes met with Borden on October 31, he could do little except seethe and weep at the injustice of the announcement of the new ministry overseas that day. The flailing Hughes saw enemies at every turn. And he was right. Liberals ahead, Tories behind. Even his own soldiers had abandoned the once powerful and influential Hughes. And his stalwart champion for over a decade, Sir Robert Borden, had turned on him, too. In Hughes's mind, Borden had sided with his enemies, and the establishment of Perley as overseas minister was the final straw. An angry and dispirited Hughes lashed out, accusing the prime minister in a November 1 missive of failing to "support him during the past two years," and, for good measure, of being a liar.[48] But such intemperate words and veiled threats no longer cowed Borden.

After consulting with the cabinet, the Ontario wing of the party, and senior representatives of the Orange Order, Borden acted with uncharacteristic speed. He wrote to Hughes on November 9, calling for his resignation, citing, among other problems, that despite his attempts to support Hughes and his countless recommendations for caution, he was unable to keep the minister in the cabinet because of his "strong tendency to assume powers which [he did] not possess." Borden noted that he no longer had the "time or energy" to deal with problems that Hughes had created, as he administered his department "as if it were a distinct and separate Government in itself."[49] While the letter did not come close to listing Sir Sam's full list of transgressions, it was enough to sound his death knell.

When Hughes received Borden's letter demanding his resignation, Colonel Eugene Fiset, the deputy minister of militia, recorded that the blood drained from the minister's face and he almost collapsed. No longer would Sir Sam lead Canada's war effort.

CHAPTER 9

Corps Commander

SIR ARTHUR CURRIE, 1917

The formation of the Overseas Ministry under Sir George Perley, and Hughes's subsequent firing, had predictably shaken up the overseas forces. By early November 1916 Perley was establishing his department, with its headquarters in London. The new minister began to clean up Hughes's mess, but he readily admitted to knowing nothing about the fighting forces. He needed a chief of staff, and either Richard Turner or Arthur Currie would be pulled back from the front to fill that important role. The new chief of staff would modernize the multiple and conflicting Canadian camps, hammer out a new training syllabus, and ensure that reinforcements reached the fighting forces in a timely manner. It would be a key position. And Currie did not want it.

The new overseas minister called a wary Currie to an interview, but the general thought it might be a trap, especially after witnessing Alderson's disastrous appointment earlier in the year. Perley's "cold and unapproachable" attitude—and this a description from his friend Sir Robert Borden—may also have put Currie on edge.[1] Perley, in turn, did not like Currie's cautious bearing and took umbrage at being reminded by the general that political interference had cost the lives of Canadians. A disgruntled Perley turned to Turner, but he was no more enthusiastic, writing to Currie that he thought the position would only be a "bag of trouble."[2] In the end Turner's hand was forced, as he had the weaker battlefield reputation and Byng had already selected Currie to be his right-hand man in instigating reforms in the Canadian Corps. A sullen Turner went back to England, putting duty before self, but making a deal with Perley to retain his seniority over Currie. He also received a promise that if a Canadian was ever considered for corps command, his name would be first on the list. As chief of staff, Turner succeeded beyond all expectations, becoming one of Canada's unsung heroes.[3] But no longer would he lead from the front: the path to the highest command was open for Arthur Currie.

When Turner resigned as divisional commander in November 1916, Currie became the senior major general at the front. Byng tasked him first with writing the corps report on the lessons learned from the Somme. He was well suited to the job, for as Sir Julian observed after the war, Currie "had a most perfect confidence in himself with a great adaptability to learn from others."[4] Currie consulted with the various commands that formed the Corps. This was a process that could have been fraught with difficulties, as soldiers blamed one another, other formations, or higher command for the deaths of their comrades. Though there was little of that rancour, as junior leaders realized that they had to learn and evolve, some hard truths had to be faced. Currie ensured that they were.

The final report was an impressive document, and Byng—with the support of Haig's headquarters—then sent Currie off with other senior British officers to carry out a similar learning process with the British and French forces. The French proved the more interesting of the two, as their experience in fighting around Verdun had been radically different from their allies' time on the Somme. Currie prodded those he spoke with and challenged what he was told. While not always making himself popular, he came away with some key lessons—perhaps the most important of which was that control over the infantry had to be decentralized from the level of the company (200 men) to that of the platoon (50 men), and possibly even down to the level of section (12 men), in order for junior officers and senior non-commissioned officers (NCOs) to operate more effectively on the battlefield. These smaller combat units also needed to be armed with more powerful weapons, primarily light machine guns (the Lewis in the case of the British and Canadians) and rifle grenades.[5] Senior British gunners emphasized to Currie—and later to one of the key Canadian gunners of the war, A.G.L. McNaughton—the importance of using a heavy artillery barrage to suppress enemy fire rather than pursuing the impossible goal of trying to destroy the enemy's entire defensive grid through bombardment, although the Canadians had already come to the same conclusion. This approach would be the key to allowing the infantry to cross No Man's Land. In January Currie wrote a detailed report for Byng, whose headquarters implemented many of the learned lessons throughout the Corps.

Returning to his division, Arthur looked older and more worn. His hair had thinned and his boyish face was lined from the stress and exhaustion of nearly two years of life at the front. His girth strained the fabric of his uniform and his double chin was more pronounced, as he had gained weight through stress and inactivity. But he embraced his work and began to prepare his division for the coming battle that was planned for April. The Canadian Corps was now facing Vimy Ridge, a German-held fortress in northern France that had been captured in the opening months of the war and had been reinforced over the last two years with concrete pillboxes, deep trenches, and miles of barbed wire.

Byng used Currie's second report, in conjunction with supporting British doctrinal manuals, to instigate major changes in the Corps, especially in the infantry platoons, which would be better armed and trained. The rest of the Corps followed suit with the reforms, and greater emphasis was placed on the need for combined-arms training—especially for forging the artillery and infantry together into a single mailed fist. A partial solution to the failure of sustaining the advance on the Somme seemed to be the leapfrogging of units through each other, thereby allowing the first waves to dig in and fortify even as the attack was being pressed forward by follow-on forces. This took time to put into practice, and there was a fear that the formations would get mixed up or shoot each other in the inevitable confusion of battle.

The attacking formations also learned to work in concert with the creeping artillery barrage. These barrages had been introduced on the Somme in late 1916, but had been refined over the last six months. Coordinated at Byng's corps headquarters, hundreds of gunners fired in unison on targets in front of the Canadian lines, and the wall of landing shells then jumped forward at a uniform pace, usually 100 yards (91 metres) every three minutes. These sweeping walls of fire would tear through No Man's Land, then the enemy's outer defensive crust, and lastly his trenches. While this wall of shellfire could not destroy all of the German strongpoints, especially those where garrison troops were holed up in deep dugouts, it suppressed enemy fire, giving the Canadian infantry time to cross the killing ground of No Man's Land and drive into the enemy trenches, where they would engage in hand-to-hand combat.[6] Again, however, carrying out this new tactic successfully required intense training, and Currie impressed on his officers the need to work with their men in landscapes that were modelled on the enemy front. Thousands of maps were also issued to junior officers and NCOs, following Currie's early recommendation that the infantry platoons had to be equipped with intelligence to effectively fight their way forward over the shattered battlefield.

The Vimy fortress was the Canadian Corps' objective as part of an April 9 British offensive, which was to preface by a week an even grander French advance to the south. This latter French operation was known as the Nivelle offensive, after the French general who orchestrated the plan.

General Robert Nivelle had risen meteorically in command during the Verdun battles, and he was a vociferous proponent of the creeping barrage–led attack. This approach was indeed a step in the right direction in solving the trench-system deadlock on the Western Front, but his plan to cut off a German-held salient along the Chemin des Dames, which would have resulted in the destruction of tens of thousands of Germans, was flawed from the start. A complete lack of control over information had resulted in the plans being leaked to the enemy, who promptly retreated from the salient, thereby shortening and strengthening their defensive line. The criminally optimistic Nivelle took it in stride, however, and carried forward with the operation. To the north, the British were to support Nivelle's unsound plan, and Byng's Corps had drawn the short straw. The Canadians were given orders to take the most difficult position on the British front: the heights of Vimy Ridge.

The ridge ran about 7 kilometres on a northwest to southeast axis, and was located 10 kilometres north of Arras. The Germans had all the advantages, as they looked down on the Canadians below them, were deeply fortified, and had a good sense as to where and when the Allies would attack. The western slope of the ridge was pitted with tens of thousands of shell craters and the rotting remains of countless Allied soldiers, as the French and British had tried three times to take the ridge and failed.[7] Vimy was already a mass graveyard.

The Vimy attack would be the first operation in which the four Canadian divisions attacked together, shoulder to shoulder. Currie's veteran 1st Division was given the most southern portion of the front, and had the furthest objectives, having to crash forward 3,500 metres. An advance of 350 metres might have been considered a deep thrust less than six months earlier; it was clear that the expectations for the Canadians at Vimy were considerably higher. Currie's divisional front was pitted with trenches and strongpoints, but the ground was fairly level, even slanting downhill in parts, and presented very different terrain than that on the heights of the ridge to the north. All of the training of the previous months would be put to good use here, as Currie ordered his attacking battalions to advance to limited objectives before digging in, with second-wave formations leapfrogging them, driving the attack, and additional waves pushing behind them—all of them moving behind a creeping barrage of shellfire.

Once the preparations were put in place, the planning devolved from divisional headquarters to the brigades and the battalions. Currie kept in close contact with his subordinates, offered helpful suggestions on proper objectives, and ensured that maps and information were distributed quickly and widely. With access to 196 light and medium guns, as well as mortars, Currie could also draw upon Byng's heavy Corps guns, which were essential in softening up strong points, shattering trench systems, and battering the deep dugouts.[8] Heavy artillery batteries also used new scientific techniques and tactics to search for enemy guns, and then attempted to destroy them with counter-battery fire. Currie was the important link in the chain between his forces at the front who were gathering intelligence on enemy positions through reconnaissance and forward observers, who would then pass along the targets to the gunners at corps headquarters. By the beginning of April, the full weight of the Corps' and divisions' guns was levelled on the German positions, pounding them ruthlessly. This assault was combined with raids ordered by Currie to gauge the enemy's defences and morale, both of which were shaken.

While snow and sleet beat down the night before the battle, many of Currie's front-line formations sheltered in underground tunnels, waiting for the first guns to go off at 5:30 A.M. When the assault went over the top, twenty-one Canadian battalions from the four divisions surged ahead to close with the enemy. At Currie's divisional command post, regular information arrived indicating the success of his forces that clawed their way forward, snuffing out opposition, overrunning the smoking remains of gun posts, and driving deep into the enemy lines. But this was no easy glide to victory behind the creeping barrage. There were vicious firefights and close-quarter battles throughout the day. Although the Germans often surrendered when the Canadians surrounded them, there were obstinate defenders along the front who continued fighting to the bitter end. By late afternoon Currie's last attacking waves were on their positions and digging in to hold them against expected enemy counterattacks. It was a victorious day, but Currie's infantry formations lost close to forty percent of their strength in wounded and killed, with more than 3,000 casualties sustained. [9]

With the 1st Division consolidating its gains by mid-afternoon, the most pressing problem for Currie was his right flank, which was unguarded by the British division there because it had been unable to keep up with the Canadians due to the fierce enemy defence. Currie tried to close the gap by sending forward his reserves to dig in and protect the open flank, but the British were slow to join hands and Currie kept an eye—as well as dozens of artillery pieces and heavy machine guns— trained on the exposed position.[10] Luckily, the Germans were in complete disarray, with the entire ridge having fallen to the Canadians by April 10, and they were never able to exploit their opponents' weakness. An excited Currie wrote of the battlefield success, "Truly magnificent, grandest day the Corps has ever had."[11]

Further behind the lines, a proud Canadian infantryman, James Jones, wrote in his diary on April 9, 1917, "Good for Hughes Rag time army."[12] While most Canadians believed this to be Byng's disciplined force rather than Hughes's ragtime army, this was a revealing statement by Jones, who associated Canada's largest overseas fighting force with the ex-minister, even if he must have surely been in the minority. Byng's boys had succeeded, even if at a terrible cost. The British to the south had not been so successful, however. After a day of deep advances on the 9th, the Germans counterattacked and drove back many of the British formations. A failure in logistics fouled up any chance of exploiting the victory, but the British attack seemed a glowing success in comparison to that of the French, who were cut apart in repeated senseless assaults. Although the mass of French guns claimed thousands of German lives, the much-hoped-for breakthrough failed abysmally and morale was shattered among the French *poilus*, many of whom came to the sudden realization that they were little more than cannon fodder for careless and callous generals. Like a contagious disease, mutiny began to spread through the French infantry, with over half of the forces by late June eventually refusing to fight in further offensive operations.

The Canadians emerged from the Battle of Vimy Ridge with a new reputation as shock troops. They had captured and held a nearly impregnable position, but at the crippling cost of 10,602 casualties over four days, making Vimy one of the bloodiest battles in Canadian history. Over the next three weeks the Corps would push across the Douai plain, intending to close with the German army. Amidst shellfire and chemical clouds, the Canadians ran up against two strongpoints: the fortified villages of Arleux and Fresnoy. Byng called on his trusted 1st Division to drive the Germans back, and issued instructions to Currie to attack on April 23. Currie protested vigorously, arguing that there was not enough time to prepare for another operation, especially as his infantry formations had been so badly cut up in the Vimy battle.[13] Byng listened to his experienced general and allowed the operation to be delayed by five days, thus making it a part of a larger British drive on the 28th.

Currie used the time to ensure that his assault formations had the latest intelligence on the enemy-held village of Arleux. As at Vimy the infantry would prepare behind the lines, practising their advance, seeking recognizable objectives, and always training not only to capture the objective but to hold it. This was the expression of the emerging Canadian battle doctrine that would be known informally as "bite and hold." The bite and hold approach to warfare was cautious, and while it was not likely to result in any breakthroughs, neither would it lead to orders that sent the infantry deep into enemy trench systems, outside the range of the protective artillery, only to be surrounded and swallowed up by the enemy. Currie mastered this methodical approach to battle, and in the end there were few other tactics used by any army on any front at any time in the war that were as consistently successful in winning ground while also minimizing casualties.

The Canadians captured Arleux on April 28, and the attack against Fresnoy on May 3 was another model operation for engaging in a limited set-piece battle. Currie had planned to take a small bite out of the enemy lines, and then to use his artillery, machine-gunners, and riflemen at the front to hold it against counterattack. While the enemy deluged the Canadians and their now lost positions in shell and gas, and threw several fierce counterattacks against the line, the Canadians held. Throughout the battle Currie could not play much of a role, but he ensured communication from his divisional headquarters to the brigadiers, encouraging and advising them, and bringing down shellfire on enemy positions. By the end of the day, Currie's men held Fresnoy in their jaws, with the general crowing in his private diary, "The British Division on the right says that but for us they could not have succeeded. Wounded German officers say we must be a special assaulting division—they wouldn't believe that we are the same division which put them off Vimy Ridge and are still at it."[14] The Canadians would eventually hold the position, but when they handed it over to the British it was lost to an enemy counterattack.

The 1st Division distinguished itself at Arleux and Fresnoy, and while there had been other Canadian formations involved, Currie received much of the credit. But Currie did not revel in his victory, instead making the effort, at times painful, to visit the fighting battalions, many of which had lost hundreds of men in the battles since Vimy. The general talked freely of the soldiers' sacrifice in taking their objectives, but he could still be rightly pleased to receive a message from First Army Commander Sir Henry Horne, declaring, "The 1st Canadian Division is the pride and wonder of the British Army."[15]

After the stunning Canadian victory at Vimy Ridge, Lieutenant-General Sir Julian Byng was elevated to command one of the five British armies on the Western Front. Haig was initially preparing to appoint another

British general to command the Canadian Corps, but Byng suggested to Haig that it was time for a Canadian to lead. The British generals agreed that it could only be Arthur Currie. To prepare the way, Currie was knighted on June 3 at Third Army headquarters. King George V was present, but the staff had no formal kneeling stool, so some ingenious officers took a champagne case, added some legs, and covered it in red baize. Everyone held their breath, hoping that it would not collapse under Currie's weight when he knelt before the King, but all was well.[16]

The knighthood was a harbinger of greater things that would come when Sir Arthur was called to Byng's headquarters three days later. There his mentor told him of his own promotion to command the Third Army and that Currie was to have the Corps and be elevated in rank to lieutenant general. It was a bittersweet moment for Currie, as he had learned much from Byng and respected him immensely, and was perhaps a bit of a surprise, too, since he had heard rumours that Turner was first in line for command of the Corps.[17] "No one realizes better than I do," Currie wrote to Newton Rowell, a politician in Canada, "the hard task that lies before me in trying to fill the shoes of our late Corps Commander, Sir Julian Byng. He was a leader who all loved and one to whom the Corps is very much indebted for its present high state of efficiency."[18] Currie had received the mantle from Byng, and would continue to fashion the Corps into an elite combat formation, but the foundation for success was put in place by the British general who, barely a year earlier, had never met a Canadian in his life.

Although Byng had told Currie he would get the Corps command, it was not in the end his decision, although he obviously had influence in selecting his successor. It was Haig who would ultimately decide, and he too was impressed with Currie. As Currie's biographer, Hugh Urquhart, observed, there was a "close friendship between Haig and Currie[,] far closer than was realized by either Haig's or Currie's friends and one unusually so for a man of Haig's reserved temperament."[19] Haig admired Currie's views on discipline and felt that he had forged a very efficient division. The field marshal had visited Currie's divisional headquarters several times before the Vimy battle and been impressed by the professionalism, cheerfulness, and hard work of the staff. Much of the credit, in Haig's mind, went to Currie. At one point the normally staid Haig bid goodbye to the corpulent Currie with a cheerful smile and a wave, saying for all to hear, "Give me fat counsellors."[20]

Canadian politicians in England agreed that it was time for one of their countrymen to command the Corps, but they were not sure if it should indeed be the forty-one-year-old Currie. His appointment in June 1917 took place even as men such as Lord Beaverbrook (Sir Max Aitken, who had by now been raised to the peerage) and Garnet Hughes were pushing to have their own champion, Richard Turner, placed in command. Turner was senior to Currie and he still had his informal agreement with Perley that, in exchange for having taken the position of chief of staff in England, he would be given priority when the corps command came available for a Canadian. Unfortunately for Turner, his failures at Second Ypres and St. Eloi had not been forgotten by the British; nor had these poor showings been fully redeemed by his victory at Courcelette on the Somme later that year, or by his fine administrative work as chief of staff in England. In fact, he had probably made himself indispensable through efficient work in England, so that he could not be spared from the ongoing reforms that were still required to sort out Hughes's mess of conflicting training camps.

Haig quickly moved to have Sir Arthur Currie installed as commander. When an unsure Currie was hesitant for fear of the intriguers in England, Haig pushed him onward, reminding him that it would be much harder to remove him after he took command. The British field marshal was right, and he made a special trip to England to ensure that Currie received the Corps, making a not-so-veiled threat to Perley and others that there was no alternative to Currie other than an imperial general, and Haig would not hesitate to select one.[21] Although the politicians in Ottawa were not happy with the *fait accompli*, Borden and his cabinet soon cabled their acceptance. In England, Lord Beaverbrook was less gracious; upon hearing that Currie had received the Corps, he was said to have remarked, "Well, I suppose we backed the wrong horse."[22]

Perley might have been appointed by the government as overseas minister, but Beaverbrook was not to be taken lightly. Nor was Sam Hughes, who, although removed as minister, remained a force to be reckoned with and placated whenever possible. If Turner would not command the Corps, Aitken and others thought they should receive some concession in exchange. It was a strange way to run a war, but the Canadian forces were still affected by political and patronage issues. As Colonel Walter Gow, the deputy commander of the overseas ministry, noted after the war, he wrestled constantly with Beaverbrook and his cabal, who acted as a "local dictatorship tinged with favouritism and a degree of nepotism."[23] Aware that Beaverbrook and Sir Sam could still cause problems, Borden felt that Currie's former 1st Division should be given to Garnet Hughes, if there were no objections. The prime minister had little to no appreciation of the qualities needed by a divisional commander; his primary goal was to buy off Sir Sam, who still remained a dangerous foe in the House of Commons and was liable at any moment to turn on the Conservatives.[24]

Currie refused to cave in to such high-level pressure. Unlike the politicians, he knew the requirements of a divisional commander. Moreover, he did not want the overseas ministry to dictate his command appointments, as this reeked of the patronage-pushing of Sam Hughes's regime. In the hope of convincing Currie to see the political realities, Lieutenant-Colonel R.F.M. Sims, a senior officer in England and a confidant of Lord Beaverbrook, made a visit to Currie's new headquarters on June 10, seeking, as Currie described it in his diary, to "dicker" about what could be offered as a reward to the Hughes and Turner supporters in England.[25] Currie refused to compromise, making it clear there would be no position for Garnet Hughes in his Corps.[26]

It was a crushing blow for Garnet Hughes. The younger Hughes had helped Currie to get his brigade in 1914, and Currie had even written a letter to him as recently as May 8, 1917, in which he seemingly indicated that he would like to see Garnet as a divisional commander in France.[27] This appears to have been an insincere sentiment on the part of Currie, as he later wrote to other soldiers that Garnet was unacceptable, noting that "the tactics are changing so rapidly, demanding the new tactics be devised to meet the changed conditions, that one who has not seen service here, or who has been away for some months, must necessarily become very much out of date."[28] Currie no doubt remembered Garnet's failure during Second Ypres, when Currie's brigade had nearly been annihilated because of his actions, as well as Garnet's mediocre performance on the Somme, when he had been one of Currie's brigadiers.[29] He also felt that the younger Hughes was not a strong disciplinarian and trainer of men. One of Currie's confidants revealed that the general had a principle that "neither in war nor in peace has friendship excused inefficiency."[30] While Currie had every right to change his mind about Garnet, his friend viewed his abrupt withdrawal of support as a betrayal.

On June 14 Currie was recalled to England and interviewed by Perley, who again tried to convince him to take on Garnet Hughes for all of their sakes. Currie refused again, annoying Perley, who could not understand Currie's seemingly high-handed and inflexible behaviour. The next night, while Currie dined with his wife, Lucy, who had crossed the ocean with the couple's two children to be closer to her husband, Garnet arrived at his hotel. The old friends retired from the dining room to talk. Garnet pleaded his case to Arthur, but the Corps commander refused to budge. Tempers flared and then burned red hot, with the three-hour discussion culminating in a screaming match. Hughes eventually stormed out, but not before promising Currie, "I will get you before I am finished with you."[31]

The experienced and much-loved Scottish-Canadian officer Archibald Macdonell—known to friends and soldiers as Batty Mac—was appointed to the command of the 1st Division instead of Garnet and was a great success among the men of the Red Patch.[32] Yet Currie paid for his insistence on merit over patronage. "From the time of my refusal," wrote Currie, Sam Hughes "never ceased to blackguard me and to minimize my influence and authority with my own men. The things to which he and his associates resorted would bring a blush of shame to the face of every decent citizen of this country."[33]

These same decent citizens might have blushed at the prewar actions of their new war hero, whose embezzlement of regimental funds was now coming back to haunt him. While Currie later claimed that he had made arrangements for friends to pay for the amount "should it be called for by the Regiment or by the Government," this was insufficient to save his reputation should the incident come to light. His lackadaisical approach to this potentially career-ending misappropriation seems out of character, even though he wrote at one point that "for nearly three years the last thing I thought of at night and the first thing in the morning"[34] was the money. Although this was likely the case, there is a curious lack of guilt or anxiety in his diary or personal correspondence. He certainly did not seem morally conflicted over the event, and even as he received a substantial rate of pay as a major general and then lieutenant general, Currie did not hasten to pay back the stolen funds.[35] His actions were bizarre and reckless, as he chose to ignore rather than rectify the problem. Currie had no doubt taken some solace from a generous Sam Hughes, who had caught wind of the problem in May 1915 and dispatched an emissary—their mutual friend, Harold Daly—overseas. Daly wrote after the war that he was "to assure General Currie that his personal interests were being looked after and that he was on no account to worry."[36] But Currie should have worried since he was placing himself in the hands of others, not the least dangerous of whom was Sam Hughes. Currie had enough experience as a businessman and as a soldier in the partisan Corps to know that this was a reckless decision.

The corps commander's past eventually came to the attention of Sir Robert Borden and his cabinet ministers in the summer of 1917, quite possibly via Hughes or forces sympathetic to the ex-minister who wished to take down Currie using his poorly kept secret. The cabinet ministers were shocked to find that their general—Canada's war hero at the front— was a trial away from being branded a felon. Perley wrote to Borden presciently: "It would be disastrous from every point of view if the matter became public."[37] Borden agreed and "greatly feared that [Currie's] default would become public scandal and destroy his usefulness."[38] Borden later burned a number of files that documented Currie's impropriety, but his cabinet ministers remained worried that the revelation of the corps commander's embezzlement would be one more nail in the collective coffin of the scandal-plagued Borden government.

An immediate crisis was contained when two of Currie's subordinate officers—Victor Odlum and David Watson—lent him the money, which he paid back over the next two years. While this averted Currie's public humiliation and possible firing, it put him irresponsibly into the debt of his juniors and, in the case of David Watson, under obligation to a major general who had been responsible for several Canadian operational debacles. By all rights Watson should have been removed from command after the disastrous March 1, 1917, gas raid, in which his division tried to use gas to smother the enemy lines and instead was itself suffocated. Other problems included the uneven performance of his forces at Vimy, as well as later failures during the August 1917 Battle of Hill 70. Despite all of this, however, Watson retained his position throughout the war. Currie was loyal to his subordinates, but he had handed Watson an ultimate trump card to use in retaining his job, for if the corps commander were to fire his subordinate, he would run the risk of the loan and the theft being revealed. It is difficult to reconcile Currie's reckless personal behaviour in relation to this impropriety with that of the public general who approached war in a methodical, careful, and informed manner.

Borden's ministers were unnerved by the embezzlement, and some were left wondering at the character of the man who commanded the nation's forces in the field. At the very least they pondered Currie's political naïveté at leaving himself so exposed to his enemies. Showing great restraint, Borden wrote after the war of Currie, "In his personal affairs he had been careless … ; rumours of default in using for his business purposes of money held in trust are still current. I received many complaints as to his conduct in this respect."[39] Brigadier William Griesbach also tried to come to grips with the uncomfortable, and uncharacteristic, act of desperation, arguing that "Currie's background must be eliminated from any discussion of his character. I think that on the day that he left Victoria he left his background behind him and became another man."[40] Indeed he was another man, but there were some things in his past that could not be outrun or avoided forever.

The Canadian Corps became (and remains) the primary national symbol of Canada's contribution to the war effort. While imperial corps were hollow shells that had divisions passing through them, the Canadian Corps maintained four permanent divisions. These formed the heart of the Corps, even though British divisions were sometimes attached to Currie's formation. The Corps was not an independent, national army—in that it fought as part of the BEF—but in 1917 the men of this formation saw themselves as part of an identifiable entity, and one that had earned an enviable reputation over the previous two years. Byng had forged the Canadians into an effective fighting machine, but now Currie would lead it forward through the final year and a half of brutal battles and stunning victories.

Currie was more than a corps commander in the BEF. Like Byng and Alderson before him, Currie had two masters to serve: the British army and Canadian politicians. At the same time, the situation of having two masters who were not in direct communication with each other offered additional room to negotiate among the powers, if one was a skilled operator. Byng, a strong-minded commander with little to lose since he would always have a place within the British army, had used the military hierarchy to protect himself against the Canadian politicians who sought to interfere. Currie would do the same, but would also occasionally use his Canadian political backers to pressure Haig's headquarters.

Before any of this manoeuvring happened, however, Currie needed to establish his Corps headquarters. Not surprisingly, Currie did not radically change the command style he had employed as a divisional commander. Wartime journalist Fred McKenzie remarked on the "air of quiet and calm that surround the man. There is no feverish rush."[41] A British war journalist, Henry Morgenthau, lunched with Currie in August 1917, and wrote about Currie's common sense, confidence, and calmness. The general remarked to him, "The Great God has given me this calm nature, which prevents my becoming excited, and I use it to study everything which I think will help to lick the Boche."[42]

Sir Arthur had an open and welcoming headquarters, where officers were encouraged to speak up, share ideas, and question assumptions. "He expected initiative in overcoming adverse circumstances.... His attitude was 'don't be satisfied with things as they are, they can generally be improved upon with initiative, forthought and endeavour,'" noted one of his staff officers.[43] Currie talked through problems with his staff, drawing on the expertise of sappers, engineers, gunners, infantry commanders, and anyone who could help. He was a good listener and often replied to issues with an "Oh," although, as one confidant observed, "he had a dozen ways of saying 'oh.'"[44] His subordinates soon learned which "oh"s were positive and which indicated the opposite. The general remained the chairman of the board, directing conversations and always listening. Major-General Archibald Macdonell remembered that Currie was open to new ideas when solving problems, but as he began to settle on a solution, he slowly offered telltale signs: "If he did not like it he unconsciously shook his head contra wise, if he approved, he nodded very slowly."[45]

Currie shouldered a crushing workload and was often ill from exhaustion during the course of the war. His youth had been plagued by a series of illnesses, and the stomach problems that had put him in hospital in the past flared up again during the course of the war. As his aide-de-camp Theodore Roberts observed, "He was under medical care and on a strict and lean diet for months at a time."[46] He suffered stomach pain that kept him up at night, gritting his teeth in the dark. When it was not pain, then it was worry, with the general often suffering from long bouts of insomnia.[47] Most of Currie's energy was focused on warfighting: he did not seem to read much during the war, and made no reference to music, but he did allow himself some time to follow professional baseball in Canada and the United States.[48] Throughout the four years of war, the general gave himself few pleasures and, despite what his girth might suggest, subordinates mentioned that he often forgot about his meals when he was working feverishly. His one gift to himself—in addition to his pipes and a single glass of Scotch a day—was a bath each morning. It was a comfort that few front-line soldiers received, but there were corps commanders throughout the British army who indulged in far more frequent luxuries.

By the time Currie took over the Corps, he had established himself as hard-working, conscientious, and morally brave. As Edmund Ironside remarked, Currie "always fearlessly expressed to his superiors what he thought his men needed."[49] Another British general, J.E.B. Seely, wrote that "again and again he nearly brought his career to an end by bluntly refusing to do things which he was certain would result in great loss of life without compensating advantage."[50] But while he was courageous in the face of his leaders, few officers found Currie to be brilliant. Yet perhaps his strength was that he was not brilliant. Despite having read military history for decades and been forced to engage in relentless on-the-job training, Currie knew his limitations. As one professional Canadian soldier wrote after the war, "The Great War brought about conditions which were new, and fresh tactics had to be devised and new instruments invented to meet them. Professional soldiers had to re-orient themselves, to forget much that they had learned and to learn afresh."[51] One of Currie's advantages was that he had less to forget, and he knew he had a lot to learn. Another senior staff officer suggested that while Sir Arthur made "mistakes, as we all did from the highest to the lowest, Currie's mistakes were genuine mistakes of a careful judgement, they were not mischances, not the miscarrying of plans, due to lack of consideration, and probably, as a consequence, Currie did not make the same mistake twice—a very great virtue in a soldier."[52] Without this internal analysis, guided by lessons disseminated throughout the BEF and from French, Belgian, and later American allies, the Corps could not have hoped to overcome the Germans, who were themselves also adapting to changing circumstances on the battlefield.

Currie's command now encompassed over 100,000 men, and his Corps headquarters was responsible for the four Canadian divisions but also for all of the formation's supporting troops, which included heavy siege guns and mortars; logistical, medical, and engineer units; motor machine-gun formations; and training schools. Currie was wise enough to devolve much of the tactical decision making down the chain of command to the divisional commanders, whom he would rely on heavily in the last year and a half of the war. The general ran a strong team and empowered his subordinates, encouraging them to experiment and take chances. Currie's divisional commanders knew their brigades and battalions better than Currie's staff at headquarters did, so it made sense for the divisional commanders to tackle tactical problems. This devolution of command would become a hallmark of the Canadian battles in the last eighteen months of the war, especially as the tempo of fighting increased and decisions had to be made closer to the front, with little opportunity to consult higher commands.

While Currie was a patient man, he did not suffer fools. He could, according to Colonel C.D.H. MacAlpine, use the most "lurid language" and had a "quick temper" that sometimes caused men to harbour grudges against him.[53] Currie's close friend, William Griesbach, noted after the war, "To his subordinates he was usually pleasant and kindly. I have known him to be otherwise. He strafed me on several occasions but I thought nothing of it and bore him no ill will."[54] War journalist Philip Gibbs observed that Currie could be "cold and ruthless at times," although he could be witty, even through the exhaustion.[55] At one point Theodore Roberts asked him about an event that had happened a year ago. "He looked at me somewhat wearily. 'A year and 12 days ago,' he said, 'How time flies! One show wears pretty thin over 377 days.'"[56] Indeed the show—as the war was often called—wore thin, and the Old Man drove himself hard. As Currie worked on less and less sleep, his temper frayed and his swearing became more common and violent.

Despite the constant strain, Currie kept his soldiers in the forefront of his decisions. Brigadier Victor Odlum wrote that his general had "earned a reputation among the members of the High Command as one of the most careful and humane leaders in the Field."[57] Andrew McNaughton, one of the most innovative gunners of the war and an army commander in the next war, echoed Odlum, observing with pride that Currie was willing to spend shells rather than the lives of his men to achieve his objectives.[58] Currie stood up for his Corps and his men, even when doing so pitted him against his friends or against respected leaders, including Sir Douglas Haig. "Sir Arthur has consistently guarded the welfare of his troops," concluded Odlum.[59]

Sir Arthur Currie had his trusted staff officers to carry out his orders, and to act as the nervous system linking his command (the brain) to his fighting and support troops (the body), but he did not fulfill the role of an isolated, imperious general in the rear. It was impossible for him to meet with all of his 100,000 soldiers, but he visited some of them behind the lines. In an age before voice-enhancing microphones, he was limited in his ability to pass along encouraging words, but at least one supporter remarked on his deep voice, which suggested "at once poise and unlimited balance."[60] One wonders if Currie should have used his voice more often. As we have already seen, he was never comfortable in simply talking to the men. While there is certainly enough evidence of his failure to display the common touch with the soldiers—evidence largely supplied by officers who liked and respected him—there are also revealing accounts of Currie having fun as a brigadier with his men at theatre shows or sporting events. What was it in rising in command to become a divisional and then corps commander that made him less willing to socialize with the men, or perhaps simply caused him to lose his touch? Was it the added weight of command or the inability of one man to connect with tens of thousands of subordinates? Like Currie's mentor, Sir Julian Byng, who taught him so much and seemed, in the words of one high-ranking observer, an "unambitious man without any desire for personal fame," Currie never seemed inclined to cultivate a cult of personality, which might have allowed him to reach out through the ranks.[61] As the third of the Corps' commanders and possibly not its last, Currie wished, remarked Brigadier-General Alexander Ross, to encourage loyalty to a "military organization," not a person.[62] Currie was deeply proud of his Corps, and often made mention of putting the Corps ahead of everything—including his own reputation.

In early July the Canadians were ordered to launch an assault against the German-held coal-mining town of Lens. It would be no easy battle, as the enemy had fortified the ruined city, setting up strongpoints in the rubble of old houses and factories, with its defenders protected by a deep series of underground tunnels. Sir Henry Horne, the commander of the First Army, ordered Currie to launch a frontal assault against the southern portion of Lens. Horne was under orders from Haig's GHQ to set up a significant diversion here in order to draw German attention and reserves away from the British forces' primary battlefield, along the Ypres sector, in what would be known as the Battle of Passchendaele. But a frontal attack against Lens was little more than a suicide plan. Horne had risen through the ranks of the British army and he had a good head for the set-piece battle, but his order to Currie was uninspiring to say the least.

The understandably nervous Currie, who was about to embark upon his first battle as a corps commander, surveyed the German front and, after consulting his divisional commanders, realized that his forces would have little hope of fighting through an urban environment. In a built-up area the enemy had all the advantages of defending their known ground, and the Canadians' fearsome gunpower—which had been essential at Vimy—would not be able to engage the enemy except through a blind battering of rubble. While Currie understood and accepted Haig's need to draw reserves away from the northern offensive that was to be launched on July 31, he sought to attack Lens on his own terms.

Currie went to see Horne on July 10 and presented his case for a new operation. If we are going to attack, implored Currie, "let us fight for something worth having."[63] This proper objective was not the ruined city, he argued, but Hill 70, a desolate, blasted chalky hill, mined and bristling with machine-gun strongpoints, to the north of Lens. It was held resolutely by the Germans, but if Currie could delude them into thinking that the main assault would be against the city, he might be able to wrestle the hill away from the enemy. Yet it was not the hill that Currie wanted; the Canadian general had made the important mental adjustment from capturing ground to killing the enemy. The capture of Hill 70, which overlooked and outflanked the city of Lens to the south, would force the Germans to counterattack across the open battlefield and, in many places, up the hill and into the mouth of the waiting Canadian machine guns, artillery, and rifle fire. Horne and Haig liked the plan, although they noted that the Germans would fight fiercely for the ground.[64] This is exactly what Currie hoped they would do. And in that fight, he would tear apart the enemy on ground of his choosing by raining down a storm of steel.

Currie's forces began to train extensively for the battle, which would involve ten front-line attacking battalions in the first phase, supported by second- and third-wave troops. "Nothing is left to chance," declared Currie, and as Vimy had shown, success rested on junior officers and NCOs knowing the terrain and their role in the battle.[65] Practice grounds, taped areas, map-readings, and lectures were used in the classroom of war before the infantry were unleashed on the battlefield. A series of large-scale raids was also carried out against the southwestern portion of the enemy defences to draw their attention there. The tactic worked, and the Germans strengthened their southern flank, while the Canadians prepared for their operation against Hill 70 to the north.

The Canadian siege guns worked day and night to level Lens in the hope of convincing the Germans that it was the primary target of the attack, but they also had to clear barbed wire along Hill 70. Horne assisted by lending army-controlled assets—especially heavy guns and machine guns—but he kept his distance, giving the Canadians time to prepare the operation. When Currie asked for a delay beyond the tentative attack date of July 31 because his guns had been unable to cut the wire, Horne replied, "My boy this is your own battle, attack when you are ready and I will hold you responsible."[66] It was exactly what Currie had desired to hear from his sympathetic and supportive commanding officer, who later wrote that Currie had "many great qualities as a leader, commander and organizer."[67]

Currie delayed the operation for two weeks, during which torrential downpours made life at the front miserable. It was far worse on the Passchendaele battlefield, where the rain, shellfire, and churned-up earth turned the landscape into a quagmire of glutinous mud and unburied corpses. On the Lens front, Currie had the luxury of waiting and not having to attack according to the timetables of others, since the operation was almost entirely Canadian.[68] He even had the audacity to ask for a few more precious heavy howitzers from the British, which Haig agreed to, even overruling his own senior artillery officer, who objected to the disruption to his own barrage plans in the Flanders region. An anxious but supportive Haig could almost be heard sighing to his diary when he wrote, "the Canadians always open their mouths very wide!"[69]

The attack was finally set for August 15, and the operation went like clockwork. The 4th Canadian Division, opposite Lens, drew fire onto its position while ten assault battalions surprised the Germans with their dawn attack, advancing behind a heavy creeping barrage. There were fierce battles, but the Germans were driven from their fortifications on the hill. More than 5,000 Canadian infantrymen dug in along the ridge, their Lee-Enfields, rifle-grenades, and Lewis machine guns trained on the enemy lines. An additional kill zone through which the counterattacking German troops would have to pass was swept by more than 200 artillery guns and about 190 Vickers heavy machine guns, the latter firing more than 500 bullets each minute.

The Germans responded as Currie had planned. They attacked into the Canadian guns. And continued to attack—again and again. After three days of brutal fighting, the Germans had launched an unprecedented twenty-one counterattacks, and had not been able to force the Canadians from the hill.[70] They left behind thousands of dead. Even the desperate use of new and terrifying mustard gas against the Canucks— which burned skin and blinded men often before they knew they were being gassed, thus reducing the effectiveness of donning their respirators—could not dislodge them. "The attacks were completely successful," wrote Currie in his diary on the 18th. "Our gunners and machine gunners never had such targets."[71]

The Hill 70 operation was as close to a perfect battle as was ever fought on the Western Front. Currie's plan had taken a conceptual leap forward: capturing ground was no longer sacrosanct; the goal was to bite off a portion of the front and force the enemy to counterattack into your own guns, thereby drawing him from his areas of strength and into No Man's Land, where all troops were vulnerable to fire. While Currie's operation had undoubtedly been responsible for the mass killing, it would not have succeeded without the tenacity of his infantry, machine gunners, and artillery men, who fought tooth and nail to hold the position against a motivated enemy. There were no easy victories on the Western Front, but here the Canadians had forced the enemy to pay a steep price: an estimated 20,000 casualties in comparison to the 5,600 suffered by Currie's Corps.[72]

The Canadians were perched atop Hill 70 and fast reducing Lens as they bounced the rubble, which created a haze of reddish dust over the city from the shattered bricks. Despite having no hope of recovering the hill, the Germans refused to relinquish the city. This was frustrating for Currie and his generals, as the enemy had been soundly beaten, but they still retained the prize. Horne's initial order to Currie back in July had been to capture Lens, and this was still what the army commander wanted. After consultation with Major-Generals Harry Burstall and David Watson of the 2nd and 4th Divisions, Currie ordered a probing attack.

Intelligence from aircraft and patrols was nearly useless for assessing how strongly the Germans held the city, but Currie was willing to try a reconnaissance in force. Two infantry brigades were ordered forward in an attack on August 21, although they had far less time to prepare for the battle and almost no maps or assessments of enemy concentrations. The operation proved a disaster as the Germans were prepared and waiting for the attackers. The Canucks fought hard in the burned-out houses and shattered factories where the enemy had established itself to throw back the incursion. But by the end of the day, the assault force limped back to its lines, having lost 1,154 men.[73]

Having failed to take Lens, Currie should have called off the attack. The butcher's bill was still wildly in the Canadians' favour, and Currie had achieved his strategic goal of tying down the German forces, even diverting two additional divisions to the front that could have been used against Haig in Flanders. "The Chief was immensely pleased," wrote Currie of Haig.[74] But unfortunately Currie allowed Major-General Watson to launch one more attack. Watson reported to Currie that

Brigadier Edward Hilliam's 10th Brigade could drive the enemy back in a final assault. Although there is no written evidence in the official records, it appears that Hilliam, Watson, and Currie still hoped to offer Horne the tangible victory that would come with capturing Lens, and shortly after the war, Currie remarked, "It was generally understood by us that we were to remain in the area until Lens fell."[75] To encircle the city, Hilliam's plan was to capture an imposing slag-heap known as Green Crassier in reference to the grass and scrub that clung to it despite shellfire. But in a bizarre manoeuvre, Hilliam offered only a single battalion to press the attack, the under-strength 44th. Hilliam and Watson had deluded themselves into thinking the operation could be a success, and the line of attack forced the 44th to advance on a narrow front, with German-held highpoints overlooking them. When the attack went in on August 23, limited success was achieved because of the grit and endurance of the troops, but the survivors were soon cut off and wiped out.

The capture of Hill 70 and the subsequent draw and defeat of the probing attack on August 21 and 23 left 8,677 Canadians listed as killed, wounded, and missing between August 15 and 25, with another 521 casualties suffered beyond the Hill 70 battlefield.[76] Haig told Currie that he regarded Hill 70 as "one of the finest minor operations of the war," and while the Canadian agreed, he also felt "it was altogether the hardest battle in which the Corps [had] participated."[77] This might have been true up to that point in the war, but the battles would get considerably harder.

Although Haig's Flanders campaign had been delayed by the Arras offensive, which dragged on longer than he expected and was far more costly in men and materiel than anticipated, the Third Battle of Ypres, or Passchendaele as it is better known, had been launched on July 31, 1917. On the afternoon of the first day of battle, the rain started, and it continued for much of the next four months. With the drainage system pulverized, the heaviest rain in years had nowhere to go, and so the water lay pooled in the shell craters. With each new offensive, the British pounded the Germans but also mulched the ground over which their infantry had to advance. And when they tried to attack without artillery barrages, they were massacred. There was nothing to do but inch forward in costly battles that raged for several months.

A desperate Haig turned to the Canadians, who had just delivered a significant victory at Hill 70. Haig needed the Canadians' powerful Corps, but Currie did not want to go north, having heard about the impassable bog. Even though he was coming off a serious bout of illness that left him, in his words, with "very sick stomach, [and] sleepless nights," he hoped that his Canadians might be attached to Byng's Third Army, which was preparing for a major tank-led offensive against Cambrai.[78] Currie saw a chance to be associated with his old mentor and was excited by the possibility of breaking the enemy line with the massed armoured attack. According to Theodore Roberts, the general raged against Passchendaele, "Let the Germans have it—keep it—rot in it.… It isn't worth a drop of blood."[79] But Haig's primary battlefield was Passchendaele, and he needed the Canadians there.

Hearing of Currie's anger, Haig took the unusual step of meeting with his Dominion general. The field marshal emphasized the importance of the battle to the morale of the forces and the need to alleviate the French, who were still recovering from their mutinies after the disastrous Nivelle offensives of April. Currie in turn tried to persuade Haig that there were easier battlefields on which to achieve victory, especially around Cambrai, but Haig reiterated his need for success in Flanders. As Currie recounted after the war:

> I carried my protest to the extreme limit, to an extent which the Canadian people do not realize, and which I believe would have resulted in my being sent home had I been other than the Canadian Corps Commander. I pointed out what the casualties were bound to be, and asked if a success would justify the sacrifice? I was ordered to go on and make the attack.[80]

Even though Currie predicted that the battle would cost 16,000 casualties, he could not go against Haig's orders. But Currie would fight the battle according to his own plan of limited attacks, and he refused to be transferred to General Hubert Gough's Fifth Army, with which the Canadians had fought on the Somme, and whose army headquarters had been guilty of poor planning, having improved little since. This was almost too much for Haig, who said, "Currie, do you realize this is mutiny?" Currie replied, "Yes Sir, but I feel I can't help myself and I must do my best for Canadians."[81] Haig swallowed his objection and allowed the Canadians to fight in Sir Herbert Plumer's Second Army.

Only detailed preparation and planning might deliver victory on this unimaginably ghastly battlefield of slimy mud and unburied corpses. Currie sent out senior staff officers to survey the ground. Since the artillery and machine-gun positions indicated on tattered, stained maps often simply did not exist, the Canadians were left guessing as to where they had been before they had been swallowed by the slurry. Those guns that could be found were in poor condition, having been worn down from incessant fire. Of the expected 550 heavy and light artillery pieces, only 290 could be located or were in working order.[82]

The reported conditions were so bad that Currie waded through the mud to check for himself, slipping and sliding in the filth, diving into scummy craters as shells dropped perilously close, and surveying the morass with his field glasses.[83] Appalled, he went to Plumer's headquarters and presented his case. When a few of the senior British staff officers derided the Canadian claim of the missing guns, Currie exploded in a fury of swearing, face mottled red, and, pointing to his muddy uniform, raged that he had been to the bloody battlefield. Had they? The shocked British officers stood in bulging-eyed, lip-quivering muteness. Plumer went to Haig, and the field marshal ensured that Currie got what he needed.

The terrain dictated the pace of Currie's operation. The lessons of Vimy and Hill 70 could not be applied fully, and this battle would be fought instead by a series of limited attacks. Massive artillery firepower would allow for bite and hold operations that would pull the Corps from the mud at the base of the ridge and onto slightly drier land, where the Germans had dug in. With the support of his army commander, Currie envisioned four limited operations—two on October 26 and 30, and then, with two fresh divisions, the final capture of the ruined Passchendaele village and what was left of the ridge on November 6 and 10.

The Canadians cautiously but relentlessly built up the infrastructure on the battlefield, focusing especially on roads, gun pits, and sheltered areas. It was slow work, and costly in men, with the Germans having nearly perfect observation over the Canadian lines, but Currie would not be rushed, and even refused to attack with Gough's forces on the 22nd, as his troops needed more time to prepare for the battle.[84] This enraged the British general, who stormed at one joint-army meeting, "Who the devil is running the Second Army?"[85] Currie did not make a habit of tweaking the nose of British army commanders, but he knew that any operation launched before full preparations were made would result in the unnecessary deaths of his boys. Detailed and overwhelming logistical support was the key to the Canadian Corps' attack doctrine, and this was no less true here in the quagmire. In the ten days before the first phase of the battle, Canadian labour groups suffered more than 1,500 casualties, largely from shellfire and poison gas. Currie lamented the losses, but the logistical work had to be pushed through "at all costs."[86]

Despite the horrible conditions, the Canadians were ready on schedule and had surprisingly high morale. The October 26 and 30 assaults were shallow pushes of less than 2,000 metres, but each step must have felt like a kilometre for the soldiers advancing through the thick mud. Through great sacrifice and endurance, the infantry achieved its goal and pulled the Canadians out of the muck onto the firmer ground at the base of Passchendaele Ridge. Currie had almost no role in the actual battle, as it fell to the brigadiers and divisional commanders to ensure that the attacking forces were supported. Although the Canadians had been aided by their creeping barrage and accurate counter-battery fire, the fighting over the week had been costly: close to 5,000 casualties were sustained, most of them spread among the attacking battalions.[87]

The third phase of the battle, on November 6, would aim to overrun what was left of Passchendaele village and key portions of the ridge. Two fresh Canadian formations, the 1st and 2nd Divisions, were rotated into the line. The British high command knew that the fighting season was winding down and German morale was low, but no one expected the enemy to fold without a fight. Before the operation Currie met with many of the new soldiers, personally greeting the incoming units of men who were likely a little shaken by the reputation of the Passchendaele battle-field. In one case Currie stood on a table and shouted to be heard by the sea of men from four battalions of the 1st Brigade, who would have num-bered several thousand. According to Canadian war correspondent F.A. McKenzie, the corps commander intoned, "The Commander-in-Chief has called on us to do a big job. It has got to be done. It is going to be your business to make the final assault and capture the ridge. I promise you that you will not be called upon to advance—as you never will be—until everything has been done that can be done to clear the way for you. After that it is up to you, and I leave it to you with confidence." The assembled troops responded to his rousing speech with "cheer after cheer."[88]

The Canadians captured the rubble of Passchendaele village on the 6th and consolidated the position as best they could amidst the horrid conditions and eviscerated dead. Over the next week, the Canadian gun-ners would fire off tens of thousands of shells to both hold the village and, in a final assault on the 10th, expand the Canadian front to make it more secure, after which Haig finally closed down the campaign. Some 16,000 Canadians were killed or wounded, just as Currie had predicted and feared, adding to the British quarter-million dead, wounded, and maimed.

Currie's victory at Passchendaele likely saved Haig's career. With time running out as the weather turned colder, had the Corps been unable to capture the muddy position, the entire BEF would have been forced to pull back almost to their original start lines, as the German guns atop the ridge would have been able to pound the exposed troops throughout the winter. Such a retreat would have been disastrous for morale, with withering casualties sustained and not even the pyrrhic victory of capturing the shattered village of Passchendaele to show for this sacrifice. As Prime Minister Lloyd George hated Haig, he might have used the opportunity to pull the field marshal's card and replace him as commander-in-chief.

Despite the Canadians' success, Currie was furious about Passchendaele in the battle's aftermath, expressing himself to one subordinate officer, Brigadier J.F.L. Embury, "very strongly on the subject and with great feeling and indignation that men should be put up against such positions to be sacrificed."[89] The Canadian Corps had reinforced its growing and sterling reputation at Passchendaele, delivering victory in the most horrific of conditions. Currie's success was recognized by the French and Belgians: on November 22 the French Minister of the Interior awarded Sir Arthur the Croix de Guerre with Palm, and observed that he hoped that Currie would someday be known as the "Duke of Passchendaele"; the Belgians followed suit the next month with the Belgian Croix de Guerre.[90]

Currie was grateful for the awards, but put the credit squarely on his soldiers. To Sir William Hearst, the Conservative premier of Ontario, Currie wrote, "Words cannot express the pride one feels in being associated with such splendid soldiers. The only regret one has, and it is a very sincere one, is that one has lost so many gallant comrades."[91] However, while Currie worked on behalf of his soldiers, pushing hard against the British to secure every advantage, many of his own men believed that Currie had sold them out to the imperials. A rumour circulated that Currie had volunteered the Corps to fight at Passchendaele to raise his own reputation and win favour.[92] It was hurtful gossip, but with morale nearly shattered during the month-long ordeal, the soldiers at the front, mired in the mud and among the rotting corpses, knew nothing of how

Currie had fought for them, putting his own career and reputation on the line. "It is no secret," wrote front-line infantry officer D.E. Macintyre, that at this point Sir Arthur "was not popular with the troops."[93] To his own soldiers, Currie was simply a château general, sending them into the line to fight and die in order to capture a few kilometres of muck.

Sir Arthur Currie was also being attacked on the home front. After the Battle of Hill 70, which was a genuine victory for the Canadian Corps, German propaganda reported that the Canadians had suffered 200,000 casualties.[94] Although that ludicrous figure was twice the total number of men in the Corps, some Canadian papers picked up on the rumour of high casualties, reporting on it with wide-eyed naïveté. Even when the extreme claims of casualties were revealed to be false, Currie was branded unfairly by some as a butcher. Putting aside those who were acting maliciously, it must be said that it was hard for Canadians several thousand kilometres from the front to distinguish a victory from a defeat, when the winners lost nearly 10,000 men.

Sir Robert Borden, having watched despairingly as the total number of recruits dropped each month since late 1916, had announced on May 18, 1917, that voluntary enlistment had reached its end.[95] The prime minister heeded the pressure and his own desire to support the soldiers at the front by implementing a system of "compulsory military enlistment on a selective basis" to keep the Canadian Corps fully reinforced to ensure that it remained "one of the finest fighting units of the Empire."[96] Borden had sought an alliance with Liberal leader Sir Wilfrid Laurier on the subject, and later a coalition government, but supporting conscription, thought Laurier, would have betrayed French Canada and his own ideals, as he did not believe that legislating compulsory service was worth tearing apart the country. Laurier refused the coalition and both parties prepared to fight the most divisive election in Canadian history.

This battle was not just about English against French, but also farmers against the government, labour against business, region against region. Given the bitter debates in the House of Commons and the apo-plectic attacks in the newspapers and by demagogues, the country seemed ready to fracture along cultural, linguistic, and class fault lines. Would the nation continue to keep faith with the soldiers overseas who needed reinforcements, or should they be abandoned to their own fate and forced to fight with weakening numbers? If they were to be sup-ported, what groups or regions were not pulling their weight through the contribution of young men? How much longer would this terrible war continue, and at what cost in lives would victory finally be secured? If conscription was not enacted, would Canada reveal itself as a nation of shirkers, and lose the hard-earned reputation won by the Canadian Corps on the battlefields? These and many other questions and accusa-tions rang forth across the country in a growing cacophony of outrage.

The din echoed overseas, and Currie could not escape the bitter debates. The former Liberal supporter had long ago cut his affiliations with the party, and he was now seen as a Conservative ally. Borden begged him several times for a favourable statement in support of the pro-conscriptionist Unionists—a new coalition party of Conservatives and renegade win-the-war Liberals who had defected when Laurier refused to join Borden. Currie wanted nothing to do with these political battles, having seen Alderson destroyed by them and being aware that he could little defend himself while fighting overseas. But as a national com-mander he felt compelled to support conscription, for he was aware that success in the attritional fighting on the Western Front would—at some level—come down to the number of men available. His own wounded soldiers, having sustained multiple injuries, were being forced back into their shattered units, sometimes not even fully healed or still suffering the effects of battle stress. Currie's loyalty was clear. "The only solution to the problem of Canadian recruiting is conscription," was Currie's public appeal in December 1917, which was much circulated in Canada during the fiercely contested election.[97]

Liberals fought back, skewering Currie as the man responsible for killing off Canadians in shocking numbers. Currie's incompetence, charged his enemies, was the reason why the country was going through this gut-wrenching process of needing more men.[98] Other Liberals, including Laurier, insinuated—or flat out lied on the hustings—that Currie had been fired for his incompetence.[99] It always took several days for the government to respond to such charges—when it heard of them at all—and some Canadians were left with the impression that a blood-thirsty incompetent led the forces overseas.

Sir Arthur was incensed. After reading about the Liberal attacks, he wrote to a friend, "I think I have a right to ask that everything possible be done to put me right before the people of Canada."[100] In vain hope, Currie appealed to Perley, asking for the Unionist government to formally deny the rumours. It did, but the damage was done in parts of the country and in segments of the population. Sir Arthur could scarcely believe that while his Corps had achieved victory at Hill 70 and Passchendaele when all others had failed, his own "countrymen should do their best to knife [him] in the back."[101]

Damned as a "murderer," the sensitive Currie was cut to the quick, and was largely defenceless in the face of his enemies at home. His meteoric rise from land developer in Victoria to national war hero had left him without the time to firm up influential political supporters. He controlled no newspapers. He had no publicity machine in Canada. Currie was a nobody before the war, and through Sam Hughes's faith in him, some chance, and his own good abilities, he had risen to fill Canada's most important military post. While Currie would soon develop more acute political antennae, he still felt betrayed by the politicians, whom he came to dislike, even despise, as a group. "It is very annoying to me to be mixed up in this party strife," he wrote disappointedly. While Currie desired to steer clear of partisan politics, this wish was naive as he was now a national figure in a divisive war effort.[102] Even as he led his

100,000 troops, he found out the hard way that the corps commander's role involved more than simply fighting battles on the Western Front.

"The year 1917 has been a glorious year for the Canadian Corps," wrote Sir Arthur to Sir William Hearst in November of that year. "We have taken every objective from the enemy we started for and have not had a single reverse. Vimy, Arleux, Fresnoy, Avion, Hill 70 and Passchendaele all signify hard fought battles and notable victories. I know that no other Corps has had the same unbroken series of successes. All this testifies to the discipline, training, leadership and fine fighting qualities of the Canadians." Currie only regretted the terrible cost to his "gallant comrades."[103] So too did the thousands of Canadian families and communities across the Dominion, who were grieving for their fallen fathers, husbands, brothers, and sons. The victories had been relentless, but so too had been the casualties. Some Canadians began to wonder when it would all end, and what would be the final total of the Canadian blood sacrifice.

CHAPTER 10

"Once so powerful"

SIR SAM HUGHES, 1917–1918

Few tears were shed for Sir Sam Hughes when he was unseated from his reign of error. One of his veteran cabinet colleagues, Sir George Foster, aptly summed up the cabinet's perspective: "The nightmare is removed."[1] Most Canadian soldiers overseas took note of Hughes's departure from the ministry, but the event was of minor concern after the terrible bloodbath on the Somme. In London, however, Sir Joseph Flavelle, an inveterate hater of Hughes, remarked that on November 11, 1916, the day when Hughes's resignation was revealed in the English papers, he observed many Canadians drunk from celebrating the announcement.[2] Canadian soldiers in England did not need much of an incentive to drink, and such revelry was by no means limited to the firing of ministers, but was the joyous remark of long-time Liberal supporter Lieutenant-Colonel J.J. Creelman representative of how the larger body of Canadian soldiers felt?

The mad Mullah of Canada has been disposed. (Sir Sam has lost his job.) The Canadian Baron Munchausen will lie to less effect, the

Louis de Rougemont of Lindsay will in vain seek supporters. The greatest soldier since Napoleon has gone to his gassy Elbe, and the greatest block to the successful termination of the war has been removed. Joy, Oh Joy! I do not like to kick a man when he is down but I am willing to break nine toes in kicking Sam in the stomach or face or anywhere else.[3]

The vitriolic observation of medical officer Harold McGill of the 31st Battalion was equally harsh, in a letter in which he admonished his sister, who had some sympathy for Sir Sam:

> I note your remarks re: the downfall of Gen. Sir Sam Hughes. There were certainly no tears shed over here when he went. You expressed a fear that he did not receive credit for all he had done. He certainly did not; otherwise he would have been tarred and feathered. Any success achieved by the Canadian militia has been in spite of him and not because of his activities. He had plenty of energy, I admit, but it was almost entirely misdirected. His infernal personal interference with everything connected to the conduct of the Canadian forces did more to bedevil the business than anything else. He was constantly active in upsetting the program of his own department. Some of his appointments of commanding officers have cost a lot of blood.[4]

Sir Sam would not be missed much among the overseas soldiers.

While Hughes's prominence in the Canadian war effort was drastically reduced, he did not disappear, even though historians have tended to ignore him and his actions during the last two years of the war. Hughes continued to sit in Parliament, an aura of anger and instability radiating from him as he now glared from his new position on the backbenches. Even though Hughes had been deposed from power, the Conservatives feared that he would be a disruptive force, for the ex-minister knew more about the war effort than anyone else except Borden. But while he was more than bitter enough to go after his old party hammer and tongs, and he often did, Hughes was also devoted to his boys, and he genuinely wanted to avoid detracting from winning the war. Journalist Britton Cooke wrote early in the war that Hughes considered every man to be one of his boys, and that he had a "fatherly heart for his great family of fighting men."[5] This feeling had not changed even after his removal from the ministry, with Hughes writing to the prime minister that he had no regrets since he always worked "for the welfare of the soldiers." But, he noted in his resignation letter to Borden that "a kindly watchful eye will be kept over them by your humble servant."[6] A kindly eye perhaps, but the other eye was concentrating on fomenting an uprising to wrest power from his former ministerial colleagues.

Almost immediately after Sir Robert Borden removed Hughes, the ex-minister's friends promised the prime minister that he would pay for his disloyalty. Sir Robert had no trouble believing this, and thought that Sir Sam would quickly "intrigue against the Government."[7] He had known Hughes for almost two decades and had seen him operate in the House and behind the closed doors of the caucus and cabinet. Hughes traded in rumours and innuendo, and he was at his most dangerous when he was attacking his enemy with wild assaults that played fast and loose with the truth. To stave off the attack that was surely coming, a well-prepared Borden immediately placed before Parliament, and thus before all Canadians, the damaging correspondence between Hughes and himself, which revealed that the ex-minister was both insolent and uncontrol-lable. It was embarrassing for Borden, insofar as some thought it made him look weak, but far worse for Hughes, who appeared as he was: intem-perate, frustrated, paranoiac, disloyal, and unstable. The experienced Borden thus took away one of Hughes's greatest weapons—his behind-the-scenes attacks of insinuation, slander, and sly digs.

Despite Borden's fear of embarrassment, however, most papers show-ered him with support, noting that he had put up with Hughes far beyond what anyone could have expected.[8] Borden's ministers backed him to the hilt, and Postmaster Minister Casgrain was informed by Conservative friends that "Sir Robert's firm action has raised him high in the estimation of everybody. It is the universal topic of conversation here, and I have not heard one single dissent from it."[9] While the Liberals had a field day with the revealing correspondence, even they knew that they had lost their easiest target now that Hughes had been sidelined.

Far more problematic for the Liberals was that the Conservatives had gained a battle-tested prime minister who had set his mind to winning the war no matter the cost to himself or the country. Such a man—in lockstep with many Canadians—would not be easy to beat in the next election. The year 1917 saw Borden become Canada's true war leader, as well as a statesman on the international stage. He was patient and conciliatory, and seemingly as firm as he was fair. The prime minister had proven he had steel in him, especially through the way he had declawed Hughes and kept on going as if it were no great matter, although Borden remarked privately, "The situation was a difficult one; perhaps more difficult than many of my friends realized."[10] Borden had revealed his strength of leadership, and the Hughes affair quickly disappeared after the publication of the correspondence. Impotent and ignored, Hughes was left to stew in his anger and to obsess over his fanciful plans of political revolt. Borden did not exactly forget about Hughes—the ex-minister was too volatile to be forgotten—but he moved forward with what he had to do as prime minister, which was, in his mind, to win the war.

If pushing Hughes to the periphery was the solution to a serious problem plaguing the government, finding able ministers to replace him was an important part of that solution. Sir Edward Kemp took over Hughes's militia department. Kemp was a corpulent Toronto industrialist who, according to historian J.L. Granatstein, had "no organizational or political genius, [but] had the virtue of being sane."[11] It was Perley who inherited Hughes's empire in England, which now fell under the newly established overseas ministry. Sir Sam despised him and attacked the new overseas minister relentlessly in print and in the House of Commons, describing him at one point as a "hopeless failure" who sacrificed "Canadian interests" in the name of "petticoat politics, party politics, wholesale discrimination and 'padding' of commissions of enquiry" to disrupt and "whitewash" various issues.[12] Perley did not lose too much sleep over Hughes's accusations, as much of what the ex-minister said could have been easily turned back on the accuser. The competent Perley and, later, Kemp, when he became overseas minister in 1918, turned their attention to untangling the knots in Hughes's conflicting overseas administrations, and the Canadian fighting forces were better for it.

"While I was sawing wood they were knifing me," complained Sir Sam to Lord Beaverbrook, referring to his many enemies in the cabinet.[13] Flavelle, White, Meighen, and practically the entire cabinet, Hughes felt, had undermined him as he worked on behalf of the country and his boys. Hughes had indeed been knifed, but he was probably guilty not only of putting the blades in his enemy's hands but also of turning his back by taking multiple trips overseas. His prolonged absences meant he was unable to defend himself in cabinet meetings against the usual intrigue that all high-ranking politicians face.

Despite his shock at being fired and then outmanoeuvred by Borden, Hughes refused to stay down. Increasingly confusing his dreams of power with harsh reality, Hughes boasted to Beaverbrook on December 8, 1916, "At the present moment, I control the situation." He hoped to let Laurier and Borden fight it out, while he "raised a third party ... [to] hold the balance."[14] Hughes had been listening to sycophants for too long.

To fulfill the dream of raising a third party, Hughes turned to Beaverbrook to convince his fellow British newspaper baron, Lord Rothermere, to buy up a number of Canadian papers to ensure both support of the war effort and, of course, Hughes's bid for power.[15] When Rothermere showed no interest in such a plan, Sir Sam implored Beaverbrook to persuade British prime minister David Lloyd George to give Borden a lordship on the Judicial Committee of the Privy Council, thereby clearing him out of the way so that Hughes could seize power.[16] While Lloyd George did not know Borden well, he certainly knew enough about Sam Hughes to avoid doing anything that might pave his way to the prime minister's office. No doubt he had been briefed by many public servants and soldiers at Whitehall or the War Office that Sir Sam was either completely unstable or partially insane.

Very little of Sir Sam's correspondence from this period has survived, but he wrote a letter to his son, Garnet, on March 7, 1917, revealing his anger and his irrationality, not to mention his paranoia. Hughes believed that his mail was being stolen and "tampered with ... and they even had detectives on prominent friends of mine."[17] Who "they" were he did not mention, but he likely assumed the culprits to be his former Conservative colleagues, although Borden was later to dismiss this conspiracy in his memoirs, noting that Sir Sam "was under constant illusions that enemies were working against him."[18] In the letter, Hughes called the Conservatives' handling of the war effort "hell on earth," and feared the war might be lost with such a spineless cabinet in power, especially "with Borden a weakling, and White a mental epileptic, and Perley an intriguing non-entity."[19] Hughes raged on about the conspiracies, convinced that his enemies had brought him down, but he rejoiced that "Borden is dead; Perley is dead; as far as the skunk can be dead, and Tom White is fast following suit."[20] There were rumours too that Flavelle was to be exposed for his pork trade profits. It was all too good to be true, thought the lip-smacking Hughes, who could only pray that his hated enemy would be outed as a profiteer; and this is what happened—although unfairly— when Flavelle, the corrupt "Bacon King," was deeply hurt and publicly embarrassed after revelations that his pork companies had raked in huge profits from war contracts. Hughes predicted that the party "will be wiped out of existence whenever there is an election." Luckily, there was one man to save it: Sir Sam Hughes. He would form a new "War Party." "My standing it seems was never so high.... I am, by all odds, twice as strong as any other man in Canada."[21]

Within this pipe dream of power grabbing, Hughes's darker fantasies of persecution now had a freer rein, especially with regard to soldier friends such as Major-General David Watson, who seemed to have abandoned him, refusing to return his correspondence, and this after Sir Sam had propped him up and cleared the way of competitors. "Whispers, and more whispers, have reached me that ... Dave Watson has failed in everything.... It came as a shock to me to learn that Dave could so readily forsake his allegiance to me." [22] The wily and politically minded Watson had not only abandoned Hughes but had also fired Sam's brother, Brigadier William St. Pierre Hughes, after the Somme battles, and William felt he had been unfairly treated. So too did Garnet and Sam, although there was little they could do about it.[23]

Borden was aware of Hughes's paranoia and intrigue, as the ex-minister was good at many things, but not at keeping secrets. Sir Sam blustered and plotted, sharing freely with political friends and enemies his plans to overthrow the government. These "confidants" promptly passed on the information to a bemused Borden.[24] The prime minister was ill, and willing to hand the reins of power over to someone else if he thought they could do a better job, but not to the lunatic Hughes.[25] Never Hughes.

"My one determination, however, is, while anxious to hold the party right, to see that the soldiers are looked after, cared for, strengthened, and given a fair chance."[26] Such was Hughes's moving statement to his son in early 1917, an indication that despite his downward-spiralling political career, he still cared deeply for his boys overseas. Although his delusional dreams of driving Borden from the party were not yet dashed, he would soon realize that the limelight was his no longer. Hughes became increasingly aware of his need to rehabilitate his reputation. The ex-minister was always most dangerous when he was threatened, and he now felt that his entire political legacy was in peril. While some men might have gone on the defensive to salvage what was left of their reputation, Hughes chose to advance into the breach of battle, and of history.

Hughes turned to defending his reputation, and on January 30, 1917, he gave a passionate defence of his work as minister. There was no one in the land who knew the state of the military better than the ex-minister, and he had buried more than a few skeletons over his quarter-century in the party. When would he begin to dig up the dead? Speaking for several hours, he talked threateningly about how "friends" had advised him to go after the government, telling him, "Your Tory colleagues have knifed you.... You are a fool to be loyal to [Borden] and the crowd."[27] While loyalty might not be the first word that came to mind when speaking of Hughes, he had been a Tory too long to switch over to the Grits, especially when, as Hughes put it, "we are engaged in a struggle for our very existence." He would not play politics while the "gallant boys at the front" fought and died, even though, as he noted gratuitously, "the verdict of history has vindicated my action in every instance."[28] Sir Sam would support the government because the Conservatives were the only party that sought to win the war and look out for the "soldiers' interests," but such an alliance would not dissuade him from lashing out vindictively and vehemently against those whom he saw as enemies of the soldiers, of the state, and, of course, of Hughes himself.

During the course of Sir Sam's extraordinary speech to the Commons, he attacked the government, especially for setting up the overseas ministry, and he directed several well-placed shots at the minister of finance, Thomas White, for mishandling the war effort and dragging the country into debt. Hughes was also up to his old tricks in unfairly attacking British officers by comparing the failures of professionals with the success of civilian-soldiers. Railing at the British, spittle flying, he offered supportive words for Currie, whom he called a "prudent and efficient officer," and suggested he should take over the Canadian Corps, or that Turner should, although he told the House callously that the Victoria Cross–winning general had arranged his own funeral by going to

England as Perley's chief of staff, something he would "regret all the rest of his days."[29] While Hughes did not understand fully why Turner had gone to England (and the general had in fact exercised little choice in the matter), it was clear that the ex-minister wanted a Canadian in command of the Corps.

Some of Hughes's behaviour in the House must have provoked wicked smiles or outright guffaws, especially his ongoing defence of the Ross rifle and his deluded assertion that he had followed the prime minister's "principle that there would be no political patronage in this war." "That met my view exactly," he lied blatantly, and then for twisted fun, suggested that he had stood his ground against unnamed cabinet colleagues who attacked him for not handing out enough political patronage appointments![30] Hughes was seemingly even delusional in his communications with his son, writing to Garnet on March 7, 1917, of the need to select the best officers, not just good Conservatives: "Do not let politics creep in. I had an awful fight to keep it out, but I kept it out."[31] From the patronage-driven Hughes the elder, such a statement was as ludicrous as it was unbelievable, revealing the power of self-delusion that constantly drove him.

In the House, Hughes continued to monitor, listen, interrupt brazenly, and attack the opposition, the government, and anyone who crossed him. While he was discredited, marginalized, and estranged from the elite in his own party, he remained a jovial member of the House. Sir Sam could often be seen talking to Tory members, and even Liberals, particularly those who had sons serving overseas.[32] Hughes was disliked by many of the Liberals, but respected by just as many more for his unwavering support of the war, or simply for his political longevity. Yet most knew that while Sir Sam might extend his hand in friendship, the other was usually looking for his opponent's throat.

Hughes had been a formidable foe, and remained so still, despite being older, feebler, and now visibly ill. But he was still dangerous, always dangerous. In the House, for instance, Hughes remained a heckler. His bad manners showed through in his constant interrupting of those questioning him, as he tried to throw them off by demanding little details of information. To bolster his defence, he would pluck obscure facts and figures from his prodigious memory or from small black books he kept hidden in his papers, hurling numbers and "evidence" at his soon flustered enemies.[33] Were they true? No one knew, although Hughes always spoke with supreme confidence. These types of attack and counter-attack—which involved never talking and only shouting, as one observer noted—were not used just for shock value, although they clearly put the enemy on the back foot. This was simply Hughes's long-established strategy in the hard battles of the House of Commons.[34]

Sir Sam's health had collapsed under the strain of the war, and his manic temperament had become far more volatile since his firing. He saw enemies all around him and he appeared to be suffering from some form of nascent dementia. His personal secretary, Charles Winter, felt that without the enormous stress of the war to keep him in constant motion, Sir Sam was losing his way. The relative calm he experienced after having lost his wartime leadership role had a "deleterious effect" on this once influential man.[35] While Winter was no doctor, it was clear for all to see that Hughes's once indefatigable strength was failing him. William Griesbach, a brigadier in the CEF, wrote of Sam Hughes:

> I think the great tragedy of his life came after he ceased to be Minister of National Defence, but was still a member of the House of Commons. Obviously he was ill. He had many grouses and grievances and was inclined to make sensational and bitter statements about those whom he thought had injured him. Newspapers quoted him fully, notwithstanding the fact that everyone knew that he was ill. The result was that many people suffered under his ill-founded allegations and Hughes himself became discredited.

Griesbach blamed the newspapers for egging him on and giving him a forum, "when they knew, as well as everybody else did, that the poor old fellow was ill."[36] Despite Hughes being ill in body and mind, the newspapers were not going to relinquish his headline-grabbing assaults; and nor was Hughes willing to give them up.

As Hughes's attacks on the government raged on, Borden continued to be wary of him, and tried to occasionally placate him with crumbs from the patronage table. These included allowing him to keep his seat in the front row with the other ministers, and supporting the appointment of Garnet Hughes to a senior command position overseas. There were minor political prizes for Hughes, too, such as sitting on a committee to determine how Canada would celebrate its fiftieth anniversary on July 1, 1917, which appealed to Sir Sam's sense of nationalism and his respect for history and commemoration.[37] It also kept him too busy, Borden hoped, to meddle in the war or devise new ways to embarrass the government.

While Sir Sam was not, therefore, completely ostracized, few could doubt that he had fallen far from his lofty perch in the government. Liberal MP Charles "Chubby" Power got to know Hughes in the final years of his life and, despite the ex-minister's garrulous reputation, he always had a cheerful word for Power, a wounded veteran from the front. Musing later, toward the end of his own life, Power wrote of Hughes, "Possibly he deserved his fate, and certainly Borden did the right and proper thing in dismissing him in 1916. He was impossible to associate or work with, but there was a pathos and sadness at the sight of this man, once so powerful, deserted and despised by all but a few firm friends, sitting in the House, only a remnant of his physical and political self."[38]

Hughes battled the government throughout 1917, accusing it of mismanagement of the conscription issue. Hadn't he raised almost 400,000 volunteers? he demanded. Was it a coincidence that upon his removal the government's recruitment system had collapsed? While there had been rot in the voluntary system since late 1916, when Hughes was still overseeing it, the government did not have a good retort to Hughes's thorny assaults, although it could more readily sniff at his paranoid insinuations that "German gold was behind the anti-recruitment movement, with so-called Labour leaders influenced by it via United States Germans."[39] Hughes railed against conscription, but he ultimately supported it, as that, he claimed, was what his constituents wanted. Sir Sam was re-elected a seventh time for Victoria-Haliburton in December 1917, with his widest margin of victory to date.

Reinvigorated by the campaign, Hughes remained an important public figure for rural Ontario. He was much loved by his constituents, who well remembered that he used his influence to ensure that dozens of improvements were effected in Lindsay and the surrounding area, as well as the building of an arsenal.[40] An anecdote that circulated about Sir Sam's connection to the people whom he represented for thirty years was particularly telling: a visitor was canoeing through the Haliburton watercourses and asked a nearby farmer the name of the area. The farmer's proud reply was "This is Sam Hughes' country."[41]

As the war entered its last year, Hughes lost none of his fire or his appeal to some segments of the country, preaching that Canada's enormous sacrifice in the war demanded that it become a full partner with Britain and the other senior Dominions in a union of Commonwealth countries: "A Dominion which sends to a European war an army immeasurably greater than the Allied armies sent to the Crimea cannot again have the issue of peace and war determined for her by a government in which she is not represented."[42] Viewed by many as a champion of an emerging Canadian nationalism, Sir Sam did not want for speaking engagements. Of course, it was his bombastic statements and claims that made him popular among some groups. He told the Canadian Club in New York on January 8, 1918, that after Germany was defeated, it should be forced to hand over its navy and its military leaders should be jailed, or perhaps executed. A day later, after hurrying back to Toronto to speak at a Masonic meeting on January 9, he reiterated his long-standing belief that all youth from ages ten to sixteen should be required to undergo universal military training. He spoke boldly in Montreal that same week, declaring that, should he again be minister of militia, he would call up Canadians under the Militia Act, and he believed there were 700,000 single men in the Dominion of eligible age for overseas service. He was firing on all cylinders that night, as he lashed out at the British too, denouncing the imperial authorities for preventing Canada from controlling its forces in England and for undermining Canadian-made equipment. That the overseas ministry now oversaw the Canadian forces was an obvious contradiction to his argument, but Hughes cared little for facts, especially those that did not support his wild accusations.[43] Throughout the war he continued to give patriotic war speeches, including a barn-burner of a talk to several thousand Torontonians at a January 1918 fundraising event, which was greeted by a standing ovation.[44]

Despite his role in supporting the war, Sir Sam was driven increasingly to the fringes of the Conservative Party. Hughes had no shortage of enemies, but he lashed out and created more. He even became suspicious of his old friend Lord Beaverbrook after several soldiers told him that the Canadian schemer was hated in the army and was playing for greater control at Hughes's expense. But when Hughes sent an accusatory letter to Beaverbrook, the adroit manipulator soothed Hughes with gentle words and a reiteration of his faith and support.[45] Beaverbrook had indeed not turned on Sir Sam, and he remained a foul-weather friend, one of the lone voices that tried to rehabilitate Hughes's reputation even after the ex-minister's fall from power, and after his death.

Sir Sam was frustrated not only by his own lack of influence but by that of his son. Garnet had risen to the rank of major general but seemed stuck in England with the 5th Division, which had once been slated for European service but now was in a purgatory of perpetual training. Garnet's isolation and lack of opportunity to distinguish himself was all the more difficult for Sir Sam to accept since he viewed Garnet as a topnotch soldier and could not understand why his son's old friend, Arthur Currie, did not assist him. In fact, throughout the summer of 1917 it became clear to Hughes that not only was the upstart Currie not a friend, but he was actively seeking to interfere with Garnet's military career, as revealed when he blocked Garnet from taking command of the 1st Division. Had not Sir Sam lent a hand to Sir Arthur at the start of the war? Was Currie like David Watson, one of the soldiers whom Hughes had supported but who now turned his back on him?

Sir Sam and Sir Arthur had never been close. While Currie had owed his opportunities to Hughes, so too did every other officer in the First Contingent. Currie had been respectful of Hughes, but he had never kowtowed. The general also believed fervently in the need for professionalism in the Corps, and that the restrictive political apron strings that led back to London and Ottawa had to be cut. For Hughes's part, he had continued to assist Currie by burying the story of his embezzlement of the regimental funds. He had even defended the general in the House of Commons when word leaked that Currie had left the front during the Second Ypres battle to gather reinforcements, which was interpreted by some as an act of cowardice. In the face of these criticisms, Hughes had stated forcefully in support of Currie that he "was there [in the rear] looking for reinforcements from the British division to help in the fight. General Currie had a perfect right to be there."[46]

Most damaging to Currie and Hughes's relationship was that, by early 1918, the latter's reputation was in free fall, while the corps commander's prestige was soaring. Despite this, or perhaps because of it, Hughes believed that Currie owed him. As C.D.H. MacAlpine, an astute soldier who knew both men, observed, "Sir Sam looked on Sir Arthur as the Currie he knew in Vancouver and never realized that Currie, with the right opportunities for his abilities, had grown into a real giant."[47] With Hughes's firing, Currie had put the ex-minister from his mind, and had turned his considerable energies to winning on the Western Front. Sir Sam felt betrayed and angry, lashing out in one letter that there "is a bad feeling growing up in the troops at the Front, and an awful feeling in England. Jealousies, hatred and favouritism are running the show."[48]

While Hughes traded in insinuations and prejudice, he knew he had enemies in Perley and Kemp, and began to suspect by the summer of 1917 that Currie might be working against him too.

The staggering casualties at Hill 70, Lens, and Passchendaele, reported with exaggeration by the Liberal press to embarrass Currie during the 1917 election, had registered with Hughes. After the bitter federal election, Hughes wrote to Borden on January 14, 1918, requesting a meeting with the prime minister in order to make him aware of "Lens, and somewhat similar massacres."[49] The ex-minister was coming after Currie. Borden refused to meet, either because he was unwilling to encourage Hughes in his smear campaign or because he simply did not believe him. While Hughes was becoming used to being ignored by those in power, he refused to let his boys down. A few months later, with his dreams for taking over the Unionist government, and the even more preposterous idea of forming a new War Party, long shattered, Hughes raged that his "purpose," presumably in life, "was to expose the whole rotten show" overseas.[50] At the head of the wormy Canadian war effort was his enemy, the new overseas minister A.E. Kemp, who had stolen Hughes's thunder and whom he despised only slightly less than Perley, who had reverted to being high commissioner, and now Currie, who was responsible for the "massacres" inflicted on his boys due to "bullhead and incompetency, [which] are traceable by the horrible casualties. Any ass can sit back and simply order battalion after battalion to go forward to certain death."[51]

Hughes was constantly pulling at the threads of the overseas bureaucracy in the hope of unravelling the entire hated organization. During a May 6, 1918, House of Commons verbal onslaught, he focused on the number of bureaucrats and soldiers involved in the overseas ministry, accusing them of shirking their duty at the front.[52] As part of the diatribe, Hughes offered his first public attack against Currie, via backhanded praise of Sir Richard Turner.[53] Hughes highlighted Turner's work in England, but argued that his talent was wasted there. Long forgotten was

Sir Richard's failure at Second Ypres and St. Eloi, and Hughes raised the question of why the Victoria Cross–winning hero did not have a battle-field command. While he was yesterday's man in the eyes of the British, Hughes praised him while levelling a thinly veiled charge against Currie. Turner was a "magnificent young officer … who always kept in view the necessity of saving the lives of his men.… He would not send his men up against the machine guns as some officers do with reckless disregard for life."[54] That reckless officer was obviously Sir Arthur Currie. Sir Sam had suffered many indignities since his removal as minister, and was increasingly wasting away from an unknown disease, but he would not be silenced when his boys were being killed indiscriminately overseas. If his soldiers could not defend themselves against their own generals, he would strike back for them. Sir Arthur would be the focus of his rage.

CHAPTER 11

Costly Victory

SIR ARTHUR CURRIE, 1918

Sir Arthur Currie had been the youngest major general in the British army and, after his appointment to corps commander, one of the youngest lieutenant generals. He stood out for many reasons. Sir Arthur was the only Canadian of this high rank fighting on the Western Front, and he was one of the most unlikely-looking generals. Overweight, jowly, and saddled with a uniform meant for trim men, he never quite looked the part. But it was perhaps his lack of a moustache that most marked him as different. Of all the generals, he was the only one to face the war without hair above his upper lip. There would be no "Charlie Chaplin" or "Old Bill" moustaches, as favoured by some of the rank and file and NCOs, nor a thin line above the lip, as worn by many officers. Perhaps Currie's lack of a moustache is not telling, yet to be the only general out of hundreds in the entire army without one was certainly a statement of some sort.

At the very least, such a choice showed in a small way that Currie knew who he was. He knew his strengths and weaknesses. The general had an open mind for the new challenges of modern warfare, but he had learned warfighting the hard way. Currie made his mistakes, and few found him brilliant. He admitted as much to one subordinate when describing his approach to planning operations: "I'm not clever enough to guess in this game. I have to set everything down and figure it out. It's harder work than being brilliant—but safer."[1] Hard work and planning were the only routes to victory. Although Currie was to become one of the most adept fighting generals in the war, even he would find that regardless of whether one's forces were winning, they were always losing. The hemorrhage of soldiers never stopped. There were no bloodless victories on the Western Front.

The Canadians had emerged from Passchendaele bloodied and nearly broken, with 16,000 casualties. They needed a rest. So did Currie, who took a short holiday to England over Christmas to see his family. "I tried to forget the war for the fortnight," he wrote, "yet such a thing was of course impossible."[2] While Currie fought to escape the battle in his mind, over the winter of 1917–1918 the Canadians underwent an extensive reorganization and implemented structural reforms to prepare for another year of battle in what Currie predicted would be "the hardest and most desperate fighting of the war."[3]

In early 1918 the British infantry divisions were also reeling from the casualties sustained during the previous year. The War Office took the desperate step of reducing the number of battalions in a British division from twelve to nine in order to create new formations. While there now appeared on paper to be more divisions, they were far less effective as fighting formations, since this restructuring reduced the infantry strength by a quarter. As well, it ripped units from their home formations, which was extremely detrimental to morale and esprit de corps. Anxious for more divisions, the British War Office pressured the Canadian overseas ministry to form a Canadian army of two corps, each composed of three divisions.[4]

Currie was urged to accept the changes, which would have taken his four over-strength divisions and divided them to create six weaker divisions in two corps. Having two corps had been Sir Sam Hughes's dream since early in the war, and he had no doubt convinced others of the importance of such a development to garnering recognition for Canada. Many Canadian officers echoed the politicians, as the reorganization would create new positions for them and greater opportunities for advancement. All expected Currie to accept the reorganization, as he would surely have been made army commander.

Sir Arthur refused. It was nothing short of shocking. Yet Currie knew his Corps: it was a hard-hitting machine. He believed that the desire on the part of some senior officers and politicians to field a national army was driven not by operational value but by national puffery. To shuffle around formations that had fought together for years was lunacy, and all for the addition of a maximum of 6,000 infanteers to the overall order of battle (4 divisions of 48 battalions vs. 6 divisions of 54 battalions). Nor were there enough trained staff officers to fill the ranks of the new command structures. "If we divide the Canadian Forces in two," argued Currie, "we weaken our strength."[5]

Currie put his head on the block, and almost had it cut off. There was immense pressure on him from the politicians in Canada and from officers in London to accept the proposed changes. But he did not break, and ultimately he prevailed. He kept his twelve-strong infantry battalion divisions. Even more important, he broke up the 5th Canadian Division in England for reinforcements, which provided another 12,000 fully trained infantrymen while the rest of the BEF was desperately turning to eighteen-year-olds or ill-trained recruits.[6] This gave him a pool of reinforcements upon which to draw in the coming year's brutal fighting.

Currie's decision was clearly right, but that did not assuage his enemies, who, according to Wilfrid Bovey, accused him of "striving to preserve his own place" as the most senior Canadian battlefield commander.[7] By breaking up the 5th Division, he also dashed the hopes of many senior officers who desired to escape their purgatory in England for a position at the front. Overseas Minister A.E. Kemp had to deal with hundreds of angry officers, and he confided to Borden, "Some of these men carry back to Canada weird tales and grievances, some of which have to be taken with a grain of salt."[8] The heaviest blow no doubt fell on Garnet Hughes, who commanded the 5th Division. As one close friend wrote, Garnet was "deeply aggrieved" at seeing his division disbanded and at being denied an opportunity to return to a battlefield command.[9] When it was clear that the 5th Division was doomed, Garnet tried to convince Kemp to force Currie to remove British-born commander Major-General Louis Lipsett of the 3rd Division, thereby creating a position for Garnet. The minister refused to intervene, aware that the sometimes chippy Currie guarded his command appointments jealously.[10] The younger Hughes was forced to accept that he would never return to the Western Front.

Sir Sam was doubly wounded, as he was a public supporter of a two-corps Canadian army, and he believed that Currie's actions had nothing to do with ensuring fighting efficiency and everything to do with mounting a personal attack against the Hughes family.[11] But even if Currie had been a Hughes family supporter, he would have had to fight Sir Sam on this issue, since six divisions would suffer more casualties than four (as they would be rotated into the line more frequently), which would put an additional strain on an ever-diminishing reinforcement pool. However, the apoplectic Hughes could only see Sir Arthur driving a stake through another of his dreams, and maligning his son in the process. He would get his revenge.

Before there were any overt attacks directed against him, Sir Arthur had to deal with the rumours. With Currie forced to travel back to England several times during his administrative battle with the politicians, stories circulated that he was leaving his men at the front for vacations, or, as one insidious whisper campaign suggested, he was undergoing a particularly resistant case of venereal disease. Where did these slurs come from? Currie blamed Lord Beaverbrook and his cabal that included Garnet Hughes and Sir Richard Turner. While there is no evidence that either Beaverbrook or Hughes were at the centre of the rumours (and certainly Turner was not), the stories were so widespread that Currie's soldiers must have contributed to them too. There were also reports circulating in newspapers that Currie was exhausted, and would probably soon be removed from command. Currie felt compelled to write to the editor of *The Daily Colonist* in Victoria to rebut the shady insinuation.[12] To another friend, General Frederick Loomis, he wrote disappointedly, "The air in London I found, as usual, to be filled with rumour and suspicion. I learned there, for the first time, just how bad my own health was. I was also told ... that I was the one who had proved to be absolutely reckless regarding the lives of the Canadians."[13]

Sir Arthur was not vulnerable to many attacks, as he had a proven battlefield record as the victor of Hill 70 and Passchendaele, but his Achilles heel was the high number of Canadian casualties. The innuendos that focused on this subject were particularly hurtful to Currie. "No one regrets casualties more than I do," wrote a distraught Currie to Premier Harlan Brewster of British Columbia. "Criticism, a public man like you has long since found out, is oft times very cruel.... I may tell you that there are some who would like to have the position in which I now am, and I am quite certain that they are the ones who initiated this propaganda."[14]

Despite Currie's denial of the rumours about his ill health, the general was indeed worn down from over three years of constant service. He was not alone, with many of the senior officers succumbing to accumulated exhaustion and on the verge of breakdowns. "Certain Commanding Officers, who have rendered most excellent and gallant service, will in a short time become so war worn as to become inefficient," wrote a sympathetic Currie from the Western Front. "If such is the case it would be unjust and cruel to adversely report upon these Officers."[15] Currie well understood the strain wrought by continuous service at the front, but he would not be forced out of his command, even if he needed a rest. As one commentator noted at the time, due to Currie's uncompromising position regarding the reorganization of the Corps, "slander had never been so reckless, unreason never so wild, suspicion never so cruel."[16]

All of this venom was directed at Sir Arthur. It took moral courage to withstand the prizes offered and the pressure executed, but Currie held to his convictions. As he wrote to Newton Rowell, president of the Privy Council, "I am dealing with everything that comes before me solely from the standpoint of what I consider to be right."[17] The general's victory in this administrative wrangling, which spanned the first quarter of 1918, strengthened his hold on the Corps, and while such manoeuvres were not the stuff to excite storytellers to hyperbole and hero worship, they marked a critical moment in the history of the Canadian Corps and the single most important battle of Currie's career.

As Currie battled the politicians in England, his forces were digging in on the Western Front, defending Vimy Ridge and the surrounding region in the face of a forthcoming German offensive. The Russian forces on the Eastern Front had succumbed to crippling casualties, absurdly bad leadership, and Bolshevism that undermined the fighting spirit of the troops, all of which allowed the Germans to make a separate peace with the revolutionary government and shift dozens of combat divisions to the Western Front.[18] Here, they planned an enormous offensive in March to crush Britain and France before the United States, which had finally entered the war in April 1917, could build up its forces in Europe.

Allied intelligence had easily pinpointed the German manoeuvres that included the stockpiling of millions of shells, the dragging forward of thousands of guns, and the movement of hundreds of thousands of men. The British high command welcomed the coming battle, believing that its soldiers would now hold the advantages of fighting on the defensive, which the Germans had enjoyed on the Western Front since just after the start of the war. Warned of the coming enemy offensive, Currie ordered a thorough fortification of Vimy Ridge and the surrounding area. His Canadians worked like demons to construct over 400 kilometres of winding trenches and lay over 450 kilometres of barbed wire, all of which was supported by hidden and mutually supportive machine-gun positions, and by deep dugouts to withstand bombardments.[19] The Corps had spilled too much blood in taking Vimy to give it up without a death struggle.

In contrast, many British formations showed little urgency. The reorganization earlier in the year had demoralized the men, and their defences were in places haphazard and poorly constructed. Currie had even heard and repeated the rumour that a general had diverted a labour battalion away from their job of reinforcing front-line trenches to build a tennis court for himself and his staff. This slackness did not bode well for the British, and it was compounded by a manpower problem, as reinforcements were held back in England on orders from Prime Minister David Lloyd George, who did not want to give Haig any more men to slaughter.[20] Adopting this position may have assuaged the prime minister's guilt, but it left a heavier burden for those soldiers at the front who faced the enemy with gaps in their ranks.

This was a period of heightened stress for Sir Arthur, as he faced both the Germans in front and unknown enemies to the rear. He also found problems on his flanks. During the frantic preparation at the front, apparently some of his Canadian soldiers had raided the supplies of the British corps next to them, commanded by Sir Charles Ferguson. Upon finding that the Canadians had looted his equipment, Ferguson wrote an angry letter to Currie, accusing him of being "in command of the greatest thieves in the world." The touchy Currie, who reacted poorly to any slight against his Corps, was furious. One observer stated that while Currie was a "very religious man, he had a remarkable command of profanity," and he turned red in the face as he unleashed round after round of obscenity in machine-gun-like fury as he read the offending letter to his staff. Shaking with rage, Currie rode off to army commander Henry Horne to demand that Ferguson apologize. Horne tried to defuse matters by joking about the incident, but Currie was in a lather. When he could get no satisfaction from Horne, he turned on his heels and said he was going to see Haig. An incredulous Horne could scarcely believe the corps commander's childish behaviour. "Surely you would not go over my head to Haig," he exclaimed. Currie spat back, "In such a matter as this, I would go to the foot of the Throne."[21] Currie was overreacting, but Horne reined in his excitable Dominion commander and ordered Ferguson to apologize. The British commander complied, but he later evened things up in his own mind by ordering a town in his lines out of bounds to the Canadians because of their rowdy behaviour, an action that further angered Currie. While it was admirable to defend one's troops, Currie was high-strung during this period, seeing enemies on all sides, and was sometimes unable to draw the line between normal slights and all-out assaults.

The Allies' true enemy struck on March 21, behind a devastating artillery and chemical barrage. Elite German stormtroopers soon overran the stunned British defenders. Even when the British Tommies held their ground, the Germans simply went around them, leaving the defenders enveloped and behind enemy lines. British formations were shattered, with survivors driven back some 20 kilometres on the first day of the offensive. More ominously, some 21,000 of the total 38,512 casualties had been lost to surrender, seeming to reveal rot in the army.[22] Haig was desperate. He pleaded with the French to reinforce him and nearly had a breakdown a few days into the battle, believing the war was lost and recommending that the British Empire make peace with Germany on any terms it could get.[23] The field marshal soon regained his composure and set his teeth to fighting the Germans, but he needed everything under his command, and he grabbed three of Currie's four divisions to shore up the most threatened part of the line.

Currie was dismayed to see his Corps broken up piecemeal, although he understood Haig's extreme anxiety. After a few days, feeling compelled to remind his commander that his Corps was not like British corps, Currie wrote gently but forcefully on the Canadian position:

> From the very nature and constitution of the organization it is impossible for the same liaison to exist in a British Corps as exists in the Canadian Corps. My Staff and myself cannot do as well with a British Corps in this battle as we can with the Canadian Corps, nor can any other Corps Staff do as well with the Canadian Divisions as my own. I know that necessity knows no law and that the Chief [Haig] will do what he thinks best, yet for the sake of victory we must win, get us together as soon as you can.[24]

The point was driven home when Canadian politicians visited Haig in the field. Currie guarded his Corps' independence and autonomy, and while he did not like to turn to the overseas ministry in England, he did so in this case in order to ensure that his formation was not broken up.[25]

Haig was more than a little annoyed by the gentle missive, and especially the political visit, feeling that he did not have time for this nationalistic nonsense as his armies were on the verge of crumbling. The field marshal sniped in his diary that Horne complained to him—which supported his own belief in his sometimes troublesome Dominion general—that "Currie is suffering from a swollen head.... He wishes to fight only as a 'Canadian Corps' and gets his Canadian representative in London to write and urge me to arrange it. As a result, the Canadians are holding a wide front near Arras, but they have not yet been in the battle."[26] Although Currie's forces were indeed not in pitched battles, they were fighting the enemy through aggressive trench raids and patrols, and, more importantly, were spread dangerously thin to free up reserves so that Haig's forces could reinforce their more threatened portions of the front. At one point in the fighting, the Canadians held almost one-fifth of the entire BEF front, while Currie's Corps was but one of eighteen on the Western Front.[27]

Two of Currie's three divisions were returned to him by early April, which left only the 2nd Division still serving with the British. The Canadians continued to hold the front, but Currie worried about the possibility of the Allied lines caving in after a renewed enemy push. Currie wrote privately, "Many British troops are not fighting well," but projected a confident face.[28] In one chest-thumping communiqué, which was distributed throughout the Corps during the desperate fighting, he intoned, "I place my trust in the Canadian Corps.... Under the orders of your devoted officers in the coming battle, you will advance or fall where you stand facing the enemy. To those who will fall I say, 'Your names will be revered forever and ever by your grateful country and God will take you unto Himself.'" While the message was extremely popular in Canada, and was reproduced in newspapers and memorabilia, Currie's soldiers, who had suffered shellfire and massed chemical attacks for over a week, sneered at his lofty message. C.B. Topp of the 42nd Battalion wrote, "The order was received by the troops with the outward cynicism that was so characteristic of their attitude toward anything approaching sentiment."[29] Other soldiers grumbled angrily that they had no intention of "falling where they stood," but if they did, they did not need a back-slap from their fat general to assure them that they had done a fine job.[30] Sir Arthur's message was offensive to many of his soldiers and they seemed to hold it against him for a long time, seeing it as another sign that he was an out-of-touch château general.

Currie's own officers often bent over backwards to praise him and to note his many fine characteristics, but almost to a man they criticized, or at least drew attention to, his failure to win the affection of the men. Why Currie could find no connection with the rank and file is strange. He was a well-liked officer before the war, but he failed to carry his good humour and common touch into his progressively larger overseas commands. Griesbach observed that "Currie was an extraordinary good looking man but he did not look like a soldier."[31] Another sympathetic general described Currie as having the physical appearance of an "overgrown baby," but perhaps this was a poor choice of words as no one else has ever made this observation in print, although a few talked openly of Currie's "baby pink face."[32] The corps commander's ungainly body drew the snide nickname from his own soldiers of "Guts and Gaiters." Did the Canadians, despite taking pride in being an army of citizen-soldiers, desire a general who looked like Haig or one of his many clones: grim-faced, lean, moustached, stiff-backed? Currie did not look like a general, which might have appealed to the unconventional citizen-army, but did not.

The general's inability to say the right thing to the men is often highlighted with reference to his "fall where you stand" message or the often repeated account of him meeting a shattered infantry battalion dragging itself off the Somme, and responding with the misplaced, even callous, remark to the dispirited survivors, "That is the way I like to see you, mud and blood."[33] While the "mud and blood" story is repeated in nearly every account describing Currie, anecdotes like this one from Joseph Hayes, the medical officer for the 85th Battalion, who wrote of Currie visiting the 12th Brigade after the terrible fighting at Passchendaele, tend to be disregarded: "He made an eloquent and touching address to the Brigade and eulogized it on the magnificent work it had done.... In conclusion he took off his cap and asked the assembly to bare their heads and bow for a few moments in silent veneration of our noble comrades who had not returned."[34] N.W. Webber, one of Currie's trusted confidants, felt that Currie was "shy by nature, and therefore sometimes out of place with the soldiers."[35] Currie had his awkward moments, but sometimes he could also find the right tone with his men.

Currie's desire to forge an effective formation based on discipline and morale also played against him, although it reinforced in Haig's mind that the Canadian was responsible for turning around the unruly Dominion troops. The field marshal remarked in the summer of 1918: "They are really fine discipline soldiers now and so smart and clean."[36] But when Currie demanded salutes and sharp discipline, he was battling against the Canadian reputation as wild and hardy frontier warriors. This image was foundational to the Canadians' sense of identity, and they bucked against his discipline.[37] It is also true that Currie sometimes lost touch with the soldiers in his Corps. He was rarely seen in the front lines in the last two years of the war. To be fair, though, it was not his place, just as the mayors of Canada's largest cities were generally not known for strolling down the back alleys or along the wharves. While his role was not at the front, Currie failed to find ways behind the lines to talk to the men in an easy manner that might have allowed them and him to drop guards. He always seemed to be inspecting rather than meeting informally, demanding a salute rather than sharing a cup of tea. While Currie worked himself nearly to death to ensure that his soldiers were well supported, he never put in the same effort to win over the rank and file. The general rarely talked about this in his letters or even his diary, so perhaps it was simply a blind spot for him, but it was held against him by many of his own troops.

Sir Arthur cared deeply for his men, but that did not preclude that at times he would be called to send them to their death. He rarely visited the wounded in hospitals. Would seeing their broken bodies shake his resolve to send men into the face of danger, as it did for Sir Douglas Haig, who also avoided the wounded? How much of Currie's perceived aloofness was a defence mechanism? While Haig could get away with his severe look— his "eyes of steel," as described by one impressed Canadian—Currie apparently could not.[38] Infantryman H.W. Johnston recounted after the war that despite Currie's operational success, "oddly enough we didn't love him…. I don't think we realized exactly how good a man we'd got."[39]

After the initial disastrous reversals of March, the British forces slowly ground the German attacks down and then out in weeks of withering fighting, during which they traded space on the battlefield and drew the enemy into prepared fire zones. Haig also got over his anger about Currie's insistence that the Canadian Corps be kept together at all times. In the dark days of April, an emotional Haig at one point remarked to Currie that despite the setbacks in the field of battle, "the one comforting thought that he had was that he still had the Canadian Corps intact, and that he should never regard himself as beaten until that Corps was put into battle."[40]

The Canadian Corps (minus the 2nd Division, which was still with a British formation) moved out of the line and into reserve in early May, for a much-needed rest. While the three divisions enjoyed the respite, a nasty rumour sprang up in the 2nd Division that Currie had abandoned the formation because he did not like them (being himself originally a 1st Division man). The rumour was reported to Currie so many times, and through such various channels, that he was sure it was a tactic in the ongoing campaign to undermine him with his men, and expressed this to one confidant: "The lie was spread so systematically that I believe it was done maliciously."[41] There is no evidence of such a plot, but Currie was now looking over his shoulder for the conspirators he believed were out to get him. Some of Currie's letters were rife with undercurrents of paranoia. But even paranoids have real enemies. That a cabal of conspirators were indeed waiting in the wings for Currie to make a mistake might have made him overly cautious. This was not the case, however, and the corps commander continued to fight the Germans in front of him, although now he was more aware of the need to watch his back.

Currie was also fighting private battles with some of the British. Although the Canadians had been aided by the British and still had many imperial officers in senior positions in the Corps, some Canadians, Currie included, felt that there were some haughty and hidebound imperials outside the Corps. While the Canadians were trying to improve through the intense study of the factors that led to victory or defeat, Currie lamented that the British were generally slower at processing these lessons, and certainly at implementing them within the larger BEF structure. He was particularly venomous in assessing General Sir Hubert Gough, who commanded the British Fifth Army, the formation that had been battered by the German forces only months before. But the British failure to learn from the battlefield was not isolated to Gough's army, and had been exposed starkly in the Battle of Arras. There, and at Passchendaele and during the March offensive, the Canadians chalked up victory after victory, while the British floundered. Some of Currie's comments about the British challenges were a little too smug as he did not acknowledge the advantages his Corps enjoyed in terms of sheer numbers of soldiers and reinforcements, or the unique structure of his fighting formation. Moreover, the chauvinism clearly went both ways, for in May of 1918 an angry Currie wrote in his diary, "I hear that Army reports that Canadians are very stout fighters, good on the defensive and also on limited objective attacks though they shake their heads at what we might do in open warfare owing to the absence of regular officers." Currie lashed out with his pen: "They forget that our leaders have seen more war in the last three years than the British Army did in its previous 100 years."[42]

Although there was no fighting for the Canadians in the quiet summer of 1918, Sir Arthur Currie was kept busy with many tasks. While his Corps was out of the line, he ordered another round of re-evaluation and training. Existing units incorporated new recruits, some of whom were the first conscripts. This brought Currie's Corps up to a strength of slightly over 103,000, with another 35,000 Canadians spread out in other formations not under his control, largely in railway and forestry units, as well as the cavalry brigade.[43]

In addition to freeing up time for training, the summer spent out of the firing line allowed Currie's men to recuperate. They played sports and enjoyed the countryside behind the trench systems. Currie had more holidays back to England, too, but he was also busy, and the letters from home never stopped. The general was a conscientious correspondent, and he often wrote directly to parents about their lost sons. His papers are filled with letters from grieving parents: "I can scarcely find words with which to express my gratitude for your kind note. It was more than kind of you to take time for writing when so many important duties are pressing upon you."[44] Currie also dealt with patronage-seekers and well-wishers, problems national and personal, and in the summer of

1918 Canada's prime minister, Sir Robert Borden, called on him for his expertise.

Sir Robert Borden and Sir Arthur Currie were less familiar with one another than one would expect of a prime minister and his wartime national army commander. Because of the distance between Ottawa and the front and Borden's own initial deference to British politicians and imperial generals in allowing them to run the war, as well as the key position held by Sir Sam Hughes, Borden had met Currie only a few times. Despite Currie's receiving the most important Canadian overseas military position in June 1917, Borden had made little effort to meet with the corps commander, as he was engaged in the thorny issue of conscription within the federal election campaign during the latter part of the year. For his part, Currie felt he had been sacrificed in that same election, and so the general had kept his distance from the prime minister.

During the German offensives of early 1918, Currie had used his political connections to effect military decisions made by his commander-in-chief, Sir Douglas Haig. Now, in the summer of 1918, the politicians turned to Currie for military advice. Since making the decision to invoke conscription, Borden had taken a more active role in the British war effort, partially in the hope that it would lead to greater independence for Canada in the Empire.[45]

As Borden met with his fellow prime ministers again in the summer of 1918, he realized he knew very little about the actual warfighting, save for the crippling casualty rates and the string of defeats in the first three years of the war. He turned to Currie to bring him up to speed and to provide him with ammunition in his discussions with the British. In preparation for his address to the Imperial War Cabinet on June 13, 1918, he sent for Currie, who was vacationing with his family in Brighton, and "directed him to put aside all considerations of military etiquette" and offer him the "unvarnished truth." Currie obliged, as was his duty, but Borden did not have to pull the general's teeth. Currie was still feeling anger toward the British after their near collapse on the battlefield, and much bile poured out in his private conversation with the prime minister. In Borden's words, "General Currie gave me a lurid picture of the situation," and was deeply critical of the British performance in preparing their defences before the German offensive.[46] Borden noted that Currie's revelations were "very depressing and I am convinced that the present situation is due to lack of organization, lack of system, lack of preparation, lack of foresight and incompetent leadership."[47]

Borden resolved to speak truth to power. He had already dragged his country through the conscription crisis that had nearly torn Canada apart. He needed to ensure that at least there would be a victory to offset the terrible sacrifices. Borden faced the Imperial War Cabinet under the impression that Currie would back him, but the Canadian general was nearly mute. "He entirely failed to give the support which I thought he had promised," wrote the mystified Borden.[48] But the Canadian prime minister was no shrinking violet. The normally reserved and retiring Borden delivered a furious barrage. Driven by the terrible casualties sustained in seemingly hopeless battles, and sensing a receptive audience among the British politicians, who shared his frustration, Borden railed about the British army:

> I am informed that there has been conspicuous failure to remove incompetent officers.... Is it or is it not the case that men of great ability who have gone into the army during this war have been systematically held down to positions no higher than Brigadier-Generals? If that is the case, I say with all respect, that it amounts to scrapping the brains of the nation in our greatest struggle of history.... We came to fight in earnest; and Canada will fight it out to the end. But earnestness must be expressed in organization, foresight, and preparation. Let the past bury its dead, but for God's sake let us get down to earnest endeavor and hold this line.[49]

Prime Minister David Lloyd George, who despised most senior army commanders in general, and Haig in particular, received Borden's fighting words with sheer delight. While it is unclear what Currie had promised to Borden in terms of supporting him, he clearly felt he could not speak in the same open manner to the Imperial War Cabinet as he could to Borden, and nor should he have. His words would surely have made their way to Haig, and he would have been crucified between his two masters.

Lloyd George had been impressed by Borden's tirade, and he knew, as well, that Currie had supplied Borden with at least some of the information. The British prime minister respected Currie's candid assessment, and would later write, "I was greatly impressed with Currie's views. They were, I felt, sane and common-sense. His great ability, his strength of purpose, and his lack of the fetishes common to the British officers were most noticeable."[50] In fact, there were rumours that Lloyd George was toying with the idea of replacing Haig with Currie as commander-in-chief, and making his chief of staff the excellent Sir John Monash, who would command one of the Australian corps by the end of the war. Both of the Dominion commanders had proven their worth on the battlefield, but there is no evidence that the British prime minister even seriously entertained the thought, and no record of this possible appointment in Currie's personal papers. Moreover, Lloyd George's elevation of the two colonials, both prewar militiamen, past the five army commanders above them, would certainly have led to mass resignations of senior generals. In any event, Currie was against deposing Haig, remarking, "It strikes me as very poor policy to swap horses at this stage."[51] Although appointment of Currie to command the BEF did not go beyond speculation and musing on the part of the frustrated British prime minister, it was at the very least an indication of Currie's enormous standing throughout the British political high command.

Currie was ambitious, but bright enough not to gun for Haig. In fact, while the two men were worlds apart, the odd couple seemed to like each other: Field Marshal Haig, friend of royalty and a soldier with several decades of experience, and Currie, the overweight civilian land-developer, somehow hit it off well. Currie respected Haig, believing him to be a gentleman and far more honourable than the devious politicians in England. "My fight," Currie wrote acidly after the war, "was not with the regular officers at all. It was with the Canadian authorities in London."[52] While the two occasionally clashed, Sir Douglas seems to have liked Sir Arthur's propensity to speak his mind. Haig knew that he needed more men like Currie in command, but he must have felt at times, with the Canadian's special considerations and demands, that perhaps one was enough.

There were no easy campaigns on the Western Front. "This is not a game of points but a process of destruction," remarked Sir Arthur Currie.[53] The general had understood after the bitter and costly Battle of the Somme that victory would not be achieved by recapturing the tens of thousands of square kilometres of occupied France and Belgium one metre at a time. Instead, the enemy's forces had to be ground down and its morale eroded, at which point its armies would collapse and retreat back to Germany. Currie had revealed this appreciation in his first battle at Hill 70, and while Passchendaele had been forced on him, he understood that the limited set-piece battle could break the power of the enemy's defensive positions. Assuming that the Allies did not wish to take decades to liberate France, their armies had to crack the German's immense defensive structure and fortifications. While Currie was considered one of the best generals of the war, and one who sought every means by which to save the lives of his soldiers, he understood that there were no bloodless battles. Careful preparation and the marshalling of resources would reduce the likelihood of an all-out slaughter, but any massed infantry attack into the kilometres-deep machine-gun-bristling defences would ultimately be costly. Currie and his force were about to find out just how strong the Germans were on the Western Front, as his Corps was employed as one of the principal spearhead forces of the BEF in the strategic counterattack launched in early August 1918 in response to the German offensives earlier in the year.

A dapper-looking Sir Arthur Currie is seen here on his way to the Cobourg courtroom in March 1928. He is carrying a vast array of legal documents. Note that Sir Arthur, then principal of McGill University in Montreal, is not wearing his multiple medals and decorations.

GONE

"MY MARKS AND SCARS I CARRY WITH ME, TO BE A WITNESS FOR ME THAT I HAVE FOUGHT HIS BATTLES WHO WILL BE MY REWARDER."

x x x

AND SO HE PASSED OVER, AND ALL THE TRUMPETS SOUNDED FOR HIM ON THE OTHER SIDE.

A full-page memorial in the Canadian veterans' magazine The Legionary *marking Sir Arthur Currie's death on December 5, 1933.*

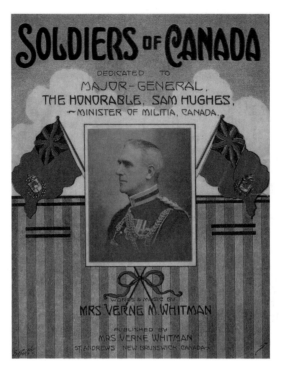

"Soldiers of Canada," a patriotic song published in Canada during the war, was dedicated to Minister of Militia and Defence Sam Hughes. There is no date on the song sheet, but it was likely written in the first half of 1915, before Hughes was knighted and raised in rank to a lieutenant general.

A portrait of Lieutenant-General Sir Arthur Currie upon receiving command of the Canadian Corps in June 1917. Currie would age significantly during the war, as a result of the crushing workload and unending stress.

A rare photograph of Lieutenant-Colonel Arthur Currie and his kilted 50th Highlanders in Victoria, British Columbia, ca. 1914.

A handsome Sam Hughes sits in this 1905 formal photograph as a fourteen-year veteran of Parliament and a war hero from the South African War.

Minister of Militia and Defence Sam Hughes inspects a Highlander militia unit in Vancouver, in 1913. Since his appointment as minister in 1911, Hughes had warned Canadians of a coming war with Germany and had garnered additional funds for the militia.

Sam Hughes striding off a ship. Hughes spent several months in England on a number of trips during the first three years of the war; whenever he arrived, the British feared the whirlwind that he brought in his wake.

Sir Arthur Currie with Sir Douglas Haig, commander-in-chief of the British Expeditionary Force. While Currie and Haig had seemingly little in common, the British general liked the younger Canadian, particularly because of his emphasis on training and discipline, as well as his moral courage.

In this 1916 photograph, Lord Beaverbrook (Sir Max Aitken), with extended stick, talks with Sir Sam Hughes and his son, Garnet Hughes. Although Beaverbrook often intrigued for his own purposes, he was a trusted ally and informant for Hughes and the Conservative government in Canada.

This Montreal Daily Star *cartoon from mid-1916 depicts a weary Sam Hughes withstanding multiple assaults against his character. The cartoon implies that his soldiers' helmet of "integrity" will protect him against "jealousy," "mean insinuation," and "spiteful attack."*

General Sir Sam Hughes' steel helmet proves a great protection.

A late 1917 photograph of Lieutenant-General Sir Arthur Currie reading a map and giving orders to his staff officers.

TROUBLE WITH THE DECEASED

This prescient cartoon, "Trouble with the Deceased," highlights the likelihood of Sir Sam Hughes rising from the grave after his firing by Prime Minister Sir Robert Borden, and damaging the Conservative Party through "talk," "speech," and "interview." The defiant Hughes, whose crypt reads "Killed in political action," holds a manifesto that begins, "It was like this." Borden looks rightly worried.

A contemplative and exhausted Sir Arthur Currie, in the war's aftermath, visiting the graves of French civilians who were executed by Germans earlier in the war. Currie anguished over the loss of civilians and his own soldiers during the course of the war.

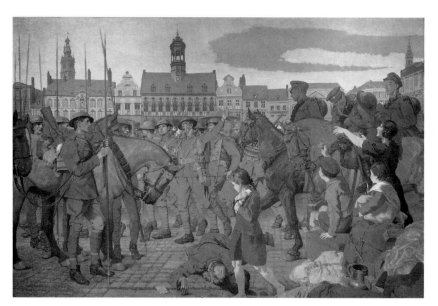

A painting by Inglis Sheldon-Williams, The Return to Mons, *depicting Canadian soldiers liberating Mons on November 11, 1918. The dead soldier in the foreground is German.*

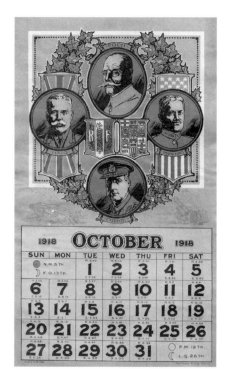

A rare 1918 calendar created by the Canadian Corps Survey Section and published in the field. Sir Arthur Currie, at the bottom, is in good company: above him, to the right, is the American commander John Pershing; at the top is Supreme Allied Commander Ferdinand Foch; to the left is Sir Douglas Haig.

The Germans had failed to knock the Allies from the war in the first half of 1918. New stormtrooper tactics, combined with crash-bombardments of high explosives, shrapnel, and gas, had stunned the Allies, but the defenders had fought hard with their backs to the wall. The enemy offensive had eventually been blunted, with the Germans suffering a crippling 800,000 casualties; many of those knocked out were the most aggressive soldiers, as they had been culled from divisions to create special attack formations.[54] Faced with increasing Allied strength as more Americans arrived every day, and having suffered a stunning defeat during the French-led counteroffensive at the Second Battle of the Marne in mid-July, the German forces were reeling and trying to hold on until the end of the campaigning season, brought by the arrival of winter.[55] Field Marshal Ferdinand Foch, who had been appointed the Allied supreme commander early in 1918, ordered the British to launch a new campaign, in order to keep hammering the tottering German forces.

The Canadians and Australians would spearhead a Fourth Army operation on the quiet Amiens front, which was garrisoned by weak German forces. Currie was only informed of the August 8 offensive on July 20, by Fourth Army commander General Henry Rawlinson, but he was sworn to secrecy, forbidden even to tell his trusted divisional commanders. An elaborate plan was needed to deceive the Germans, for they had long regarded the appearance of the Canadian Corps—a force that one captured enemy document called "magnificently equipped and highly trained in storm tactics"—as a signal of an attack.[56] Several Canadian formations travelled north to the Ypres front, with deliberately sloppy signals intelligence alerting the enemy to the move. The ruse worked and the Germans thought the Corps was ordered north, when in fact it was preparing to move to the Amiens front on the Somme.

Although the surprise assault would be important in shocking the enemy, Currie's Corps had little time to prepare for the battle. Divisional commanders were not told of the operation until July 29, and all lower commands had to scramble to move the 100,000-man city that was the

Canadian Corps—with all of its guns, ammunition, war materiel, food, and hospitals—dozens of kilometres to the battlefield for August 8.[57] The Canadian Corps' senior staff worked around the clock, and one journalist who watched Currie's gut-wrenching pace described him as the leader "whom one left studying battle reports at two in the morning and heard at breakfast that he had been in the field since six o'clock."[58]

There was enormous confusion in getting the combat formations to Amiens, but three of the four Canadian divisions were in the line by the night of August 7, with the fourth in reserve to exploit success. At 4:20 A.M. on August 8 the German lines were chewed through by a creeping barrage from 646 guns, behind which infantry units advanced in loose diamond formations in order to manoeuvre on the battlefield and outflank enemy strongpoints. A heavy fog helped to mask the Canadian push, but pockets of German resistance held up the advancing infantry, who shot, bombed, and stabbed their way forward. While there was an enormous tank armada of 168 metal beasts, many of them were lost in the fog or arrived too late to influence the firefights.[59] Nonetheless, Currie described the first day of battle as a success: "The surprise had been complete and overwhelming."[60]

On the other side of the hill, the German reaction was most telling: "August 8th was the black day of the German Army in the history of the war," lamented General Erich Ludendorff, who directed much of the war effort as part of the German high command. Along the Amiens front, three entire divisions had been shattered, and an astounding 5,033 Germans had been captured.[61] But "black day" did not equate with end-game. While the Canadians had advanced 13 kilometres, and the Australians 11 in their spearhead role, the second day of the battle was very difficult for the Allied troops, especially as the enemy high command rushed reinforcements to backstop the front.

Despite excited and breathy talk of a breakthrough, the fighting on the 8th had been intense and the Canadians had lost 1,036 killed and 2,803 wounded.[62] Moreover, the Canadian infantry were now spread wider over the battlefield and out of range of many of their own artillery. The logistical support for sharp-end formations was enormous: new roads and rails were built; guns were dragged forward by men, horses, and tractors; and tens of thousands of shells moved east while thousands of wounded soldiers moved west.

The set-piece battle was like a sledgehammer: when it crashed down, it was hard to get it back to the shoulder to smash again. The Germans were prepared for another day of offensive operations and the Canadians gave it to them, but these were now frontal attacks with far less artillery support. The Canadians pushed on, but paid for it. The 6-kilometre advance on the 9th cost the Corps 2,574 killed and wounded.[63]

Even though the Germans had been handily beaten, Currie was shaken when he visited the medical units to offer some comfort to his wounded soldiers. It was a searing experience: "I saw ambulance after ambulance full of wounded men, some shrieking, some groaning, some dying, some dead, some just suffering in patience, waiting to get to the hospital gate.... The terrible smell of gas gangrene from some of the wounds, the sickening odour of ether, the white faces of the worn-out nurses, the blood-stained hands of the doctors, who had to work as fast as butchers—only to save and not to kill—made a scene of horror that I can never forget."[64] Some of the wounded Canadians blamed Currie for the late arrival of the medical units at the front. To some degree Sir Arthur was to blame—although more guilt should have been attributed to Fourth Army headquarters' insistence on secrecy. The rushed planning period had required the delaying of medical care units in order to get the fighting forces and materiel of war to the front, and the wounded soldiers had paid for it in agony and avoidable deaths. But these were among the hard choices forced on commanders in war.

The fighting continued officially for another four days, although with far fewer forces, as much of the Canadian Corps dug in to consolidate their victory. On August 13, Currie and Australian commander John Monash appealed to their superiors to call off the battle.[65] Haig and

Rawlinson listened and, after facing Allied supreme commander Ferdinand Foch's anger about reducing the pressure on the enemy, ended the fighting. Haig had learned from his past experiences of prolonging a battle to the point of diminishing returns, and he must be given credit for drawing down the Amiens offensive against Foch's wishes.

During the course of the Amiens battle, which continued to see minor operations for another week, the four over-strength Canadian divisions in the Corps met and defeated elements of fourteen German divisions, capturing 9,311 prisoners, 201 guns, 152 trench mortars, and 755 machine-guns.[66] This was fighting of the most testing nature. The Canadian Corps, at the outset a little under 102,000 strong, suffered 11,822 casualties, and most of these losses fell on the infantry.[67] While Amiens was a crushing victory for the Allies, more were needed before the German forces would fold under the hammer blows, and this series of campaigns, from August until the end of the war, would be known as the Hundred Days.

Foch's strategy on the Western Front was straightforward and brutal: relentlessly attack the enemy to use up his reserves and shatter morale. Currie, too, believed in hammering the Germans, telling a group of soldiers after the war, "You must assault the citadel of the enemy if you hope to vanquish the foe."[68] The Canadian Corps, now as part of Sir Henry Horne's First Army, would be the primary battering ram to smash one of the most heavily fortified German positions: the Hindenburg Line, east of Arras.

The Hindenburg Line was not a single trench but a series of strong defensive positions 30 kilometres in depth on the Canadian front. This line was centred on and around the 1916 Somme defences and the former British trenches that had been lost during the fighting in the earlier part of 1918. Concrete pillboxes and tunnels offered protection against all but the heaviest of artillery bombardments. A kilometre and a half behind the forward line centred on Monchy le Preux was the Fresnes-Rouvroy Line, and the strongest of them all, the Drocourt-Quéant Line, was another 2 kilometres to the east and situated along a series of key topographical positions, including hills atop river-cut valleys. Behind the Drocourt-Quéant Line was the yet unfinished Canal du Nord, which incorporated marshes and numerous trench systems into its defences, and then the heights of Bourlon Wood and, further to the east, Cambrai, a key logistical and railway hub. Throughout the German defensive system, machine-gunners, riflemen, gunners, and mortar teams were dug-in and situated on the most advantageous positions.

Army commander Henry Horne's broad instructions to the Canadian Corps had been to attack "eastwards astride the Arras-Cambrai Road, and by forcing its way through the Drocourt-Quéant line south of the Scarpe to break the hinge of the Hindenburg System and prevent the possibility of the enemy rallying behind this powerfully organised defended area."[69] Horne, who trusted Currie, allowed the Canadians to plan the battle as they saw fit. It would be a smash-and-advance operation, although the Corps was less effective now than at Amiens, with wounded combat veterans replaced by conscripts. While the conscripts would eventually fight as well as any other new recruits, sending them in at this point was a prospect the corps commander did not relish. But Currie still commanded an enormous force, with 101,599 Canadians and, for this battle, another 46,491 British troops attached—for a combined force about two and a half times as large as Wellington's army at the decisive Battle of Waterloo.[70] Because of the depth of the enemy defences, Currie ordered two divisions into the line, each of which would cycle one of their three brigades over the next three days. At the end of that period, two fresh divisions would assume the drive to the Drocourt-Quéant Line. The terrain largely precluded the effective use of tanks, so this would be a hammering operation in which infantry and artillery worked together, supported by machine guns, tactical airpower, chemical weapons, and mobile mortar teams.

There was little opportunity for a surprise strike like the one at Amiens, but Currie did his best to assist the soldiers at the front by moving the start time back to 3 A.M., a few hours earlier than the usual dawn attacks.[71] Brigadier G.S. Harrington, Currie's trusted senior staff officer in the Corps, remembered that the night before the Arras battle he found Currie awake in the early hours, reading a history of Stonewall Jackson, too anxious to sleep.[72] The commander had, moreover, been suffering from serious stomach illness since the Amiens battle, a problem that would plague him for at least another month.[73] The stress was eating away at Currie, but he knew that good commanders had to be willing to gamble, although he had tried to stack the odds in his favour through detailed planning and gaining solid intelligence on the enemy.

An earth-shattering 762 Allied guns opened up on the enemy lines under a bright moonlit sky in the early morning of August 26. While the gunners' counter-barrage smothered the long-range enemy artillery fire, and the creeping barrage wreaked havoc on the barbed wire, many of the enemy defenders fought tenaciously. Front-line Canadian formations attacked through and around these strongpoints, knocking them out when they had to, but often leaving them for mopping up units. These deep attacks sowed confusion in the enemy lines and severed communication from front to rear, and were not dissimilar to the German stormtrooper tactics used earlier in the year.

The harsh fighting and close-quarters combat continued into the second day. There were some set-piece battles, but much of the fighting consisted of confused, chaotic engagements led by small groups of desperate warriors, often cut off from their headquarters and battling for their lives. As at Amiens, the German defence stiffened considerably on the second day, particularly when two divisions and several elite machine-gun companies were rushed in to backstop the crumbling lines.[74] The fighting came to a climax on August 28, as the spent Canadians again pushed into the enemy lines, although they were still to the west of the Drocourt-Quéant Line. The logistical chain was stretched to the breaking point and the Canadian forces were now dispersed and disorganized, with heavy guns mired in the rear and the enemy prepared for another round of Canadian assaults. The situation had the makings of a slaughter. And it would be.

Currie rarely made mistakes, but he should have pulled his tired divisions from the front at this point, or postponed the operation. Instead, he gambled and pushed them for one more day. Infantry battalions were savagely reduced in strength, and some went into the line with as few as 200 men or as composite units. They were ordered to frontally assault through uncut barbed wire and in the face of enemy fire that was unsuppressed, as the supporting artillery fire was ragged and weak. Brutal battles were carried out all along the front, with the Canadians finding ways to advance, but always against raking fire. While the individual infantry fighting units employed sophisticated fire and movement tactics, overall it was smash-and-plunge-ahead warfare. The two Canadian divisions were rotated out on the 28th after suffering almost 6,000 casualties.[75]

Having clawed their way through a few kilometres of enemy trenches, Currie's Corps aimed to crash the primary obstacle, the Drocourt-Quéant Line. "I regard the fighting in which we are about to engage as the most serious we have taken on for many months," wrote Currie in his diary.[76] The objective would not fall easily. Currie cycled his 1st and 4th Divisions through, with assistance from the 4th British Division, but only a few tanks were allotted to the Canadians. From August 28 to September 1, the Canadians fought a series of minor engagements to clear out enemy resistance and gain better jumping-off positions for the main assault.

The barrage came down at 4:50 A.M. on September 2, with the infantry advancing behind their storm of steel. In the hope of breaking the Drocourt-Quéant Line and bouncing the Canal du Nord behind it, Currie had allowed Brigadier Raymond Brutinel, commander of the Machine Gun Corps, to throw his armoured cars into the line. These cars had worked effectively at Amiens by racing down roads to surprise the enemy, but here the Germans stopped them cold with felled logs and heavy fire. The attack was even more costly to the Canadian infantry, as the Corps' gunners had been forced to call off their barrage on this sector in order to prevent friendly fire casualties. This left the armoured cars and their supporting infantry with much-reduced firepower as they faced German strongpoints. In Currie's guarded words, "The enemy resistance, free of the demoralising effect of our barrage stiffened considerably, the open country swept continually by intense machine gun fire."[77] In reality, the Canadians were slaughtered, but still the tenacious infantry found a way to inch forward under the withering fire, and punched through the Drocourt-Quéant Line by the end of the day. Currie was guilty of neither callousness nor recklessness in trying to find a way to put his armoured cars into action and to break through the enemy lines. That the operation failed revealed that Sir Arthur was not infallible, but also that he learned from his errors, as he did not again allow the armoured cars to dictate the pace of an operation. This was cold comfort to the thousands of dead.

Elements from at least seven German divisions had been met and defeated on the Canadian front: 10,492 prisoners had been captured and sent to holding cages behind the lines, as well as 123 artillery pieces, 99 trench mortars, and an astonishing 927 machine guns, in what one British newspaper called "the greatest fighting exploit in the annals of the Canadian nation, and [which] stands unsurpassed in the entire war."[78] But another 12,000 Canadians had been killed or wounded.

The Canadian Corps had achieved two significant victories at Amiens and Arras. Sir Arthur Currie wrote to one friend that Sir Julian Byng had told him on the sly, "High French and British officers think that our smashing of the Queant-Drocourt line was the turning point in the campaign."[79] But the Corps was nearly shattered during the ordeal. The two battles had cost the Canadians almost 25,000 casualties, more than 80 percent of which had been gouged from the infantry.[80] Even though most of the Canadian infantry battalions were back to a full fighting strength of 900 to 1,000—almost double that of British infantry battalions—after the costliest month of fighting in the war, the survivors might justifiably have believed that they had earned a rest. Combat soldiers such as A.J. Kelley recounted that they were "too tired to think, much less sleep."[81] Other Canadian infantrymen grumbled that the true military objective of the Arras campaign had not been to break the enemy trenches but to win "another decoration for Currie."[82] Many of the Canadian soldiers were frustrated, angry, and saddened by the ghastly losses, but we must also take into account eyewitness observations such as that of engineer George Hannes, who, while also in the thick of battle, wrote to his wife at home that Sir Arthur Currie "is the idol of the army," noting further, "I think he is a great Canadian and a great general."[83]

After being driven from the Arras trench system, the Germans retreated behind the Canal du Nord. Half of the vaunted Hindenburg Line had been breached, but the canal strongpoint, subsequent trench systems, and Cambrai were still formidable enemy obstacles facing the Canadian front. German high command ordered that no further retreat was possible.[84] To lose the Hindenburg Line would be nothing short of disastrous.

Currie and his senior staff had about three weeks to prepare for the battle. While the canal was not much of an obstacle, at only 40 metres wide, the Germans had flooded the surrounding region. Currie refused to order his men into another Passchendaele-like bog. He searched for another way, and his staff found it in a dry gap about 2,600 metres wide, but this was a dangerously narrow path through which to send a corps. If the enemy held up the Canadians here, the operation would be shattered, along with much of the front-line forces.

With few other options available, this is where Currie planned to attack, even though, as he admitted, the plan was "fraught with difficulties."[85] Yet he had faith in his forces, and felt they could kick in the door and rush through it to the eastern side of the canal before the Germans could react. It was a dangerous move, and army commander Horne thought it perhaps too dangerous. The British general met with Currie in the days before the battle, and it is reported that "three times on the way back to his own headquarters he turned to his senior staff officer to say, 'I don't believe I ought to let them do it.'"[86] The concerned Horne made two more visits to Currie's headquarters and even brought along Byng, who spoke to Currie in a fatherly way: "Do you realize you are attempting the most difficult operation of the war? If anybody can do it, the Canadians can do it, but if you fail it means home for you."[87] Currie must have been a little shaken, but this was the only way to breach the line, even though a setback here would result in the death of thousands of his troops, damage the Canadian Corps' reputation and, as Byng warned, probably bring about Currie's removal from command.

The operation would consist of an artillery and infantry attack in a set-piece battle, but Currie's combat engineers would play a key role in building bridges across the canal to allow the artillery and follow-up formations to support the units that would be crashing through the enemy trenches.[88] A rapid advance was essential, as the German defenders were echeloned in depth, with three divisions in the line and five in reserve. The Canadian 1st and 4th Divisions faced them across No Man's Land and were ready for the launch at 5:20 A.M. on September 27.

British and Canadian guns and mortars, 785 strong in total, laid down a massive barrage that tore its way through the German lines. Canadian fighting units surged forward, punching through the narrow opening to spread out on the eastern side of the canal. After breaking the barrier, the assaulting infantry engaged in open warfare, striking deep into the enemy lines and then defending against enemy counterattacks, and often with no flanking units for support. Although the enemy artillery was smothered by counter-battery fire, the Germans had responded to this tactic by moving their guns forward to shoot in a direct-fire role. Only through countless acts of bravery and sacrifice did the Canadians succeed in knocking out enemy strongpoints centred around machine guns and light artillery.

By the end of the first day, Bourlon Wood fell to four Canadian infantry battalions supported by machine-gun units that drove through the woods, moving around areas of resistance. Over the next few days, the Canadians continued to pierce the enemy trenches, but the supporting artillery barrage became increasingly sporadic, and more and more battles involved frontal assaults against dug-in defenders. On the 29th and 30th, the third and fourth days of battle, almost no tanks were left to support the infantry and the enemy had rushed forward six additional backstopping divisions and thirteen elite machine-gun companies to the Canadian-defended front. In contrast, on the British portion of the front, which was twice as large, the Germans had ordered forward only three divisions and a brigade.[89]

Too few Canadians were now called on to do too much against nearly impossible odds. The constant orders to attack, sent down from army, corps, and divisional headquarters, were increasingly reckless, allowing less time to plan and placing the burden on exhausted combat units further down the chain of command, as the corps, division, and occasional brigade headquarters were out of touch with their forces. Currie was not unaware of the struggle at the sharp end, writing in a letter to Prime Minister Borden that the breaking of the canal and its eastern defences during the last five days was "of the bitterest fighting we have ever experienced.... It was attack and counterattack every day of the five days."[90]

The battle ground to a halt on October 1, when the Canadians, having driven through dozens of German trench systems, were stopped at the gates of Cambrai. The enemy held the city in strength and Currie's forces were hamstrung as Foch's headquarters ordered that it not be bombarded, as it was an important logistical centre that had rails and roads leading to and from it. Exhibiting the moral bravery that he had shown throughout the war, Currie refused to send his men into the city without artillery support. The rank and file knew nothing about their commander's stance. Instead, rumours circulated among the Canadian soldiers that Currie would drive them forward regardless of the cost. Albert West of the 43rd Battalion offered angry thoughts in his diary: "We hear Gen. Currie has said he will have Cambrai 'tho he lose 75% of his corps. If so he is a fool and a murderer."[91] Despite the rumours, Currie would not send his men into Cambrai without adequate support, and so the Canadian Corps waited a week. They were preparing for an assault on October 8 when the Germans, realizing their position was hopeless, finally retreated. The all-important railway hub of Cambrai was left in Canadian hands, and the battle dribbled to an end over the next week. Currie proudly recounted in his diary the words of one captured German brigadier: "In the German Army everyone agreed that the Canadian troops were most to be feared in all the Allied Armies."[92]

"The hardest part of this whole job—was having so often to sign the death warrant for a lot of splendid Canadian lives," recounted an anguished Currie to one senior staff officer.[93] As hard as it was, Currie was willing to accept the casualties in exchange for victory. He had to be—that was his role in the war—but he devoted himself to ensuring that those losses were as low as possible. In return, however, Currie was hungry for publicity. The general had always taken deep pride in the accomplishments of his soldiers, and certainly during the pounding battles of the Hundred Days, they deserved the full credit of their success. Yet Currie also needed the recognition because of the unusually high casualty rates. Without the people at home knowing about the victories—the countless trenches and fortified villages that fell to the Corps—they would only see the long lists of dead and maimed. A distrustful Currie believed that the British newspapers were downplaying the accomplishment of his Corps deliberately. "We are British, certainly, and proud to be called such, but a certain section of the English press are evidently determined on a policy to ignore the word 'Canadian,'" wrote an angry Currie to a sympathetic Prime Minister Borden, who was fighting his own battles for Canadian recognition.[94] As Currie reiterated, if the Canadian people think we only took "two miserable little villages" for the high number of casualties, "no one can blame them for thinking that casualties were unduly heavy."[95]

Whether or not Currie was accurate in assessing that the Corps' achievements were being ignored—several British generals were on record for complaining that the Dominion forces received more than their fair share of the credit, as they were a more identifiable fighting formation—he could still rightly bask in the Canadian victories in the Hundred Days. As Currie wrote to one friend, "The Canadian Corps gained a wonderful reputation here.... No force of equal size ever accomplished so much in a similar space of time during the war."[96] Haig had relied heavily on his Canadians in the final push. Currie regretted the casualties the Corps had suffered, but wrote, "I do not consider that anyone can regard them as excessive when the extent and severity of the operations are considered. You cannot meet and defeat in battle one-quarter of the German Army without suffering casualties."[97] Yet the Canadians' crippling 45,835 killed and wounded in the Hundred Days campaign between August 8 and November 11, 1918, represented an eighth of the total casualties for the entire BEF, which stood at 379,000. These losses cast a deep shadow over the battlefield success.[98]

Sir Arthur Currie "had an almost fanatical hatred of unnecessary casualties," wrote Brigadier J.E.B. Seely, the British general who commanded the Canadian Cavalry Brigade for much of the war. "Of all the men that I knew in nearly four years on the Western Front, I think Currie was the man who took the most care of the lives of his troops."[99] Major-General Archibald Macdonell, who worked closely with the corps commander, used almost the same words in observing that "Currie had almost a fanatical horror of losses."[100] Yet there was no escaping that, as a commanding officer, he had to put his men in harm's way. Currie dealt with the crushing weight of command by turning more fully to his faith. A war correspondent at the time talked of Currie's "sincere, simple, piety." Even when taking into account the rhetoric of a sympathetic correspondent, one pauses at the statement, "In the hour of distress he turns naturally and with complete faith to a higher power."[101] As one of Currie's prewar Victoria militia friends observed, "It was very curious to notice how responsibility sobered his character and gave him a very real and deep under-current of religious conviction which was certainly not there prior to 1914."[102] This faith in a higher power helped Currie to deal with the stress of sending his men into battle, and of ordering some to their deaths.

But there was steel in Currie too. While he lamented the loss of his brave boys, and relied on coping mechanisms and faith, he never once considered pulling men from the line. He would see the fighting through the bitter end. Even at the Canal du Nord, Currie was finding ways to push his soldiers across the battlefield while his army commander was warning him of the danger (although offering no other viable solution to completing the operation). Currie knew his Corps and he succeeded, but should he have pulled back and let other formations do the fighting? No, that was impossible, in Currie's mind. His Corps was bigger, stronger, and, frankly, better than almost any other British fighting formation. His Corps had missed the worst of the fighting in the early half of the year, and while it had been cut up badly since Amiens, the flow of reinforcements from England had not abated. Currie knew the danger of trading experienced NCOs and hardbitten privates for new, untested men, but his Corps could still absorb the blows better than other British and Dominion forces, all of which were down to the bone.[103] Currie would neither avoid his duty nor pass the suffering on to other British formations. However, his men only saw the death and destruction around them. As one of Currie's officers noted of the harsh fighting, "The ordinary Tommy who, having been used to the regular sequence of relief from the front line, could not understand the necessity of being continually returned to the attack during the last 90 days of open fighting and claimed that he was worked to death for probably Currie's glorification."[104]

After the Hindenburg Line was broken, the Germans were in full retreat, with the Canadians pursuing them as they fled eastward to their frontier. While the German army appeared in ruins, its morale shattered and desertions rampant, Currie believed it was still far from folding. Surely the intensity of battle during the Hundred Days was proof of that: "We have never known the Boche to fight harder. He is like a cornered rat, and I believe will fight most desperately until beaten absolutely and totally."[105] With these words, Currie was echoing what he was hearing from his superiors, although it was supported by his own observation and experience, and after the enemy's tenacious defence during the last four years, few thought the Germans would give up before 1919. The battle had to be pressed onward.

Currie always sought to build on victory and learn from defeat. The lessons of the Arras and Canal du Nord battles were studied, and war diaries read intently for lessons of recent fighting; and when Currie felt he needed more information, he talked directly to the men.[106] In the aftermath of the Canal du Nord and its terrible casualties, Currie bravely went to speak to the survivors of the 42nd Battalion. He called in the officers, and his opening remarks revealed his desire to learn first-hand of hard truths: "Gentlemen, I want you to forget that I am the Corps Commander to tell me quite frankly just what you think went wrong with the last show. I want to know exactly what you are thinking, whether you believe mistakes have been made by higher commanders or not. I want you to feel quite free to speak to me as man to man and nothing you say will be held against you."[107] Currie listened intently and he and his small staff took notes on success and failure. For the corps commander to face the survivors of the battalion took moral courage.

As the Canadians hounded the retreating enemy, few pitched battles took place from mid-October to the end of the month. The Germans would typically leave behind sacrificial screening forces of machine-gunners to hold up the Canadians nipping at their heels, thereby using soldiers' lives to purchase time and allow the main force to keep marching east. Although these last-stand German forces were smothered with artillery fire or poison gas, and then systematically knocked out, the process always cost Canadian lives. The enemy stopped retreating at the last major French city in the Canadian sector still under their control, Valenciennes. The Germans dug in—on ground of their choosing, among civilians, and with strong forces. The Canadians launched their final set-piece battle of the war here on November 1, and behind a devastating artillery barrage, they drove through the enemy lines. It was an overwhelming Canadian victory, and the bodies of over 800 Germans were gradually located among the ruined buildings and open fields after the fighting ended on the 2nd.

The last ten days of the war saw the Canadians engaged in a series of minor battles and skirmishes, but some of these involved multi-battalion engagements of several thousand men. All of the Canadian vanguard units suffered killed and wounded casualties, with more than 645 sustained during a four-day period by just two of the four Canadian divisions.[108] Currie could see that the Germans were beaten, but were they shattered? His forces had crushed the enemy at Valenciennes, but rearguard elements were fighting hard. On November 7, Currie noted hopefully in his diary, "It begins to look as if the end is coming fast."[109]

As the Canadians drove eastward, they encountered the Belgian moated city of Mons. While it had no strategic value, Mons was a nearly mythical town for the British army. It was the place the British had been driven from in August 1914, in the face of overwhelming German forces and firepower. Its capture would starkly reveal the reversal of fortunes in the war, although more than a few cynical soldiers must have grimaced that the British Empire had spent four years and millions of lives in trying to get back to the start line.

Currie knew that the capture of Mons would be a symbolic victory, and one heeded throughout the Empire. Currie's commander—General Henry Horne—wanted to capture Mons as he had been a part of the retreat four years earlier, and so did Sir Arthur, although neither was willing to trade many lives for the city.[110] The bloodbath that was the Great War was clearly winding down. The Allies were pursuing the beaten German army across the front and the Canadians had already suffered close to 3,000 casualties in this frustrating fighting since the capture of Cambrai in early October. But rumours of the war's end had circulated since the first months of the conflict, and few put much faith in them. Currie had orders to advance. He obeyed.

On the outskirts of Mons on November 10, Currie ordered probing attacks against the enemy line to see if the German defenders would fall back. The 42nd Battalion and Royal Canadian Regiment of the 7th Brigade scouted for passages across the bridges that guarded the city, but enemy machine-gunners protected most of these, laying down heavy fire every time the Canadians tried to push forward. In fact, the Germans took an aggressive stance here, launching a number of sorties from the city that pushed into the Canadian positions before being repulsed. Currie wrote to Borden after the armistice, "We could have taken Mons on Sunday, November 10, but it would have cost too much to do so."[111]

Indeed, how much was Mons worth? Not much, if the war was soon to end, but Currie had orders to keep pressure on the enemy, as there was widespread speculation that the Germans might simply be using the armistice as a ruse to buy much-needed time to prepare a defensive line closer to their border.[112] There was certainly no let-up to the north of Mons, with Major-General Harry Burstall's 2nd Division experiencing determined resistance on November 10 and 11.[113] In the face of this stiff defence, Currie ordered that unnecessary risks should not be taken, but there was no thought of stopping and digging in with the hope that the fighting would end through the sacrifice of another national force. Although some Canadian soldiers grumbled at the thought of risking their lives when the war seemed to be dribbling to an end, the Royal Canadian Regiment and the 42nd Battalion found soft spots in the German defences and crossed a series of bridges in the early hours of November 11, infiltrating through the city. The Germans had no stomach for a battle and by dawn most of the enemy defenders were in retreat. Belgians in Mons awoke to freedom after four years of occupation.

Around 6:30 A.M. Currie's headquarters received a wire from First Army headquarters that the armistice would come into effect at 11 A.M.[114] The prize of Mons had fallen to the Canadians before the end of the war. There were few celebrations throughout the Corps, or even at Currie's headquarters. At the armistice hour, the general addressed a small group of men. "Ten minutes ago the last shot of the war was fired," reported Currie. "I think we should all bare our heads and thank the God of Battles for what has happened."[115] It was a sombre moment, but in the days that followed the Mons liberation, Currie's headquarters was inundated with congratulatory messages from throughout the British army, including missives from Sir Julian Byng and Sir Douglas Haig.[116] The symbolic capture of Mons signified an important victory for the BEF at large, and the Canadians in particular. Yet, even as the last shots were fired on the Western Front, new forces were arming themselves for the War of Reputations.

CHAPTER 12

Currie Accused

1919

Following the armistice on November 11, 1918, two Canadian divisions were selected to be a part of the army of occupation in
Germany, with the other two divisions stationed in Belgium. Anxious to
go home, the troops were quarrelsome and receptive to rumours. There
was no easy solution to the problem of demobilizing several million
Allied soldiers, and as the painfully slow process unfolded, Sir Arthur
Currie and his generals tried to keep their men busy with sports and
educational classes.[1] Still the soldiers grumbled, complained, and groused.
Private William David Bradley recounted his anger at hearing Currie
speak to his battalion in February 1919:

> We had an inspection yesterday by our beloved Corps Commander
> General Sir A Currie C. M. J. K. L. M. P. R. S. T. A. O. G. and I don't
> know how many more [awards] that he isn't entitled to and he told
> us that from when the first soldiers of the third division arrived
> home it would be 3 months until the last man of the 4th division
> arrives, the division which I am in but he is full of hot air. He also
> had the nerve to tell us this in front of 4 BN's that he knew of men

that were getting better food and better billets and more than they had before they enlisted. I expected to see something go flying through the air at him but lucky for him there wasn't but everybody booed him until he started on another subject. I see in the paper where he will run for the Premier of Canada. Good gracious I say God help Canada if he gets a hold.[2]

As the frustrated soldiers stewed in boredom, virulent rumours passed from man to man, and from unit to unit. Most were tall tales and fabrications, but they soothed some listeners with insight into the unknown future. When soldiers would go home and where they might next be posted were popular topics of discussion, with all manner of nefarious and absurd commentary in between.

The general malaise and disagreeable mood resulted in some of Currie's own men spreading rumours about him. He had, according to the snipes, sacrificed the Canadian soldiers, volunteering them for every battle, and all in the name of elevating his reputation among the British. After one coldly unemotional inspection by Currie, infantryman James Pedley of the 4th Battalion came to the opinion, which he carried throughout his life, that "there was something inhumanly arrogant to me in Currie, something which impressed me with a distaste I shared with many others. 'Guts-and-Gaiters' the boys called him. He lacked the winning personality that makes a man beloved as well as great."[3] Currie knew that his soldiers were unhappy, but he blamed the problem on the conscripts who had recently joined the Corps and who had "not yet acquired the proper esprit de corps."[4] Whether there was only a disaffected minority or signs of larger discontent, Currie observed to one friend, "We have always had a rumour producing factory in the Canadian Corps … I cannot see how I can stop it."[5]

But the expression of the soldiers' discontent was not limited to the spread of rumours. While Currie was busy during this period, he became aware of the steady, low-level anger of his soldiers, which smouldered rather than exploded. At one point his car was trying to pass one of his infantry battalions on a narrow road, and the infantry at first refused to move. After some embarrassing minutes, his car inched past the filthy and marched-out soldiers, with Currie greeted by dirty looks and leering comments.[6] Here was hard evidence of his soldiers' dissatisfaction. The general was shaken.

Currie had also been warned of conspirators in England who were working against him. Friends advised him that intriguers were visiting hospitals, consoling the wounded, and "intimating to the latter that the casualties in the Canadian Corps [had] been altogether too high."[7] Currie was still recovering from several months of seventeen-hour days during the worst of the fighting, and his tired mind sought old enemies, including Garnet Hughes and Richard Turner, whom he thought were working to undermine him to even wartime scores.[8] In particular, Currie had heard from supporters that Argyll House—Turner's headquarters in England—had kept up a "sustained but veiled attempt to create amongst Canadians in England a feeling antagonistic to the Corps Commander."[9] Such talk, and Currie's increasingly desperate attempt to find the enemies who he believed had turned his men against him, left him frustrated: "From the time I first became associated with Canada's Overseas Forces, I have met with opposition, and found it almost as difficult a task fighting political soldiers as I have fighting Germans."[10]

Although Turner had an uneasy relationship with Currie, he had always done his best to assist the corps commander. Sir Arthur did him a disservice in lumping him in with his real enemies. In trying to locate the source of the rumours, Turner reported to the overseas ministry, "The malicious lying statements regarding intrigue against General Currie ... are without a doubt bred and fostered by ... disgruntled and discredited officers" from broken-up battalions in England.[11] Many of these angry officers, thought Turner, blamed Currie for their isolation in England, as the corps commander had a well-known policy of not accepting officers from disbanded units unless they had combat experience on the Western

Front. But not all the blame could be ascribed to these officers. Victor Odlum, the respected commander of the 11th Infantry Brigade and a good friend to Currie, recalled in early 1919 that, following the armistice, the rumours had been rife throughout the camps: "Sir Arthur, in order to acquire honour for himself, had sacrificed men needlessly, and some of them were very bitter on this score.... In short, they charged him with having no regard for the lives of his men."[12] Brigadier-General A.E. Ross remembered being startled upon hearing a fellow officer in the mess call Currie "a butcher," and then realizing with even more shock that this was a common expression used by the rank and file.[13] These accusations were not just the invention of a malevolent group of embittered conspirators; Currie's own soldiers believed and even embellished the rumours, and both officers and enlisted men whispered against him. As one of Currie's closest friends concluded, "The cruel fact [is] that this propaganda against the Corps Commander was fostered, if not begun in the literal sense, within the CEF."[14] The operational success of the Canadian Corps during the Hundred Days had elevated the Canadian reputation to that of elite shock troops; but this level of respect had been purchased at a high price: first the 45,000 casualties and now the ruin of Sir Arthur's reputation in the eyes of his own men.

Sir Arthur had scented problems after the armistice: first in the ranks, then in England, and perhaps most dangerously in Ottawa. As in the war, he had enemies on all fronts. Even after the warfighting stopped, however, he had no time to run the attackers to ground. He was too busy, too tired. "The war took out of all of us a great deal more than we realized," wrote a still exhausted but candid Currie a year after the armistice. "There are often times when one believes that the only possible way to feeling normal again would be to take a long rest of a year or so. Some days you feel all right while at other times, your nerves are all on edge; you are irritable and find difficulty in getting your brain to work hard."[15]

The general knew from friends in Canada that Sir Sam Hughes was still looking to embarrass him publicly, but he felt incapable of striking back at the former minister, whom he described as "a liar ... at times insane, and apparently ... a cur of the worst type."[16] Surely his record and that of his Corps, Currie believed, spoke for themselves. They did, but not loudly enough. And the truth was often drowned out beneath a cacophony of anger and dissatisfaction from those who had suffered, and who continued to suffer in the war's aftermath.

Within a month of the armistice, Currie realized that he had perhaps miscalculated in his assessment of the potential threat from home. While friends such as Brigadier W.A. Griesbach had advised him "to sit tight and do nothing" about Hughes, Currie now felt that something had to be done, as there was no respite from the worried letters to the general by friends who despaired about the relentless rumour campaign against him.[17] Even as Currie was lauded as the conquering hero among the overseas Allies, Hughes denounced him in Canada as a "murderer, a coward, a drunkard, and almost everything else that is bad and vile."[18] A dispirited Currie did not know how to defend himself against the madman, but he knew that the unstable ex-minister would not stop of his own volition.

Currie was at a loss as to why anyone would listen to the ex-minister's rants against him, especially since, in the general's eyes, Hughes was responsible for arming the Canadians with the "Ross rifle which killed men unnecessarily." Further, he had run the CEF like his own personal patronage-ridden fiefdom, placing in command positions officers whose only merit had been "their willingness to lick his boots."[19] In Currie's mind, Hughes had saddled the Canadians with enormous burdens, while he himself had always worked on their behalf. In a letter of late December, when rumours were circulating widely through Canada, Currie reassured his sister—and perhaps himself—that "there will not be a word of truth in what he says, but Sam Hughes is a vindictive and bitterly disappointed man, and so is his son Garnet."[20]

Despite Sir Sam Hughes's fall from grace, the ex-minister still had friends and backers in the Canadian militia. The corps commander, on the other hand, had surprisingly few close friends among senior politicians. While Currie had supported the Unionists during the war, he had had little time to develop any close relations with influential ministers. The cold and sometimes aloof Sir Robert Borden had not gotten any closer to Currie, despite the general's assistance during 1918. When the rumours began to circulate freely, Sir Arthur's enemies came out of the woodwork, like ticks smelling blood, and this emboldened and then spurred Hughes to insinuate more openly that the high casualties were due to reckless command decisions rather than the hard-pounding nature of the fighting. Neither detractors nor supporters had any hard evidence to rely on, as the war records were still under lock and key in the various historical units, but selective anecdotes based on the rumours from wounded veterans lent some credence to the accusations against Currie. Hughes had evidently heard enough to convince him of the general's culpability.

Sir Sam had already expressed his concern to Borden and others about Currie's suitability to command. Hughes's charge in early January 1918 had been ignored by the prime minister, and he had written a second letter in October of the same year, condemning the "useless massacre of our Canadian boys, as needlessly occurred at Cambrai," reminding Borden, "I have on other occasions drawn your attention to the massacres at Lens, Passchendaele, etc, where the only apparent object was to glorify the General in command…."[21] Borden was familiar with Hughes's outbursts and attacks, and so he again brushed them aside, especially when Sir Sam demanded the removal of Currie and his incompetent "Black-hand Gang."[22]

With no movement from the prime minister, Sir Sam had commenced a rumour campaign against Currie, as he had done in the past against enemies such as Flavelle and Perley. The ex-minister shared some of his twisted thoughts with his old co-conspirator, Lord Beaverbrook:

"Currie was a coward at St. Julien and a damned fool ever since. He was the cause of practically having murdered thousands of men at Lens and Paschendaele [sic], and it is generally supposed the motive was to prevent the possibility of Turner coming back with the Second Army Corps, and to prevent Garnet from commanding a Division." In short, Hughes argued, Currie had murdered his own men to ensure that his rival would not be able to make it back to the front, thus ruining Canada's opportunity to step onto the battlefield and the world stage with a full army of two corps.[23] The rumour campaign went on for several months, but it was coming to an end in late February when informants passed on information to the government that Hughes was going to voice his accusations against Currie in the House of Commons.

To pre-empt this public harangue, Minister of Militia Sydney Mewburn asked Currie in February 1919 for information that could be used as ammunition against Hughes.[24] Surprisingly, Currie dragged his feet in responding to the minister, and, when he did, he cited that regulations did not allow him to send documents that showed the success of the Canadians on the battlefield unless proper chain of command was followed. Currie's unhelpful actions were shockingly short-sighted at this point, although perhaps understandable. As a victim of past political crossfires, he was leery of being caught in another war of words. The general wrote to a Canadian politician, "I am not going to become involved in any newspaper controversy, for the people who are making the charges would pass readily from one set of lies to another."[25] But Currie did himself no favours in sticking to his principles—or perhaps hiding behind them.

Currie's decision not to offer a public defence was born of other considerations as well. The corps commander was exhausted and suffering from what we now recognize as post-traumatic stress disorder. "Looking at him," wrote an upset William Lyon Mackenzie King in May of 1919, "one would think him a man between fifty and sixty, rather than forty-three."[26] The war had worn him out terribly and he seemed on the brink of a breakdown. "I am tired, Colonel, very tired, and now that the strain is over I am feeling it more than ever," wrote Currie to a friend in Canada in the war's aftermath.[27] The general believed that he had worked diligently for his country and his soldiers, and—perhaps naively—did not feel he needed to justify his actions. "If my record in this war can be tarnished by such as [Hughes]," he commented wearily, "then I don't much care."[28]

Although Currie was disillusioned and dispirited, and perhaps even fatalistic in believing that Hughes could not be dissuaded, Currie still hoped he would not face the charges alone. A strong word from the government in his support would put the ex-minister in his place. Currie wrote pleadingly to Sir Edward Kemp on February 27 about the mean gossip and rumours circulating in England and Canada, arguing, "It seems to me that I have the right to ask for protection" from the untrue allegations "about my being a murderer of Canadian troops, about my being bombed, and shot at, and boo-ed, and God knows what else."[29] Currie requested that Borden defend him in the House of Commons against these "malicious lies," but the prime minister was in Paris at the time and felt no urgency to take part in this new war of reputations. In fact, Borden actively dissuaded Kemp from investigating the rumours, as he feared what such an action might reveal. Were there more embezzlement scandals linked to the general? Had the casualties during the war indeed been too high and, if so, was not the government partially to blame for not having listened to Sir Sam Hughes, the country's expert on the war? No, Borden chose the safe course of action and went back to remaking the world at the peace conference, leaving Currie to fend for himself.

As a desperate Currie was being rebuffed politely by Borden and then Kemp, Hughes launched his public assault against Currie within the protective sanctity of the House of Commons on March 4, 1919. The Parliament buildings had burned down in 1916 and so the seat of democracy had been moved temporarily to the castle-like Victoria

Memorial Museum (now the site of the Canadian Museum of Nature). While the Senate was housed in a room where one cheeky wag had affixed the museum label, "Prehistoric Fossils," members of Parliament were in the two-storey, semi-circular salon on the third floor.[30] It was here that Hughes rose to speak.

The frail ex-minister launched into a condemnation of his colleagues in the Union government, focusing on the enormous costs of the war and the draconian powers that had been adopted under the War Measures Act, which had allowed for censorship, the suspension of habeas corpus, and other government powers in the name of winning the war. With deliberate spite, Hughes drew an inflammatory comparison with the recently defeated enemy: "If we are going to have autocracy in time of war, let us have it in time of peace, too, and send for the Kaiser to run the country." It was typical Hughes bombast. Next, the ex-minister took aim at one of his favourite targets, Sir Joseph Flavelle. His reference to Flavelle as the "owner of this Government" provoked guffaws of laughter from the Liberals, and the stand-up comic Hughes had to wait a while for the House to settle.[31] As an old hand at the theatre of politics, Sir Sam pivoted easily from engaging in jokey banter to condemning Flavelle as a shameless war profiteer. The baiting and battering of Flavelle was comfortable terrain for Hughes. Unionists cringed; the Liberals cheered him on. The ex-minister was enjoying the limelight, and he felt some of that rush of old, when once he had stood nearly centre stage in the House. Hughes was on a roll, and he now trained his sights on a new victim: Sir Arthur Currie.

He read first from the damning letter that he had sent Borden dated October 1, 1918, to ensure that it would become part of the formal public record of the country. In it, he had demanded that the prime minister remove the "incompetents and have this needless slaughter, for I can call it nothing else, of our Canadian lads stopped."[32] He then launched into the second phase of his verbal assault on Currie. Hughes lamented what he saw as the needless casualties suffered by Canadian soldiers during the war, and he again blamed Currie, without naming him, asking, with reference to the final capture of Mons on November 11, "why any man of common sense would send soldiers in there, unless it were for his own glorification." The operation at Mons—coming as it did at the end of the grinding battles of the Hundred Days—was another example, thundered Hughes, of Currie's casual habit of "needlessly sacrificing the lives of Canadian soldiers." Any general ordering such an attack, he argued, should be "tried summarily by court martial and punished so far as the law would allow." In the shocked silence that followed, he advised the House wickedly, "You cannot find one Canadian soldier returning from France who will not curse the name of the officer who ordered the attack on Mons."[33]

Hughes's charge, according to one member of Parliament, caused "a considerable sensation, but I think that nearly everyone was quite disgusted."[34] Hughes was certainly an unstable force, but this man, a general and former defence minister, who knew more about war than anyone in the House save for perhaps Borden, was levelling harrowing accusations. Moreover, many in the House had heard the whispers and rumours about misconduct of the senior high command overseas, and some even from veterans of the front. Were the casualties not gut-wrenchingly high? Who was to blame?

As one of the most excoriating attacks in recent memory raged through Parliament, with a former minister accusing Canada's most important, accomplished, and famous general of murdering his own soldiers, it is shocking that no MPs came to Currie's defence. The corps commander's old friend, Lieutenant-Colonel Cy Peck, had recently returned to Canada to take up his seat in the House of Commons. Although he had traded his kilt for a suit, he still wore the Empire's highest award for bravery, the Victoria Cross. On his first day in the House he was understandably unsure of himself, and certainly unready to respond to Hughes, despite the encouragement he received from his fellow backbenchers. But there were other experienced MPs who could have taken on Hughes. As Peck later wrote to Currie, "I thought that some member of the Government [by which he meant a cabinet minister] ought to have replied in your defence."[35]

But it was difficult for MPs or cabinet ministers to respond to the charges in the absence of proper information, a situation that of course never inhibited Hughes. With Borden away, some of the Unionists were also unsure about the nature of their collective response, as they were about many other issues facing the government.[36] And there was the added disincentive of confronting the aging yet still dangerous war horse, who snapped and kicked at any and all who came against him. Despite his physical frailty and ailing mind, Hughes remained a force unto himself. "Everybody seemed to be scared of him," wrote an astonished Peck, who had spent the war at the front and thought of Hughes as little more than a farce.[37] Furthermore, Currie's past financial misdeeds, the high casualty levels during the Hundred Days, and the widespread rumours among returning troops all seemed to cast a shadow over Currie's success in leading one of the finest fighting formations on the Western Front. There were few politicians willing to stick their neck out for the general, who had last been in Canada half a decade ago. While the government could have launched an investigation to clear Currie's name, it chose to do nothing, as if Hughes's tirade could be forgotten, swept away, or buried. Delay, avoidance, and obfuscation were all tactics of successful governments, but one Canadian friend warned Currie, "You have been subjected to all sorts of criticisms. The people who hear the same criticisms repeated many times take it for granted there is something in it."[38]

Although the politicians refused to be drawn into the emerging battle, Canadians were not silent in the face of Hughes's assault. Several veterans' organizations issued rebuttals reaffirming their faith in Currie, and brushed aside Hughes's words as malignant and unrepresentative of the returned soldiers' perspective.[39] On March 5, the *Toronto Daily Star* published a front-page defence of Currie's tactics at Cambrai, which documented how the infantry swept around the town, assisted by tanks—

a far different retelling of the battle than Hughes's clumsy depiction of a mad frontal assault. A day later, the *Toronto Globe* wrote, "The terrors of the war have been great and manifold for our gallant men in France, but Sir Sam Hughes is a greater terror than any of them. The enemy never dealt a fouler blow than that directed by Sir Sam Hughes against the leaders for the Canadian Army still in the field and unable to defend themselves."[40] Another editorial writer mused about Hughes's unbalanced mind, but thought the issue of high casualty numbers in the Hundred Days should be investigated; however, the writer wondered mischievously if the investigation "should be a parliamentary, a military, or a medical one."[41] Hughes had been reduced to an incompetent, even loony, caricature—a sick and unstable man who needed a medical doctor or psychiatrist to examine him after his outrageous charge. With the rebuttals offered by newspapers and some veterans' groups, the general's supporters might have seen a silver lining in this cloud: surely the rumours would be buried quickly now that they had been brought into the harsh light of public opinion, perhaps even with Hughes forced to issue a public *mea culpa*.

But Sir Sam would do no such thing. In fact, as was typical, Hughes dug in to defend his position. And despite the backlash from many vocal editors, concerned Canadians writing to their newspapers, and veterans' groups, the government was slow to respond to Hughes's serious charges, with only two backbench defenders speaking up for the maligned general. South Vancouver MP Richard Cooper called Currie a great soldier and accused Hughes, and men like him, of mean-spirited conniving, as they "stand back 3,500 miles and, without full information to guide them, undertake to criticize."[42] A more powerful denunciation of Hughes was made ten days after Sir Sam's attack, by Currie's old friend Cy Peck, who recounted the event to Currie: "[The] House was packed as well as the galleries. I got a very fine reception when I arose to speak.... As you will see, I went after Sam hammer and tongs, and the poor old boy sat dumbfounded." Peck defended Currie's actions, and noted that he was using his "privilege as a member of Parliament to defend the leaders of the Canadian Corps, because they are not here to defend themselves." As a participant in the battle for Mons, the Victoria Cross winner told the House that the operation had resulted in few casualties—fewer than any other major battle fought during the course of the war. He also ridiculed Hughes's tactical appreciation of fighting on the Western Front and described Currie as "one of the greatest Canadians, one of the great commanders of the war."[43] Peck further accused Hughes of running a "campaign of infamy," and hoped he would cease his dastardly actions, as further inaccuracies would be "unfortunate for the reputation which the Canadians have won for themselves."[44] For his defence of the general, Peck received applause, cheers, and "reams of congratulations from both sides of the House and from across the country."[45]

Currie was grateful that "Sandy," as he called Peck affectionately, had stood up for him in the House as a "sturdy defender."

> I should never want for a better one, and I would like, Peck, from the depths of a very grateful heart to thank you for what you said in my behalf. Of course we both had heard that this attack was to be made, but yet one could scarcely realize that the people of Canada would elect to a seat in the House of Commons a man who could do such a cowardly, mean and vicious a thing.[46]

Currie was mystified that other senior ministers, and even the prime minister, would not speak on his behalf. Lamentably, the government's response got little better with time. Sir Edward Kemp offered faint praise of Currie in May when, in support of tabling the overseas ministry report, he spoke of the general: "He has made a high place for himself in history; he measures up to a proud standard as compared with other great generals of the war; he was ever considerate of the men under him, and always exercised patience and foresight in dealing with problems which came before him."[47] "Ever considerate" and "dealing with problems"? Surely Canada's government was not made up of timid neophytes, unable to put up little more than a shambolic, understated defence against a discredited, unstable, and generally disliked ex-minister? Were there not more supportive words to describe Canada's greatest battlefield general? The government's weak defence left many Canadians uneasy; in the days after the initial March 4 attack, the *Toronto Daily Star* captured the sentiment of many across the country: "Sir Sam makes accusations before Parliament and the people of Canada more serious than anything known in the history of the country."[48]

It is tempting to see the sick and aged Hughes as simply bent on carrying out his revenge against Currie, whom he saw as an imperial toady who had turned his back not only on himself, but also on his son. Hughes had used public denunciations and rumour-mongering against his enemies in the past, and had gone far further in his bitter attacks against Joseph Flavelle. In this case, however, the ex-minister seemed to have been genu- inely moved to action by the rumours he heard about the "butcher." As the self-appointed guardian of Canada's overseas soldiers, Hughes felt he was one of the few politicians who had the right to take the general down.

Was Sir Sam's attack against Sir Arthur—several more of which would follow over the next two years—the result of jealousy and bitter- ness or of a heartfelt desire to punish the man who had thrown away lives? The two motives are intertwined and, since Hughes was not the introspective sort, it is likely that even he was not sure which one was more dominant. But having seen combat in South Africa, and knowing well how personal bravery and action had led to victory there, Hughes simply could not understand why the generals could not overcome the unholy trinity of the wire, the shell, and the spade. This war of industrial might, enormous resources, and shocking casualties was frustrating and foreign to the ex-minister, whose mind could not grasp the complexities of the modern battlefield. Sir Sam looked, as he always did, for someone to blame, and he found his target in Sir Arthur Currie.

The most puzzling dimension of Sir Sam's attack was his decision not to bring down Sir Arthur with charges of financial embezzlement.[49] Despite being an old veteran of gloves-off political brawling, Hughes never dredged up Currie's regimental misdeeds. He might have been able to destroy Currie with that accusation, and certainly much of the general's angst over Hughes's attack in late 1918 and early 1919 was based on his worry that the ex-minister would brand him publicly as a thief. But Hughes never revealed Currie's financial misdeeds in the House, and even if he felt constrained by the fact that he might be implicated somehow in the cover-up, he had long developed the technique of insinuation, which would have allowed him to raise the issue for others to explore. Instead, the ex-minister hammered away at the senseless casualties suffered by his boys. Had Hughes, in fact, taken the high road in his accusations against Currie? This was a road rarely taken by the minister, but it seems uncharacteristic of him not to have dredged up Currie's pilferous past. Perhaps Hughes's reason for refusing to deliver the *coup de grâce* is revealed in a letter to his son, Garnet:

> I created him on your recommendation; made him what he is; covered up his blunders; hid his cowardice and his reward for my decency was giving it to you in the neck and, as far as possible, to me. He is even worse than David Watson. However, all those not guilty of butchering men are behind me.[50]

In his mind, Sir Sam had given Sir Arthur his start, as well as covering up his failures on the battlefield and his prewar embezzlement, and there had been no loyalty in return. It would appear that Hughes believed he had enough evidence of Currie's wartime failure to avoid destroying him over his prewar thieving.

While much of the above passage from Hughes to his son reveals Sir Sam's unhealthy ego, in his defence, surely there was some self-contained logic behind his accusations. To any who, like Hughes, did not directly witness the ongoing difficulties in the fighting on the Western Front, such operations, which cost thousands of casualties for the capture of only a few thousand metres of muddy wasteland, must have seemed like senseless slaughter. Moreover, the characteristics that made Currie a great general were not always clear or publicly visible; his careful planning, attention to detail, and moral courage were often overshadowed by his lack of charisma and his unease with the rank and file. Was Hughes so wrong to accuse Currie of causing the deaths of thousands? Was the general not in command during this horrific slaughter, and therefore responsible for it? With the hindsight afforded by time and historical study, it is easier to appreciate the corps commander's accomplishments. At the time, however, Hughes's vanity, bitterness, and compassion for his boys made it difficult for him to view Currie as anything other than a bloodthirsty martinet sacrificing Canadians to build his own reputation. Hughes's self-aggrandizing and destructive actions have made it too easy for historians to brush him aside as an unstable megalomaniac. He was a more complex figure, guided by actions and urges not always visible behind his wildly inaccurate accusations and newspaper-grabbing tirades. And perhaps Hughes's focus on Currie's wartime actions instead of his past misdeeds is an indication that the ex-minister was indeed concerned about the soldiers overseas rather than simply bent on destroying the general. However, given his fanatical behaviour, his contemporaries could be forgiven for thinking him little more than a madman.

CHAPTER 13

The War of Reputations

1919–1921

Canada's greatest battlefield general returned to Canada on August 17, 1919, his ship mooring at the Halifax harbour. Delays had pushed the arrival to just after midnight, and only a cold breeze and a handful of sleepy junior dignitaries were on hand to greet Sir Arthur as he walked down the gangplank, Lady Currie on his arm. It appeared to some that the general had slunk back into the country. The next day was a Sunday, and the celebrations were decidedly muted in Halifax as the general and his wife were escorted to the city hall. The *Chronicle* reported disapprovingly that while there was a guard of honour and hordes of officials, Sir Arthur was received in solemn silence.[1] Canadians did not have a lot of experience in welcoming home new royalty, and perhaps it was thought that quiet dignity was the way to go. Whatever the case, the atmosphere of the event, noted the *Chronicle*, seemed more like a funeral than a hero's coronation.

The next leg of Currie's trip was to Ottawa, which started out more promisingly. A special train transported him to the capital, arriving late on the 18th. The soot-stained Central Station was nearly bursting with an excited crowd that strained dangerously to catch a glimpse of the general. To the cheering throngs of civilians and veterans, a band played "See, the Conquering Hero Comes." Currie straightened up and waved to the crowd. He was greeted by the acting prime minister, Sir George Foster, a long-serving veteran of the Conservative party.

Currie and entourage were whisked off to Canada's temporary Parliament, where the crowds were larger, although they showed more restraint, clapping politely. Unlike at the train station, this crowd seemed to be formed more by curious gawkers than by delirious patriots. Currie was no doubt disappointed by the absence of Prime Minister Sir Robert Borden and several prominent cabinet ministers who were in New Brunswick greeting the Prince of Wales. The top tier of the government was missing in action. The warm reception for Currie seemed to disappear as he passed through the great wooden doors of Canada's temporary Parliament. Those present seemed strangely uneasy. There were few of the flowery speeches that Canadian politicians normally heap effusively on returned heroes, and it was even reported that a small group of women in the gallery hissed at Currie's name.[2] Something had gone very wrong. The shaken general put on a brave face, but he must have realized that Sir Sam Hughes's charges still hung heavily in the air. After fighting for four years on the Western Front, Currie would have to face a new war, this time for his reputation, and against an elusive enemy.

Despite the lukewarm public receptions that met his return home, Currie was promoted to full general upon his arrival in Ottawa, becoming the first Canadian in the Dominion's history to attain that rank. He was also made inspector-general of the Canadian Armed Forces, a new position that was created for him alone and that carried the distinction of being the government's primary military advisor, thereby trumping the existing chief of the general staff. With these appointments, it appeared that Currie had gone some way toward putting behind him Sir Sam's charges, but it remained "a time of stress" for the general, wrote one friend.[3] For one thing, Sir Arthur and Lady Currie were not well off financially. Although as a lieutenant general Currie had made a significant salary of $41.24 a day, or $15,000 a year, much of that had gone toward paying off his debt.[4] His firm in Victoria had suffered in his absence, and like many veterans who survived the war, Currie found that his company had been lost while he was away. This was a heavy blow, and years later the general remarked that the loss made him "sick now to think of it."[5]

In England a grateful King and citizenry greeted Field Marshal Haig as "the hero of the British people," awarding him £100,000, a fortune in that day.[6] Sir Robert Borden believed that Currie deserved a "reasonable sum" from the government "as he had sacrificed his business interest," as well as led the Corps in the Empire's War for Civilization, but he noted, "my colleagues and the caucus … did not in the least favour the proposal, which had to be abandoned." Borden did not appear to have pushed too hard, however. Perhaps the scandal of Currie's embezzlement had got round Ottawa, and certainly the rumours passed on by returned veterans were damaging enough for Borden to believe that "Currie was not highly popular either in the Canadian army or in Canadian public opinion."[7] Throughout his life, Sir Arthur carried a deep wound from the fact that Parliament had not even offered him an official vote of thanks.

Liberal Party leader William Lyon Mackenzie King, who always had his ear to the ground in Ottawa, was concerned about Currie, whom he admired very much. He wrote in his diary in August, "There are damnable efforts being made to destroy his reputation, by saying he was indifferent to life."[8] But while Currie knew that he needed to defend his reputation from the slanderous attacks of Hughes and others, he instead chose to talk about the Canadian Corps. As Currie wrote to one correspondent, "There are so many things in connection with the war that I would like to tell the Canadian people.… I refer principally to the reasons why certain campaigns were lost, and continued. Yet one hesitates to do so because statements I would have to make would reflect on the conduct of the troops, Allied and otherwise, with whom we fought."[9] To justify his own interpretation of events, Currie would have to skewer others, including Haig, and he was not willing to do that. But he felt that his own actions were justifiable; as he wrote to one supporter in early 1919, "I have never done anything since coming to France of which I am ashamed nor concerning which I am afraid to let in the full light of day.... I am not at all afraid what future history will decide."[10] But Currie was not a political naïf, and he would find ways to set the record straight.

Sir Arthur Currie buttressed his own reputation with the general public and future historians by compiling a favourable account of the war. He knew that the Canadian Corps' reputation for excellence, proven throughout the war, had been sealed in the Hundred Days, but after the Hughes attacks, friends in Canada had warned Currie about an alarming lack of knowledge on the part of Canadians. As one of them had noted, "The general public is not so well informed and nothing has struck me since my return as to the curiously incomplete idea in the public mind as to the achievements of the Canadian Corps, particularly since August 8th. The fact was that the brilliant record was overwhelmed to some extent in the general tide of victory."[11] In short, because of wartime censorship, many Canadians did not know about the Canadian Corps' remarkable record of victories during the Hundred Days, and were instead inundated only with the long lists of casualties.

Currie had taken note of this problem, and in December 1918 had established the Canadian War Narrative Section (CWNS), a small group of officers that would have access to all official records created or held by the Corps in order to craft a compelling narrative of battle, with a focus on the Hundred Days.[12] The CWNS would help Currie control the first draft of history. The unit's only historical monograph was eventually published as part of the 1919 overseas ministry report, officially known as the *Interim Report on the Operations of the Canadian Corps during the Year 1918*.[13] It emphasized the hard-pounding nature of the fighting during the Hundred Days, which helped to explain why almost 20 percent of all

Canadian battlefield casualties in over four years of fighting had occurred during these ninety-six days of battle. As a spearhead force, the four over-strength Canadian divisions met and defeated elements of 47 German divisions, effectively destroying 15 of them, while also liberating 228 cities, towns, and villages, and capturing 31,537 prisoners.[14] The Currie-sanctioned monograph was an important step in setting down the record of the Corps' success and the reasons for its high casualties, although the report's small print run and dry-as-dust tone ensured that few read it. But at least Currie's success was now in print and on record.

"The history of the Canadian Corps," wrote wartime gunner Andrew McNaughton, "is inseparably linked with the name of General Sir Arthur Currie."[15] And although it was not just the Corps but the entire Canadian war effort that impelled Canada forward to a new sense of nationhood, Currie and his men were important symbols for the Dominion's claim for greater influence in international affairs. Yet the exhausted and worried general knew that his personal war was not over, and he steeled himself to restore his reputation against the smear campaign that was quietly but effectively levelled against him.

One of Currie's first public speeches in Canada was at the Canadian Club at the Château Laurier in Ottawa on August 19, 1919. The room was packed, and the enthusiastic crowd cheered the general when he entered the dining room. During the course of his anticipated talk, Currie invoked the comradeship of the Corps and its hard-won victories on the Western Front: "Our great strength lay in the fact that we were one big fighting machine and we were all doing our share as we saw it."[16] Those in attendance could not have failed to notice that Currie was throwing down the gauntlet to Hughes and his ilk, when he proclaimed, "I can stand here tonight and face every man, woman and child in Canada and say that I have no excuse to offer for anything I have done."[17]

A week later he spoke in Montreal to enormous crowds made up of veterans and civilians, and then led them in an impromptu march. "We are all comrades here as we were all comrades there," he told a large group of veterans. "The rest of my life, as far as I am able, will be devoted, first, to helping the widows and orphans of those who are not coming back; and, next, to helping you boys who exposed your bodies as the living bulwark against dangers that threatened the world."[18] On the next leg of his trip, a huge group of cheering civilians and veterans greeted him at the train station in Toronto on August 29, including over 500 singing schoolchildren. He spoke forcefully later that day at Massey Hall, without a prepared speech, dazzling the audience with his intimate knowledge of the war. In praising the accomplishments of the Corps, he took the opportunity to remind listeners that it was he who called off the Amiens battle when it had run its course, and he let it be known that when the Corps was sent in to capture Mons, the Canadians were simply following orders from the British army in which his formation served. The *Toronto Globe* noted the day after his talk that Currie had "effectively answered the cruel slander" of Sir Sam Hughes, an "armchair critic three thousand miles from the field of battle."[19] Everywhere Currie went that late summer, he was greeted by large crowds and prolonged cheers. "Of all the men I have met," wrote a star-struck Mackenzie King, "he seems to me more likely than any other to become a prominent political figure, and I should not be surprised to see him Prime Minister of Canada some day."[20]

In late September, Currie went west after having spent more than two weeks with his mother in Strathroy. At every stop on his tour to Winnipeg, Regina, Calgary, Vancouver, and Victoria, Currie told the tales of his Corps and of the bravery of the Canadians in battle. Out of the destructiveness of war, Currie intoned, should come something "more priceless than peace—a Canadian national sentiment."[21] This declaration of support for a new Canadian nationalism was, ironically, a position that Hughes would likely have embraced. As part of the tour, however, Currie was clearly trying to rehabilitate his reputation, which he did, talk by talk. The *Manitoba Free Press,* echoing the eastern newspapers, suggested that Currie's speaking tour had put paid to the "charge which has been in circulation throughout Canada, that as commander of the Canadian forces, he sacrificed the lives of many Canadian soldiers the day the armistice was signed, by ordering the capture of Mons."[22] The rumours were never far from Currie's mind, but his frank and charismatic speeches helped to push them further to the periphery. *Saturday Night* magazine gushed that few Canadians had made a "finer impression on the Canadian public than has General Sir Arthur Currie.... The remarkable personality of Gen Currie, and the wisdom of his speeches, have had the effect of silencing criticism that was ready to leap from the lips and pens of the uninformed."[23] This was an optimistic assessment, and more than a few of Currie's enemies, as well as his former soldiers, continued to blight his name, although they must surely have constituted a minority, and a shrinking one.

For Currie, still reeling from the war's exertions, the speaking tour proved too much. "Each day, as [I] got farther away from the cessation of war, [I] continued to feel even more fatigued," the general recalled to one politician.[24] To another friend, a sheepish Currie wrote, "I suppose we did not realize just how much a rest was necessary."[25] The combination of exhaustion and untreated post-traumatic stress brought on his collapse at the end of the tour. "I am under doctor's orders," he wrote from his bed, "to cease attending any functions, or to engage in any work entailing any brain energy. I received the same orders on my arrival in Canada but refused to obey them, with the result that now I know I must or else go to hospital."[26] The fleshy Currie rapidly shed weight during this period, and friends were shocked by his appearance as his clothes hung off his sickly body. The war exacted much from Currie and it would take years for him to recover from the strain wrought by more than four years of service on the Western Front.

A worn-out Currie took over as inspector-general and councillor to the government on militia matters on December 10, 1919. He sought to reform the Canadian forces and, despite his long career as a civilian-soldier, aimed to establish a strong cadre of permanent soldiers. Almost immediately, however, Currie found that the debt-ridden country could not sustain his planned reforms. His 10,000-strong permanent force was cut in half, with too many of these positions already filled by useless old soldiers who had not even served overseas during the war. Contrasting the situation with his overseas command, Currie lamented, "One finds it harder to clean house."[27] The glacially slow bureaucracy, ensnared in its own red tape, ensured that few reforms were put into place. The general's trusted officers of the Canadian Corps had returned to their lives and Currie was now an outsider at the helm of a ship that was content to putter along.

Sir Arthur soon had the distinct and unpleasant feeling that his position was a sinecure, and that not much was expected of him. He raged in one letter that there were many members of Parliament who hoped he would simply be satisfied with his plum position and, in the general's words, "loaf for the balance of my life." Currie spat, "I want no favours from a Government who did not even say 'thank you' to any members of the CEF."[28] The government had in fact thanked the Canadian soldiers, but it had not singled out Currie for any special recognition. Still smarting from the cold shoulder, Canada's greatest general would write that he felt that he "was in the same class as the man who runs an elevator in a public building": he had a role to play, but he was all but ignored by everyone of importance.[29]

Sir Arthur was still a young man at forty-four, and he was not content to sit out his life in Ottawa, a city that he and his wife found too cold in the winter, too humid in the summer, and terminally boring all year round. Currie pushed on in the face of systemic inertia. "Defence of the realm is the duty of every citizen," he lectured, yet his plan for universal and compulsory military service was met with politically realistic shrugs.[30] He was soon engaged in administrative battles over the fate of his beloved Canadian Corps. The units and formations that had fought within the Corps were swallowed up by existing militia regiments, although Currie used his influence to ensure that some hybrid amalgamations would survive; for example, the 50th Gordon Highlanders and the 16th Battalion were combined to form a new Scottish regiment. But what was to be done with militia units such as the Queen's Own Rifles, whose members had served in at least twelve different CEF battalions? Militia commanders pushed back and, by stacking key committees, eventually watered down Currie's plans to the extent that the Canadian Corps was all but assimilated by existing militia units.[31] Currie was not accustomed to losing battles, but in Ottawa he faced defeat at every turn. Some people want to forget, he wrote sadly, "that there was such a thing as the Canadian Corps."[32]

A miserable Currie received a spring gift on the morning of April 12, 1920. It came in the form of a letter from McGill University in Montreal, one of Canada's most distinguished institutions of higher learning, but one that had been slowly sliding into decrepitude over the previous decade. Currie had no affiliation with McGill or Montreal, but, as Canada's largest city, Montreal had contributed the most men and units to the CEF, and more than 3,000 McGill professors, students, and graduates had served, with 363 killed and three times that many wounded.[33] The general had many friends in the cosmopolitan centre of business and finance, and hundreds of his Corps veterans were now enrolled at the university.

The letter from Frank Adams, a former CEF man and the acting principal of McGill, was intriguing. Sir Arthur was offered his second honorary doctorate of law—the first having come from Cambridge a year earlier. The honour was no doubt gratifying for a man who had only finished high school, but the communiqué seemed to hold promise of more, as Adams asked to meet with Currie on another pressing matter. The general likely knew that McGill had already begun an international search for a new principal.[34] McGill Governor W.M. Birks led the search committee and he had sent out letters to presidents of universities in

North America and Britain. The short list already included President H.M. Tory of the University of Alberta, several distinguished McGill professors, wartime gunner and former McGill professor Andrew McNaughton, and Principal W.L. Grant of Upper Canada College. But Sir Auckland Geddes, who had been principal of McGill for a short time after the war before taking the ambassadorship to Washington, pushed for Currie, despite his lack of academic qualifications. "Mark my words, Currie is your man—when the history of the War comes to be written and certain things can be said that cannot now be said while certain people are living, Currie's name will be greater than it is today. I speak from inside Cabinet information—his name will be one of the very great names of the War. He has all the organizing ability, qualities of leadership and a name to conjure with, from Halifax to Vancouver."[35] This testimonial seems to have been the tipping point for the search team.

"The offer to go to McGill came like a shot out of the blue," remarked Currie.[36] The general was gratified to be considered for the position, but he protested—perhaps half-heartedly—that he was not qualified, especially since he had never been to university.[37] Nonetheless, Sir Arthur went to Montreal in early May and, after discussions with the university governors, accepted the position. There seems to have been no worry or mention of the gossip and rumours that plagued the general. In turn, Currie was less concerned about the rumours and more about the fact that he did not have a university degree; but, in his words, "they believed I had other characteristics which made up for my deficiencies."[38] The general's reputation as a builder and a leader of men, a well as his international standing, excited the governors. As for Currie, he welcomed the opportunity to "meet thousands of young men every year," noting, "I hope that I may be of some help in starting them on the main portion of life's highway with proper ideas of citizenship."[39] This statement resonates as especially poignant, for Currie already felt that the high ideals that the Canadian Corps represented overseas—universal camaraderie and devotion to duty—had been shunted aside in the harsh postwar years as

Canadians revealed "little indication of any growth of national spirit."[40] Perhaps at McGill, Currie hoped, he could make a difference.

The announcement of Currie's appointment as principal and vice-chancellor of McGill University was made at spring convocation, where the general also received his honorary degree. Left out of the announcement was his generous salary of $17,500 and the included benefits of a house and a directorship with the Bank of Montreal that paid several thousand dollars, which were not insignificant incentives for the cash-poor Currie family. McGill expected Sir Arthur to be worth his weight in gold. His primary tasks were to raise millions of dollars to engage in a massive rebuilding program and to restore the university's reputation. At the convocation ceremony, when Currie went to the podium to receive his degree, many of the McGill governors and senior university staff held their breath. How would the rambunctious students and prickly professors receive this relatively uneducated soldier? The administrators need not have worried, although they had planted class president John O'Brien in the crowd to lead a round of cheers upon the announcement. When Currie's position was revealed, the students erupted with "a spontaneous outburst of applause and cheering."[41] Many of the loudest were Currie's veterans. Sir Arthur had found a new home.

Sir Sam Hughes had once written, "One has not many years to live but a long time to be dead."[42] Few would deny in 1921 that the ex-minister had lived a long and full life, and one not lacking in success. But the two years since his first denunciation of Currie in March of 1919 had been difficult, marking a sad end to his memorable career as one of the Dominion's longest-serving politicians. Sir Sam's erratic behaviour had only deepened in the months that followed his public hammering of Sir Arthur, and he was all but shunned by his old colleagues, thrashed in the House of Commons by Peck and other members, and now castigated by veterans groups and newspapers. Nonetheless, he would not back down in his attack on Currie.

Bitterness had poisoned Hughes, but so too had disease. Hughes's doctors diagnosed him with pernicious anemia, a wasting illness that was winning the battle against the once hard-as-nails minister. Now, with gaunt face, emaciated body, and trembling voice, he was little more than a broken man. But although he had lost his push and pull, he found some solace in lashing out at the supposed intriguers who had brought him down. Little of Sir Sam's personal correspondence from this time period has survived, but one revealing letter from May 1919 to Garnet provides evidence of the ex-minister's fragile mental state. Seeing enemies at every turn, both real and imagined, he believed there were conspiracies against him, and these largely directed by Currie.

> Re Curry [sic]—I told you years ago that he was a four-flusher. Of course he knew if Lipsett had got one corps and he another, he would not last six weeks and you would naturally come in for the second corps.... I have the fullest evidence now that upwards of nine months or more ago, instructions have been issued in a propaganda form to certain writers and correspondents, 'On every occasion, Sir Sam must be overshadowed by others.' And in several instances I have the definite instructions, 'Under any and every circumstances Sir Sam must be completely overshadowed by Sir Arthur Curry.'[43]

Much of Sir Sam's anger was a result of his fall from grace. In his mind, others had orchestrated his descent, and with regard to Currie, he clearly believed that his one-time subordinate deserved to be knocked down a notch—or perhaps destroyed completely—for what he had done to the Hughes family.

Sir Sam hammered away at the general in the last years of his life, although it was increasingly apparent that Hughes's physical health, and perhaps his mind, was failing. There were rumours of him spending time in a mental hospital. A concerned Duke of Devonshire met Hughes in June 1919 in Ottawa and remarked to his diary, "He is certainly an odd man but he must have had a stroke."[44] Few of Sam's fellow parliamentarians wanted to be seen as attacking the old warhorse when he was soon to be put down. Yet Hughes still had fight in him. During one verbal lashing in the House on September 29, 1919, Hughes battered away at his enemies, primarily Flavelle and Currie, guided by "knowing the honest convictions of [his] own heart and conscience." Hughes had even changed his tune regarding Currie's actions at Second Ypres. Where once he had defended Currie on this subject in the House, he now condemned him, arguing that no orders had been found directing Currie to Snow's headquarters, and so the only conclusion was that the general had run away from his command. Jumping ahead in the war to 1918, Hughes railed that Currie was to blame for the Canadians having missed the opportunity to further distinguish themselves with an army of two corps, and, since he had no problem beating a dead horse, he again lashed into Currie for capturing Mons on the last day of the war. The town was, he noted facetiously, "a nice little place, but to sacrifice the lives of Canadians on the eve of the armistice was quite out of place."[45]

During this tirade, both William Griesbach and Cy Peck, former Corps veterans, challenged Hughes repeatedly, arguing that the ex-minister did not have a grasp of the battles or the nature of warfighting in the Hundred Days. Hughes's appreciation was always at the tactical level—the level of the soldier that he was and of the boys he so dearly cared for—and he neither understood nor seemed to care about the difficulties and challenges of sustained operations over a long period, such as those that took place during the Hundred Days. Moreover, Hughes's charges had by now ceased to be shocking, and were more than a little embarrassing. Sir Sam was a mere shadow of his former robust and ruthless self, with his voice in parts of his speech reduced to a mere whisper, and in repeating the old charges, he elicited little response from his fellow MPs. One observer noted that Sir Sam's speech was "pitiable in the extreme," adding, "He disclosed the fact that his real complaint was loss of prestige and loss of that flattery and adulation upon which his soul has fed for the past six or seven years." Hughes ranted for some time and made some "extraordinary statements," but when he sat down, there "was no applause ... only perfect silence." Most of the members of the press gallery had left in disgust during the tirade, with one journalist commenting, "It was almost pathetic to see" this once formidable warrior shuffle along his by now well-worn path of slander and suspicion, "singing his old song to an empty gallery."[46]

Hughes's final attack against Currie on June 16, 1920, was similar, if perhaps more bitter. In a rambling speech, Hughes dismissed Currie's fame as little more than "propaganda," and argued that there were scores of Canadian officers who "are regarded throughout the length and breadth of this country in military circles as infinitely superior to General Sir Arthur Currie as a general or as a gentleman." Hughes insinuated that the general had been promoted above his rank and before all of the "facts" had become known about his cowardly military actions at the Battle of Second Ypres. "Had I remained in office six weeks longer, not only General Currie, but several other officers would have been asked to hand in their resignations." After declaring, "I created General Sir Arthur Currie," he finished with one of his most shocking statements in the House: "I have no hesitation in saying that many Canadians would be above the sod today if he had not carried out his tactics and strategy in relation to Cambrai."[47]

While many believed the old man was deranged—"not responsible for what he says," in the words of one of the saddened Corps' veterans who read about the tirade—some Canadians paid heed to the public condemnations, which were reported on widely across the country.[48] Even though Sir Arthur had been celebrated by civilians and veterans, rewarded with a plum military position, and an even more prestigious principalship at McGill, Hughes's attacks dogged him. Currie refused to respond to the parliamentary broadsides, but he had many who were willing to fight on his behalf. The *Toronto Star* was but one of many papers that took it upon itself to openly support Currie: "In ignoring these attacks upon him it is probable that General Currie makes the most effective of all answers."[49] Silence had always been a formidable weapon against Hughes, but the unanswered charges nonetheless weighed heavily on Currie. The general also felt constrained by his embezzlement. Sir Sam Hughes continued to hold the trump card that Currie had walked away with more than $10,000 from his regiment, and any face-to-face encounter or high-profile rebuttal might provoke the ex-minister to tell the Canadian public about the stolen money. Although Currie made no record of this dread in his diary or papers, it is clear that he had to endure Hughes's attacks for fear of provoking stronger retaliation. The general's inability to fully respond to the charges ate away at him like cancer. "It is hard indeed," wrote a distressed Currie, "that I must ... defend myself against the base calumny of a lying and dying rattlesnake."[50]

Sir Sam was indeed dying. He was in his sixty-ninth year and he would not see another. After receiving his third blood transfusion in the summer of 1921, Hughes was advised by his doctors that he would not recover, and he decided to return home to his riding, to be surrounded in his final days by loved ones, friends, and admirers. But he did not leave Ottawa as a pariah. Sir Robert Borden had written to his ex-minister when Hughes's last letter was read to the caucus in late May 1921, noting that it was greeted by a "fine cheer."[51] "The friends of Sam Hughes were not all of them staunch in the hours of trial," wrote his grandson of the same name, "but in every corner of the country, in every walk of life, he left men and women behind him who generally speaking wished him well,"[52] and this group included his former colleagues in the Conservative party. Hughes's name still carried enough clout to ensure that a private railway car was donated to bear him home. As the train pulled out of Ottawa, a conductor came back to the Hughes car and asked the pale and nearly lifeless Sir Sam if the engineer should be told to travel slowly for his comfort. Hughes rose from his bed, looked the man square in the eyes, and barked, "No! Tell 'em to go like blazes!"[53]

Hughes would live his final weeks in his family home, which was built in 1917 to look like a hunting lodge with hand-hewn beams and masonry, a magnificent fireplace, and fourteen rooms. Here he rallied and fell back again, and hung on to life for weeks beyond what his doctors—whom he derided as "quacks" to their faces—had predicted. All the while he was visited by important constituents and countrymen looking to pay their respects.

Sir Sam still enjoyed scandalizing the great and the good and he took delight in teasing the clergymen who came by to offer him consoling words. When one Methodist minister lectured to him about the afterlife, Sir Sam spat from his deathbed, "Don't you bother about me. Pretty soon I'll be sitting on the right hand of God, and I'll be able to arrange things all right enough."[54] Civilized people simply did not say things like that in early-twentieth-century Canada. The minister fled the Hughes house, fearing that Sir Sam was perhaps headed for an afterlife amid smoke and sulphur.

On a warm Friday on August 26, 1921, Hughes was buried in Lindsay, Ontario. In "Sir Sam's country" almost every store was closed that morning, with windows draped in black and purple or with coloured lithographs of Sir Sam staring out defiantly. The flags flew at half mast. Some 20,000 mourners and onlookers, thousands of citizens whom the former minister had represented for three decades, as well as some of Hughes's old enemies, paid their respects to "Lindsay's foremost citizen," as one of the two town papers intoned. It was appropriate that Sam's bronze casket, glass-topped to reveal the old warrior, was displayed in the high-ceilinged armoury, which he had secured funds to build.

Six Great War veterans carried the coffin slowly through the black-draped doors of the armoury and out into the sunshine and the silent crowds that lined Lindsay's streets. The muffled roll of the drums added to the solemnity of the procession and the loading of the coffin onto the waiting gun-carriage. The mid-afternoon sun beat down on the polished medals adorning hundreds of uniforms, and Hughes's coffin was paraded past the thousands of mourners, led by his old militia unit, the 45th Victoria Regiment, and followed by the traditional riderless black horse with boots reversed in the stirrups. The procession moved through Lindsay to the Riverside Cemetery, outside the town limits, where Sir Sam was finally lowered into the ground to the notes of the "Last Post," played by Bugler Arthur Rhodes, a one-armed veteran of the Great War. Field artillery guns fired fifteen salutes.[55]

Sir Sam had been a force in Parliament and throughout the Dominion, and with his death the country had lost one of its most dynamic and disturbing sons. Few could discount his effect on the nation, for good and ill, and while eulogizers highlighted the former rather than the latter, historians would not be so kind to the general and minister. In 1921, however, Hughes's death seemed to represent the passing of an era. When Sir Sam died, he returned to the land from which he sprang. Yet, while his body was now gone, his ghost lived on. And it had not yet finished with Sir Arthur Currie.

CHAPTER 14

Forging a New Legacy

PRINCIPAL SIR ARTHUR CURRIE,
1920–1927

Sir Arthur Currie wrote to a newspaper editor in November 1921, defending one of his former generals, A.E. Ross. No stranger to damaging gossip, Currie raged, "The slandermonger is a cunning coward, knowing full well that rumors once spread can never be overtaken and that the man who starts the rumor on its foul way can seldom be definitely placed."[1] Despite Currie's ongoing success in postwar society, "foul" rumours continued to haunt him, too. While Sir Sam Hughes was gone, the insinuations against Currie lived on. The general had been unable to determine the source of the persistent rumours, and he felt further victimized by his government, which had failed to reward him or defend his reputation.

Currie also had to contend with his former Victoria business partner, R.A. Power. When Currie's prewar real estate company had been wiped out in the financial crash, his old partner had had to carry much of the burden. To Power, it appeared that his partner had left him saddled with debt and problems while he had gone off to become one of the Empire's

300

most respected soldiers. Power complained bitterly that Sir Arthur had stiffed him, even though Currie had lost all his own money as well.[2] In some circles in Victoria, Currie's name continued to be blackened.

Currie's uneasy relationship with veterans' groups in the first half of the 1920s added tinder to the slow-burning fire of resentment, with some angry veterans continuing to slag him, as he was seen as having abandoned the veterans' groups and their fight for greater rights and a wartime bonus. No one knew how many veterans listened to and spread the wartime rumours about Currie the Butcher, but the gossip persisted across the country—although not, it appears, abroad, where Currie remained lauded as Canada's war hero. The general continued to be war-haunted.

The Canadian Corps' third and last commander became McGill's eighth principal on May 31, 1920, and a rejuvenated Sir Arthur attacked the problems at McGill as he had dealt with challenges during the war. Newspapers across the country celebrated the appointment, each outdoing the next in offering accolades for Currie and the university. Even *The Times of London* chimed in, raving that McGill had shown "boldness and optimism" in selecting the "great military commander Currie to direct the fortunes" of the university.[3] Yet perhaps the most revealing commentary was from the *Ottawa Journal*, which observed that the principalship was an important recognition for Currie "because he has been so little honoured by his own country since his return."[4]

Principal Currie's first and most important task was to raise funds for McGill. Many of the campus buildings were in a decrepit state, and the war had restricted the hiring of new professors. In the fall of 1920, Currie spearheaded a $5-million fundraising campaign. This was an enormous sum for postwar Canada, burdened as it was by debt, but Currie toured the country enlisting support and opening chequebooks. Within a year he could proudly point to the $5 million, plus an oversubscription of another $1.4 million.[5] As one newspaper reported, "The tributes paid to Sir Arthur Currie's influence in the result were many."[6]

The re-energized Currie worked hard, although he still had time to puff on his pipe up to twenty times a day. But he was in good form, and his booming, infectious laugh rang through the halls at the university—especially, as his secretary remembered, when in the company of his friend, McGill professor and famed humorist Stephen Leacock.[7] An admiring Leacock observed of Currie, "Beside him was his pipe with plenty of strong tobacco and plenty of strong language to keep it burning.... He said what he thought and he said it in his own way—which was a forceful one. He knew some of the strongest words in our language. Nor was there ever such honesty as his."[8]

Sir Arthur's blunt assessments and refusal to stand on authority made him popular with students, and his prodigious memory often astounded young men and women on campus. According to McGillite G.B. Puddicombe, "This was a man—tall, erect, dignified, yet possessed of the common touch so often apparent in the truly great. Who of that era does not recall his unhurried walk down the tree-lined avenue of the campus, his hat doffed to each shy, admiring co-ed, addressing male undergraduates, to their astonished delight, 90 per cent of the time by name."[9] Currie was a fan of many of the McGill sports teams, and he could be seen sitting in the stands of Percival Molson Memorial Stadium—named after the former student who had been killed on the Western Front—or cheering from the sidelines in rain, sleet, or snow. He lunched with many of the students, a disarming quality in a university principal, and, even more astonishing, would visit them in their dorm rooms, occasionally sitting on their beds as he asked questions or listened carefully to their concerns.

Currie had a moralistic side, and he urged students to follow a strict code of personal conduct.[10] He could be prudish, as revealed in a 1919 remark to a group of soldiers; objecting to the sight of men and women together, especially in parks, he declared that something had to be done to "stop the shameful cuddling that offends the eye almost everywhere you go."[11] While such beliefs certainly put him out of touch with most young people, the McGill student body did not seem to hold it against him. Perhaps he was more in tune with school spirit and student sentiments when he championed fair play and loyalty. In one speech to the Arts undergraduates in 1930, Currie intoned, "I prefer the spirit that lasts, that is loyal to the university in days of adversity as well as in days of success, the spirit that is faithful to ideas, that believes that McGill has ideals in sports as in anything else, that would prefer to see McGill go down to defeat in every game played in every sport rather than that she should depart in the smallest degree from what is amateur, or fair or honourable."[12] Yet he could easily shift from the idealist to the pragmatic. Gerald Halpenny, president of the Student Council, recounted the story of an attack that the *McGill Daily* had made in late 1932 on the Student Council, the faculty, and the university, when it sniped in one issue that the McGill Union was little more than a brothel. Currie summoned Halpenny into his office to offer some gruff advice: "Halpenny, if any person ever called my home a whorehouse, I'd knock him down and if he was able to get up, I'd knock him down again."[13] Currie's suggestions to students were often more gentle, but he could revert to the hard-talking general when the situation called for it.

Unlike Currie the divisional or corps commander, who had sometimes floundered in finding the right words to appeal to the rank and file, Principal Currie had developed the gift of reaching out to students. As he observed to his old friend Victor Odlum, "The association with the student life is fascinating and I know of no position in Canada which offers better opportunities for useful service to the common welfare."[14]

The war hero turned principal did not stand on his former position as general. In fact, he never appeared on campus in uniform, and only wore his medals on Remembrance Day. His office was Spartan, even shabby: the university's administrative headquarters had a large wooden desk, worn from much use, and little else except for some beaten-up yellow school chairs, threadbare Persian carpet covering a bare linoleum floor, and curtainless windows. One of the university secretaries described it as a wartime barrack room.[15] Currie was too busy to consider upgrades, as there was always a pressing financial demand somewhere on campus that he wished to attend to before addressing his own needs. But, as Stephen Leacock noted of Sir Arthur, though his office was barren, it was "accessible to all of us."[16]

Currie also seems to have mixed well with the professors. While he admitted that he did not always understand how professors functioned, he supported their right to be unique, and even at times odd. As he had during the war, Currie had a good eye for nurturing leaders and allowing the gifted to have their head. Even his critics grudgingly acknowledged this quality in him. McGill professor and respected writer Sir Andrew Macphail liked the general, but was uncomfortable seeing a non-academic lead an institution of higher learning; yet still he wrote of Currie, "In no long time he mastered every detail with a thoroughness that astonished even those who have spent a life-time within these walls. He entered into the inscrutable mind of the professor; and, more difficult of all, he discerned and dominated the mind of the student, who is equally alert for any sign of weakness, or of strength misapplied."[17]

Where Currie had achieved success in the war partially because he had been adept at delegating tasks to trusted subordinates, Principal Currie ran the McGill ship with an intrusive hand. He insisted, for example, on being involved in almost every hire at the university, often personally interviewing potential professors. Such an intense workload was too much for one man, especially in addition to his pressing duties at the Bank of Montreal, his regular involvement in the community and church, and the demands of his family.

Despite the constant pressure Currie experienced on multiple fronts, he was happy in Montreal, and his family remained ensconced at the Baumgarten residence at 3450 McTavish Street, which would later be converted into a faculty club. Sir Arthur spoke no French, and rarely even tried to work a few French words into his speeches, although this appears not to have hindered him in the city, since much of Montreal's upper crust was English-speaking. As leading members of the city's elite, the Curries were called on for all manner of social functions. Sir Arthur found such socializing to be time-consuming but enjoyable. "My days are full and there are many evenings taken up in University work," he wrote to one friend. "I have tried to do a little more than I can stand."[18] Currie worked as hard as he had done as a general on the Western Front, but the war had destroyed his health. Although he seemed to have the same powerful stamina—in that he worked long days, and with few holidays—his health was now more prone to sudden breakdowns.

Yet the fundamental question arises when comparing the principal to the general: How did General Sir Arthur Currie, the distant, uncomfortable, seemingly cold military leader change in only a few years to the approachable, thoughtful, even warm Principal Sir Arthur Currie? Currie makes no mention of this transformation in his own papers or in his personal diary. But he did leave a clue: he observed once that he could not think of his McGill students without remembering his boys in France and Flanders. He had cared for them deeply but had been placed in the agonizing position of sending many to their deaths. Perhaps what he could not do for his soldiers at the front he now sought to do for the young academics in Montreal, who could be nurtured in less fearful environments.[19]

As he worked successfully to put McGill on a more stable financial footing, Sir Arthur's own health increasingly deteriorated. The university governors pleaded with him to rest more, and Currie was forced to take longer absences from work in the early 1920s. But he always felt guilty about leaving McGill unattended, and usually returned early from his holidays and sick leaves. His wartime reputation and postwar success also brought constant calls for attendance at the unveiling of memorials, invitations to social events, and offers of other honours. By the midpoint of the decade, for instance, Currie lamented to one veteran that since the war he had been asked to write "at least fifty and probably one hundred" forewords for works of military history, and that he had sadly been forced to turn most of them down.[20] Furthermore, a steady stream of businessmen, politicians, social reformers, inventors, parents, and even patients in lunatic asylums wrote to him asking for his advice or support. He also kept up correspondence with soldiers and veterans, both in Canada and overseas. Many veterans wrote asking for assistance, a good word to get a job, or help with a difficult pension claim. Currie often went out of his way to extend a hand, and although he was not always successful, he had some influence in bettering former soldiers' lives, one at a time.

Another result of his fame was that Currie was inundated with an avalanche of invitations to give speeches, many of which he accepted. He developed a flair for connecting with his audience, often speaking without notes and always with passion and conviction. Currie's sheer size and deep voice commanded attention, and he was certainly a more comfortable speaker than he had been during the war, when he had almost always needed to have a prepared text on hand, even if he had memorized it. Now his addresses were homey and lacking in pretension, leading Sir Andrew Macphail to observe that Sir Arthur had the "gift of rhetoric."[21] He was attracted to many subjects, but not surprisingly, he often spoke of the Canadian Corps, the need to recognize the sacrifice of veterans, and the role of education in fostering a better and rejuvenated Canadian society. Currie intoned in the early 1920s, "It is for us to remember the deeds of our brave countrymen and cherish the memory of their high fight, their cheerful bearing, their proud and willing service. We would do well to take their example for our ideal and make it a vital part of our being, so that it may be transmitted to our children's children from generation to generation."[22]

Currie avoided politics. While he had been a prewar Liberal, and a useful wartime ally to Borden's Conservatives/Unionists, he found politics unrewarding, even immoral, writing at one point shortly after the war, "Why is it that so many men seem to lose their sense of right and fair dealing just as soon as they enter political life?"[23] Currie had been scarred by the attacks on his character during the 1917 conscription election, and his helplessness at responding to the politically motivated assaults had left him bitter and unwilling to engage in party politics. His return to Canada had occasioned much speculation and loose talk about his joining the Conservatives as a star candidate, but he quashed such rumours almost immediately.[24] Still, for someone of Currie's status, there was no avoiding politics entirely, and the ruling parties often consulted him on matters military or related to foreign affairs. When William Lyon Mackenzie King became prime minister in 1921, Currie was astute enough to offer his congratulations, even though he was wary of King, who had not served during the war and had always been unclear about his views regarding Canada's role overseas.[25] Despite Currie's ambivalence toward King, the prime minister was attracted to the big general. He even offered Currie the ambassadorship to the United States in 1923, no doubt because of the general's international fame but also perhaps because he wished to keep Currie out of politics, as the rumours that he was to succeed Conservative leader Arthur Meighen periodically filled the air in Ottawa.[26] Currie turned down the ambassadorship, and the next year, when the gossip about his potential to replace Meighen as Tory leader was prevalent, he noted to Victor Odlum, "Recently a great deal of pressure has been brought to bear upon me to enter political life, but I have steadfastly refused to accept the bait and will continue so to act."[27]

In 1924 an international attack was launched against Currie's reputation. As the veterans had got on with their lives, the historians had begun to grapple with writing the war. Yet since access to the official war records— the reports, orders, casualty returns, and war diaries created by formations, units, and commanders during the course of battle—was denied to academics, journalists, and even veterans for reasons of national security, it was only the official historians, appointed by their respective governments, who were tasked with writing the first authoritative accounts of the war.

In Canada, Colonel A.F. Duguid, a decorated wartime artillery officer and prewar engineer, was assigned the enormous challenge of first arranging the war records—the pages of which numbered in the tens of millions—and then trying to make sense of them to write a coherent narrative of Canada's war effort. He projected it would take eight volumes to complete the task.[28] In London, Sir James Edmonds, another distinguished soldier and a recognized military scholar, waded through the entire breadth of the war records in his multi-volume history that would eventually tell the story of the Empire, including the Dominions, at war.[29] Edmonds and Duguid had passed a few official notes back and forth in the early 1920s, but the imperial historian only rarely consulted the Canadian, who was not far along in his work.

In late 1924 Edmonds sent draft chapters of the 1915 Battle of Second Ypres to Duguid for his comments, and asked him to distribute them to senior officers for a check of their accuracy. Duguid read the chapters with growing alarm, and quickly dispatched the drafts to dozens of surviving officers. An incredulous Currie nearly wept with frustration when he read Edmonds's draft history. It was misleading, disrespectful, and mean-spirited. The imperial historian had downplayed the role of the Canadians in the battle, often making them appear consistently in need of British assistance. There was almost no allowance for the confusion that reigned at the front, the shattering effects of overwhelming enemy fire, troops, and gas, and little acknowledgment of the chaos behind the Allied lines as the high command dithered and dragged its feet in stabilizing the front where the Canadians were fighting for their lives.

Currie, who had always fought for the reputation of his troops and who was in a constant struggle to defend his own wartime reputation, believed that an officially sanctioned imperial condemnation would be devastating, and might add fuel to the still-simmering coals of Canadian discontent surrounding the memory of the war. Moreover, he saw the history as a deliberate anti-Canadian attack by the imperials, especially by professional soldiers like Edmonds. Indeed, Currie believed that

Edmonds was colluding with Snow—the official historian's hero of the battle, and whom he had served as a staff officer during the war. Currie lamented to Sir J.H. MacBrien, a former wartime infantry brigadier and now Canadian chief of the general staff, that Edmonds's final assessments were "ungenerous, unjustifiable and untrue, if not contemptibly base," adding, "I feel that his evident conclusions are founded on absolutely false premise and his mind must, to some extent, have been poisoned."[30]

The British official historian had struggled with Currie's actions during Second Ypres, and especially with his unorthodox departure from the front to gather reinforcements in the rear at around noon on April 24, 1915. Edmonds had offered a literary wink of sorts to Duguid, suggesting that he had covered up Currie's embarrassing retreat from the front. When Duguid duly passed the comment on to Currie, the general was outraged, noting, "There was nothing to cover and I certainly have never attempted to cover it at any time or any place. To suggest that it needs covering is mean and dirty."[31] Currie provided his version of events—the need to get reinforcements, as well as Snow's poor treatment of him—and Duguid turned this, along with an avalanche of criticism supplied by Canadian officers, into a May 1925 rebuttal to Edmonds that ran to fifty-three pages of errors and commentary.

The bewildered Edmonds thought the nitpicky Canadians were trying to corrupt his history, and in 1926 he wrote, "There was no limit to their lying."[32] No doubt Edmonds felt he was correct in his harsh assessment, but he had been guilty of minimizing the Canadians' role, and was far too flippant about the desperate Canadian stand at Ypres. In the end, Duguid and the surviving Canadian veterans persuaded Edmonds—by pleading and threatening, and by marshalling the official war records to back their claims—to rewrite the history and make it less offensive to them.[33]

The draft history was a stark warning to Sir Arthur, who offered this somewhat cynical observation toward the end of his life: "Soldiers fight battles, but historians make the history of them."[34] But by this, he did not mean to suggest that the soldiers—or in Currie's case, the generals—were helpless in the face of history. Currie realized that the war of reputations, which by 1926 had in one form or another lasted twice as long as the Great War itself, would require constant vigilance, resilience, and a willingness on his part to go to battle when required. In his mind, the history of the war was too important to be left in the hands of the historians.

In this new war of words, Currie was not above enlisting history in defence of his own reputation. The Canadian War Narrative Section's 1918 report of operations, which Currie had ordered to be compiled, had been one of the vehicles he had used to try to deflect Hughes's attack against him by noting the success of the Canadian Corps in destroying German formations, capturing prisoners, and liberating French and Belgian towns and territory. But the report's success in refuting Hughes was only marginal, as its distribution had been limited and the text written in the form of an operational report rather than a narrative history.

A more effective weapon in the war of the pens was the official Canadian medical history of the Great War written by Sir Andrew Macphail, a wartime veteran and celebrated writer. In the war's aftermath, most official historians aimed to be staid and reserved, and to offer only the most careful of judgments, but Macphail took the opportunity to even some old scores. He was a vehement opponent of Sir Sam Hughes and used the history to flay him. While Macphail's medical study was a potted and uneven offering, and far too rushed to be an enduring work, it was nonetheless an effective weapon against Hughes. Sir Sam was openly accused of meddling behaviour and administrative incompetence so severe that it brought the army "to the verge of disaster; and wrenched the Canadian constitution so severely that it has not yet recovered from the strain." For good measure, Macphail sniped that "the Minister in time lost the confidence of his colleagues; he never had the confidence of the army after it became an Army." As Macphail had served overseas as a medical officer, he wrote from personal experience, concluding that when Hughes resigned, the men of the CEF let out a sigh of relief and collectively felt "a sense of deliverance."[35]

Fellow official historian A.F. Duguid was deeply worried about the polemical tone of the medical history. But since Macphail owned intellectual rights to his work, the Department of National Defence could not force changes on him, and authorities in the department believed Macphail when he told them that he would publish the work independently if they did not allow the history to go forward. Duguid found a compromise in asking Macphail to send draft copies to expert readers, who included several prominent Canadian Army Medical Corps officers and Sir Arthur Currie.[36] The readers generally lauded the text, but many of the medical officers had their own scalpels to grind with Hughes since he had attacked the medical corps as incompetent.[37] Currie, of course, must have felt vindicated as he read the text, and he later endorsed it with no qualms; his only instruction was, "Publish it without altering a single word.... When published it will create a good deal of comment for he has painted the Minister of Militia in 1914 in his true light."[38] Duguid remained concerned, but was able to persuade Macphail to tone down his most vitriolic attacks against Hughes. Even then, however, the text contained many damning comments; it was clear that the official medical historian was intent on firing a heavy barrage in the war of reputations.

Sir Sam was four years in his grave when Macphail's book was published in 1925, and the former minister had few champions, but the book nonetheless drew harsh condemnation. As the *Winnipeg Free Press* observed, *The Medical Services* "produced a storm all over Canada," with many reviewers condemning the official censure of Hughes as unfair.[39] The *Toronto Daily Star* devoted the front page of its July 11, 1925, edition to the book and highlighted Macphail's attacks on the ex-minister.[40] "We fought a war to end war," continued the same paper a few weeks later, "and the few remarks of Sir Andrew have started one of their own." An unintended result of Macphail's book was also noted: "Sir Andrew has resurrected Sir Sam."[41] In a surprising twist, most papers leapt to Hughes's defence, noting his good work at the start of the war and focusing on the raising of the First Contingent. Even the *Toronto Star*, which had been an enemy of Hughes when he was minister and had rarely missed an opportunity to besmirch his actions during the war, observed that justice had not been served in this one-sided historical assault: "No doubt Sir Sam Hughes made serious blunders, but it was a time for blundering and everyone was at it, here and everywhere else."[42] In response to Macphail's history, the *Toronto Telegram* observed, "The ghost of Sir Sam stalks through his pages."[43] He also continued to stalk Sir Arthur Currie's mind. And with Hughes dead, Currie believed he would never have a chance to bury the ex-minister's allegations for good.

Sir Arthur ought to have considered writing his memoirs. Many of the British generals had followed this route in order to get their stories down on paper. In England, Sir Douglas Haig had two loyal staff officers write a semi-official history, *Sir Douglas Haig's Command*, in 1922.[44] While Haig was not the author, his fingerprints were all over the narrative, as he actively sought to bolster his reputation against emerging criticism. Haig's important work in supporting the Legion also ensured that many veterans in the 1920s looked fondly upon their old leader.[45]

Sir Arthur Currie cared deeply for his reputation and that of the Canadian Corps, but he seems to have lacked the political skills Haig demonstrated in protecting his honour with a literary shield. Currie's disinterest in writing his memoirs was also a result of his being a generation younger than Haig. Only in his late forties, Currie was not financially secure enough to stop working and devote himself solely to charities, veterans' causes, or writing. Nor did he want to. His life was far from over, and, after being appointed to the principalship at McGill, he believed he had much important work to do.

Throughout the 1920s, Currie fielded periodic inquiries from concerned citizens or editors looking to score a publishing coup, as well as from friends imploring him to get his memoirs down on paper. But Sir Arthur could not force himself to take on the task, and he noted in 1923,

I have often thought about writing Memoirs, not particularly for publication, but merely in order to set down what I know of my own knowledge concerning events, but the fact of the matter is that I have not yet had time to look through my papers. All of them are still in the boxes in which they came from France.[46]

Although Currie was undoubtedly busy with his work at McGill, more intangible forces seem to have prevented him from confronting his wartime activities in print. Was he simply a man not comfortable expressing himself in writing, or was he unable to turn his mind back in a forceful way to consider his wartime actions, the painful and the proud? Even when others offered to ghostwrite his memoirs, Currie seemed uninterested. This reticence is particularly hard to explain since Currie continued to fight to achieve recognition for the Canadian Corps. Sir Arthur would go to his grave without leaving a literary legacy, although his archival collection of personal papers, letters, and reports would provide the bare bones for future generations of historians to build on.

While Currie's support for the Corps was unwavering, his relationship with veterans was more conflicted. During the 1920s Sir Arthur was almost always greeted positively in public or at lectures by former soldiers who were proud of their commander, but he had a strained relationship with veterans' organizations in the first half of the decade. Although many veterans in the immediate postwar years were simply happy to reconnect with loved ones, the pervasive financial strain of the early 1920s was hard on all Canadians. The enormous national wartime debt that stood at over $1 billion made it nearly impossible for the government to move toward shaping a new Canada based on the returned soldiers' dreams of prosperity. Veterans' desire to shift the brotherhood of the trenches to the streets and farms across the Dominion meant that, within a few years, tens of thousands came together to form a number of organizations. As there were many groups, some in competition to attract members, the veterans spoke with no single voice, but they were increasingly militant, as they believed that the shirkers and profiteers had done well out of the conflagration, while they and their comrades had borne a disproportionately heavy burden.

Many of the veterans' groups were infused with militancy and classism, and in the largest organization, the Great War Veterans Association, senior officers like Currie and his fellow generals were not welcome. Victor Odlum wrote derisively to Currie in April 1924 that the soldiers' organizations were controlled by "batmen" (officers' servants) and low-level "ne'er-do-wells." Such organizations did not want "senior leadership" and instead looked to "exploit grievances." While Odlum and Currie both felt sure there were some "heroes" in the veterans' groups, they believed in the early 1920s that the veterans were going through a "grievance phase," and Odlum went so far as to say that he was waiting "for the disease to run its course."[47] These were harsh, if private, words about former soldiers, but many veterans remained strident, especially during a nearly decade-long battle with successive governments over a demanded $2,000 bonus for each returned soldier. Conservative and Liberal governments felt that the national debt precluded this reward, and Canadians seem to have agreed, as few publicly supported the veterans, who burned through a lot of their goodwill in the "bonus battle" that was ultimately lost.

Currie, too, did not believe in the "bonus battle," and he disassociated himself from the veterans' groups. He had an opportunity to repair this frayed relationship when Earl Haig (Sir Douglas had been raised to the peerage in 1919) wrote to him on March 30, 1925, about his upcoming visit to Canada and his desire to be reunited with "those gallant Canadians who did so much to help us to victory in the Great War."[48] Haig asked Currie to use his influence to unite a number of the disparate veterans' groups, but a bitter Currie turned down his old leader, not wishing his name to be associated with "a failure."[49] Sir Arthur felt that the veterans' organizations were ineffective, noting that their leaders simply "keep up the old shouting that the country owes a living to every returned soldier. It is always a popular cry, but makes little impression on anyone except those who feel they would be benefited."[50] This was a harsh judgment from the veterans' former corps commander, and by taking this stance he missed the opportunity to become a conciliator. Currie was a man of the establishment and he supported the establishment, so that his attitude toward the veterans was at times ungenerous, bordering on callous. This mindset did not help his reputation among some segments of the veteran population.

Neither Edmonds's all-out historical assault nor Currie's apparent lack of empathy for the veterans had permanently damaged his reputation on a national level. He was still popular among Canadians, was seen increasingly as an elder statesman, and was called upon frequently to represent veterans or attend commemorative events such as the erection of memorials across the country. Currie's papers are filled with invitations to take part in ceremonies and poppy campaigns, to give Remembrance Day addresses, and to attend veterans' reunions. He was also called upon to offer his opinion on commemorative iconography. Architect T.C. Pomphrey consulted Currie in April 1925 about which eight battles should be placed on the Toronto War Memorial Cenotaph to be erected in front of City Hall. Currie picked Ypres, Somme, Mount Sorrel, Vimy, Passchendaele, Amiens, Arras, and Cambrai. He felt that Mons was not necessary to include, as it had not been much of a battle and was only memorable as "it marked the end of the war and happened to be the place where the first battle was fought in 1914 in which British troops were engaged. We fought no particular action there and so it is not identified in any outstanding way with courage or self-sacrifice."[51] Currie was increasingly a touchstone for how Canadians would remember the war, with his reputation intimately linked to that of the Canadian Corps and its slain and surviving members.

THE MADMAN AND THE BUTCHER

During his years in Montreal, Currie was visited by national and international luminaries. His fame spread and he was eventually awarded nineteen honorary degrees for his service to Canada and the Empire.[52] He served as president of the Conference of Canadian Universities from 1925 to 1927 and was involved in several charities, including (as president) the Dominion Council of the Last Post Fund, which offered funerals for destitute veterans.[53] Throughout this period of growing fame and influence, Sir Arthur kept in touch with senior officers and his mentor, Sir Julian Byng.

Byng had come to Canada in 1921 to assume the post of governor general. Currie had pushed hard behind the scenes for his former commander's appointment, and Byng was a popular choice among the veterans. Baron Byng of Vimy, who had selected his title to denote his most important battle, remained a respected figurehead for the Canadian Corps, and hosted annual Vimy Day dinners that attracted hundreds of officers. Everywhere he went he had a special word for war veterans, but in early 1926 he was placed in a difficult situation by Liberal prime minister William Lyon Mackenzie King, in what political watchers later dubbed the "King–Byng affair."

King suffered a defeat in the 1925 federal election, receiving fewer seats than the Conservatives, but he continued to govern with the support of the Western, agrarian party, the Progressives. Scandals and indifferent leadership on the part of the Liberals eventually resulted in the Progressives pulling their support in early 1926. Unable to form a government, King went to Byng to dissolve Parliament and have him call a new election. The governor general knew that Canadians did not want another election and he believed that Arthur Meighen of the Conservatives deserved a chance to form a government, as he had won more seats in the election and seemed to have the swing vote of the Progressives.

Byng was correct to allow Meighen the chance to form the government, and the Conservative succeeded, but only for a few days before losing a crucial vote. Byng then dissolved Parliament.[54] During the subsequent election, King dragged Byng's name through the mud, accusing the monarch's representative of interfering in Canadian politics, and even of undermining responsible government. The wily King and the Liberal press smeared the governor general mercilessly, and Meighen refused to offer much of a public defence of Byng, believing that King's accusations were meaningless and fraudulent. But in accusing Byng of attempting to destroy the Canadian governmental system and of conspiring to block Canada's path toward independence through his imperious decision, King had great appeal at the grassroots level. He mercilessly tarred Byng, who, along with Currie, had done more than any other man to foster a unique Canadian spirit through the Canadian Corps. The Liberal accusations were a factor in the election outcome, although Meighen's unpopularity in Quebec, due to his role in the wartime conscription crisis, also continued to dog him. King was returned as prime minister and a wounded Byng left Canada that year. He would spend most of his remaining years as chief of police in London, before dying in 1935.

Currie was disgusted. While he once had tolerated King, he now thought the prime minister immoral, a man who had "summoned to his side all the radical, non-imperialists and anti-Empire people in our country and all those who are constantly involved against the established order of things," and declared unreservedly, "I think he is the most dangerous public man who has appeared in our country."[55] King's actions also confirmed Currie's belief in the corrupt nature of politics. The prime minister's rough handling of Byng seemed to suggest that the old soldiers who had done their duty to the Dominion and the Empire were now at the mercy of the slaggers, politicians, and detractors, and that the Canadian Corps, and what it represented to Currie and veterans like him, was in danger of being marginalized, even forgotten, by a society that was anxious to leave the war in the past. The King–Byng affair, as well as Currie's own battle against the British official historian, reinforced his belief that the soldiers would have to take ownership of the Great War and its place in Canadian society, and to fight against those who disparaged that sacred memory.

CHAPTER 15

The Ghost of Sam Hughes

1927–1928

"**I** have heard stories of our heavy casualties on Armistice Day, and how I rode into Mons like a conqueror through the dead Canadians, along the road," wrote Sir Arthur Currie to veteran S.N. Walker in November 1927. "The fact is that not a Canadian was killed on November 11th ... our records prove it." Walker accepted his former corps commander's word regarding the final day of action in the War to End All Wars, but he wrote freely that he too had been privy to rumours and stories about Currie. Walker had even heard "young children say that 'Currie was a butcher.'"[1] Repeating what they heard at home or at school, children sang ditties and spoke rhymes about Currie as if he was some sort of boogeyman. And countless others passed around rumours tainting Currie's reputation. No one knew how many Canadians believed them, but they must surely have been a minority as Currie was certainly no social pariah. He had shown that he could lead in both war and peace. One informal magazine poll in a May 1927 issue of *Maclean's*, entitled "Who is the Greatest Living Canadian?," ranked Currie sixth, ahead of the uncharismatic Prime Minister W.L.M. King, but behind Frederick

Banting; Sir Charles Saunders (who developed a robust strain of wheat); Sir Robert Borden; Borden's wartime deputy prime minister, Sir George Foster; and Jack Miner (an environmentalist).[2] Currie had not been condemned as a warmonger and banished to a crypt at defence headquarters, but neither had he been fully honoured by his nation.

Sir Arthur Currie had redeemed his reputation to a great extent by becoming a respected educator, but the allegations of his wantonly sacrificing his men during the war continued to plague him. Or was it that Currie was simply haunted by ghosts that others could not see? The sixth most popular living Canadian was unquestionably more hero than goat. All wartime leaders suffered mean and malicious assaults from their legions of detractors, and Borden, Meighen, and Laurier, to name but a few high-profile Canadians, had not escaped the war with their reputations intact among some segments of the population. Why should Currie have thought that he would do so? Was it his inexperience with fame that created such an expectation, or his misplaced belief that if he steered clear of politics and simply soldiered on, he might not be tarred by his opponents? Whatever the case, Currie found the rumours particularly galling because he was a man who attacked problems head on. Through study, hard work, and application he found solutions, as he had demonstrated on the Western Front. But in the war against rumours, he could not face the enemy squarely. How could one fight a ghost?

Then one of the ghosts materialized in the form of a newspaper editorial. The *Port Hope Evening Guide*, a small-town newspaper, offered a shocking opinion on its June 13, 1927, front page. In response to the *Globe*'s coverage of a ceremony in Mons, where Canadian officials and veterans had been honoured by the still grateful citizens of that liberated city, the owner and publisher of the *Evening Guide*, sixty-seven-year-old Frederick Wilson, encouraged political muckraker and journalist William Preston to write an opinion piece. Both men thought the Canadian coverage of Mons was far too self-congratulatory while downplaying the sacrifice in lives on the last day of the war.

Wilson and Preston remembered Sir Sam Hughes's charge in the House of Commons that not only had Currie ordered the attack for his own glory, but the poor bloody infantry—the ordinary Canadians who paid for it with their lives—had been forgotten. Moreover, Preston had his own axe to grind with Currie. At seventy-six, and with half a century of journalistic and political battles behind him, Preston had acquired the strange nickname "Hug the Machine." And as a bagman for the Liberals, he had been involved in several high-profile scandals during the previous decades, although the party had rewarded his fierce partisanship over the years with minor government patronage appointments.[3] He was a frequent target of enraged Conservatives, who missed no opportunity to vilify him because of his own legacy of unrestrained attacks on them. All political parties needed and had men like Preston working quietly in backrooms and local constituencies, but most preferred to keep them far from the seat of power until they were needed. Preston had been involved in the divisive 1917 election in the unenviable position of ensuring that overseas soldiers had the opportunity to vote Liberal. He had made little impact and over ninety percent cast their vote for the Unionists. A frustrated Preston accused the officers of the CEF of unduly influencing their men to vote for the Unionists' conscription platform, going so far as to suggest that the high command had sent known Liberals on suicide missions to reduce their numbers.[4] He tarred Currie as the leader of this alleged political assassination program and as an incompetent amateur commanding the Canadian overseas war effort, or so he suggested later, in his memoirs.[5] Deeply partisan, Preston saw Currie as an enemy.

In his 1927 editorial, Preston penned for Wilson's paper an assault that reached new levels of vitriol. It read in full,

Cable dispatches this morning give details of the unveiling of a bronze plaque at the Hotel de Ville (the City Hall) at Mons, commemorative of the capture of the city by the Canadians on November 11th, 1918. This is an event which might very properly be allowed to pass into oblivion, very much regretted rather than glorified.

It was the last day; and the last hour, and almost the last minute, when to glorify the Canadian Headquarters staff the Commander-in-Chief [Currie] conceived the mad idea that it would be a fine thing to say that the Canadians had fired the last shot in the Great War, and had captured the last German entrenchment before the bugles sounded eleven o'clock, when the armistice which had been signed by both sides would begin officially.

Canadian Headquarters sounded the advance upon the retreating Germans, unsuspecting that any mad proposal for further and unnecessary fighting was even contemplated. The men were sent on in front to charge the enemy. Headquarters, with conspicuous bravery, brought up the rear. The fighting may have been more severe than was expected. Certain it is the Germans did not take the attack lying down.

Of course the town was taken just at the last minute before the official moment of the armistice arrived. But the penalty that was paid in useless waste of human life was appalling. There are hearts in Port Hope stricken with sorrow and mourning through this worse than drunken spree by Canadian Headquarters. Veterans who had passed through the whole four years of war lie buried in Belgian cemeteries as the result of the "glories of Mons."

Headquarters Staff assembled in the centre of the town as the eleven o'clock signal sounded that the official armistice was effective from that hour. Along the route that they had carefully and with safety made their way to the centre of the town, passing the dead and dying and the wounded, victims of their madness. It was common talk among the soldiers that while the staff were congratulating themselves upon the great victory and enjoying the pride upon having "fired the last shot in the Great War," a sergeant advanced and whispered to one of the Staff that unless they withdrew immediately to a place of safety, they would not be allowed to leave the place alive, as the guns of the indignant

Canadian soldiers were already trained on them. In less time than it takes to tell the story, Headquarters got into motors and were fleeing for their lives.

It does not seem to be remembered that even Ottawa, neither by government nor Parliament, gave Sir Arthur Currie any official vote of thanks, or any special grant as an evidence of the esteem or appreciation for his services. And this is the only case of the kind in connection with any of the high commanding officers of the war. He was allowed to return to Canada unnoticed by officials of the government of Parliament and permitted to sink into comparative obscurity in a civilian position as President of McGill University. The official desire to glorify Mons, therefore, deserves more than a passing or silent notice. Canadian valour won Mons, but it was by such a shocking useless waste of human life that it is an eternal disgrace to the Headquarters that directed operations.[6]

While it is impossible to gauge the impact of editorials on the reading public, it is quite certain that this attack-piece would have sunk into obscurity had Peter Brown, the proprietor of the *Port Hope Times*, the *Evening Guide*'s competitor, not sent the offending article to Sir Arthur Currie, in the hope that he might respond. Brown aimed to stir the pot and perhaps score a publishing coup; instead, he sowed a whirlwind.

Sir Arthur must have read the article in late July 1927 with a growing sense of despair. "Waste of human life"; a "mad proposal"; "the guns of indignant Canadian soldiers" trained on him and his staff? And a particularly sore spot for Currie, the taunting reminder that "neither government nor Parliament gave Sir Arthur Currie any official vote of thanks." The bitterness he had carried for years, the inability to strike back at his tormentors, the flashes of anger he saw in the faces of returned veterans or their still grieving families—all of this had been a heavy burden. Indeed, lesser men would have been crushed by it. Currie had led one of the most impressive fighting formations on the Western Front, and his countrymen had emerged from the war with a new sense of what it meant to be Canadian. The prime minister had used the success of the Canadian Corps to demand greater political autonomy. Yet Currie's government had barely thanked him, instead shepherding him like the black sheep of the family into an impotent job in Ottawa. When Currie's mentor Byng had been torn apart by the wily King, he had been forced to watch in near silence. And now it appeared that he was next in line, as he witnessed the return of the "propaganda indulged in during the closing months of the war," brought back, he believed, by that "same gang."[7] The ghost of Sam Hughes had come rattling his chains again.

Very quickly, however, Currie shifted from despair to hardened resolve. After ten years of whispers and slander, he wrote, "I thought the time had come when, once and for all, this spreading of lies should cease."[8] Preston's article would finally allow him to confront and defeat the long-circulating rumours. Currie believed the source had been Sam and Garnet Hughes and Beaverbrook during the war, and that the same cabal was still pursuing him. This amounted to paranoia on Sir Arthur's part, as Sam was dead and the others had gone on with their lives. But perhaps Currie could be excused for such feelings since the long-standing nature of the rumours seemed to suggest that there truly had been a sustained effort by someone or some group to bring him down. Since he could never come to grips with the reality that some of his own veterans had spread the postwar rumours about him being a butcher, Currie found solace in pinning the blame on his old enemies. As he observed to one friend, the conduct of those who had supported Sam Hughes's actions was "hard to forget or to forgive."[9]

Yet Currie's plan to strike back at a small-town newspaper that specialized in writing about local softball games and lawn parties was questionable. More than a few friends thought the move unwise, and pleaded with him to ignore the article and its odious writer, Preston, who revelled in any sort of notoriety. Victor Odlum cautioned him that taking the issue to trial—which was the most extreme of Currie's options—was risky, and that "no matter what the verdict" he had "everything to lose." Odlum believed that "only a few thousand people of the lower stratum of character and intelligence [had] even heard of the gossip" against him.[10] Currie was indeed worried about a trial and its possible outcome, but as he told Walter Gow, a prominent Toronto lawyer and the former deputy minister of the overseas military forces in London, "[If] I had passed [the attack] by it would have been followed by another.... I believe the Canadian people ought to have sufficient pride in themselves to stop this particular type of scandal-mongering."[11] Sir Arthur's friends could never know how much the general had been hurt by accusations that he had recklessly led his boys to the abattoir.

Currie also felt more confident about bringing the case to trial after consulting with Canada's official historian, A.F. Duguid, whom he asked to look through the official "war records for casualty figures, wartime orders and lists of sympathetic officers," and specifically for the circumstances behind the attack on Mons.[12] Duguid informed him that the records seemed to support Currie's memory: that he had not ordered his forces to attack Mons, but was carrying out orders that originated from First Army headquarters. "For ten years now it has been said that we, for our own glorification, practically slaughtered the men in the Canadian Corps in November 11th," raged Currie to one of his former junior officers in the war,[13] noting further that, "because I have been hurt so much in the past over the repetition of these lies," they had to be stopped. And now he had both a direct opponent and the records to back up his defence.[14] By stomping on Preston and the newspaper editor who had published his article, Currie might finally be able to fully restore his reputation and put an end to the rumours that had hounded him. Sir Arthur could also finally strike back at Hughes, now in his grave six years.

Currie had set his mind on suing the *Port Hope Evening Guide*. Accusations of libel are grounded in an individual's belief that his or her reputation has been damaged by the claims of a second party. While Sir Arthur would sue for money, he hoped for a symbolic victory rather than financial restitution, and he had in any case been warned by friends that it was unlikely that a small-town newspaper with a readership of about 1,000 would be able to pay much in damages. The money did not matter; Currie wanted public vindication. In this civil action case, Currie became the plaintiff and Wilson the publisher and Preston the journalist were the defendants. Currie's lawyers knew well that the burden was on the defendants in a libel case like this, as they had to prove that every word they had written was based on the truth. It was not sufficient under the law that the defendants believed that what they wrote was true—its veracity had to be proven. As a series of lawyers told Wilson and Preston, this requirement put them at a decided disadvantage, and at the centre of a likely unwinnable case.[15] Moreover, neither man had served overseas during the war; they had access to almost no reliable histories; and the official records had been closed since the war, and could only be opened by subpoena and examined at the trial. Given these limitations, how would they prove the claims made in the editorial?

Although many signs pointed to victory, Currie was wary of having to relive the war and justify his actions. If the defendants had to prove the truth of their claims in court—such as that Mons had been a "deliberate and useless waste of life"—would this process allow them to re-examine other parts of the war? Perhaps battles such as Passchendaele and the Somme, or Currie's actions at Second Ypres? Might the Mons accusations be proven false but Currie's reputation still be damaged by vindictive lawyers or armchair strategists posing questions within the comfort of a courtroom a decade after events and with the fog of war burned clear by time? A civil case such as this included a pretrial examination for discovery, which gave each side an opportunity to question the other in order to probe for information and develop trial arguments. Currie was rightly concerned that the defendants might use this pretrial examination to embarrass him to the point of dropping the case, for fear of what unsavoury information might be revealed to the public. Moreover, could a general and university principal from Montreal receive a fair trial from a jury likely composed of clerks and farmers? These were worrisome thoughts. Therefore, through intermediaries, Currie offered the newspaper's publisher, Frederick Wilson, the opportunity to come to Montreal, hear the truth from Currie, and print a retraction. Even as Currie looked for vengeance, this outcome would be better than a no-holds-barred libel suit, which could make him vulnerable to further attacks.

Wilson visited Currie on November 5, 1927. It would not be a pleasant experience for the small-town publisher, who had a reputation as a kindly and able journalist. Being called out onto the carpet before a prepared and angry Currie was not the way he had wanted to meet the general. But Wilson believed in journalistic integrity and, it seems likely, in the veracity of the Mons story. He had never been sued before, but if he folded in the face of Currie's pressure tactics, what would this say to other journalists and newspapers—that the rich and powerful, aided by their moneyed friends, could stifle the truth through intimidation in court? For his part, Currie did not simply stand on his formidable reputation, or try to bludgeon Wilson into a *mea culpa*. He prepared maps and archival documents for Wilson to study as he walked him through the battles of the Hundred Days, the challenges facing the Corps, including the density of enemy troops and the difficult trench systems, especially at Arras and to the east of the Canal du Nord. At the end of the presentation, Currie asked Wilson what he planned to do about the article now that he had seen the evidence. The silent Wilson, who had spent most of the time listening, replied boldly, "Sir Arthur, I am going to do just what I think is right."[16]

Wilson left the meeting feeling that even if Currie was not guilty of ordering the attack on Mons for his own glorification, in the postwar remembrance ceremonies the Canadian soldier—who had done the fighting and dying—had been pushed aside, with the glory going to the senior officers. No, it was time to remind Canadians about the cost of the war.[17] He would not publish a retraction as Currie wished; he would fight the general's suit against him, his paper, and the editorial's author, Preston. Wilson steeled himself for battle.

Even before he met with Wilson, Currie had begun to prepare for the court battle. Thorough preparation was the hallmark of his "way of war," and here he was on ground of his own choosing. Wilfrid Bovey and Allan Magee, both successful lawyers who had served with Currie on his wartime staff, spent weeks collecting names and information from fellow officers who would testify on Currie's behalf. Maps were drawn, instructions and orders were gathered, and all information regarding the armistice was pulled together from Currie's own papers. Yet the best source for understanding the war was the defence archives controlled by Colonel Duguid in Ottawa. In the multitude of records were buried the casualty numbers for the last day of the war, as well as the orders and instructions from all levels of command. Currie asked Duguid for sources to support his claims that contradicted the accusations in the article, but he was particularly interested in evidence from the unit war diaries and in official records on the number of casualties suffered by all Empire forces. "They are going to try to shew [sic]," wrote Currie, "that the Canadians were used too much, that the British gave them the hardest tasks, and that our losses were unnecessarily and unfairly high."[18] Sir Arthur would have to be ready for a battle.

Canadian Corps veteran A.F. Duguid initially assisted Currie and his team with putting together their case, but the defence also requested access to the records. Duguid was unsympathetic to the newspapermen, offering them little, but the minister of national defence, Liberal James L. Ralston, was subject to political pressure to act fairly with regard to the trial.[19] Ralston was a decorated battalion commander from the war and a friend to Currie, but Liberal Party supporters urged him to back longtime party member Preston. Ralston's only solution was to walk a careful path and deny both sides access to the defence archives. Currie was disappointed that Ralston seemed to be putting politics above loyalty to the Corps, but the general had already received significant information from Duguid, and he had his own personal archives and experiences to draw upon. Having searched his records, amassed evidence, and turned his mind back to the final months of the war, Currie felt he had put together a strong case, but he spent long nights worrying that he was walking into an ambush set by the Hughes family and the dark intriguers who waited in the shadows.

If Currie was worried, for their part Preston and Wilson should have realized they had little chance of success in the case. Currie had the support of the military elite in the country and he had influential friends who the defendants rightly assumed were bankrolling the general. The McGill principal had a team of lawyers led by W.N. Tilley, widely regarded as one of the most accomplished barristers in the Dominion, who had frequently argued cases before the highest courts in Canada and England. This was indeed an example of David vs. Goliath. It would also be a high-profile event, and soon the press began to call it "Currie's $50,000 libel case," as those were the damages Currie's lawyers were seeking.

In contrast to Currie's high-powered team, the defendants had several lawyers refuse to take their case for fear of being tarred in the dirty fight that would likely transpire. After much disappointment, Wilson finally turned to Frank Regan, a forty-two-year-old lawyer from Toronto who saw an opportunity to defend the underdogs and no doubt raise his profile from the local to the national level. Regan was a card-carrying Liberal, and while he had not served in the Great War, he had been involved in patriotic work on the home front. He would lead the defence's case.

The first hurdle for Currie was the pretrial examination for discovery in early March 1928, which allowed the two parties in the lawsuit to probe each other's case through detailed questions before a judge, but without a jury. Currie took the train to Cobourg, where he and his defence team set up a "war headquarters" in the Dunham Hotel. The media, too, flocked to the small town, with newspaper editors across the country sniffing an enormous story, or willing to turn it into one. They would not be disappointed.

On March 10, Currie arrived at the stone-built Victoria Hall, which housed the courtroom. Wearing a dapper suit and a top hat, he looked very much a university administrator rather than a general. He did not, for instance, wear his chest of medals, but he was equipped with his pipe, which he smoked throughout the process. He looked older and was much thinner than during the war, but he still had enormous energy and presence. The goal of Currie's team during the examination period was to keep the defendants constrained to the narrow topic of Mons, the subject of the offending article, and not to allow the defence team's lawyer to refight the entire war in court. But these discovery questions were meant to be exactly what their name suggested—an opportunity to discover and probe the merits of the case—and so judges generally allowed much leeway in the questions.

On the first day of the pretrial, Currie stood next to a large map—multicoloured and enormous, at about 1.5 by 3 metres—illustrating the Canadian operations during the Hundred Days, and lectured on the battles with deep knowledge and conviction. Frank Regan began by probing Currie's memory of the Mons operation, primarily attacking the claim that it was ordered by his commanders and was part of normal fighting. Currie had been well coached and knew his own Corps' history intimately, and he made sure to specifically structure his answers so that they refuted the story from the *Port Hope Evening Guide*. While the campaign in the last week of the war had been costly, with the Germans giving ground but fighting hard, Currie was at pains to note that it was not he who had ordered the attack on Mons "on the last day, almost the last hour and last minute," as the editorial phrased it. It was the British high command that had ordered the advance, and the directive had gone out to dozens of divisions all along the front.

Currie had a few more surprises for the defence team. In responding to questions about the need to capture Mons, and the glory the victory had brought the corps commander, Currie answered that there really had been no specific attack on Mons. The Canadian advance was part of a wider operation that swept through the last remnants of Belgian occupied territory, and Mons had simply been on their front. While Currie was perhaps disingenuous in refusing to acknowledge the importance of Mons—especially its symbolic value—he was accurate in saying that Mons was but one of many objectives in the final days of the war, although it was clearly the most recognizable.

An increasingly frustrated Regan continued to hammer away, hoping to draw blood or at least wear the general down. Jabbing his pipe at Sir Arthur like a dagger, he tried to shake loose from him the casualty numbers for the final day—which was at the heart of the story. Currie refused to offer up the goods. When he suggested that the records revealed that not a single Canadian soldier was killed in liberating Mons, the defence snorted in disbelief. But Currie seemed correct—the limited number of records available at this stage in the trial appeared to show that no Canadians had been killed on November 11, 1918. As the questioning continued, it was clear that the blood toll was not run up during the capture of Mons, but as a result of the fighting since August 8, which had produced staggering losses. While Regan later realized this fact, and would try hard to highlight the brutal nature of the Hundred Days in the trial the following month, during the discovery process he was hamstrung by the article, which had only mentioned Mons, and was therefore forced to limit his questions to that battle and to exclude the wider campaign.

Hour after hour, Regan chipped away at the steadily tiring Currie, who was being beaten down under the relentless questioning by the lawyer. But the general's answers opened up few chinks in his armour. Over time, however, Regan sensed a weakness in Currie's defence that he was simply following orders from the British high command. He tried to force Currie to admit that he could have called off the operation, but the former corps commander would not be baited. Instead, Currie reiterated that his orders to his subordinate divisional commanders—especially to Frederick Loomis of the 3rd Division, which was in the vanguard of the fighting—were that the fighting formations at the spearhead of the force should not advance if they encountered heavy opposition. Currie did not highlight that his artillery was forbidden to level Mons, but he was correct in stating that the decisions as to how the assault was to be carried out were left to the 42nd Battalion and the Royal Canadian Regiment, the two infantry battalions that engaged the city's German defenders. Regan pressed Currie on this order, suggesting that he was lying about simply following orders from above, noting that he had some discretion regarding which objectives should be attacked and captured. Although Currie agreed that all senior commanders had some leeway in translating orders into actions, he testified that he could not have avoided Mons. "If we had not continued pressing," replied Currie in impassioned tones, "I would have violated my orders. I would have acted unsoundly from a tactical point of view. I would have been traitorous to the troops on my right and left who were going on."[20] This was surely the correct answer for a general, although Regan may have believed he had found a weakness in Currie's argument, as his assessment of the situation seemed to leave the general's actions open to some interpretation.

During the course of the long day, Regan returned feebly to the limited official records from the Department of National Defence that he had been allowed to see. The extracts from the war diaries, he triumphantly exclaimed, made note of the heavy fighting in the final days of the war. This severity of battle Currie openly conceded, but it had nothing to do with the decision to attack Mons. Regan began to flail. The local judge, L.V. O'Connor, allowed the defence lawyer much freedom in his wide-ranging inquiries, but he steadily lost his patience with the torrent of questions, few of which seemed relevant to the case. By the end of the exhausting day, Regan was not yet finished and the judge agreed to adjourn the examination until the next Friday, March 16. The week's reprieve gave the defence a chance to catch their breath and reappraise the process. All knew it was going poorly.

Newspaper publisher Frederick Wilson was visibly uncomfortable during the court proceedings, but William Preston seemed to be enjoying himself. While the two were both named in the libel suit, Wilson had put up the money for their lawyer, Regan, but the muckraking Preston reserved the right to represent himself in court. He wanted the opportunity to speak in his own defence, although he was content to let Regan do much of the heavy lifting at this early stage of the trial. Preston would strike when he saw his opening. In the meantime, he added fuel to the fire, no doubt so that the glow of controversy would light him fully for the journalists to document. He spoke at a Liberal association meeting in North Toronto on Thursday, March 15, the night before the discovery examination was to reconvene in Cobourg, remarking provocatively that he had received a flood of letters from veterans supporting his case and speaking ill of Currie, letters "which, if published today, would, I think, shock this country to its very foundations."[21] This may have been true, but he never produced the letters, nor did he call any of the veterans to the stand during the trial. It seemed that Preston, like Sir Sam Hughes before him, knew much about fighting in the war of reputations, especially when falsehood could be used to score points against one's opponents. The journalists, who smelled blood, had been angry that the judge had refused them admittance to the courtroom during the discovery period of the trial. Needing to file stories, many of them turned to innuendo, rumours, and the republishing of old charges, including Hughes's House of Commons attacks. Others were caught trying to spy on the proceedings or bribing sheriffs or others for information. The defence likely leaked favourable information too, knowing it could use the newspapers to its advantage, especially to get its message out to potential jurors. The first phase of the "Third Battle of Mons," as the trial was soon labelled, was as much about winning the war of perception in the media as it was about uncovering the truth.

The second sitting of the examination continued on the Friday, but because Currie's lawyers were late coming in from Toronto by rail, the proceedings did not begin until 9 P.M. and continued past midnight. Fewer quarrels took place between Currie and Regan this time, and

Currie mainly stood close to the map, walking those in attendance through the operations. As one journalist reported, likely spying through a window from the darkness outside, "There was little or no cross-firing between counsel, and the examination continued as quietly but with much less formality, as a class receiving instructions from a teacher on a blackboard. The tall figure of the principal of McGill University with the pedagogical horn-rimmed glasses as the instructor and Mr. Regan the pupil."[22] Such a deferential role on the part of the defence lawyer did not bode well for the defendants' chances. Regan knew this and resolved to come out swinging on the final day of examination the next morning.

The judge allowed the media into the courtroom on the Saturday. And with journalists present, Regan took the opportunity to drop a bomb. He proclaimed that the discovery questions had exposed a dastardly deed: the official war records had been doctored to cover up the reckless murder of Canadians. He thundered to an astonished crowd, "We say the records have been deliberately falsified, and we propose to bring men here to say so, men from every unit engaged at the Battle of Mons."[23] Regan promised 75 to 100 witnesses, as journalists scratched down his words at a fever pitch. A government conspiracy? An official military cover-up involving the falsification of records? What else had been revealed in the closed sessions? asked the hungry reporters. Surely the defence was continuing the case because it had found something damning against Currie? Conjecture and rumours were rife.

Currie's lawyers rightly objected to the unproven accusations. If the defence could not find records to support its fabricated newspaper article, was it not more likely that the defence was wrong or lying rather than suffering under the burden of an army-wide conspiracy? But Sir Arthur was increasingly worried. During the discovery questions, Regan had pressed him about the Battle of Passchendaele and the reasons why it had been fought. Was it not indisputably callous, he demanded, to send soldiers into that quagmire? Attacking the general's credibility, Regan also explored Currie's actions during Second Ypres, which had always been contentious but were now twisted into a failure of courage in the face of enemy pressure. During the discovery examination period, Currie was bombarded with 2,645 questions, of which 285 alone dealt with Second Ypres.[24] Moreover, Regan had clearly been informed of Currie's prewar embezzlement of regimental funds, possibly by Currie's old partner, R.A. Power, who still carried a grudge. But when he introduced the subject, Currie's lawyers acted quickly by objecting to the line of questioning. The defence countered by arguing that if this was a case about reputations, did they not have a right to examine Currie's entire wartime career? The otherwise lenient judge refused to entertain such a broad query, rightly telling the defence that it fell outside the scope of the offending newspaper article, but Currie was more than a little shaken by the revelation that his old enemies seemed to be feeding the defence information with which to ruin him. He blamed Garnet Hughes for the "smear campaign," and believed that "the threat he made to me in London when I refused to take him as GOC 1st Division is being carried out at the present time."[25]

A note handwritten by Currie during the course of the examination observed that the "enemys [sic] plan of battle" was to prove that Currie knew the armistice was coming and should have stopped the attack; that his attack on Mons was clumsy and wrong-headed; that he "was only a civilian or insurance agent soldier"; and that he was, throughout the war, "reckless of life." He was sure that the ultimate goal of Regan and his clients was to "hurt [his] reputation in every way possible" and to intimidate Currie to such an extent that he would withdraw his case.[26] But Currie had entrenched; there was no possibility of retreat now that his reputation was on the line. Moreover, if Currie had proven anything throughout his long career, it was that he was not easily intimidated. The former corps commander had also begun to see the proceedings as not only an attack against him but as an assault on the memory of the Canadian Corps. "Apparently, another battle must be fought," he noted wearily, "and, as in all battles, someone will be wounded."[27] Currie was willing to accept those wounds on behalf of his soldiers. Yet he worried that, in a courtroom, a decade removed from the conflict, his wartime decisions appeared far less difficult to others; everything looked simple on a colour-coded map showing clearly marked lines of advance and enemy positions. As Currie observed worriedly to a friend, the defence planned to "fight the whole war all over again."[28]

CHAPTER 16

Trial of the Decade

APRIL 1928

T he trial of the decade was stoking Sir Arthur Currie's paranoia. But perhaps he had every right to worry, as the defence was indeed out to get him. Currie was equally concerned that the trial that he had demanded was going too well. Despite being harassed and hounded, Currie and his lawyers knew that they had suffered no grievous blows in the examination of discovery round, and it seemed evident that the defence could not hope to win its case. But this worried Currie even more. Who was stiffening the backbone of the defence? If they could not win, why fight? Currie believed increasingly that the Hughes-led wartime cabal had been resurrected to drive a stake through his reputation. As an anxious Sir Arthur wrote to Brigadier H.M. Dyer, "I sometimes think that the whole thing is a plant. They knew I was particularly tender concerning the gossip.... It may be that the article was written in order to induce action on my part, and then having succeeded in this they propose to introduce as much irrelevant matter as possible, in order to besmirch what little reputation I may have."[1]

Currie's wartime record was going to be picked apart in the coming trial. Insinuations would be made that Currie was a failed real-estate developer and weekend warrior who had risen far beyond his abilities, and that, to keep his reputation intact with his British masters, he had sadistically and relentlessly forced his men into the mouth of the guns. Currie had sued the *Port Hope Evening Guide* to finally put an end to the rumours and speculation. Now he feared that, instead, his reputation might be damaged beyond repair as Canada's Great War was refought in a Cobourg courtroom, the outcome being decided not by armies, but by lawyers, judge, and jurors. The most influential witness at the trial would be Sir Arthur, who needed to convince the court, Canada, and now perhaps himself that he had worked in the best interest of his men and that the original charges brought by Sir Sam Hughes had been lies.

Justice Hugh Rose was assigned to Currie's case in the spring of 1928. The judge for the examination phase of the trial had been generous in allowing the defence to ask Currie hundreds of questions that were outside the scope of the trial, but Rose—who had been called to the bar in 1894 and had been a judge for over a decade—would prove to be more strict in keeping Regan and the defence restricted to the content of the offending article. Although Rose was respected among lawyers for his patience in his courtroom, he was virtually unknown to the public. He wanted to remain that way and was not seeking to use the high-profile trial to further his own career. Rose refused to grant interviews despite multiple requests by journalists, remarking at one point, "I don't believe in publicity and that sort of stuff."[2]

Rose may not have believed in publicity, but there was no escaping it for anyone involved in the trial. Journalists from across the country flocked to Cobourg for the start of the trial on the cool and sunny Monday, April 16, 1928. The upper floor of the courthouse was equipped with telegraph equipment, which reporters could use to wire their stories to eagerly awaiting editors throughout the Dominion and the Empire. The snow had melted during the unusually warm weather, and the courtoom at Victoria Hall—an architectural marvel that had been standing proudly for over sixty years, with a courtroom modelled after the Old Bailey in London—would be unbearably hot over the coming two weeks. The room was filled to capacity with the legal teams and a horde of journalists, veterans, and the curious. The seats went quickly and there was always a throng of disappointed would-be spectators each morning, as the sheriff's men turned away the overflow.

On the first day of the trial, Sir Arthur arrived wearing a dark blue suit and sat with his team of lawyers. Preston, Wilson, and the lawyer, Regan, seemed an old and under-equipped team, an image that was perhaps cultivated to visually enforce the idea of an underdog local newspaper facing the corporate might of famous and rich out-of-towners. The two sides would face off in the largest courtroom in the hall, with panelled walls, a mahogany ceiling, and an enormous coat of arms behind the bench. The case of *Currie v. Preston and Wilson* was called at 2:30 P.M.

Currie's lawyer, W.N. Tilley, opened the trial by addressing the jury of twelve and reading the offending article aloud and in full. The case, as he presented it, was about Wilson and Preston's grossly unfair and libellous statements. Tilley instructed the jurors that in a libel trial it fell to the defendants to prove their allegations—in this case, primarily that Currie had ordered the attack on Mons in a callous manner and with disregard for the lives of his soldiers. Without revealing too much more, Tilley reminded the court that the Canadians did not fight as an independent force during the war and that Currie was simply following orders on the day in question. Tilley did not have to go much further, as the burden of proof was on the defendants, and he closed his opening statement after less than two hours.

Regan had probably assumed that Currie's team would take the full day to argue their case, but he was not unprepared. He started by grandstanding for the jurors: in one of his first statements, he moved for a nonsuit, arguing that the plaintiffs had failed to establish that the article in question was about Sir Arthur Currie, even though the general had been named in the piece. Judge Rose would have none of this and instructed Regan to proceed with his case. Regan showed little surprise or disappointment when his theatrics failed, and began to call a series of witnesses.

Although Regan had crowed to journalists a few weeks earlier that he would produce 100 veterans to testify against Currie, his witness list contained far fewer. Yet there were some veterans willing to speak for the defence, and their words carried the power of those who had seen and served. The first was Harold Fox, a signaller in the 21st Battalion who had been wounded during the Amiens battle but had rejoined his unit a few days before the end of the war. The jurors and audience waited anxiously for his testimony, as here was a combat veteran who might offer the first nails with which to crucify the corps commander. Fox described the 21st Battalion's advance in the direction of Mons on November 10, during which a private was killed and several others were wounded. He also testified that, upon entering Mons on the 11th, he saw a handful of slain Canadians.[3] Regan prodded Fox, noting triumphantly that Currie had testified in the discovery period that he knew of no Canadians killed on the last day of the war. While Fox would not call his former commander a liar, as Regan seemed to hope, he noted that if the soldiers had been killed on the 10th, they would not have remained lying around by the side of the road a day later.

Regan continued to chip away at Currie's case, hoping that perhaps through the testimony of soldiers—most of whom were sympathetic figures to the jury, and certainly to the reporters, who gave them prominent coverage in their stories—he might dredge up the truth that, as he saw it, was buried behind an official conspiracy of silence and cover-up. One of Regan's tactics was to call veterans who could offer only hearsay evidence—stories heard through the rumour mill about severe casualties on the 11th—and to hope that the jury took their testimony under consideration even when the exasperated judge ruled it inadmissible. But a few of the defence's witnesses worked against its own case—such as William Teddiman, a sergeant in the 52nd Battalion, who testified candidly that although on the morning of the 11th there was news of the armistice coming into effect at 11 A.M., he and his comrades took little notice of it since they had heard that same rumour nearly daily for years. This was a common statement, made by several of the veterans, and while Regan did his best to downplay the soldiers' belief in the inaccuracy of rumours, the jury could not help but notice the trend in the testimony: while the cessation of hostilities seemed imminent in early November, no one—not even the fighting men at the front—believed that the war might soon come to an end.[4] This perspective mattered, of course, since the newspaper article accused Currie of deliberately ordering the attack to capture Mons just before the armistice came into effect.

From the start of the case, Regan was determined to refute Currie's previous claim that no soldiers had been killed on November 11. Veterans' testimony revealed that several Canadian corpses had been seen in Mons, which seemed to contravene earlier public statements by the Historical Section and Currie. While there was no way to prove that the slain soldiers had actually died in Mons (instead of on the outskirts), the admission of the presence of bodies seemed a minor victory for the defence, and may have shaken some of Currie's confidence in his claims that very little fighting had occurred in the liberation of Mons. But a few dead soldiers did not prove that Currie was a heartless butcher who had sent legions to the gallows.

Over the course of the second day of the trial, Regan used his veterans again, this time to try to confirm Currie's unpopularity among his soldiers. Yet every time he tried to prod a veteran into offering his opinion, Currie's lawyers rightly objected that the man's statement was simply hearsay or that it fell outside of the parameters of the libel case, since the offending article in question was about Mons and not what soldiers at the front had thought of Currie. The judge had some sympathy for Regan and the defendants, especially for Regan's contention that a case about a damaged reputation demanded some investigation into Currie's entire wartime career. Currie eventually told Tilley to drop the objections, either not worrying about the state of his reputation among his men or not wanting to appear that he worried. And so, later in the day, Regan asked witness Albert Mason about how Currie was regarded among the rank and file. After some deliberation, Mason replied carefully that "reputation or popularity may be different." Indeed they were, but when pressed by Regan, Mason testified, "He was not as popular as the others." This comment Currie's lawyers objected to, rightly querying who the "others" were and how any accurate comparison could be made, but Regan ran with the statement, theatrically pondering Mason's response: "He may be a very skilful commander, and at the same time he may be a man, as we say, who would order his men into battle up until one of them was killed at 3 minutes before 11 o'clock. That is two different things—head and heart, and if I may put it in a blunt way … I am dealing with his humanity, how he felt towards the private soldier."[5] Here, Regan clearly showed that he intended to reveal Currie's callous nature (his lack of humanity) not by questioning his tactical wisdom—although he would chip away at this well-remarked quality in the general—but by hammering him over his seemingly reckless, self-interested actions in the final days of an already long and bloody war.

One of Regan's challenges in pressing home his defence was that while several veterans testified under oath that they felt that Currie should not have pushed the Corps to capture Mons on the last day of battle, they generally did so hesitantly, and for the most part seemed to be uncomfortable second-guessing their commander's wartime conduct. Regan had a difficult time understanding why the veterans of the battlefield would not take the opportunity to strike back at a commander who had seemingly stepped over the corpses of their comrades as he advanced into victory, and history. Yet the lawyer, safe in a courtroom, could not hope to understand the loyalty that many veterans had to the Corps and to Currie, or the understanding on the part of many of the old soldiers, even the embittered ones, of the hard decisions that Currie had confronted every day of the war. Of course it was mad to send Canadian troops into Mons when German machine guns were firing 500 bullets a minute to guard against the advance. It must have seemed mad in 1918, too, but for soldiers who carried out such orders, and did so day after day, it was what was expected of them.

Regan was doubly disappointed to find that the official war records— crates of which had been brought to Cobourg—showed that few Canadian soldiers had been killed in the last days of the war, and none on November 11. Although Regan had seen some of the records during the discovery phase, he had hoped that these newly arrived documents would refute Currie's claim of low casualty levels. Having now read through many of the relevant records, he was frustrated that they did not match the witnesses' accounts of dead Canadian soldiers being seen in Mons.[6] This was a potentially fatal blow to the defence's case.

But a desperate Regan had already tipped his hand in the examination period, regarding how he planned to sidestep the issue of archival records. Now he played it. On the fourth day of the trial, he stunned the court by accusing the Department of National Defence in perpetrating a cover-up. "We say that these records which deal with the publication of the casualties to the world were deliberately falsified for the purpose of keeping from the world the knowledge of the loss of life."[7] This tampering had been carried out under the orders of Currie, or at least with his collusion, Regan charged. This was a bold statement to make, and all the more so given that he had no evidence. But Regan clung to his story, questioning how the records could indicate that no Canadians had been killed on the 11th while veterans had testified to having seen Canadian corpses both in Mons and on the outskirts of the city.

Before Currie's lawyers could object to the outlandish accusation, the judge intervened and ordered Regan to offer some proof or withdraw his statement. A stuttering and backpedalling Regan knew he could do neither without damaging his case, and Currie's lawyers, not displeased that Regan had taken a long piece of rope and put it around his neck, were willing to see if he would tighten the noose. With false innocence, Tilley also declared his desire to know if the records were falsified, avowing that Currie would not stand for this—if it were true. Duguid and other veterans were also quick to offer evidence of the absurdity of Regan's claims, pointing out that any conspiracy would have involved hundreds of soldiers in multiple headquarters falsifying the records without leaving any trace; it was also incredible that there would have been no leaks about the conspiracy for over a decade. Regan retreated awkwardly from his position, feebly withdrawing the statement after suffering further humiliations at the hands of the judge, who noted that the article didn't refer to such problems with the records, and so he had best stay on message. Further cross-examination of key defence witnesses by Tilley scored additional points for Currie's team, as Duguid and Judge Advocate-General Reginald Orde admitted to providing Currie with some erroneous information that no soldiers had been killed on November 11. The two men were not simply falling on their swords for the ex–corps commander; the records were voluminous, numbering in the hundreds of thousands of pages for this part of the war alone, and it was easy to overlook specific casualty figures. The war's historian determined that a closer examination of the records raised the number of dead from zero to one, and that this one soldier was killed to the north of Mons. Having been suitably chastised by the judge, and then flayed by Tilley, Regan could only whine again about the difficulty the defence had experienced in accessing and evaluating the war records.

On Saturday, a week after the case had begun, Regan called Wilson to the stand. The strain of the trial had noticeably aged the newspaper editor. He appeared exhausted and spoke with a barely audible voice. Regan hoped to strengthen his case by asking about the origins of the offending article. And although the judge had previously disallowed the inclusion of Hughes's 1919 House of Commons attack on Currie, Regan hoped to work it in here, as the attack had shaped Wilson's opinion of Currie, something he testified to in response to the discovery questions. While Tilley objected strenuously to the backdoor introduction of Hughes's damaging words, the judge eventually relented and allowed them to be entered in as evidence, as he considered them relevant in assessing Wilson's state of mind and his belief that Currie was responsible for the terrible wartime casualties. In response to further leading questions, Wilson testified that he asked Preston to write the article because he "wanted to see the privates get their share of taking Mons, that is, the glory."[8] Given all the rumours about the senseless slaughter, declared Wilson, he also felt it was safe, and perhaps time, to settle the issue. Although Wilson added little to the case, his quiet defiance, his noticeably ill health, and his refusal to fold in the face of Currie's pressure may have swayed the jury from his own community to look upon him with sympathy, even admiration.

"Mons Captured in Three Days, Legal Battle Enters Second Week," ran the cheeky headline in the *Toronto Telegram* on April 24, 1928.[9] The trial had dragged on longer than most had expected due to Regan's detailed questioning and his relentless attempts to bring hearsay evidence into the trial. At one point, he employed the dubious tactic of reading into the record the entire examination of discovery transcript, a task that took mind-numbing hours to complete. Regan had argued non-stop for nearly two weeks, but in the end he rested his case without delivering the knockout punch. However, he would still have the opportunity to try to tarnish Currie's integrity and reputation during his cross-examination of the general's supporting witnesses.

The veterans testifying for the defence had made an impact on the court with their wartime eyewitness accounts, and Currie's lawyer, W.N. Tilley, now hoped to reverse the effect of their commentary by calling in his own sympathetic soldiers. The prosecution's veterans had been hand-picked to provide support for the general. They offered positive remarks about Currie and tough rejoinders to Regan, often ridiculing his questions or being insolent to the point that the judge was forced to intervene. Regan was undeterred, however, and returned consistently to his main message about Currie's callousness. He picked strange, but perhaps understandably blatant, examples to underscore the prevalent image of the general as blimpish and out of touch with his men. Regan had already established during the discovery period that on the morning of the 11th, when the message of the pending armistice came in from First Army headquarters around 6:45 A.M., Currie had been taking a bath at his headquarters at Valenciennes about 30 kilometres from Mons. And during the trial, the defence again made much of Currie's having been bathing while his own soldiers were still fighting and dying for Mons, invoking images of a lazy and slightly comical general.

Regan also used his cross-examination to try to minimize the impact of Currie's witnesses who spoke of the relatively light fighting on the 11th. The testimony of Sergeant Major James Page of the 42nd Battalion was particularly damning for Regan's defence. The *Port Hope Evening Guide* had claimed that the rank and file had been on the brink of turning their rifles on Currie and his staff when they entered Mons, and that they had been forced to make a hasty retreat from the liberated city lest they be executed by their own men. Page testified that although his unit had fought its way into Mons, he and his men had been ordered to parade for Currie after the battle. "We gave three cheers for General Currie in the usual manner, which was generally done on all parades, and we gave it with good heart."[10] Here was evidence that contradicted the claim that Currie's own men were seconds away from assassinating their commander. Other veterans testified that the attack on Mons was not nearly as violent or costly as the set-piece battle ten days earlier against Valenciennes. When Regan pressed Eric Findley, a company commander in the 42nd Battalion, about the special place of Mons in the annals of the BEF, Findley recounted that all of his men had known of its importance as they prepared to attack, but that for them it was simply another objective:

"Mons was in the path of the ground that we wanted to occupy."[11] All of this testimony countered Regan's argument that the attack on Mons had been maliciously ordered, haphazardly planned, and particularly brutal.

An exasperated Regan, sensing the tide turning against him, rashly accused several of the veterans of collaborating with Currie's team to get their stories right—of being coached by the general in what he denigrated as the "War College." The witnesses hotly refuted the accusation to a man, and Regan's only evidence to support his claim was that most of the officers were staying at the same hotel. As his temper frayed, Regan addressed some veterans with open hostility. They, in turn, did not hide their disdain for the lawyer. In the crowd, the veterans hooted with derision, clapped loudly, snickered asides, and stamped their feet in approval. And when they took the stand, testy exchanges raged back and forth between them and Regan, with the judge at times seemingly helpless to do little but intervene and ask for more cordiality from both lawyer and witness. When Royal Ewing, former commanding officer of the 42nd Battalion, was in the witness box and offering evidence in support of Currie's case—specifically, that no one expected the war to end on November 11—Regan tried to pry out of him an admission that it might have been better if the Canadians had remained where they were on that final day instead of advancing. Ewing retorted quickly, "You mean if we hadn't gone to France at all?"[12] The crowd in the courtroom roared with laughter, but the remark bit deep, as more than a few of the veterans had sneered at Regan's decision to avoid military service during the war.

Regan also badly misjudged the situation with regard to Milton Gregg from the Royal Canadian Regiment, a much revered war hero. Regan was unaware that Gregg had been awarded the Victoria Cross, and after a quarrelsome series of exchanges, he could not understand why the emotional temperature seemed to be dropping in the courtroom. Soon, the audience turned against him, at times even booing him for his line of questioning. Only after Gregg left the stand was a note passed to Regan informing him that he had been shabbily treating a Victoria Cross winner. Offering an immediate apology did little to relieve the lawyer's embarrassment, and the incident further revealed that the defence was at an extreme disadvantage. As they were trying to argue a case without having the intimate knowledge of events, they were often unable to ask the right questions or find evidence to support their own suppositions.

In the end, Currie's witnesses—his former comrades—fully endorsed him. With their high levels of confidence, education, and comfort with public speaking, they were a formidable body. And they believed in the cause. As General J.H. MacBrien, the former chief of the general staff, testified in one hostile exchange with Regan, Currie would have the soldiers' loyalty and support, as he was "fighting the battle for us again in peace, as he had done in war."[13]

Despite the limitations imposed on the defence, which restricted their understanding of the intricacies of the warfighting on the Western Front and their access to the official records, Regan had proven himself an adept lawyer, relying on flourish and hard-hitting questions as he stretched the limits of what was acceptable in a libel case in order to make up for a lack of evidence. The defence team had scored some minor victories, not only in bringing to light that it seemed that more than one Canadian had been killed on the last day of the war—according to witnesses who testified to seeing several Canadians slain in parts of the city—but also, perhaps more importantly, in taking a step toward tearing down Currie's reputation. Regan's snide remarks and insinuations about Currie's extravagant behaviour of keeping three aides-de-camp instead of the single aide who normally supported a corps commander, and even the bizarre line of questioning about his bathing habits, had together probably scored a few points, although one could never be sure with a jury.

Currie's lawyers had probably done more than enough to refute almost all of the points raised in the newspaper article. But victory could only be ensured by having Currie take the witness stand, for the general not to speak in his own defence would surely have been viewed as a sign of weakness. And in any case, Currie did not wish to avoid the stand, as the main goal of having the trial was to clear his name and to finally refute the decade-old charges made against him. He now had an audience and countless journalists who were ready to listen. He was ready, even eager, to fight his last battle of the Great War.

On the eleventh day of the trial, Currie took his place in the witness box. The courtroom was packed, as the sheriffs seemed to have let even more spectators into the room. Currie looked calm in his civilian attire and heavy glasses, and he wore none of the trappings that would distinguish him as a general. Tilley and his team had no doubt advised Currie of the need to watch out for Regan's ploys, and to stay above the fray in order to keep the jury onside. Currie knew the importance of presenting such a calm veneer, although he too must have worried about what pools of grievance lay within him, long festering as he had endured wave after wave of attacks against his character. The tension that had been building throughout the trial assumed potentially explosive proportions. Indeed, one of Currie's lawyers was later to write that he could feel on that day "the violent events of history swirling about [the] Cobourg courtroom."[14]

Tilley's examination of his client was brief. He reminded the courtroom that Currie's orders to capture Mons had indeed come from First Army headquarters, and that since the Canadian Corps fought as part of the BEF, its commander could not question orders, even in the final days of the war. After a mere forty minutes, Tilley rested his case. A startled Regan had expected a lengthier period of questions and answers from Currie's team, perhaps a day or two, which would have allowed the general to bring his knowledge and commanding personality to bear on the courtroom. But the defence lawyer was nonetheless ready. The only way for his clients to win this case was by his destroying Currie's reputation. He set out to do it.

Regan began his cross-examination by using Tilley's short question period as a cudgel against Currie, suggesting that there was more to the story of Mons than the general's lawyers had covered in forty minutes, and that he was perhaps giving too little consideration to the seriousness of the case by refusing to share his experiences with the court. On his back foot from the start, Currie defended his lawyer, noting that much had already been presented during the course of the trial, although he admitted that Regan was right in arguing that perhaps the jury would have liked to have heard more from him.

A smug Regan almost immediately switched subjects, drawing Currie's attention to an interview he had given to the *Star Weekly* on November 5, 1927, right after he had decided to sue the Port Hope newspaper. Regan portrayed the interview to the jury as a clear attempt to influence public opinion about the case, but he also cleverly used Currie's own words to pervert the once-heroic narrative of the Cambrai attack. Focusing on General Horne's uncertainty about Currie's daring plan to cross the Canal du Nord, Regan tried to paint Currie as a recklessly dangerous general, and one who acted contrary to his army commander's better judgment. This was a mean-spirited twisting of events, especially since Currie's bold operation had succeeded, but Regan argued that the incident supported the thesis that Currie had a tendency to gamble—and not well—with his soldiers' lives.

Regan also argued that while the last set-piece battle of the war was on November 1, 1918, at Valenciennes—where the Canadians had unleashed an unprecedented weight of shells in their prebattle bombardment—the Mons operation, in contrast, seemed a half-hearted attack, with no barrage. This lack of protective firepower, Regan insinuated, revealed Currie's heartless desire to capture the city before the armistice came into effect, regardless of the cost. Currie would not be tricked by Regan's selective interpretation of events, and he held fast to what he believed, declaring that the Corps "was not going to let them [the Germans] get away from us."[15] He described the thinking at the time: if the armistice was, as many believed, only a ruse on the part of the Germans for a much-needed pause in order to prepare another series of trenches to the east of Mons, or if it remained the temporary respite it was meant to be, then the Canadians would have to attack Mons and other positions at some point in the future, at the cost of more lives since the enemy would have used that time to dig in and fortify. But Regan refused the argument, badgering Currie to admit that he had known the war would soon be over, especially after the Valenciennes battle. Currie did no such thing.

Regan could find no opening, so he exploited Sir Arthur's weakness: the rumour campaign against him. Using the 1927 *Star Weekly* interview extensively, Regan quoted Currie's words back to him, focusing on the general's description of the rumours as "some foolish talk about my ordering an attack on Mons after the armistice came."[16] But the rumours were more than that, of course. Currie was forced to admit on the witness stand that they were not just idle chatter, but that they had been swirling for ten years. This comment Regan seized upon, suggesting that if the rumours had had legs to last ten years, surely Wilson and Preston had a right, even a journalistic duty, to write about this event that had become common knowledge. Moreover, Currie had done well since the war, Regan argued, having been rewarded by the nation and given the prestigious principalship of McGill. It was absurd to suggest that his reputation had suffered because of the rumours; and if it had, how could this article of less than 600 words, published in a paper read by about the same number of people, have further damaged Currie's reputation? This line of questioning seemed to catch Currie no matter which direction he turned: either the rumours were insignificant and Currie therefore had no legitimate reason to sue the newspaper, or the rumours had been around for ten years and therefore it was unfair to sue the newspaper for simply repeating what was commonly known and discussed. Yet Currie responded with passion, telling the courtroom that he had pursued Wilson and Preston because they were the first to put the rumours into print, and to therefore place themselves in a position to be called out for libel. However, the nuances of the law may not have resonated with the jurors, and certainly Regan sensed a weakness here, among Currie's otherwise strong rebuttals.

Regan returned to chiselling away at Currie's reputation, suggesting that he had not been honest about the number of casualties on the last day—having, during the course of the trial, modified the total from zero to a single Canadian. Currie refused to acknowledge that there were more, rightly noting that any evidence presented to the contrary was hearsay and that the official records supported his claim. Again, Regan was foiled and remained unable to apply pressure to Currie in a way that would confirm the newspaper story's claim of a senseless mass slaughter at Mons.

A frustrated Regan decided again to go after Currie's bathing habits, noting that while his soldiers were fighting and dying on the front lines, Currie didn't let the news of the armistice "interfere with [his] ablutions."[17] This image of Sir Arthur as a château general was damning, even if it had nothing to do with the case. Currie was angry about Regan poking fun at his baths, and lashed back passionately that Regan did not understand the feeling of the soldiers, speaking as he did a decade later and from the dislocated confines of a courtroom. Currie spoke movingly about how none of the soldiers cheered upon hearing of the armistice, for "the feeling was too deep." It took "days before you appreciated that this thing had ended."[18] Regan left this comment alone, not knowing how to respond without denigrating the men, but he did return to the matter of the casualties. Noting that the general had every right to take pride in the Canadian Corps' accomplishments, he asked, with feigned innocence, why on the day of the Mons battle he was not "satisfied with the fact that there had been in the Canadian Corps 215,542 casualties," and why he had apparently been willing to increase this number.

Currie angrily denounced the implication that he had intentionally driven his men into the mouth of the guns, but Regan coyly read from the *Star Weekly* interview, in which Currie had said, "God, I'd like to see them at the Boche again." "General," Regan shouted, as he set up his knockout blow, "Look at me and tell me what you meant by it—'God, I'd like to see them at the Boche again'—with a quarter of a million casualties, approximately, in your Corps. Weren't you satisfied they had done enough fighting?"[19]

"Absolutely satisfied," retorted an angry Currie, "and I know a great deal more about casualties, Mr. Regan, than do you.... Yes, I lived through the months of war there, I saw those magnificent battalions go into battle and come out badly decimated, and I have feelings about it that you can never appreciate." Regan came back at Currie relentlessly, returning to the heavy fighting of the Hundred Days, in which the Canadian Corps had defeated forty-seven enemy divisions. "Don't you think, Sir Arthur, that in the dying days of the war you might have spared your men a trifle more than you did?"

"No," thundered Currie. And he turned the tables on Regan. "You are the man," he raged, "that is suggesting that those men who did that should lie down and quit within two days of the final victory." A backpedalling Regan defended himself: "I didn't say that." "Oh yes," charged Currie, "you say spare them, you say quit."

Regan had gone too far and Currie pressed his advantage. His voice rose, emotion-laden yet powerful: "No, no, you would have them disobey an order, you would have them be guilty of treason, disregard the instructions of the Commander in Chief, disregard the instruction of Marshal Foch, and act in an unsoldierly way, right at the very last. Those were not the men who did that sort of thing."[20]

Silence.

Then the courtroom exploded into a cacophony of applause and cheering.[21] All knew that Regan had lost. Although he continued to snipe at Currie, the tension between the two men leaked away, as it was obvious that the defence lawyer would be unable to prove that Currie had knowingly sent his men to their death.

But perhaps the defence still had a puncher's chance. The crusty William Preston, the author of the article, had been waiting for his opportunity to cross-examine Currie. Preston had chosen to represent himself because he wanted the opportunity to personally cross swords with Currie. He had been silent for almost the entire two weeks, taking notes, and now he was sure he had Currie where he wanted him.

Preston started his examination by musing about Currie's prewar militia days. An increasingly anxious Currie knew that this could only be going in the direction of revealing the embezzlement, a subject that, to date, had been suppressed each time the defence had tried to raise it. Tilley jumped in as Preston began his probing assault, and the tired judge agreed that the questions had to be focused on Mons. Preston dropped the issue, perhaps having raised it only to unnerve Currie.

The journalist then took up another subject that was painful for Currie: the rumour campaign. And he did so in a level, measured, and professional interrogation that lasted for most of six hours. Currie, on the other hand, had been pushed to the brink by Regan's questions, and was now clearly out of sorts. His face was flushed, his voice rose, and his answers had an identifiable tone of indignation. Preston rattled the bones of Sir Sam Hughes by resurrecting the ex-minister's House of Commons accusation, and Currie had to suffer through hearing those damning words yet again. A weary Tilley challenged the relevance of this material, but Preston was ready: "If these speeches have come to the attention of the plaintiff for years, and there has been no reply by him to them, no attempt or effort on his part to prove their falsity," why was he now attacking a small-town newspaper, and himself as author of the article?[22] The judge thought about it and let Preston continue with the line of questioning. Sam Hughes walked again.

Currie replied that until now he had had no method of refuting the rumours, but one wonders if the jury believed that one of Canada's best-known figures, who had engaged in cross-country lecture tours and had friends in high places, could not have found a way to address the injustices against him. Currie was hamstrung in that he had never publicly shared his own incapacitating postwar trauma, and especially the war-haunted dreams that returned him to the battlefield night after night, and didn't wish to do so now. Instead, he offered a more genuine comment: "I had come back to my own country after four years of war, and I did not think that I should be called upon to defend every charge that anybody made against me.... I felt too hurt to enter into any conflict of the kind at that time. I did not think the thing would be believed, but apparently it has for ten years."[23] Preston did not believe the general, noting incredulously, "And you preferred to remain under a cloud of that kind rather than defend yourself?" In response, Currie noted again, his voice rising in anger, that there was no way to "contradict rumour."[24]

Preston next turned to the matter of his own article.[25] Here, he lied openly. He told the court that the article had been reprinted in the *Ottawa Citizen*, a paper with a much larger circulation than the *Port Hope Evening Guide*. So why, he asked, turning to the jurors, had Currie made the decision to harass a small-town paper instead of suing the larger paper, which was defended by a legion of lawyers? Currie had no effective answer to this question, as the *Citizen* had not in fact reprinted Preston's article, and had featured only a few excerpts of it to show that Preston was a scoundrel who deserved to be sued for his libellous remarks![26] Sir Arthur might have destroyed Preston's credibility here if he had revealed the defence's twisting of events, but under the strain of the hours of cross-examination he failed to refute the fabricated claim. Through bluff, bravado, and deception, Preston seemed to have scored points. Currie's team of lawyers must have worried that the jury had been persuaded about Currie's strategy of avoiding the powerful *Citizen* in favour of destroying the hometown paper and its long-time diligent owner.

The defence began its final arguments on Monday, April 30. The trial had now entered its third week and almost every paper in the country featured it as front-page news. In Cobourg, there had been long lineups to get into the courtroom, and some onlookers had been in their seats for over four hours before the lawyers began the proceedings at 1:30 in the afternoon. "Spectators crawled every inch of space," wrote one journalist, and those who could find no seat jostled in the main lobby for the best standing-room view.[27]

Regan's defence, and perhaps his career, hinged on his closing arguments. He had made himself unpopular with his attacks against veteran witnesses and Currie, and if he failed to close the case, his own reputation might be irrevocably ruined. Success, on the other hand, might vindicate his use of severe methods. It was clear from the evidence presented that the defence could not win the case under the existing libel laws. Regan had not proven every point that had been made in the article—perhaps not even a single point—and so he had been forced to expand his argument to encompass a broader context: the attack on Mons as well as the operations that preceded it. Since the judge was often frustrated by Regan's searching questions—and eventually ruled out of order an astonishing 861 of the queries—no one was sure how many of those off-topic, yet still damaging remarks had lodged with the jury.[28]

Having played loose and fast with the parameters of the case, Regan now had only a few hours in which to hammer Currie again. He impressed upon the jury his conviction that the general before them may or may not have been guilty at Mons, but he was certainly guilty of recklessness during the course of the war. And even on that fateful day, Regan argued, although Currie may not have given the orders to capture Mons, it was well within the general's power to have issued modified orders to prevent the needless sacrifice of his men. Regan was repeating much of what he had tried unsuccessfully to establish during the trial, and he still clung to the viability of alternative ideas, such as going around Mons, even though many veterans had mocked him for his armchair tactics. He also returned to his now discredited claim about the doctored records, suggesting again that the casualties on the 11th had been backdated to the 9th or 10th to assuage the general's guilt. Regan argued that seventy-three Canadians were killed in the taking of Mons, an absurd number he came up with by adding up all the bodies observed by multiple witnesses.[29] The fictional statistic failed to account for the possibility of different men seeing the same bodies, or of the bodies being left behind from the previous day's battle.

These were the facts, as Regan saw them, but what about the emotions involved, he asked? What about the parents and widows and orphans who had been denied a lifetime with their loved ones? Did Currie not have to answer to them? Whether the count was seventy-three dead or fewer, wasn't it incumbent upon the corps commander to call off the operation if he knew that the Germans were soon to give up? At the very least, surely Wilson and the Cobourg paper had a right to raise these questions. "All that old man Wilson—brave man that he is—asked for is that these brave men be given their share of the glory of Mons." His voice rising dramatically, Regan reminded the room that it was time to remember the privates and NCOs who had died in the name of taking Mons and raising the reputation of their general. The officers had received recognition and gallantry awards while the privates had been cast aside. "Glory for the officers, but graves for the men," he growled. He then addressed Currie's suit.

"Does Currie deserve $50,000?" No, give him nothing, implored Regan, as he wound down his case with a flourish. "We have tried to do our duty to the living. We have tried to do our duty to the dead." It was a moving end to a powerful speech that reduced many of the pro-Currie crowd to silence. Weeping could be heard from a group of women, and an elderly man collapsed in sobs—perhaps the father of a soldier killed in the war.

Preston was the next to sum up his case, and he came out swinging. He had no regrets about what he had written. He had heard nothing in the trial to convince him of Currie's innocence in ordering the attack on Mons. Moreover, while he had believed what he had written to be true, he had based it on Sir Sam Hughes's far more public attack on the general—an attack, he emphasized, that Currie had chosen not to respond to for over a decade. For the former corps commander and current principal of McGill to raise the issue at this time, and with a small-town paper, revealed some hidden defect in Currie, insinuated Preston. What if there had been no article? Would Currie have gone to his grave forever haunted by the ghost of Sir Sam? Was not this war of reputations actually Currie's fault since he had not dealt with the accusations when they were first made? "Give a lie 24 hours start and the bells of eternity will ring before you catch up with it. Give it ten years and where are you?"

Preston scored some points with these arguments, but, perhaps emboldened by his success, became more aggressive, then mocking, and finally mean-spirited. By the end of a long tirade, he was comparing Currie unfavourably to British generals who, according to the journalist, would never have sent their soldiers into hopeless battles. Preston maintained that "this master tactician, this war lord trained in a real estate and insurance office" had been the one driving his men toward death. It was too much. A shocked crowd hissed and booed. Whatever rewriting of history was going on in the courtroom, few were willing to entertain the idea that Currie was a simple real estate man playing at senior officer. Undaunted, Preston conjured up images of Canadian bodies carpeting the streets of Mons, with Currie striding over them toward his own personal glory without a glance toward the fallen. "I impeach Arthur Currie before this bar on behalf of the widows who lost their husbands, the mothers who lost their sons, the sons who lost their fathers, and the fathers who lost their support, in the needless, frightful, reckless warwaste of life in the attacks on Mons."[30]

Currie had sat through seven hours of relentless assault. It was surely one of the worst days of his life. He had been accused of callousness, brutality, and incompetence. He had been reminded that his soldiers' deaths had profoundly traumatized the loved ones who were left behind to pick up the pieces of their shattered lives. It must have been agonizing to wait for his lawyer to respond. Accusations hung heavily in the air.

When Tilley stood up to address the jury, it was 6:30 P.M. Everyone in the room was exhausted and hungry. Tilley could have asked for a recess and begun his closing remarks the next morning, but by then the accusations would have had a chance to fester in the jury's minds. Currie's team had to respond now. They would not give the lies twenty-four hours to take hold.

In opposition to Regan's impassioned statements and Preston's scathing oratory, Tilley chose the mien of an elder statesman. His tone was even and he spent much of his time reminding the jury what the trial was not about. It was not about refighting the war, as the defence had tried to do relentlessly; it was not about Currie's reputation as a general; it was not about anything other than what had been written in the offending article. The defence could not win their case, argued Tilley, and so they had resorted to the worst form of infamy by repeatedly attacking Currie's reputation. "The article was mean but the conduct of the trial was meaner," he declared. The defence had not proven that there was an "appalling loss of life"; in fact, he noted, "There is absolutely not one sentence in this article that has a dirty sting to it that has been justified." The defence knew nothing of the strategy or tactics used in the war, observed Tilley, and he justified this statement by reminding the jury of the many veterans who had scorned Regan's fanciful tactical solutions to the fighting the Western Front. Tilley also allowed himself some theatrics to match Preston's appeal to the loved ones left behind. Wilson and Preston's article had hurt Currie, he argued, but it had devastated the survivors with its suggestion that the soldiers' sacrifice had been worthless, merely something to elevate a general's reputation.

He pressed on, pointing out that Currie had given the defendants a chance to retract their story. They had refused, and now, said a reproachful Tilley, they should be punished. Tilley reminded the jury of his strong case but finished by saying, rather lamely, "I am proud to suggest to you that General Currie did his part." It did not matter. Many spectators applauded and whistled. Judge Rose adjourned the session. He would begin his charge to the jury the next morning.

*   *   *

At 9:30 A.M. on May 1, 1928, the judge instructed the jury on the law of libel, reminding them that the burden of proof fell on the defendants. While deciphering the finer points of the law, Rose made it clear that writers could not rely upon rumour and "common talk," as the defence called it during the course of the trial, in order to damage someone's reputation. In relation to the fanciful line in the article, stating that the staff had been forced to retreat to their cars and flee "for their lives," Rose asked the jury if they had heard any evidence of this during the trial. They had not; in fact, only the opposite. Most of Rose's instructions seemed to favour Currie's case, although he did note that the $50,000 asked for by the plaintiff need not be adhered to. He suggested that the jury could find a sum that would compensate Currie, but seemed to imply that it might not have to be the full amount sought.[31] The jury began their deliberations a little before lunch.

Three hours later, the verdict came in. A buzz went through Cobourg, as citizens and journalists raced back to the courtroom. The foreman led in the jury. The room was silent, save for the occasional cough or rustle of clothes. Currie and Preston were at their tables, but Wilson had been unable to withstand the strain and was not present. The foreman turned to the judge and said, "On behalf of the jury, I beg to submit the finding that the Defendants are guilty of libel, and that the award of five hundred dollars be given to the Plaintiff."[32]

It was over just like that. Currie had won. He looked stunned, but soon his friends and old comrades were cheering and slapping him on the back within the pandemonium of victory. Currie turned to the jury and shook each of their hands, including the sole dissenter, veteran George Mouncey, who had voted against Currie—as revealed publicly when Regan demanded that each member of the jury be polled for his verdict. Tearful and overwhelmed, the general was older and wearier for his ordeal. But the nightmare was over. He had exorcised the ghosts that had haunted him for over a decade. Hughes was back in his grave.

CHAPTER 17

Reputation Restored

SIR ARTHUR CURRIE, 1928–1933

*C*urrie vs. Preston and Wilson, the Third Battle of Mons, or the $50,000 Currie trial—whatever Canadians called it, the spectacle in Cobourg, according to one of Sir Arthur's friends, had for weeks been "the sole topic of conversation among Canadians."[1] The *Ottawa Citizen* described the trial as "one of the most sensational litigations in the history of Canadian jurisprudence ... [and] one followed with an intensity of interest throughout Canada which perhaps no other litigation has attracted."[2] Scores of journalists had sent nearly a million words of reportage over the courthouse wires, across North America and around the world.[3] The trial had been a brutal affair for all involved, although it had been particularly harrowing for Currie. In the aftermath, Currie wrote that he had been warned by many concerned friends to avoid the confrontation, but noted, "I had to do it, I could not die with such a charge unanswered, I wanted the people of Canada to know the truth, I wanted to prove Sam Hughes a liar."[4] With his victory in Cobourg, Currie had finally pried loose the dead hand of Hughes from his throat.

"Ten years have passed since we came home, and we have never been more united since the conflict ceased," spoke a drained but jubilant Sir Arthur to a huge group of well-wishers at Montreal's Windsor Station at 10 P.M. on May 2. News had spread through the city that Currie had returned. A boisterous crowd consisting of Montreal citizens, veterans, and McGill students converged on the station. A military band from the Royal Montreal Regiment and pipers from the Royal Highlanders of Canada could barely be heard over the din of cheers, bonhomie, and songs that rose through the crowd in wave after wave of revelry. While a reporter described Currie as "pale and tired, and showing signs of great fatigue," the principal had enough energy to launch into an impromptu speech.[5] "Once more we have come through a dirty fight, and once more we have won," he exulted. "The Corps is once more united as it was in the fields of France and Flanders."[6] Although Sir Arthur was the returning hero of McGill, he had chosen to tether his victory to his beloved Canadian Corps.

The coming days brought additional celebrations, including an officers' dinner attended by 400, a turnout that Currie described as "remarkable evidence of that fine comradeship and loyalty which binds us so closely together."[7] Over 2,000 telegrams and letters flooded the Currie household, sent by admirers ranging from Prime Minister King and British generals to Currie's former soldiers, all congratulating the victor and suggesting that the ordeal had finally removed all lingering traces of scandal. Veteran N.C. Diespecher stated that he had heard for years many of the rumours directed against the general, but now he hoped "that this action will settle once and for all, the mean and petty attacks to which you have been subject since your return from overseas."[8] Currie fully deserved the acclaim he now received, stated William Beattie, a wartime padre—acclaim that would have been his years before, "had not 'the enemy' at home poisoned the public mind against you with poisonous lies."[9] In a revealing letter from Dr. W. Salem Caldwell, the war veteran and an alumni of McGill admitted to having once believed that Currie was responsible for butchering his own men: "Laboring under the untruthful reports of the last days of the war repeated in the *Guide* article, I, too, often wondered how you could have been so honoured by the Governors of McGill University." The trial had finally put an end to the disturbing rumours for Caldwell, and for many others. "It makes me extremely happy to have regained pride in, and respect of, our Ex-commander in Chief," he wrote, "and to now know that there was *not* a needless sacrifice before Mons."[10]

Although the trial had been costly to Currie's health, it had restored his reputation among the vast majority of Canadians, and the general believed that it had also helped to weld "together the [men of] Canadian Corps."[11] An attack on Currie, stated hundreds of veterans who supported him in print after the trial, was an attack on the Corps. "I think every man who was in the CEF owes you a debt of gratitude," wrote veteran Gregor Barclay.[12]

Three weeks after the verdict came down, and as the supportive messages were still flooding into Currie's home, William Preston and Fredrick Wilson filed legal papers to appeal the Cobourg decision. Currie's health had always been fragile—from the stomach ulcers he had suffered in his youth through his wartime illnesses, and later compounded by the mental trauma resulting from post-traumatic stress disorder—and the sixteen-day trial had stretched his constitution to the breaking point.[13] As one witness wrote after the trial, "No one will ever know, certainly he never made it known, what he suffered in mind and spirit during these weeks."[14] Currie had barely begun to recover from the ordeal when he received notification of the possibility of another trial.

He collapsed. "The main trouble," wrote Currie, "arose from a complete nervous break-down caused largely by the worry of the trial and by the narrowing thought that ten years after the war one was forced to fight another battle to retain a hold of any good name one had."[15] Even though Currie's lawyers assured the general that the defendants had no grounds on which to appeal the case—and they were subsequently proven correct—it was too much for Currie, who became bedridden for weeks. The shock to his system was severe and he lost over fifty pounds in the coming months, which reduced him to a gaunt and frail figure.[16]

Currie took solace in the judgment, although he must have been disappointed by the award of $500, which was a hundred times less than what he had asked for. To some, the skimpy sum was a sign that Sir Arthur's victory was a qualified one, although the general comforted himself with the knowledge that the judge had instructed the jury that it could reduce the sum from $50,000 to whatever amount it deemed appropriate, and perhaps $500 was seen as a significant punishment by the farmers and labourers who made up the jury. That said, the award certainly fell well short of meeting Currie's lawyer fees, which had climbed to $14,000. But the general had friends in high places, and Sir Edward Beatty, chairman of the Canadian Pacific Railway and of the McGill Board of Governors, used his influence to raise $30,000 for Currie. Beatty wrote to Sir Arthur while he was still recovering, asserting, "I doubt if there is any man in Canada but yourself who could receive such a tribute."[17]

The losing defendants were not so lucky, however. Newspaper editor Frederick Wilson was driven into debt, as the $500 award was soon dwarfed by more than $5,000 in added costs for the trial and a portion of Currie's legal fees. But although he had ended as a loser in both the legal court and the court of public opinion, he had conducted himself with dignity during the difficult proceedings. Any openminded observer who had witnessed Wilson during the trial sensed his genuine belief in journalistic integrity and his desire to see the rank and file receive their just recognition. His actions may have been misguided, but his values were understandable, and many believed that he paid for his stand with his health, as he died in October 1929.

The motivations of Regan and Preston were not so easily understood by Canadians, and both men became social pariahs. Preston's scornful and shameless treatment of Currie, both in his article and during the trial, had only reinforced his reputation as an unrestrained character assassin. Even his Liberal Party handlers turned their backs on him. Preston fled to England, but he returned in 1933 to unsuccessfully sue P.D. Ross, the publisher of the *Ottawa Journal*, for libel—the focus of the suit being damage to Preston's reputation caused by statements relating to his published memoirs. He lost the case, but the grizzled political warrior lived to the age of ninety-two, passing away in England in 1942.[18]

Frank Regan, the lead lawyer for the defendants, was also caught in the smouldering ruins of the trial's aftermath, with his reputation shredded. Regan had mounted an effective if desperate defence at times, even though he was often at a grave disadvantage in not fully understanding the nature of warfighting on the Western Front, as well as in having limited access to the official records. Regan had not only been deeply identified with the defendants and the offending story, but he had been their champion. Many thought he had stepped over the line in his conduct during the trial, and that while his ultimate strategy—the diminishment of Currie's wartime character and reputation—had been partially effective, it had been fully brutal.

Currie's friends, and presumably many Canadians, felt that the defence lawyer had gone too far in his "horrible inquisition," as one veteran described it. One young woman, Jennie Kerr, wrote to Currie that if she had been in Cobourg during the trial, she "would have given that insulting devil of a Regan such a blow between the eyes that it would have knocked him out for all time to come." And then, for good measure, while he was down, she would have "scratched his eyes out."[19] With sight intact but reputation in tatters, Regan's practice limped on. In 1930 he sought to run as a member of Parliament, but found his nomination blocked by those who saw him as a political liability. A desperate Regan even wrote to Currie, asking for his help, but the still bitter principal refused to bury the hatchet, unless it was in Regan's head.

Currie recovered slowly from his breakdown, which was later diagnosed as a minor stroke. He was on a strict diet and took long periods of rest. But the requests for speaking engagements did not abate. In June 1928 Lady Currie took her husband to Europe to escape the limelight in Canada, a trip that allowed him time to relax, see old wartime friends, and play golf. The respite was intended to last only a few weeks, but Sir Arthur would actually be gone from McGill for almost a year, as his health took another turn for the worse. The fifty-four-year-old Currie contracted what his doctors diagnosed as paratyphoid. He recovered and extended his trip, eventually spending several months in Egypt in early 1929. The Curries finally returned to Canada in May, greeted by friends and McGillites. Many worried about Currie's appearance, as he had not fully regained the weight lost during his prolonged illness.

Currie dove back into his work at McGill, anxious to re-exert authority over the university. His doctors cautioned him to put in fewer hours at the office, avoid weekend work, and reduce his heavy public-speaking load. But he could not—it was in his nature to work hard, and there were always too many groups and associations aching to have him support their missions. Currie always spread himself thin. His new secretary, Dorothy McMurray, met him in 1929 and described him as "A very big, a very tall man," adding, "I found him awe-inspiring. He looked very tired."[20] He was hospitalized later in November of that year with a nasty flu that, in Sir Arthur's words, "disorganized my digestive organs," and also resulted in a rather distressing five days of straight hiccupping.[21] Currie recovered, but he seemed vulnerable to flus and colds. Friends noticed that he stooped more and always looked fatigued, and that even his smooth, roundish face had taken on a lined appearance. He looked a decade older than he was.

Currie's legal victory seemed to mark a sea change in his rapport with the Great War veterans. While it is unfair to suggest that Currie had been disliked by the Corps' ex-soldiers, his relationship with the various veterans' associations in the first half of the decade following the war had not been easy. However, this changed in 1925, when the Legion of the British Empire Service League was formed by amalgamating a number of disparate organizations to create the largest veterans' group. As the veterans had by this time failed to secure their $2,000 bonus, and many of the more radical leaders had left, the Legion became more inclusive of senior officers. Even before the trial, Currie's popularity in the Legion was evident, as he was elected as its president in 1928, and from 1929 to the end of his life he held the post of grand president, an honorific position but one that held significance for him and others after his previously strained relationship with veterans' organizations.

Although Currie had interceded in pension cases for veterans who had appealed directly to him, he had not been deeply involved in the fight for collective rights in the immediate aftermath of the war. By the latter part of the decade, however, he began to focus more energy on helping veterans, especially with their administrative battle to secure just pensions. Canada's pension system had been generous compared to that of Great Britain or the financially decimated France or Germany, but it was still a bureaucracy within which veterans often felt humiliated in front of pension boards made up of supposed experts who poked and prodded them, studied their files, and demanded proof that wounds were suffered in battle rather than in the prewar or postwar years.[22] An impersonal and slightly bizarre system assigned pension allotments for lost arms or missing eyes—thus quantifying a veteran's pain and loss—with less visible wounds, especially psychological breakdown or gas poisoning, scoring very low, when they were recognized at all.[23]

"They Served Till Death—Why Not We?" wrote Currie of his veterans, minting the phrase later adopted by the Royal Canadian Legion as its official motto.[24] While Currie lamented the loss of the fallen, he pushed hard for the rights and welfare of those still alive, some of whom seemed reduced to the living dead, as they shuffled through life in physical pain and emotional agony. In one much-discussed letter that he published with the *Toronto Star* in April 1927, Currie stated, "The health of almost everyone who served throughout the war was, to some extent, adversely affected. Men may not have been wounded nor have suffered from any illness, but I do not believe that any man could go through the campaigns of the Great War without his power to resist disease being minimized."[25] Currie wanted to see pension regulations revised, with a more sympathetic eye toward the veterans. He argued that they should have greater access to their own records and encounter fewer bureaucratic hurdles, especially in the case of veterans who were in isolated rural areas and could not easily access information relating to the Pensions Act, and who found their appeals denied because of administrative red tape. No doubt Currie felt for his boys because he too was a victim of the illness now known as post-traumatic stress disorder, which was poorly understood by society at the time.

Currie shared his views at the Legion's annual convention in Regina in 1929, in a passionate letter that was read by another since Sir Arthur was too ill to attend; he wrote that he was "not only amazed but ashamed that eleven years after the war it is necessary not only to plead but to fight for justice."[26] When he was healthy again, he threw his full weight into the battle and rallied the support of important newspapers. Currie kept up the pressure, and the next year, in March 1930, he addressed the Pensions Committee in Ottawa. Although he appeared old and wasted—"delicate," as described by Prime Minister Mackenzie King—he put on a "masterly performance."[27] He talked for over an hour without notes, his emaciated body radiating with energy, his voice rising in anger, and his command of facts and stories of ignored veterans moving many in the room to tears.[28] The government soon revised the legislation, but the new system did not work as well as the veterans had hoped—and, in fact, the pension board took advantage of its inefficiencies to appeal decisions that were favourable to veterans. But a few more years of battle ensured that a fairer system was created with the establishment of the Canadian Pensions Commission in 1933.[29]

While Currie did not have the same energy that he once had, he continued to agitate for veterans' rights and for public recognition of the Canadian Corps, which he believed had been unjustly ignored. Currie fervently hoped that the powerful ideals that underpinned the Corps— which had brought Canadians from across the country together to fight for a common cause, to overlook their petty and regional jealousies, and to unite them as countrymen—could be resurrected in the harsh postwar years. If the "old spirit" of the Corps could be "revived once more in the men of this country," he declared, "many problems now apparent would disappear."[30]

It would take more than camaraderie for the Corps' veterans to withstand the financial meltdown of 1929 that rocked Canada and the world, leading to a decade-long economic depression. Like many Canadians, Sir Arthur had much of his finances tied up in stocks, and by the fall of 1931 he had lost most of his fortune. McGill, too, was feeling the financial constriction, with major building projects abandoned. Currie threw his energies into raising money to keep McGill afloat and to retain important programs such as the School for Graduate Nurses that was slated for closure. He fought hard to save it and ultimately succeeded.[31]

Sir Arthur achieved a few such victories during the Great Depression, the most important being the establishment of McGill's world-class neurological institute. Currie went cap in hand to businesses and wealthy Montrealers, prodded the city and the province, and then used his international reputation to secure over a million dollars in funding from the Rockefeller Foundation in the United States. There were many who helped found the neurological institute, but Currie could rightly lay claim to being an essential player.[32] The building was erected in 1933, and the institute's success was one of the few bright lights on a dark horizon, as Currie and the governors were forced to sell McGill assets, cut salaries (including his own), and raise tuition fees. These were bleak years, but Currie helped guide McGill to recovery. As one observer noted of Currie and McGill, "The personality of the Principal permeated the whole place, down to the lowliest labourer picking up trash from the grass. Everyone knew him, almost felt they knew him personally. They were a little in awe of him, and yet somehow he seemed near to them. They felt he understood their lives; he himself had been through worse times than most of them, and had survived."[33]

Currie continued to be haunted by the war. Writing as late as a decade after the armistice, he confessed to W.H. Langley, a friend in Victoria, "Very often I have dreams about the war. In those dreams it is never ended and still goes on and I remember what a horrible feeling of disappointment I have. Sometimes the Germans are winning and sometimes we are; the war is fought in all sorts of strange places—sometimes the front line is east of Arras, at others through my old home in Western Ontario."[34] He might have added that his mind was now the battlefield. Currie was not alone in realizing that the dead continued to claw at the living, refusing to be banished to their cemeteries. And Currie, for his part, did not want the silent legions to be forgotten, or their sacrifice wasted. Too many of his boys had paid the ultimate sacrifice in the "war to end all wars," as the Great War was sometimes known, but Currie was terrified that war would come again.

Guided by this worry, Currie embraced one last passion late in his life. Canada's most respected general became a voice for disarmament. "Those who have seen it [war] and experienced it realize the horror of its frightful waste and extravagance," Sir Arthur averred.[35] He believed that the Great War had been fought to ensure a long peace, but in the early 1930s he revealed publicly that he was "disillusioned" with the idea, and feared a coming war.[36] As an avid watcher of international affairs, Currie observed with dismay the military armament and aggressiveness in Japan, Italy, and Germany. He had little faith in the League of Nations or peace treaties, as evidenced in a radio address he made on November 11, 1931: "The history of the past has taught us, and the history of the present confirms most emphatically, that these solemn engagements are easily disregarded."[37] Currie believed that the next war would be even more savage than the Great War, with weapons unleashed against civilians in the form of aerial bombardments, poison gas, and even biological agents. Whole nations would be laid to waste. Although Currie was no pacifist—and he publicly spoke of serving his country when war came again, as he expected it would—he refused to side with those soldiers, many of whom were his friends, who called for the Allied nations of the world to rearm.[38] In a widely publicized speech at a meeting of the National Republican Club of New York in January 1932, Currie declared that, without disarmament, "the world is doomed to destruction."[39] His hope was that diplomacy and reason would prevail. Spending on arms and weapons not only took away from investment in health and education, he argued, but stockpiles of such weapons nearly begged to be used. In high-profile speeches in Canada and the United States, Currie pushed for peaceful dialogue. "For only on the knowledge of facts, interpreted in the spirit of understanding and goodwill, can peace be made secure."[40]

"We who were once members of the Canadian Corps are bound by the ties of a common remembrance," wrote a melancholic Currie in the first days of November 1933, in preparation for his annual Remembrance Day speech.[41] Early November was a difficult time for him. Sir Arthur was always deeply involved in Remembrance Day, as Armistice Day had been renamed in 1931, with his approval. He felt the weight of the dead keenly on that sacred day—a day that was bittersweet in stirring up "memories of pain—the pain of parting, the pain of hardship and physical suffering."[42]

Currie had made his name as a soldier, but he had cemented his reputation as an educator. For thirteen years he had functioned as the face of McGill, and while his health had been precarious, he had seemed in good spirits throughout 1933. However, on Sunday, November 5, while composing his Remembrance Day message, he collapsed. Found slumped on the floor in his study, surrounded by war trophies and souvenirs from his beloved Canadian Corps, he was rushed to the Royal Victoria Hospital.

The hospital assembled a team of its best doctors, but the diagnosis was grim. Sir Arthur had suffered a massive stroke. His family, McGillites, and many Canadians across the country kept a steady vigil. On the eleventh of November, the doctors issued a proclamation that Sir Arthur seemed to be improving. Although Currie never regained consciousness, the grip of his hand would tighten on occasion when his wife Lily, or his two children, Garner and Marjorie, would talk to him. But then bronchial problems set in around November 19. He fought the infection, but began to fade fast when he contracted pneumonia.[43] Sir Arthur Currie joined his comrades in the silent Canadian Expeditionary Force at 2:50 A.M. on November 30, 1933.

Newspapers across the country carried front-page stories of Currie's death, and of his funeral a week later. The *Montreal Daily Herald* devoted the entire front page, above and below the fold, to an enormous portrait of Currie, along with the title, "A Nation Mourns."[44] McGill closed for a full week and flags in Montreal flew at half mast.[45] Currie's funeral was the largest the country had ever witnessed, and the newly established Canadian Radio Broadcasting Commission carried a live, coast-to-coast broadcast of the procession and funeral.[46] On December 5, which would have been Sir Arthur's fifty-eighth birthday, the funeral was carried out in two phases, one civil and one military, as befitted Canada's most important civilian-soldier.

Sir Arthur's casket, draped with the Union Jack and McGill's red-and-white flag, lay in state at Christ Church Anglican Cathedral in downtown Montreal. Thousands of Montrealers passed slowly by the casket, paying their respects. Currie's ceremonial sword, his field cap, and his medals and decorations were on display. At 10:45 A.M., the civil ceremony commenced, with Prime Minister R.B. Bennett, the governor general, the Earl of Bessborough, senior army commanders, McGillites, and old comrades-in-arms in attendance. A memorial service was also held in

London's Westminster Abbey to mark the passing of one of the Empire's most prominent generals.

Through the grey, cloudy skies, a light rain began to fall on Montreal. When the service ended, the casket was carried out to a waiting hearse. One of the pallbearers was an old friend—Garnet Hughes, who had buried his anger toward Currie after the trial.[47] The hearse took Currie's body to the McGill campus and stopped in front of the Arts Building, where the coffin was transferred to a gun carriage drawn by eight war horses. A full military escort assembled, composed of hundreds of cavalrymen, infantry, and gunners, and behind them was the traditional empty-saddled horse, boots reversed in the stirrups. The long procession of mourners followed the coffin as it moved down the streets of Montreal, which were lined several rows deep with an estimated 150,000 witnesses who stood in the slush and cold rain.[48] No one could remember a larger crowd ever having assembled in the city.

The procession moved at a slow pace as deafening artillery gun salutes reverberated through Montreal's streets. When the horses finally reached Mount Royal cemetery, a short private ceremony took place, and then the light faded for the last time on Sir Arthur Currie, principal of McGill and commander of the Canadian Corps.

CONCLUSION

Revered and Reviled

THE LONG WAR OF REPUTATIONS

"**S**uch a man does not die," wrote the *Montreal Daily Star* in its eulogy to Sir Arthur Currie. "He will be remembered and quoted and recalled as an inspiration long after the men who talked with him and heard his living voice have themselves passed from the scene. He becomes one of the imperishable possessions of the Canadian people."[1] In death, Currie's reputation was fortified. His funeral was awe-inspiring with its huge crowds and nationwide coverage, and was a clear indication that he had been fully embraced by his country. R.B. Bennett's government took a kinder view of Currie than Borden's 1919 cabinet had, and it finally acknowledged the general's service with a cash gift of $50,000 to Lady Currie. During the 1935 House of Commons debates, the leader of the opposition, William Lyon Mackenzie King, observed that it was "unfortunate that after the war ... no recognition whatever, so far as I know, was given by parliament of the distinguished services of eminent generals and others who participated in the war."[2] Now the general would be recognized, although it was only after his death that he received his due from Parliament.

"Neither Sir John A. Macdonald nor Sir Wilfrid Laurier received such a tribute," wrote Sir Robert Borden of Currie's enormous funeral. "The future historian will have to judge whether Currie's service was comparable with theirs."[3] Though there can be no doubt that Macdonald and Laurier are better remembered today, Currie has certainly not faded from historical memory. Although the Great War undoubtedly remains a defining moment in the country's history, the constructed and at times contested memory of the war rests on two enduring but contrasting images. First, the war is remembered as a terrible and forlorn slaughter, as evoked by the ghastly record of more than 60,000 dead and another 173,000 wounded in body, mind, and spirit. The memorials to the fallen in every community are evidence of the bloody swath this war tore through the country. Second, the war is accurately portrayed as an important turning point in the nation's history—a time when Canadians began to see themselves differently and when others started to view Canada as a country instead of a colony.[4] Currie's place in history is now very much tied to the latter memory strand rather than the former, although his purported role in the terrible slaughter plagued him for much of the decade after the war.

Currie the militiaman, who felt the hard hand of war on the cruel Western Front, but excelled, has come to represent and even embody Canada's own evolution during the course of the war. Given his status as a symbol of the national maturation process that occurred from 1914 to 1918, it is perhaps not surprising that Currie's reputation is also intertwined with the victory at Vimy—one of the war's defining moments. The erection of Walter Allward's stunning memorial in 1936 has cemented the place of Vimy in the hearts of Canadians, who continue to make pilgrimages to the memorial site at Vimy Ridge each year by the thousands. Vimy is part of the nation's creation myth, the place where Canada came of age, and an important story that we instill in each generation. Currie, in turn, remains closely linked to the battle, and it is common, almost frequent, to hear Currie instead of Sir Julian Byng referred to in the media or among Canadians as the corps commander at Vimy. The myth of Currie as the commander at Vimy remains resilient.

No doubt many Canadians have been influenced in this regard by the wishful myth-making episode of the much-viewed *Historica Minutes* educational video series that devoted a segment to Vimy. The popular segment presents Currie as the senior commander of the battle, and includes a scene in which the Canadian general explains to the mystified British how the battle will be won. In reality, although Currie played a key role in planning and executing the battle, if credit must go to one person, it belongs to Byng. To ascribe the battle's success to Currie amounts to nationalistic rewriting of history, and Canadians might be excused for wondering why Baron Byng of Vimy adopted this particular title!

But even if he is not known as Sir Arthur of Vimy, few would argue against acknowledging Currie as one of the finest battlefield generals in the war. He excelled at each of his commands, regardless of the growing challenges and complexities. He was not without his faults, but he seems to have recognized his own limitations, a trait that has eluded generals throughout history, from Napoleon to Patton, to whom the term "brilliant" applies more easily. Currie knew that his success came from blood, sweat, and study rather than from an innate understanding of war. He succeeded more than he failed, but there were failures. This fact does not tarnish his reputation, however; it merely reveals that he was human.

Sir Arthur agonized over the casualties the Corps sustained in the war, but he also knew that success on the Western Front necessarily required casualties, sometimes at crippling levels. To some this recognition made him appear callous, even cruel. But it is, in the end, one that all commanders must confront. Currie was far from reckless, and his aggressiveness on the battlefield, especially at Hill 70, Arras, and the Hindenburg Line, led directly to victory. His methodical approach to fighting—of biting and holding in set-piece battles—was the only way to succeed in the battles of the Great War, and it consistently produced results. All of these factors must come together in any assessment of Currie, who is regarded widely as one of the finest generals of the war.

Currie wrote that while it was the soldiers who fought and bled on the battlefield, it was the historians who would make sense of, and pass judgment over, their actions. He was right, and historians have been kind to Sir Arthur over the years—far more so than to most generals, who tend to die and fade away without a sympathetic biographer. After Currie's death, one of his loyal veterans, Colonel Hugh Urquhart, who had been severely wounded while leading his men at the front, began to compile records relating to Currie's life. Supported by official historian Colonel A.F. Duguid, and having canvassed the opinions of Currie's wartime comrades, Urquhart wrote a celebratory account of his general. *Arthur Currie: The Biography of a Great Canadian* was ready for publication in 1939 but was delayed by the Second World War and did not reach Canadians until 1950.

A decade earlier, in 1940, one of Currie's loyal friends, Theodore Roberts, had lamented, "I fear Arthur Currie is today no more than a dead corps commander to the national consciousness."[4] Sir Arthur's name no longer resonated with Canadians, and he continued to fade from public memory. When A.M.J. Hyatt began his doctoral dissertation research on Currie in the late 1950s, he noted that the general was, at that time, "'an unrecognized hero.' He was hardly mentioned in textbooks on Canadian history and was frequently misidentified."[5] And General Andrew McNaughton, one of Canada's most celebrated soldiers, observed in the early 1960s, "Even with the favourable verdict of the court and all that has since been written and published in praise of the Canadian Corps and its commander, there still comes an occasional echo of past criticisms and insinuations."[6] From the 1940s to the early 1960s, Currie was forgotten or misremembered, much like the Great War itself, which was overshadowed by the "Good War" against Hitler and his Nazi legions.[7]

But if Currie remained a murky figure in the Second World War's aftermath, he has been better recognized since the late 1960s, with historians helping to keep his memory alive. The general left a rich archive of material, including official reports that he authored; thousands of letters from him and about him; and many documents that revealed much about his approach to warfighting, if less about Currie the man.

Currie was written back into the nation's history in the 1980s, although historian Robert Demill met several elderly individuals around this time, who informed him that their parents' "hatred" for Currie had never faded or been assuaged with time.[8] The successful court verdict had done little to convince them that Currie did not have blood on his hands. It is worth remembering, however, that Currie did in fact have blood on his hands, as all generals and most soldiers did. The Canadian Corps was not a peacekeeping force. Its primary role was to destroy the enemy. And soldiers had to die on both sides to achieve this goal.

The twenty-first century has not seen Sir Arthur Currie's presence diminished in the nation's history books. He is the fulcrum on which turn most of the army histories and is featured prominently in the First World War permanent gallery at the Canadian War Museum, which is visited by several hundred thousand visitors each year. Currie is also one of fourteen Valiants, a collective memorial of statues and busts of military men and women who represent courage and service to the country over four centuries. These statues were erected in late 2006 near the National Memorial in Ottawa and caused a minor controversy among historians, who wondered what criteria were used to choose these particular figures and why it was being done at this point in the nation's history, although most Canadians seemed unperturbed by such questions. Currie remains on duty near Parliament Hill in all his bronzed glory.

Streets and schools across the country carry Currie's name, and Currie Barracks in Calgary and Currie Hall at the Royal Military College of Canada also memorialize the Great War commander. A Sir Arthur Currie University was never established, though his counterpart in Australia, Sir John Monash, did receive this honour. But in public memory, Currie's image and name continue to register widely. The CBC's

2004 vote-in program *The Greatest Canadian* allowed Canadians to cast their vote for the "greatest" living or historical figure. These types of surveys always include the latest flash-in-the-pan stars, questionable iconoclasts such as Don Cherry, and celebrities such as Pamela Anderson, but Currie scored high, achieving twenty-fourth place. It is interesting that three other Great War figures—the Unknown Soldier, Billy Bishop, and John McCrae—made the list of Top 100 Great Canadians, not to mention prime ministers Lester B. Pearson and John Diefenbaker, both of whom served in the Great War, but neither of whom was voted in because of their military service. No service personnel from the Second World War or Korea were represented, other than Farley Mowat (who was surely selected for his contributions as an author and activist rather than for his career in the infantry in the Second World War), and of the military figures included, only General Romeo Dallaire, best remembered as the traumatized peacekeeper in Rwanda, placed ahead of Currie. Although the results of such surveys are highly unscientific, Currie's high standing is nonetheless noteworthy.

Lord Byng wrote of his protegé after his death, "I often wonder whether history will do justice to Arthur Currie."[9] It has certainly done so, although Sir Arthur has periodically been subjected to renewed salvoes in the war of reputations. While Currie has by now shed much of his butcher image, it was dredged up again in the 1988 television documentary *The Killing Ground*, in which director and writer Terry McKenna raised the issue of the useless waste of life in the battle at Mons:

> Currie decided that a last-minute assault of the Belgium city of Mons would be a glorious way to close out the war.... His men ... were horrified when the order was given.... When the battle was over 26 Canadian soldiers were buried in the fields of Europe.... The circumstances of their tragedy have been distorted and mythologized for 70 years.[10]

While there was some outrage on the part of academics and veterans toward the rehashed claims in *The Killing Ground*, the documentary is all but forgotten now; but writer-director Paul Gross's 2008 epic blockbuster film, *Passchendaele,* is likely to live on in public memory for decades. Although its focus is on the soldiers in the mud and misery of the Flanders front, the film contains a brief mention of Currie when an experienced colonel speaks of his predicting the casualties that would be sustained at Passchendaele—a prediction that he never shared with the men, of course. The colonel remarks that "the general is never wrong." Gross no doubt wanted to fit in some good words about Currie, and even if what is included amounts to little more than a sound bite, it carries some resonance, especially in its implication that Currie was not to be blamed for the battle since he had warned the British about how much the victory would cost in lives. For good measure, the hyper-patriotic fool of a recruiting colonel in the film, who is mean, vindictive, and pompous, is named Dobson-Hughes. The name can be no accident. The madman lives on, still clutching at Canadians from beyond the grave.

Sir Sam Hughes's career was so bizarre and unsettling that it reads like a novel, and perhaps an unbelievable one at that. He was a colossus of Canadian politics for three decades, though he remains largely forgotten, or, if remembered at all, as little more than a conceited lunatic. Vain, outrageous, and at times monstrous in his views, this barmy bully stood his ground in every fight. "Sam Hughes was truculent, ruthless and bombastic. He was arrogant, impetuous and eccentric"—and this from Alan Capon, one of his biographers, who argued that Hughes deserved better from historians! But Capon notes more sympathetically, "He was also, however, a brilliant man of action, complex and hard-driving and in military matters, so far ahead of his contemporaries that he was to suffer a prolonged and frequently undeserved barrage of criticism both during and after his service as Minister of Militia."[11] Another of the handful of

Hughes champions in the court of history was wartime veteran and long-time premier of Ontario, Leslie Frost, who wrote in the mid-1960s, "Sam Hughes has been done great injustice by contemporary writers to date. Perhaps the time has come to set the record straight." Although Frost acknowledged that Hughes was not without his faults, he argued that he had been unfairly "labelled as a mad man," adding, "He was the man on the spot who did things, which, in retrospect, dwarf the weaknesses and the errors."[12]

Sir Sam's grandson, who carried on the name and was a talented historian and Ontario Supreme Court Judge, wrote that his grandfather did himself no favours in preparing his legacy. He noted that, as a man who clearly understood his place in history and who had a "highly developed talent for notoriety, such as few Canadian politicians have possessed, Sir Sam must often have dwelt upon his future reputation, but through either carelessness or impatience he gave little heed to the task of the historian. He kept few private papers and none organized after the manner of men who have an eye for biography. The few which he left are the unsatisfactory gleaning of brief periods of inactivity."[13] The dearth of Hughes's own views on the war was compounded when much of his official and departmental correspondence was destroyed in the 1920s. It is unclear why this occurred, though it was more likely an instance of the periodic vetting of files that takes place among historically blinded bureaucrats than any sort of conspiracy to do in Hughes.[14] The Hughes family and descendants withheld other inherited correspondence and even a partially written memoir from historians—who they believed had done and would continue to do Sir Sam an injustice—although that material has now been donated to the Library and Archives of Canada, and was used in this book.

Hell hath no fury like a historian scorned, and without Sir Sam's records to sift through and make sense of his service to the country, generations of historians have too readily relied upon what Hughes's enemies had to say about him. And they had a lot to say—little of it nice. Hughes needs rescuing from the historical prison—or perhaps the better analogy is historical Bedlam—to which historians have consigned him.

Hughes's first biographer was his military secretary, Brigadier Charles Winter, who published a chatty book in 1931. "There is some doubt whether a full-dress biography of the late Sir Sam Hughes is either necessary or desirable," wrote reviewer B.K. Sandwell of Winter's short offering. "The duty of the biography is to help us to understand the mental process of the person described; but Sir Sam's mental processes were of the simplest, and elucidation would be wasted on them."[15] Sir Sam clearly deserved better than such dismissive reviews that reduced him to nothing more than a simpleminded, war-bent hillbilly. Perceiving this need, sympathetic journalist Alan Capon aimed to rehabilitate Hughes's image four decades later, although he did not seek to hide the unpleasant side of the minister's character. The first and only scholarly biography of Hughes, by Royal Military College professor Ronald Haycock in the mid-1980s, offered a fair treatment of its subject, providing insight into Hughes's actions and the ways in which he was shaped by time, place, and circumstance. It was a history grounded in a deep understanding of Canadian military, politics, and society, and constructed from wide archival research, but *Sam Hughes: The Public Career of a Controversial Canadian, 1885–1916*, along with the two earlier biographies, had little impact in rehabilitating Sir Sam's reputation, as public memory of Hughes as a malignant force was too firmly entrenched.

So why is Sir Sam still the madman of history? Hughes effectively burned almost every bridge he crossed in his long life, except those between himself and his constituents. By constantly attacking his own party in the last years of his life, he drove away all but a few friends there. Hughes was always difficult, both as a colleague and as an opponent, except when he was cravenly apologizing for and weeping over one of his periodic outrages. Over the course of a long and lively career, he cultivated multiple hatreds, which, it should be noted, were shared freely and passionately by many in return. Prime Minister Sir Robert Borden, who put up with so much from his unruly minister during the war, pulled out the carving knives in his two-volume memoir, which was published in 1938, a year after his death. Historians followed suit in condemning Hughes throughout the rest of the century, presenting him less as a man, warts and all, and more as a caricature, warts and warts.

Since Hughes is remembered prominently as Currie's nemesis, and as the general has been elevated steadily over the last century to his rightful place in the pantheon of Canadian heroes, the movement of the scales has inevitably led to Hughes being pulled further down, revealed in all his nuttiness. He was an easy mark. Popular historian Pierre Berton wrote of Hughes in his 1986 best-selling *Vimy* that Sir Sam's brave actions to ensure that the Canadians fought together as a coherent force "have to be taken into account," but that they should be "weighed against the mountain of gaucheries, barbarities, vulgarities, and blunders that have made him the laughing stock of history."[16] Such negative sentiments were echoed by journalist and military historian Daniel Dancocks, who reviled Hughes, blasting the ex-minister in his biography of Sir Arthur Currie, and by Ralph Allen, who wrote that Hughes "would have had the greatest difficulty passing a standard medical test for sanity."[17] Over the last ninety years, almost every academic historian has taken the opportunity to throw a shovelful of dirt onto Sir Sam's now cold grave. Historian Michael Bliss offered a judgment representative of most historians' in his withering assessment that "Borden's worst mistake, a decision he ought to have reversed long before any shot was fired, was to maintain Sam Hughes as Minister of Militia.... At best, Hughes was possibly qualified to be Minister of Militia in Stephen Leacock's 'Mariposa.' As Minister responsible for the Canadian division in a world war Hughes was pathetically and obviously out of his depth."[18] Almost without exception, Hughes has been excoriated in print, media, and public memory. In 2007, Canada's national history magazine, *The Beaver*, conducted a quirky quiz on the "worst Canadian" in our history.[19] Various interest groups hijacked the unscientific online poll, but a separate survey conducted by historians placed Hughes as one of the top contenders. No matter what Canadians think of Hughes, the label "worst Canadian" seems more than a little harsh.

There can be no doubt that Hughes's reputation has suffered over the years at the hands of historians who have reduced him to a maniacal, failed administrator who represented the worst of the amateur and politically partisan Canadian war effort. Such broad characterizations are true to some degree, but this book has also tried to reveal the full spectrum of Hughes's contributions and duty to his country, as well as to occasionally explain the psyche that drove and shaped his activities and actions. Vindictive, unreasonable, cocksure, bigoted, and egocentric he was; less evident among historians' writing have been his easy charm, magnetic charisma, powerful speaking style, and unflagging energy and drive. And let us not forget his successes. Contemporary journalist J. Castell Hopkins noted that despite all of Hughes's faults, he had, as minister of defence during the first twenty-eight months of the war, "blazed a pathway to efficient success in matters of recruiting, munitions-making, transport and training of troops; he had overcome a public inertia in certain points which required an almost dynamic energy to move; he had driven the fear of the Minister, if not the fear of God, into a Militia system which had lacked cohesion and discipline."[20] How can such achievements be reconciled with Hughes's sometimes repellent personality, insatiable ego, and street-fighting tactics? The simple answer is that Hughes was a complex character. Unstable and dynamic; shrewd in some matters, naive in others; inclusive at times but bigoted about other issues; thick-skinned against insults but prone to break down into tears of contrition, he defies easy categorization. History is messy, and so are people. Biographers cannot tie up all the loose ends of a life with a perfect bow. There are some of Sir Sam's urges, actions, and motivations that we will never understand. We may take some solace in the fact that he likely did not understand them either.

Hughes's raising of nearly 400,000 men in a volunteer war effort is surely an indication that he achieved some success as war minister. His inability to engage Quebec can be explained by his regional and religious background, but also by his fervent desire to ensure that the war effort remained volunteer-driven. If French Canadians did not want to serve, that was fine with Hughes.[21] He did little to encourage them, and not a little bit to dissuade them, but he was certainly let down by his Quebec colleagues in the cabinet. In fact, with cabinets formed from representatives of all the regions, it fell to the Quebec ministers to play a key role in the war, especially in the raising of soldiers from their province. Hughes failed to win over French Canada, but he has also surely been scapegoated over the years for the low number of recruits from that region, and it seems likely that no other minister in Borden's government could have done any better.

Hughes succeeded in raising an enormous volunteer fighting force, and his ability to carve a war munitions industry from nothing—which involved convincing a wary group of Canadian industrialists who in 1914 were still mired in economic depression—speaks further to his strength of character and singleminded drive. His relentless pursuit of munitions contracts brought in hundreds of millions of dollars from British orders, placed Canada on a war footing, created a new heavy industry, and eventually put more than 250,000 Canadians to work.[22] Few historians have ever considered that Hughes may have played the most significant individual role in dragging Canada out of its prewar depression.

Hughes succeeded in raising men and encouraging the manufacture of munitions, but his relationship overseas was also essential, as he always pushed for external recognition for Canada. His ability to stand up to the British—even to intimidate them—is not to be underestimated. Hughes's demands for greater autonomy and recognition, as well as his insistence that Canadians receive key command positions, represent the types of assertiveness most Canadians would applaud. Although Hughes may not have actually confronted Kitchener in his office, he certainly besieged the old field marshal with missives and threats of mad action to ensure that the Canadians would indeed fight together. His deliberate policy of Canadianization should be considered no mere footnote in appraising his success as a war leader. During the first two and a half years of the war, the Canadians fought an essential and ongoing battle to establish recognition and status as an independent fighting force, and while the laurels for this success belong to no single Canadian, Hughes would be at the top of any list of candidates.

Despite these accomplishments, however, Hughes was a menace to the goal of professionalizing the Canadian Corps and to the need for its senior officers to shed the partisan interference that was impeding success on the battlefield. Here he remained the old-style politician at his worst and his most intrusive. But Hughes's demand that the Canadians use Canadian-made equipment was not entirely outrageous, partially because he believed the equipment was better made than similar British kit, but also because using national materiel kept his countrymen employed. Was this wrong? Yes, of course, when the boots dissolved or the rifles did not work, but many Canadians, and almost all politicians, would have supported Hughes's Canadian-first sentiment. Where Hughes failed was in his inability to acknowledge his own mistakes. Such a lack of self-awareness and -analysis amounted to a form of sociopathic behaviour, and for this he deserves some of the harsh condemnation he has received from history's hangmen.

One wonders how Hughes would fare in our history books—and more particularly if he would still be a cartoon character—if he had remained minister throughout the war, or if he had gone overseas as a commander. He would likely have been impossible for superior officers to handle in either case, and might have caused even more damage than his bull-in-a-china-shop actions did during the first two and a half years of the war. But perhaps not. The entire Canadian war effort and the overseas fighting forces matured during the war, and as part of this process, Canadians in positions of power learned to fight more effectively and to better support the war through a variety of means. Sir Sam's performance might similarly have improved over time. Hughes was rarely guilty of deliberate ministerial malfeasance; it was his amateurism that led to inefficiency at best and chaos at worst. Yet much of the early war effort suffered from this same non-professional approach, and Hughes was not alone in some of his failings, joined as he was by cabinet ministers, the prime minister, and most of the senior soldiers overseas. To push this musing further, what, for example, would we think of Sir Arthur Currie had he been removed from battlefield command at the end of the Somme in late 1916, like the now forgotten Sir Richard Turner, deprived of the chance to redeem his mediocre showing on that cruel battlefield, and also of the opportunity to strive ahead during the battles of Vimy, Hill 70, or the Hundred Days? The historical profession is not well equipped to engage in counterfactual history and the "what if" questions, but perhaps such reflections lend some weight to the argument that Sir Sam might have improved as the war went on, and certainly that he was a force for good as well as chaos.

Putting such speculations aside, however, we are left with a historical actor who was unstable, unliked, and, by late 1916, unneeded. For many Canadians before the war, Hughes represented the fringe of the Conservative Party. Even today, one can only understand Hughes as a man of his time, and one schooled in late nineteenth-century politics, whose actions appear awfully harsh one hundred years later. Hughes thrived in his personal battles, seeming to feed off them. In the coarse arena of the House of Commons, he was one of the most hostile and belligerent fighters, wielding skills that left him feared and hated.

At the core of this book is the question of what drove Sir Sam Hughes to denounce Sir Arthur Currie. Hughes's motivations were never fully elucidated in his own writings, and it is dangerous to believe his own justifications, if only because he often convinced himself of the righteousness of his own actions and was sometimes simply a blatant liar. It is clear, however, that Hughes had experience with character assassination. Perhaps he had been on the receiving end so many times that he simply believed such assaults to be a part of the grim battles of early-twentieth-century politics. Sir Sam's maniacal attacks against Flavelle and some of his colleagues, especially White, Kemp, and Perley, were typical of Hughes after his removal from power. In 1916 Hughes despicably savaged the reputation of an able officer overseas, seeking retaliation for attacks against him by the officer's brother, P.D. Ross, the Conservative editor of the *Ottawa Journal*.[23] For Hughes, the best defence was always a strong, wild, and at times flailing offence, and his accusations against Currie can be seen as a continuation of these well-honed and rough tactics. Moreover, though we will never know how age and illness had damaged Hughes's mind, or be able to gauge the depths of his anger upon being removed from power and abandoned, it remains true that he cared for his boys overseas. And they were killed by the thousands. Who was to blame? Most Canadians pointed to the Germans, some the British commanders, and fewer still Sir Arthur Currie. Hughes focused his attack on all three.

For his attack on Currie, and other questionable acts, does Hughes deserve to be ensconced in Canada's rogues' gallery, or to be condemned forever as evil? What if Sir Sam's lashing assaults were brave and selfless attempts to uncover gross incompetence on the part of callous generals sacrificing Canadian boys to pad their own reputations? They were not viewed in this way, but Hughes saw himself—or wanted himself portrayed—in this light. It is the terrible casualties that go to the core of Hughes's assault on Currie. They were gut-churningly high, but were they too high? How do we measure triumph when there is no benchmark to measure it against? Are high casualties evidence of success on the battlefield or of gross bungling? Answering such questions requires recourse to contextualizing information and an understanding of the complex circumstances at play. At what point did the Canadian Corps' reputation as shock troops lead to their overuse by the British high command, who believed correctly that Currie's men could deliver victory, no matter the difficulty or the cost? The Canadians' list of battlefield accomplishments dwarf that of almost any other fighting formation of an equivalent size; at the same time, they suffered higher casualties as a result of being engaged in nearly constant battle. While Currie had more manoeuvrability than British corps commanders, he was still part of a hierarchical chain of command. He had his orders to keep attacking, and he could not have pulled his forces from the line even if he had wanted to, although there is no indication that he desired to end their role in the fighting. The general felt the pain of seeing his men being torn apart in battle, but he was not at the front with the soldiers, nor did he share their fear, exhaustion, and agony. The view from the front was very different from the one from the rear, and again very different back in Canada. It is likely that these differences wrought by distance played no small part in the accusations brought by Hughes, who could see none of Currie's hard work and only the terrible red wastage of war.

The memory of the Great War is complex, and has been constructed and reconstructed over time as different generations have infused the worldwide conflagration with changing values. The war's history has been shaped by the deeds of ordinary and extraordinary people, the records that documented these actions, the various perceptions of these events, and their chroniclers. No general emerged from the war with reputation unscathed, yet Currie was one of the most caring, deliberate, and cautious of all. That he should have been singled out as a butcher sheds some light on the memory and myth, valorizations and accusations that lingered around the 60,000 dead. All who served closely with Currie knew of his dedication to his soldiers. Moreover, it can surely be said that while the war made Currie's reputation, it also led to his premature death. He drove himself too hard and he never fully recovered. He worked for his soldiers, absorbing the lessons of battle, pushing his subordinates to evolve, and railing against his superiors. That his own men never loved Currie is not difficult to understand. Currie's lack of ease among them, his enforcement of discipline, and his unsoldierly appearance all worked against him. Reputations are fickle things, and it usually takes much longer to build one up than to tear one down. And what has remained impressive to fellow generals, subordinate officers, and generations of historians was not always apparent to those fighting at the sharp end.

While Sir Sam Hughes seems destined to remain on the lunatic fringe of history, Sir Arthur Currie's reputation has been rehabilitated and enhanced since the late 1920s, not only by the events and aftermath of the "trial of the century," but also by historians, educators, journalists, and the Canadian public. But there are no final exchanges in the war of reputations, and the next generation may look back on these titans of history and decide that a re-evaluation is in order. The echo of that long-ago war continues to reverberate over time, and we still hear it and pay it heed. The ghosts of the Great War walk among us still.

BIBLIOGRAPHY

PRIMARY SOURCES, UNPUBLISHED

Library and Archives of Canada, Ottawa, Private Papers
Lord Beaverbrook (Sir Max Aitken), MG 27 II G 1
R.B. Bennett, MG 26 K
Sir Robert Borden, MG 26 H
J.J. Creelman, MG 30 E8
Sir Arthur Currie, MG 30 E100
Harold Daly, MG 27 II F 9
Duke of Devonshire, MG 27 II B 4
W.A. Griesbach, MG 30 E15
Sir Sam Hughes, MG 27 II D 23
A.E. Kemp papers, MG 27 II D 9
William Lyon Mackenzie King diaries online
Sir Wilfrid Laurier, MG 26 G
Sir John A. Macdonald papers, MG 26 A
D.E. Macintyre, MG 30 E241
Victor Odlum, MG 30 E300
Sir George Perley, MG 27, II D 12
Newton Rowell, MG 27 II D13
Sir Richard Turner, MG 30 E49

Library and Archives of Canada, Ottawa, Government Records
Records of the Department of Militia and Defence (RG 9)
Records of the Department of National Defence (RG 24)

Records of the Department of External Affairs (RG 25)
Records of Veterans Affairs (RG 38)
Records of the Overseas Ministry (RG 150)

McGill University Archives
Hugh Urquhart papers, MG 4027

Directorate of History and Heritage, Department of National Defence
A.F. Duguid biography file

Canadian War Museum, Military History Research Centre
William David Bradley, 20090115
J.H. Brown, 19830003-020
Sir Arthur Currie, 19801226
John McClung, 20030153-001
Sir Richard Turner, 19710147-001

HISTORICAL RESOURCES ONLINE
Canadian Letters and Images Project: www.canadianletters.ca
Dictionary of Canadian Biography Online: www.biographi.ca

SECONDARY SOURCES
Articles
Anderson, W. Hastings. "The Crossing of the Canal du Nord." *Canadian Defence Quarterly* 2.1 (October 1924) 236–54.
Barr, Niall and Gary Sheffield. "Douglas Haig, the Common Soldier, and the British Legion," in Brian Bond and Nigel Cave (eds.) *Haig: A Reappraisal 70 Years On* (Barnsley: Pen and Sword, 1999) 228–30.
Black, Robson. "General—The—Honorable—Sam: An Uncensored Character-Sketch of the Minister of Militia." *Maclean's* (January 1915) 38–9.
Bliss, Michael. "War Business as Usual: Canadian Munitions Production, 1914–18," in N.F. Dreisziger (ed.) *Mobilization for Total War: The Canadian, American and British Experience, 1914–1918, 1939–1945* (Waterloo: Wilfrid Laurier Press, 1981) 43–56.
Boire, Michael. "Vimy Ridge: The Battlefield before the Canadians, 1914–1916," in Geoffrey Hayes et al. (eds.) *Vimy Ridge: A Canadian Reassessment* (Waterloo: Wilfrid Laurier University Press, 2007) 51–64.

Bovey, Wilfrid. "General Sir Arthur Currie: An Appreciation." *Canadian Defence Quarterly* 11.2 (January 1934) 371–9.

Brennan, Patrick. "'Completely Worn Out by Service in France': Combat Stress and Breakdown among Senior Officers in the Canadian Corps." *Canadian Military History* 18.2 (Spring 2009) 5–14.

Brown, Robert Craig and Desmond Morton. "The Embarrassing Apotheosis of a Great Canadian: Sir Arthur Currie's Personal Crisis in 1917." *The Canadian Historical Review* 60.1 (March 1979) 41–64.

Brown, Robert Craig and Donald Loveridge. "Unrequited Faith: Recruiting the CEF, 1914–1918." *Revue Internationale d'Histoire Militaire* 51 (1982) 53–79.

Brown, Robert Craig. "'Whither are we being shoved?' Political Leadership in Canada during World War I," in J.L. Granatstein and R.D. Cuff (eds.) *War and Society in North America* (Toronto: Thomas Nelson and Sons, 1971) 104–19.

Carson, C.H.F. "Last Battle of Mons—in a Canadian Court." *Canadian Lawyer* 5.1 (February 1981) 6–11.

Clarke, Nic. "'He was my best subaltern': The life and death of Lieutenant Herrick S. Duggan, 70th Field Company, Royal Engineers." *Canadian Military History* 17.2 (Spring 2008) 21–32.

Cook, Tim. "From Destruction to Construction: The Khaki University of Canada, 1917–1919." *Journal of Canadian Studies* 37.1 (Spring 2002) 109–43.

Cook, Tim. "The Politics of Surrender: Canadian Soldiers and the Killing of Prisoners in the Great War." *Journal of Military History* 70.3 (July 2006) 637–65.

Cook, Tim. "Literary Memorials: The Great War Regimental Histories, 1919–1939." *Journal of the Canadian Historical Association* (2002) 167–90.

Cook, Tim. "Documenting War & Forging Reputations: Sir Max Aitken and the Canadian War Records Office in the First World War." *War in History* 10.3 (July 2003) 157–87.

Cook, Tim. "'We are hammering Fritz to pieces': The Gunners at Vimy," in Geoffrey Hayes et al. (eds.) *Vimy Ridge: A Canadian Reassessment* (Waterloo: Wilfrid Laurier University Press, 2007) 105–24.

Cooke, Britton B. "Major-General Sam Hughes." *Canadian Magazine* 45 (1915) 391–4.

Corry, J.A. "The Growth of Government Activities in Canada, 1914–1921." *Canadian Historical Association Annual Report* (1940) 63–73.

Fetherstonhaugh, R.C. "General Sir Arthur Currie: Tribute of the Graduates' Society of McGill University." *Canadian Defence Quarterly* 11.2 (January 1934) 152–5.

French, David. "Sir Douglas Haig's Reputation, 1918–1928: A Note." *Historical Journal* 28.4 (December 1985) 953–60.

Goodspeed, D.J. "Prelude to the Somme: Mount Sorrel, June 1916," in Michael Cross and Robert Bothwell (eds.) *Policy by Other Means: Essays in Honour of C.P. Stacey* (Toronto: University of Toronto Press, 1972) 145–62.

Gosselin, Daniel P. "Spirited Imperialism: The Formation and Command of the First Canadian Expeditionary Force in South Africa." *Canadian Military History* 17.3 (Summer 2008) 5–20.

Granatstein, J.L. "Conscription in the Great War," in David Mackenzie (ed.) *Canada and the First World War* (Toronto: University of Toronto Press, 2005) 62–75.

Gray, Charlotte. "The New Biography." *Queen's Quarterly* 108.2 (Summer 2001).

Harris, Stephen. "From Subordinate to Ally: The Canadian Corps and National Autonomy, 1914–1918." *Revue Internationale d'Historie Militaire* 51 (1982) 109–30.

Haycock, Ronald. "'Getting Elected in Spite of Them ...' Sam Hughes Gets into Parliament, 1892." *Ontario History* 75.2 (June 1983) 153–74.

Haycock, Ronald. "The Proving Ground: Sam Hughes and the Boer War." *Journal of Canadian Studies* 16 (Autumn–Winter 1981–1982) 14–25.

Haycock, Ronald. "Sir Sam Hughes: A Canadian General—Why Bother!" in Lieutenant-Colonel Bernd Horn and Stephen Harris (eds.) *Warrior Chiefs: Perspectives on Senior Canadian Military Leadership* (Toronto: Dundurn Press, 2001) 17–41.

Hughes, Sir Sam. "Some Observations on the War." *Empire Club of Canada* (Toronto: The Bryant Press, 1917) 265–74.

Hughes, Sam. "Canada's Future within the Empire." in E.A. Victor (ed.) *Canada's Future: What She Offers after the War* (Toronto: Macmillan Company, 1916) 10–15.

Hughes, Sir Sam. "The War and Our Duty." *Address Delivered before the Canadian Clubs of Ottawa, 1915–1916* (Ottawa: The Davidson-Merrill Press, 1916) 50–7.

Hughes, Sam H.S. "Sir Sam Hughes and the Problem of Imperialism." *Report of Annual Meeting of the Canadian Historian Association* (1950) 30–41.

Hyatt, A.M.J. "The Military Leadership of Sir Arthur Currie," in Lieutenant-Colonel Bernd Horn and Stephen Harris (eds.) *Warrior Chiefs: Perspectives on Senior Canadian Military Leaders* (Toronto: Dundurn Press, 2001) 43–56.

Hyatt, A.M.J. "Sir Arthur Currie and Politicians: A Case Study of Civil–Military Relations in the First World War," in Richard Preston and Peter Dennis (eds.) *Swords and Covenants* (Croom Helm: Rowman and Littlefield, 1976).

Hyatt, A.M.J. "Sir Arthur Currie and Conscription: A Soldier's View." *Canadian Historical Review* 50.3 (1969) 286–96.

Iacobelli, Teresa. "Arbitrary Justice?: A Comparative Analysis of Canadian Death Sentences Passed and Commuted during the First World War." *Canadian Military History* 16.1 (2007) 23–36.

Iarocci, Andrew. "The 1st Canadian Division: An Operational Mosaic," in Geoffrey Hayes et al. (eds.) *Vimy Ridge: A Canadian Reassessment* (Waterloo: Wilfrid Laurier University Press, 2007) 155–70.

Madsen, Chris. "Canadian Troops and Farm Burning in the South African War." *Canadian Military Journal* 6.2 (Summer 2005) 49–58.

MacFarlane, John. "The Right Stuff? Evaluating the Performance of Lieutenant-Colonel F.-L. Lessard in South Africa and His Failure to Receive a Senior Command Position with the CEF in 1914." *Canadian Military History* 8.3 (1999) 48–59.

Macmillan, Margaret. "Canada and the Peace Settlements," in David Mackenzie (ed.) *Canada and the First World War: Essays in Honour of Robert Craig Brown* (Toronto: University of Toronto Press, 2006) 379–408.

Macphail, Sir Andrew. "Sir Arthur Currie: The Value of a Degree." *Queen's Quarterly* 41 (Spring 1934) 1–19.

McCarthy, Chris. "Queen of the Battlefield: The Development of Command Organisation and Tactics in the British Infantry Battalion during the Great War," in Gary Sheffield and Dan Todman (eds.) *Command and Control on the Western Front: The British Army's Experience 1914–1918* (Spellmount, 2002) 173–94.

McNaughton, A.G.L. "The Development of Artillery in the Great War." *Canadian Defence Quarterly* 6.2 (January 1929) 160–71.

McRandle, James and James Quirk. "The Blood Test Revisited: A New Look at German Casualty Counts in World War I." *Journal of Military History* 70.3 (July 2006) 667–702.

Michel, Robert. "The General Portrayed: Sir Arthur Currie and his Painters." *Fontanus* 7 (1994) 73–102.

Miller, Carman. "Framing Canada's Great War: A Case for Including the Boer War." *Journal of Transatlantic Studies* 6.1 (April 2008) 3–21.

Miller, Carman. "Sir Frederick William Borden and Military Reform, 1896–1911." *The Canadian Historical Review* 50.3 (September 1969) 265–84.

Miller, Carman. "The Crucible of War: Canadian and British Troops during the Boer War," in Peter Dennis and Jeffrey Grey (eds.) *The Boer War* (Canberra: Army History Unit, 2000) 84–98.

Monger, David. "'No mere silent commander'? Sir Henry Horne and the Mentality of Command during the First World War." *Historical Research* 82.216 (May 2009) 340–59.

Morton, Desmond. "French Canada and the Canadian Militia, 1868–1914." *Social History-histoire sociale* 3 (April 1969) 32–69.

Morton, Desmond. "The Limits of Loyalty: French Canadian Officers and the First World War," in Edgar Denton (ed.) *Limits of Loyalty* (Waterloo: Wilfrid Laurier University Press, 1980) 79–98.

Morton, Desmond. "'Kicking and Complaining': Demobilization Riots in the Canadian Expeditionary Force, 1918–19." *The Canadian Historical Review* 61.3 (1980) 334–60.

Neiberg, Michael. "'What True Misery Is': France's Crisis of Morale 1917," in Peter Dennis and Jeffrey Grey (eds.) *1917: Tactics, Training and Technology* (Canberra: The Chief of the Army's Military History Conference, 2007) 105–24.

O'Brien, Mike. "Manhood and the Militia Myth: Masculinity, Class and Militarism in Ontario, 1902–1914," in Jeffrey Keshen and Serge Marc Durflinger (eds.) *War and Society in Post-Confederation Canada* (Toronto: Nelson, 2007) 39–54.

Penlington, Norman. "General Hutton and the Problem of Military Imperialism in Canada, 1898–1900." *The Canadian Historical Review* 24.2 (1943) 156–71.

Pugsley, Christopher. "Learning from the Canadian Corps on the Western Front." *Canadian Military History* 15.1 (Winter 2006) 5–32.

Robbins, Simon. "Henry Horne," in Ian F.W. Beckett and Steven Corvi (eds.) *Haig's Generals* (Barnsley: Pen and Sword, 2006) 97–121.

Scott, John. "'Three Cheers for Earl Haig'": Canadian Veterans and the Visit of Field Marshal Sir Douglas Haig to Canada in the Summer of 1925." *Canadian Military History* 5.1 (Summer 1996) 35–40.

Sheffield, Gary and Niall Barr. "Douglas Haig, the Common Soldier and the British Legion," in Brian Bond and Nigel Cave (eds.) *Haig: A Reappraisal 70 Years On* (Barnsley: Pen and Sword, 1999) 223–39.

Simkins, Peter. "Building Blocks: Aspects of Command and Control at Brigade Level," in Dan Todman and Gary Sheffield (eds.) *Command and Control in the British Army on the Western Front* (Stroud: Spellmount, 2004) 120–141.

Simkins, Peter. "Haig and the Army Commanders," in Brian Bond and Nigel Cave (eds.) *Haig: A Reappraisal 70 Years On* (Barnsley: Pen and Sword, 1999) 78–106.

Stewart, Robert. "The Obsessions of Sam Hughes." *The Beaver* (October–November 2003) 14–20.

Strachan, Hew. "The Morale of the German Army," in Hugh Cecil and Peter Liddell (eds.) *Facing Armageddon: The First World War Experienced* (Barnsley: Pen and Sword, 1996) 221–7.

Todman, Daniel. "'Sans Peur et Sans Reproche': The Retirement, Death and Mourning of Sir Douglas Haig, 1918–1928." *The Journal of Military History* 67.4 (2003) 1083–1106.

Travers, Timothy. "Allies in Conflict: The British and Canadian Official Historians and the Real Story of Second Ypres (1915)." *Journal of Contemporary History* 24 (1989) 301–25.

Travers, T.H.E. "From Surafend to Gough: Charles Bean, James Edmonds, and the Making of the Australian Official History." *Journal of the Australian War Memorial* 27 (October 1995) 15–25.

Vance, Jonathan. "The Soldier as Novelist: Literature, History, and the Great War." *Canadian Literature* 179 (Winter 2003) 22–37.

Walker, Jonathan. "'An Unforgivable Sin': The Actions at St. Eloi Craters, 1916." *Journal of the Centre of the First World War Studies* 2.3 (November 2005) 158–9.

Wilson, Barbara. "The Road to the Cobourg Court Room: New Material from the Archives of the Canadian War Museum on the Sir Arthur Currie–Sir Sam Hughes Dispute, 1918–19." *Canadian Military History* 10.3 (Summer 2001) 67–73.

Wood, Colonel William. "Behind the Scenes of Canadian War History, The J. Clarence Webster Lectures for 1925–6." *The Argosy* 4.1 (Sackville, New Brunswick, June 1926) 1–45.

Books

Allen, Ralph. *Ordeal by Fire: Canada 1910–1950*. Toronto: Doubleday Canada, 1961.

Anderson, Peter. *I, That's Me: Escape from a German Prison Camp and Other Adventures*. Edmonton: Bradburn, 1924.

Andrews, E.M. *The Anzac Illusion: Anglo–Australian relations during World War I*. Cambridge: Cambridge University Press, 1993.

Beahen, William. "Sam Hughes on Canada's Military Role in the British Empire, 1896–1911." University of Ottawa: MA thesis, n.d. [ca. 1970s].

Lord Beaverbrook. *Friends*. London: Hinemann, 1959.

Becker, John Harold. *Silhouettes of the Great War: The Memoirs of John Harold Becker*. Ottawa: CEF Books, 2001.

Beckett, Ian F.W. and Steven Corvi. *Haig's Generals*. Barnsley: Pen and Sword, 2006.

Berger, Carl. *The Sense of Power: Studies in the Ideas of Canadian Imperialism, 1867–1914*. Toronto: University of Toronto Press, 1971.

Berger, Carl (ed.). *Conscription 1917*. Canadian Historical Readings, No. 8.

Berton, Pierre. *Vimy*. Toronto: Random House, 1986.

Blake, Robert. *The Private Papers of Douglas Haig, 1914–1919*. London: Eyre and Spottiswoode, 1952.

Bliss, Michael. *Right Honourable Men: The Descent of Canadian Politics from Macdonald to Chrétien*. Toronto: HarperCollins, 2004.

Bliss, Michael. *A Canadian Millionaire: The Life and Business Times of Sir Joseph Flavelle, Bart., 1858–1939*. Toronto: Macmillan of Canada, 1978.

Bond, Brian and Nigel Cave (eds.). *Haig: A Reappraisal 70 Years On*. Barnsley: Pen and Sword, 1999.

Boraston, J. and G. Dewar. *Sir Douglas Haig's Command, 1915–1922*. Boston: Houghton Mifflin, 1922.

Borden, Sir Robert. *Letters to Limbo*. Toronto: University of Toronto Press, 1971.

Borden, Sir Robert. *Robert Laird Borden: His Memoirs* (2 volumes). Toronto: McClelland & Stewart, 1938.

Borys, David. "The Education of a Corps Commander: Arthur Currie's Leadership from 1915 to 1917." University of Alberta: MA thesis, 2006.

Bothwell, Robert, Ian Drummond, and John English. *Canada, 1900–1945.* Toronto: University of Toronto Press, 1990.

Brandon, Laura. *Art or Memorial? The Forgotten History of Canada's War Art.* Calgary: University of Calgary Press, 2006.

Bridle, Augustus. *Sons of Canada.* Toronto: J.M. Dent, 1916.

Bridle, Augustus. *The Masques of Ottawa.* Toronto: The Macmillan Company, 1921.

Brown, Ian Malcolm. "Lieutenant-General Sir Arthur Currie and the Canadian Corps 1917–1918: The Evolution of a Style of Command and Attack." University of Calgary: MA thesis, 1991.

Brown, Robert Craig. *Robert Laird Borden: A Biography* (2 volumes). Toronto: Macmillan of Canada, 1975 and 1980.

Brown, Robert Craig and Ramsay Cook. *Canada, 1896–1921: A Nation Transformed.* Toronto: McClelland & Stewart, 1974.

Capon, Alan R. *His Faults Lie Gently: The Incredible Sam Hughes.* Lindsay: Floyd Hall, 1969.

Carnegie, David. *The History of Munitions Supply in Canada, 1914–1918.* London: Longmans, Green, 1925.

Cassar, George. *Beyond Courage: The Canadians at the Second Battle of Ypres.* Ottawa: Oberon, 1985.

Chisholm, Anne and Michael Davie. *Beaverbrook: A Life.* London: Hutchinson, 1992.

Clark, C.S. *Of Toronto the Good: A Social Study: The Queen City of Canada as It Is.* Montreal: Toronto Pub., n.d.

Clyne, H.R.N. *Vancouver's 29th.* Vancouver: Tobin's Tigers Association, 1964.

Collard, Edgar Andrew (ed.). *The McGill You Knew: An Anthology of Memories 1920–1960.* Don Mills: Longman, 1975.

Cook, Tim. *No Place to Run: The Canadian Corps and Gas Warfare in the First World War.* Vancouver: University of British Columbia Press, 1999.

Cook, Tim. *Clio's Warriors: Canadian Historians and the Writing of the World Wars.* Vancouver: University of British Columbia Press, 1999.

Cook, Tim. *At the Sharp End: Canadians Fighting the Great War, Volume I: 1914–1916.* Toronto: Viking, 2007.

Cook, Tim. *Shock Troops: Canadians Fighting the Great War, Volume II: 1917–1918.* Toronto: Viking, 2008.

Currie, John Allister. *"The Red Watch": With the First Canadian Division in Flanders.* Toronto: McClelland, Goodchild & Stewart, 1916.

Dafoe, John Wesley. *Clifford Sifton: In Relation to His Times.* Toronto: The Macmillan Company of Canada Limited, 1931.

Dancocks, Daniel. *Sir Arthur Currie: A Biography.* Toronto: Methuen, 1985.

Dancocks, Daniel. *Gallant Canadians: The Story of the Tenth Canadian Infantry Battalion, 1914–1919.* Calgary: Calgary Highlanders Regimental Funds Foundation, 1990.

Dancocks, Daniel. *Spearhead to Victory: Canada and the Great War.* Edmonton: Hurtig, 1987.

Demill, Robert Scott. "The 1928 Cobourg Trial of Sir Arthur Currie and the Port Hope Evening Guide: The Rehabilitation of the Reputation of a Corps Commander." University of Ottawa: MA thesis, 1989.

Donaldson, Gordon. *Sixteen Men: The Prime Ministers of Canada.* Toronto: Doubleday, 1980.

Duguid, A.F. *A Question of Confidence: The Ross Rifle in the Trenches,* edited by Clive M. Law. Ottawa: Service Publications, 2000.

Duguid, A.F. *Official History of the Canadian Forces in the Great War 1914–1919.* Ottawa: King's Printer, 1938.

Durflinger, Serge M. *Lest We Forget: A History of the Last Post Fund, 1909–1999.* Montreal: The Last Post Fund, 2000.

Edmonds, Brigadier-General Sir James E. and Captain G.C. Wynne. *History of the Great War based on official documents by direction of the Historical Section of the Committee of Imperial Defence. Military Operations: France and Belgium, 1915. Volume I: Winter 1914–15: Battle of Neuve Chapelle: Battle of Ypres.* London: Macmillan, 1927.

English, John. *The Decline of Politics: The Conservatives and the Party System, 1901–20.* Toronto: University of Toronto Press, 1993.

Farr, Donn. *The Silent General: Horne of the First Army.* Solihull: Helion and Company, 2007.

Fetherstonhaugh, R.C. *The 13th Battalion Royal Highlanders of Canada, 1914–1919.* Montreal: self-published, 1925.

Flick, C.L. *'Just What Happened': A Diary of the Mobilization of the Canadian Militia, 1914.* Privately published, 1917.

Freeman, Bill and Richard Nielsen. *Far From Home: Canadians in the First World War.* Toronto: McGraw-Hill, 1999.

Frost, George William. *Sincerely Yours.* Victoria: The Inditer, 1998.

Frost, Stanley Brice. *McGill University: For the Advancement of Learning, Volume II: 1895–1971.* Montreal-Kingston: McGill-Queen's University Press, 1984.

Frost, Leslie. *Fighting Men.* Toronto: Clarke, Irwin, 1967.

Frost, Leslie. *The Record on Sir Sam Hughes Set Straight.* Unpublished pamphlet held at the Canadian War Museum, Military History Research Centre, n.d. [ca. 1960s].

Gaddis, John Lewis. *The Landscape of History: How Historians Map the Past.* New York: Oxford University Press, 2002.

George, David Lloyd. *War Memoirs of David Lloyd George, volume VI.* London: Ivor Nicholson and Watson, 1936.

Gerritsen, Maarten. "Corps Identity: The Letters, Diaries and Memoirs of Canada's Great War Soldiers." Memorial University: Ph.D. dissertation, 2008.

Glazebrook, G.P. de T. *Sir Edmund Walker.* London: Oxford University Press, 1933.

Godefroy, A.B. *For Freedom and Honour: The Story of the 25 Canadian Volunteers Executed in the Great War.* Ottawa: CEF Books, 1998.

Graham, Roger. *Arthur Meighen, A Biography: And Fortune Fled.* Toronto: University of Toronto Press, 1963.

Graham, Roger. *The King–Byng Affair, 1926: A Question of Responsible Government.* Toronto: Copp Clark, 1967.

Granatstein, J.L. *Canada's Army: Waging War and Keeping the Peace.* Toronto: University of Toronto Press, 2002.

Granatstein, J.L. and J.M. Hitsman. *Broken Promises: A History of Conscription in Canada.* Toronto: Oxford University Press, 1977.

Granastein, J.L. and R.D. Cuff. *War and Society in North America.* Toronto: Thomas Nelson, 1971.

Green, Andrew. *The Great War: Sir James Edmonds and the Official Histories 1915–1948.* London: Taylor & Francis, 2003.

Greenfield, Nathan. *Baptism of Fire: The Second Battle of Ypres and the Forging of Canada, April 1915.* Toronto: HarperCollins, 2008.

Griesbach, W.A. *I Remember.* Toronto: Ryerson Press, 1946.

Gwyn, Sandra. *Tapestry of War.* Toronto: HarperCollins, 1992.

Hadley, Michael L. and Roger Sarty. *Tin Pots and Pirate Ships: Canadian Naval Forces and German Sea Raiders 1880–1918.* Montreal-Kingston: McGill-Queen's University Press, 1991.

Hamilton, General Sir Ian. *Report on the Military Institutions of Canada.* Ottawa: King's Printer, 1913.

Harris, Stephen J. *Canadian Brass: The Making of a Professional Army.* Toronto: University of Toronto Press, 1988.

Haycock, R.G. *Sam Hughes: The Public Career of a Controversial Canadian, 1885–1916.* Ottawa: Canadian War Museum, 1986.

Hayes, Joseph. *The Eighty-Fifth Canadian Infantry Battalion: Nova Scotia Highlanders in France and Flanders.* Halifax: Royal Print & Litho, 1920.

Hickson, Arthur O. *As It Was Then.* Nova Scotia: Acadia University, 1988.

Hillmer, Norman and J.L. Granatstein. *Empire to Umpire: Canada and the World to the 1990s.* Toronto: Copp Clark, 1994.

Hopkins, J. Castell. *Canadian Annual Review of Public Affairs, 1919.* Toronto: The Canadian Annual Review Limited, 1920.

Hopkins, J. Castell. *Canada at War: A Record of Heroism and Achievement, 1914–1918.* Toronto: The Canadian Annual Review Limited, 1919.

Houston, Cecil. *The Sash Canada Wore: A Historical Geography of the Orange Order in Canada.* Toronto: University of Toronto Press, 1980.

Hughes, John (ed.). *The Unwanted: Great War Letters from the Field.* Edmonton: University of Alberta Press, 2005.

Hughes, Sam. *Steering the Course: A Memoir.* Montreal-Kingston: McGill-Queen's University Press, 2000.

Humphries, Mark. *The Selected Papers of Sir Arthur Currie: Diaries, Letters, and Report to the Ministry, 1917–33.* Waterloo: Laurier Centre for Military, Strategic and Disarmament Studies, 2008.

Hyatt, A.M.J. *General Sir Arthur Currie: A Military Biography.* Toronto: University of Toronto Press and Canadian War Museum, 1987.

Iarocci, Andrew. *Shoestring Soldiers: The 1st Canadian Division at War, 1914–1915.* Toronto: University of Toronto Press, 2008.

Kerr, Wilfred. *Arms and the Maple Leaf: Memoirs of Canada's Corps 1918.* Seaforth, Ont.: Huron Expositor, 1943.

Keshen, Jeff. *Propaganda and Censorship during Canada's Great War.* Edmonton: University of Alberta Press, 1996.

Kirkconnell, Watson. *County of Victoria: Centennial History.* Lindsay: John Deyell Limited, 1967.

Kitchen, Martin. *The German Offensives of 1918*. Stroud: Tempus, 2005.

Livesay, J.F.B. *Canada's Hundred Days: With the Canadian Corps from Amiens to Mons, Aug. 8–Nov. 11, 1918*. Toronto: Thomas Allen, 1919.

Lucas, Sir Charles. *The Empire at War, volume II*. Oxford University Press, 1923.

Magnuss, Philip. *Kitchener: Portrait of an Imperialist*. London: Penguin, 1968.

Macphail, Sir Andrew. *The Medical Services*. Ottawa: F.A. Acland, 1924.

Macphail, Sir Andrew. *Official History of the Canadian Forces in the Great War: The Medical Services*. Ottawa: King's Printer, 1925.

Macfie, John. *Letters Home*. Meaford: Oliver Graphics, 1990.

McGillicuddy, Owen E. "Sir Arthur Currie: Leader of Men." Unpublished manuscript held at the Canadian War Museum, Military History Research Centre. n.d., [ca. October 1925].

McKenzie, F.A. *Canada's Day of Glory*. Toronto: William Briggs, 1918.

McMurray, Dorothy. *Four Principals of McGill: A Memoir*. Montreal: The Graduates' Society of McGill University, 1974.

McMurray, Dorothy. *Only Grandfathers Wore Beards*. Unpublished memoir held at the Canadian War Museum, Military History Research Centre. n.d., [ca. 1960s–1970s].

Miller, Carman. *Painting the Map Red: Canada and the South African War, 1899–1902*. Montreal-Kingston: McGill-Queen's University Press, 1993.

Miller, Ian Hugh Maclean. *Our Glory and Our Grief: Torontonians and the Great War*. Toronto: University of Toronto Press, 2002.

Morrison, E.W.B. *With the Guns in South Africa*. Hamilton: Spectator Printing Company, 1901.

Morton, Desmond. *A Peculiar Kind of Politics: Canada's Overseas Ministry in the First World War*. Toronto: University of Toronto Press, 1982.

Morton, Desmond. *When Your Number's Up: The Canadian Soldier in the First World War*. Toronto: Random House, 1993.

Morton, Desmond. *Ministers and Generals: Politics and the Canadian Militia, 1868–1914*. Toronto: University of Toronto Press, 1970.

Morton, Desmond. *The Canadian General: Sir William Otter*. Toronto: Hakkert, 1974.

Morton, Desmond. *Canada and War: A Military and Political History*. Toronto: Butterworths, 1981.

Morton, Desmond and Glenn Wright. *Winning the Second Battle: Canadian Veterans and the Return to Civilian Life, 1915–1930.* Toronto: University of Toronto Press, 1987.

Morton, Desmond and J.L. Granatstein. *Marching to Armageddon: Canadians and the Great War 1914–1919.* Toronto: Lester & Orpen Dennys, 1989.

Moss, Mark. *Manliness and Militarism: Educating Young Boys in Ontario for War.* New York: Oxford University Press, 2001.

Murray, W.W. *The History of the 2nd Canadian Battalion, (Eastern Ontario Regiment) Canadian Expeditionary Force in the Great War, 1914–1918.* Ottawa: Mortimer Ltd., 1947.

Nasmith, George G. *On the Fringe of the Great Fight.* Toronto: McClelland, Goodchild & Stewart, 1917.

Nicholson, G.W.L. *The Gunners of Canada: The History of the Royal Regiment of the Canadian Artillery, Vol. 1: 1534–1919.* Toronto: McClelland & Stewart, 1967.

Noel, S.J.R. *Patrons, Clients, Brokers: Ontario Society and Politics, 1791–1896.* Toronto: University of Toronto Press, 1990.

Norris, Marjorie Barron (ed.). *Medicine and Duty: The World War I Memoir of Captain Harold W. McGill.* Calgary: University of Calgary Press, 2007.

Overseas Military Forces of Canada, Report of the Ministry, Overseas Military Forces of Canada, 1918. London: H.M Stationery Office, 1919.

Peat, Harold. *Private Peat.* New York: Grosset and Dunlap, 1917.

Peck, Edward. *Cy Peck, V.C.: A Biography of a Legendary Canadian.* Vancouver: privately printed, 2006.

Pedley, James. *Only This: A War Retrospect, 1917–1918.* Ottawa: The Graphic Publishers, 1927.

Porter, Neal. "From Logistics to Open Warfare: The State of Logistics in the Canadian Corps, August to November 1918." University of Ottawa: MA thesis, 2002.

Prang, Margaret. *N.W. Rowell: Ontario Nationalist.* Toronto: University of Toronto Press, 1975.

Preston, R.A. *Canada and Imperial Defence: A Study of the Origins of the British Commonwealth's Defense Organization, 1867–1919.* Toronto: University of Toronto Press, 1964.

Preston, William Thomas Rochester. *My Generation of Politics and Politicians.* Toronto: D.A. Rose, 1927.

Radley, Kenneth. *We Lead, Others Follow: First Canadian Division 1914–1918*. St. Catharines: Vanwell, 2006.

Rawling, Bill. *Death Their Enemy: Canadian Medical Practitioners and War*. Ottawa: self-published, 2001.

Rawling, Bill. *Surviving Trench Warfare: Technology and the Canadian Corps, 1914–1918*. Toronto: University of Toronto Press, 1992.

Robertson, Ian Ross. *Sir Andrew Macphail: The Life and Legacy of a Canadian Man of Letters*. Montreal-Kingston: McGill-Queen's University Press, 2008.

Robbins, Simon. *British Generalship on the Western Front, 1914–1918: Defeat into Victory*. London: Frank Cass, 2005.

Russenholt, E.S. *Six Thousand Canadian Men: Being the History of the 44th Battalion, Canadian Infantry, 1914–1919*. Winnipeg: Printed to the order of Forty-Fourth Battalion Association by the Montfort Press, 1932.

Schreiber, Shane. *Shock Army of the British Empire: The Canadian Corps in the Last 100 Days of the Great War*. Westport, Conn: Praeger, 1997.

Schull, Joseph. *Laurier: The First Canadian*. Toronto: Macmillan of Canada, 1965.

Seely, J.E.B. *Adventure*. London: Heinemann, 1931.

Sharpe, Robert J. *The Last Day, The Last Hour: The Currie Libel Trial*. Toronto: Osgoode Society, 1988.

Sheffield, Gary and John Bourne. *Douglas Haig: War Diaries and Letters, 1914–1918*. London: Weidenfield and Nicolson, 2005.

Soye, Edward. "Canadian War Trophies: Arthur Doughty and German Aircraft Allocated to Canada after the First World War." Royal Military College of Canada: MA thesis, 2009.

Stacey, C.P. *Canada and the Age of Conflict, 1867–1921*. Toronto: Macmillan of Canada, 1977.

Stevens, G.R. *A City Goes to War*. Brampton: Charters, 1964.

Stevens, Paul and John Saywell (eds.). *Lord Minto's Canadian Papers, volume I*. Toronto: The Champlain Society, 1981.

Stewart, Robert. *Sam Steele: Lion of the Frontier*. Toronto: Doubleday, 1979.

Stewart, William. "Attack Doctrine in the Canadian Corps, 1916–1918." University of New Brunswick: MA thesis, 1982.

Strachan, Hew. *The First World War*. London: Simon & Schuster, 2003.

Swettenham, John. *To Seize the Victory: The Canadian Corps in World War I*. Toronto: Ryerson Press, 1965.

Taylor, A.J.P. *Beaverbrook.* New York: Simon & Schuster, 1972.

Terraine, John. *Douglas Haig: The Educated Soldier.* London: Hutchinson, 1963.

Thompson, Austin Seton. *Jarvis Street: A Story of Triumph and Tragedy.* Toronto: Personal Library, 1980.

Todman, Dan. *The Great War: Myth and Memory.* London: Hambledon and London, 2005.

Topp, C.B. *The 42nd Battalion, CEF. Royal Highlanders of Canada in the Great War.* Montreal: privately printed, 1931.

Travers, T.H.E. *The Killing Ground: The British Army, the Western Front, and the Emergence of Modern Warfare, 1900–1918.* London: Allen & Unwin, 1987.

Tunis, Barbara. *In Caps and Gowns.* Montreal: McGill University Press, 1966.

Tupper, Reginald H. *Victor Gordon Tupper: A Brother's Tribute.* Toronto: Oxford University Press, 1921.

Urquhart, Hugh M. *Arthur Currie: The Biography of a Great Canadian.* Toronto: Dent, 1950.

Vance, Jonathan. *Death So Noble: Memory, Meaning, and the First World War.* Vancouver: University of British Columbia Press, 1997.

Wallace, W. Steward. *The Memoirs of the Rt. Hon. Sir George Foster.* Toronto: Macmillan Company of Canada, 1933.

Ward, Norman (ed.). *A Party Politician: The Memoirs of Chubby Power.* Toronto: Macmillan of Canada, 1966.

Wells, George Anderson. *The Fighting Bishop.* Toronto: Cardwell House, 1971.

Wemyss, Lady Wester. *The Life and Letters of Lord Wester Wemyss.* London: Eyre and Spottiswoode, 1935.

White, Thomas. *The Story of Canada's War Finances.* Montreal: Blackwell, 1921.

Williams, Jeffrey. *Byng of Vimy.* Toronto: University of Toronto Press, 1983, 1992.

Willson, Beckles. *From Quebec to Piccadilly and Other Places: Some Anglo-Canadian Memories.* London: Jonathan Cape, 1929.

Wilson, David. *The Orange Order in Canada.* Dublin: Four Courts Press, 2007.

Winter, Charles F. *Lieutenant-General the Hon. Sir Sam Hughes.* Toronto: Macmillan Company of Canada, 1931.

Wood, H.F. *Vimy!* Toronto: Macmillan of Canada, 1967.

Wood, James A. "The Sense of Duty: Canadian Ideas of the Citizen Soldier, 1896–1917." Wilfrid Laurier University: Ph.D. dissertation, 2006.

Endnotes

Introduction

[1] Sandra Gwyn, *Tapestry of War: A Private View of Canadians in the Great War* (Toronto: HarperCollins, 1992) 269.

[2] House of Commons Debates (Hansard), 4 March 1919, 207.

[3] Tim Cook, *Shock Troops: Canadians Fighting the Great War, Volume II: 1917–1918* (Toronto: Viking, 2008) 3; David Lloyd George, *War Memoirs of David Lloyd George*, v. 6 (London: Ivor Nicholson and Watson, 1936) 3367.

[4] McGill University Archives (hereafter MU), Hugh Urquhart papers, M.G. 4027, box 1, file 12, Macdonnel to Urquhart, n.d. [ca. 1934].

[5] Library and Archives Canada, Sir Arthur Currie papers [hereafter LAC CP], MG 30 E100, v. 43, diary [hereafter Currie's diary], 7 February 1918.

[6] MU, Urquhart papers, box 1, file 13, Impressions of A.C. by E.S. Hoare-Nairne.

[7] Jean-Paul Sartre, cited in Charlotte Gray, "The New Biography," *Queen's Quarterly* 108.2 (Summer 2001) 248.

[8] John Lewis Gaddis, *The Landscape of History: How Historians Map the Past* (Oxford University Press, 2002) 137.

Chapter 1: A Fighter

[1] Alan R. Capon, *His Faults Lie Gently: The Incredible Sam Hughes* (Lindsay: Floyd Hall, 1969) 24; on Lindsay, see Watson Kirkconnell, *County of Victoria: Centennial History* (Lindsay: John Deyell Limited, 1967) 126.

[2] R.G. Haycock, *Sam Hughes: The Public Career of a Controversial Canadian, 1885–1916* (Ottawa: Canadian War Museum, 1986) 28.

[3] Robson Black, "General—The—Honorable—Sam: An Uncensored Character-Sketch of the Minister of Militia," *Maclean's* (January 1915) 39.

[4] LAC, Sir Sam Hughes papers [hereafter LAC, Sam Hughes papers], MG 27 II-D-23, v. 1, file 3, Hughes's untitled memoir, n.d. [written 1919–1921], page 1. Hereafter Hughes's memoir.

[5] Hughes's memoir, 17.

[6] For Hughes's militia appointments, see LAC, Sam Hughes papers, v. 1, file 1, biographical notes, n.d.

[7] For an early history of Hughes's employment, see LAC, Sam Hughes papers, v. 1, file 4, Educational Standing, Certificates, Testimonials, etc., of Mr. Samuel Hughes.

[8] Capon, *His Faults Lie Gently*, 22.

[9] Hughes's memoir, 69.

[10] Dictionary of Canadian Biography Online, Robert Craig Brown. Sam Hughes biography.

[11] Charles F. Winter, *Lieutenant-General The Hon. Sir Sam Hughes* (Toronto: The Macmillan Company of Canada, 1931) xv; Austin Seton Thompson, *Jarvis Street: A Story of Triumph and Tragedy* (Toronto: Personal Library, 1980) 143; Hughes's memoir, 6.

[12] Sam Hughes, *Steering the Course: A Memoir* (Montreal: McGill-Queen's University Press, 2000) 9.

[13] *Victoria Warder*, 4 October 1889.

[14] Leslie Frost, *Record on Sir Sam Hughes Set Straight* (pamphlet, no date) 5.

[15] Haycock, *Sam Hughes*, 26–7.

[16] Hughes's memoir, 34.

[17] Sam H.S. Hughes, "Sir Sam Hughes and the Problem of Imperialism," *Report of Annual Meeting of the Canadian Historical Association* 29.1 (1950) 32.

[18] LAC, Sir Robert Borden papers, MG 26 H C-4214, Hughes to Borden, 26 November 1914, page 12600.

[19] See David Wilson, *The Orange Order in Canada* (Four Courts Press: Dublin, 2007) and Cecil Houston, *The Sash Canada Wore: A Historical Geography of the Orange Order in Canada* (Toronto: University of Toronto Press, 1980).

[20] See Carl Berger, *The Sense of Power: Studies in the Ideas of Canadian Imperialism, 1867–1914* (Toronto: University of Toronto Press, 1971).

[21] Stanley Brice Frost, *McGill University: For the Advancement of Learning, Volume II: 1895–1971* (Montreal: McGill-Queen's University Press, 1984) 98.

[22] For the election, see Ronald Haycock, "'Getting Elected in Spite of Them ...' Sam Hughes Gets into Parliament, 1892," *Ontario History* 75.2 (1983) 153–74.

[23] C.S. Clark, *Of Toronto the Good, A Social Study: The Queen City of Canada as It Is* (Montreal, Quebec: Toronto Pub., n.d.) 30.

[24] See William P. Beahen, "Sam Hughes on Canada's Military Role in the British Empire, 1896–1911" (University of Ottawa, Masters, n.d.).

[25] See William Christian, *Parkin: Canada's Most Famous Forgotten Man* (Toronto: Blue Butterfly Books, 2008) and Berger, *The Sense of Power*.

[26] *Victoria Warder*, 13 May 1887.

[27] Desmond Morton, *Ministers and Generals: Politics and the Canadian Militia, 1868–1914* (Toronto: University of Toronto Press, 1970) 17.

[28] Carman Miller, "Sir Frederick William Borden and Military Reform, 1896–1911," *The Canadian Historical Review* 50.3 (September 1969) 265–84.

[29] LAC, Sir Wilfrid Laurier papers, MG 26 G, v. 124, 37197, Laurier to Borden, 5 September 1899.

[30] Hansard, 1899, 7328-29; also see LAC pamphlet, no. 2565, Correspondence touching on the conduct of Lieutenant-Colonel Hughes, MP in connection with his volunteering for active service in South Africa, 7–9.

[31] See Daniel P. Gosselin, "Spirited Imperialism: The Formation and Command of the First Canadian Expeditionary Force in South Africa," *Canadian Military History* 17.3 (Summer 2008) 5–20.

[32] Haycock, *Sam Hughes*, 72.

[33] Paul Stevens and John Saywell (eds.), *Lord Minto's Canadian Papers*, v. I (Toronto: The Champlain Society, 1981) 372.

[34] LAC, pamphlet, no. 2565, Correspondence touching on the conduct of Lieutenant-Colonel Hughes, MP... , Hughes to Hutton, 28 August 1899.

[35] Harris, *Canadian Brass*, 87.

[36] LAC, Sam Hughes papers, v. 2, file 3, Hughes to Sir Frederick Borden, 20 December 1910.

[37] Ralph Allen, *Ordeal by Fire: Canada 1910–1945*, (Toronto: Doubleday, 1961) 37.

[38] John Swettenham, *To Seize the Victory: The Canadian Corps in World War I* (Toronto: Ryerson Press, 1965) 22.

[39] Beckles Willson, *From Quebec to Piccadilly and Other Places: Some Anglo-Canadian Memories* (London: Jonathan Cape, 1929) 106.

[40] Desmond Morton, *The Canadian General: Sir William Otter* (Toronto: Hakkert, 1974) 167; for Hutton's previous objections to Hughes, see LAC, Sam Hughes papers, v. 2, file 1, Hutton to Borden, 28 October 1899.

[41] For the Canadian guerrilla and anti-guerrilla war, see Chris Madsen, "Canadian Troops and Farm Burning in the South African War," *Canadian Military Journal* 6.2 (Summer 2005) 49–58.

[42] For Hughes in South Africa, see Ron Haycock, "The Proving Ground: Sam Hughes and the Boer War," *Journal of Canadian Studies* XVI (Autumn–Winter, 1981–2). For Hughes's own account of his service, see Hughes's memoir, A-1 to A-16.

[43] E.W.B. Morrison, *With the Guns in South Africa* (Hamilton: Spectator Printing Company, 1901) 110.

[44] Ronald G. Haycock, "Sir Sam Hughes: A Canadian General—Why Bother!," in Lieutenant-Colonel Bernd Horn and Stephen Harris, *Warrior Chiefs: Perspectives on Senior Canadian Military Leadership* (Toronto: Dundurn Press, 2001) 22.

[45] Britton B. Cooke, "Major-General Sam Hughes," *Canadian Magazine* 45 (1915) 393.

[46] Carman Miller, *Painting the Map Red: Canada and the South African War, 1899–1902* (Montreal-Kingston: McGill-Queen's University Press, 1993) 202–3.

[47] LAC, Sam Hughes papers, v. 2, file 3, Hughes to Lord Roberts, 27 November [no year, but likely 1910].

[48] Gordon Donaldson, *Sixteen Men: The Prime Ministers of Canada* (Toronto: Doubleday, 1980) 81.

[49] Robson Black, "General—The—Honorable—Sam: An Uncensored Character-Sketch of the Minister of Militia," *Maclean's* (January 1915) 39.

Chapter 2: War Hero and Martial Madman

[1] Swettenham, *To Seize the Victory*, 22.

[2] Norman Hillmer and J.L. Granatstein, *Empire to Umpire: Canada and the World to the 1990s* (Toronto: Copp Clark, 1994) 23; Carman Miller, "Framing Canada's Great War: A Case for Including the Boer War," *Journal of Transatlantic Studies* 6.1 (April 2008) 13–14.

[3] Augustus Bridle, *Sons of Canada: Short Studies of Characteristic Canadians* (Toronto: J.M. Dent & Sons, 1916) 160.

[4] On the two VCs, see LAC, Sam Hughes papers, v. 2, file 3, Hughes to Laurier, 13 April [no year, but likely 1910]; Allen, *Ordeal by Fire: Canada 1910–1950*, 38.

[5] Haycock, *Sam Hughes*, 98.

[6] Schull, *Laurier*, 438.

[7] See Hansard, 22 May 1908, 7030; and 17 April 1907, 6907.

[8] Hansard, 5495 to 5518; 5511–21, 5545 and 5575–6.

[9] Capon, *His Faults Lie Gently*, 38.

[10] W. Steward Wallace, *The Memoirs of the Rt. Hon. Sir George Foster* (Toronto: Macmillan, 1933) 129.

[11] Capon, *His Faults Lie Gently*, 33.

[12] Hansard, 13 May 1909, 6442–4.

[13] LAC, Sam Hughes papers, v. 1, file 11, Address upon the subject of Canadian Assistance to the Imperial Navy, delivered by Col. Sam Hughes, M.P., 17 February 1910.

[14] Joseph Schull, *Laurier: The First Canadian* (Toronto: Macmillan of Canada, 1965) 496.

[15] For the naval debates, see Michael L. Hadley and Roger Sarty, *Tin Pots and Pirate Ships: Canadian Naval Forces and German Sea Raiders 1880–1918* (Montreal: McGill-Queen's University Press, 1991).

[16] See Hansard, 1907–08, 9330; J. Castell Hopkins, *Canadian Annual Review* (hereafter *CAR*), 1907, 438, 473–4.

[17] Haycock, *Sam Hughes*, 115.

[18] Haycock, *Sam Hughes*, 130.

[19] LAC, Borden papers, Hughes to Borden, 25 September 1911, 65082.

[20] Robert Borden (ed.), *Robert Laird Borden: His Memoirs* (Toronto, 1938) I/330.

[21] Borden, *Memoirs*, I/330.

[22] Michael Bliss, *A Canadian Millionaire: The Life and Business Times of Sir Joseph Flavelle, Bart., 1858–1939* (Toronto: Macmillan of Canada, 1978) 276.

[23] Capon, *His Faults Lie Gently*, 34.

[24] Haycock, *Sam Hughes*, 139.

[25] *CAR* 1912, 285; also see Hansard, 10 December 1906, 741; and Hansard, 11 July 1905, 9192; and LAC, Sam Hughes papers, v. 1, file 8, Hughes to Borden, 17 October 1916.

[26] On cadets, see Mark Moss, *Manliness and Militarism: Educating Young Boys in Ontario for War* (New York: Oxford University Press, 2001); and Desmond Morton, "The Cadet Movement in the Moment of Canadian Militarism, 1909–1914," *Journal of Canadian Studies* XIII.2 (Summer 1978).

[27] Donaldson, *Sixteen Men*, 81.

[28] J. Castell Hopkins, *Canada at War: A Record of Heroism and Achievement, 1914–1918* (Toronto: The Canadian Annual Review Limited, 1919) 63.

[29] James A. Wood, "The Sense of Duty: Canadian Ideas of the Citizen Soldier, 1896–1917" (Wilfrid Laurier University: Ph.D. dissertation, 2006) 280; *CAR* 1914, 133–4.

[30] LAC, Sam Hughes papers, v. 1, file 12, Hughes's private notebook, "Militia and Defence, 1914," no pagination.

[31] Borden papers, C-4344, Hughes to Borden, 25 September 1911, 65082.

[32] Morton, *The Canadian General*, 291.

[33] W.L.M. King diaries, digitized, online at the Library and Archives Canada website, 27 January 1911.

[34] Robert Craig Brown, *Robert Laird Borden*, v. 2 (Toronto: Macmillan of Canada, 1980) I/253; Duguid, *Official History of the Canadian Forces in the Great War 1914–1919*, 3.

[35] Mike O'Brien, "Manhood and the Militia Myth: Masculinity, Class and Militarism in Ontario, 1902–1914," in Jeffrey Keshen and Serge Marc Durflinger

(eds.), *War and Society in Post-Confederation Canada* (Toronto: Nelson, 2007) 49.

[36] See Morton, *The Canadian General*, 309–10.

[37] Gwyn, *Tapestry of War*, 196.

[38] Robert Stewart, "The Obsessions of Sam Hughes," *The Beaver* (October–November, 2003) 19.

[39] Haycock, *Sam Hughes*, 167–9; General Sir Ian Hamilton, *Report on the Military Institutions of Canada* (Ottawa: King's Printer, 1913).

[40] Hansard, 1912–13, 4942.

Chapter 3: Civilian-Soldier

[1] LAC, CP, v. 16, file 48, Currie to Thompson, 23 November 1921.

[2] Owen E. McGillicuddy, *Sir Arthur Currie: Leader of Men* (unpublished manuscript held at the Canadian War Museum, Military History Research Centre, n.d. [ca. October 1925]) chapter II, 4.

[3] For some school anecdotes, see *Star Weekly*, 22 February 1930.

[4] McGillicuddy, "Sir Arthur Currie: Leader of Men," chapter III, 2.

[5] Frost, *McGill University*, 116.

[6] A.M.J. Hyatt, *General Sir Arthur Currie: A Military Biography* (Toronto: University of Toronto Press, 1987), 5; Frost, *McGill University*, 116.

[7] MU, Urquhart papers, box 1, file Unsorted correspondence, undated note on Lady Currie.

[8] Daniel Dancocks, *Sir Arthur Currie: A Biography* (Toronto: Methuen, 1985) 11–12.

[9] Hugh M. Urquhart, *Arthur Currie: The Biography of a Great Canadian* (Toronto: Dent, 1950) 21.

[10] Dancocks, *Currie*, 14–15.

[11] McGillicuddy, "Sir Arthur Currie: Leader of Men," chapter III, 5.

[12] Wilfrid Bovey, "General Sir Arthur Currie: An Appreciation," *Canadian Defence Quarterly* XI.2 (January 1934) 141.

[13] Dancocks, *Currie*, 18.

[14] MU, Urquhart papers, 4027, box 1, file 12, Scudamore to Urquhart, 5 March 1935.

[15] Hyatt, *General Sir Arthur Currie*, 8.

[16] Urquhart, *Arthur Currie*, 25–6.

[17] The *Daily Times*, 15 August 1913.

[18] Augustus Bridle, *The Masques of Ottawa* (Toronto: The Macmillan Company, 1921) 155.

[19] Urquhart, *Arthur Currie*, 18.

[20] LAC, Records of the Department of National Defence (RG 24), v. 1815, file 4-40, Extract from John Nelson's "Currie—Now it can be told," The *Toronto Star Weekly*, 1 May 1926, 3.

[21] The *Daily Columnist*, 21 and 22 November 1913; Hyatt, *General Sir Arthur Currie*, 10.

[22] In Currie's class of sixteen, he scored fourth highest on the "Examination in Theoretical Portion of Militia Staff Course." See RG 24, v. 1815, file 4-40.

[23] The *Daily Columnist*, 19 December 1913.

[24] LAC, Borden papers, v. 361, Currie to Matson, 29 September 1914.

Chapter 4: Canada's Warlord

[1] Charles F. Winter, *Lieutenant-General the Hon. Sir Sam Hughes* (Toronto: The Macmillan Company of Canada, 1931) 32–6.

[2] G.P. de T. Glazebrook, *Sir Edmund Walker* (Oxford University Press, 1933) 115.

[3] *CAR* 1914, 182.

[4] Stephen J. Harris, *Canadian Brass: The Making of a Professional Army* (Toronto: University of Toronto Press, 1988) 24.

[5] Hansard, 26 January 1916, 292.

[6] Brown, *Borden*, 6; Hillmer and Granatstein, *Empire to Umpire*, 54.

[7] A.F. Duguid, *Official History of the Canadian Forces in the Great War 1914–1919* (Ottawa: King's Printer, 1938) 91.

[8] George G. Nasmith, *On the Fringe of the Great Fight* (Toronto: McClelland, Goodchild & Stewart, 1917) 2–3.

[9] Sir Robert Borden, MG 26 H, R6113-46-1-E, personal diary [hereafter Borden's diary], 6 August 1914.

[10] Borden, *Memoirs*, I/463.

[11] Borden, *Memoirs*, I/463-4; also see Britton B. Cooke, "Major-General Sam Hughes," *Canadian Magazine* 45 (1915) 391.

[12] Haycock, *Sam Hughes*, 159.

[13] Griesbach, *I Remember*, 345.

[14] Gwyn, *Tapestry of War*, 52.

[15] W.W. Murray, *The History of the 2nd Canadian Battalion (Eastern Ontario Regiment) Canadian Expeditionary Force in the Great War, 1914–1918* (Ottawa: Mortimer Ltd., 1947) 3.

[16] Allen, *Ordeal by Fire*, 65.

[17] Borden papers, reel C-4214, Sam Sharpe to Frank Cochrane, 18 September 1914, 12481; Ibid., Sharpe to Borden, 18 September 1914, 12488.

[18] CWM, J.H. Brown papers, 19830003-020, Horace to Uncle Clarence, 15 September 1914.

[19] MHRC, *Blaming it on Valcartier*, publication no. 24 (Ottawa: Central Information Office of the Canadian Liberal Party, 1915) 4.

[20] Borden papers, reel C-4214, Hughes to Borden, 10 September 1914, 12469.

[21] Borden papers, reel C-4214, Hughes to Borden, 26 November 1914, 12600.

[22] *CAR* 1914, 213–4.

[23] Urquhart, *Arthur Currie*, 40.

[24] See C.L. Flick, '*Just What Happened*': *A Diary of the Mobilization of the Canadian Militia, 1914* (Privately published, 1917) 4, 8–9; also, Roger Graham, *Arthur Meighen: And Fortune Fled, 1920–1927* (Toronto: University of Toronto Press, 1963) v. 1, 108.

[25] John MacFarlane, "The right stuff? Evaluating the performance of Lieutenant-Colonel F.-L. Lessard in South Africa and his failure to receive a senior command position with the CEF in 1914," *Canadian Military History* 8.3 (1999) 48–58.

[26] See Desmond Morton, "French Canada and the Canadian Militia, 1868–1914," *Social History-histoire sociale* 3 (April 1969) 32–50.

[27] LAC, Borden papers, v. 361, Currie to Matson, 29 September 1914.

[28] Brown, *Borden*, II/15.

[29] Peter Anderson, *I, That's Me: Escape from a German Prison Camp and Other Adventures* (Edmonton: Bradburn, 1924) 23.

[30] Wallace, *The Memoirs of the Rt. Hon. Sir George Foster*, 177–8; Graham, *Meighen*, I/109.

[31] Robert Craig Brown and Ramsay Cook, *Canada, 1896–1921: A Nation Transformed* (Toronto: McClelland & Stewart, 1974) 214.

[32] LAC, Sam Hughes papers, v. 1, file 8, Hughes to Borden, 24 July 1916.

[33] Borden papers, C-4214, Craven to Borden, 25 September 1914, 12526.

[34] Cited in Capon, *His Faults Lie Gently*, 57.

[35] Borden papers, C-4214, Borden to Perley, 19 October 1914, 12544.

[36] Haycock, *Sam Hughes*, 187; Borden private diaries, 8 and 25 August 1915; Canada, *Department of External Affairs, Documents on Canada's External Relations, 1909–1918* (Ottawa, 1967) 64.

[37] Hansard, 26 January 1916, 288; Borden papers, reel C-4214, Borden to Perley, 13 August 1914, 12464.

[38] Desmond Morton, *When Your Number's Up: The Canadian Soldier in the First World War* (Toronto: Random House of Canada, 1993) 6.

[39] Bill Freeman and Richard Nielsen, *Far From Home: Canadians in the First World War* (McGraw-Hill, 1999) 1.

[40] G.W.L. Nicholson, *The Canadian Expeditionary Force, 1914–1919: Official History of the Canadian Army in the First World War* (Ottawa: Queen's Printer, 1960) 17–18.

[41] Borden, *Memoirs*, I/465.

[42] Harold Peat, *Private Peat* (New York: Grosset and Dunlap, 1917) 14.

[43] Bridle, *The Masques of Ottawa*, 141.

[44] Borden papers, C-4214, J.B. Maclean to Borden, 30 November 1914, 12608.

[45] Capon, *His Faults Lie Gently*, 70.

Chapter 5: The Brigadier

[1] LAC, RG 24, v. 1812, file GAQ 4-6, Notes on Conversation with Major-General G.B. Hughes, 11 January 1934.

[2] Robert Craig Brown and Desmond Morton, "The Embarrassing Apotheosis of a Great Canadian: Sir Arthur Currie's Personal Crisis in 1917," *The Canadian Historical Review* LX (March 1979) 41–63.

[3] Mark Humphries, *The Selected Papers of Sir Arthur Currie: Diaries, Letters, and Report to the Ministry, 1917–33* (Waterloo: Laurier Centre for Military, Strategic and Disarmament Studies [LCMSDS], 2008) 18.

[4] LAC, Borden papers, v. 361, Currie to Matson, 29 September 1914.

[5] T.G. Roberts, "I Remember Currie," *Ottawa Journal*, 6 April 1940.

[6] MU, Urquhart papers, 4027, box 1, file 12, Scudamore to Urquhart, 5 March 1935.

[7] Ibid.

[8] Urquhart, *Arthur Currie*, 41.

[9] Borden papers, C-4430, Memorandum respecting the late Sir Arthur Currie, 13 August 1934, 150487.

[10] *CAR* 1914, 196.

[11] Morton, *When Your Number's Up*, 16–18.

[12] DCB Online, Desmond Morton, Sir E.A.H. Alderson biography; Borden papers, C-4238, Carson to Borden, 8 January 1915, 22813.

[13] H.F. Wood, *Vimy!* (Toronto: Macmillan of Canada, 1967) 55.

[14] MU, Urquhart papers, 4027, box 1, file 12, Alderson to Currie, 11 July 1917.

[15] Urquhart, *Arthur Currie*, 50.

[16] Flick, *Just What Happened*, 28.

[17] For the Canadian reputation in 1914, see Tim Cook, "From Destruction to Construction: The Khaki University of Canada, 1917–1919," *Journal of Canadian Studies* 37.1 (Spring 2002) 109–143.

[18] Dancocks, *Currie*, 35.

[19] Wood, *The Sense of Duty*, 354, note 12.

[20] LAC, Records of the Department of Militia and Defence (RG 9) III-A-1, file 10-4-12, McRae to Perley, 3 March 1917; Nicholson, *CEF,* 26-7.

[21] LAC, Sam Hughes papers, v. 1, file 8, Hughes to Borden, 1 September 1916.

[22] LAC, J.J. Creelman papers, MG 30 E8, diary, 18 October 1914.

[23] *CAR* 1914, 217.

[24] Lady Wester Wemyss, *The Life and Letters of Lord Wester Wemyss* (London: Eyre and Spottiswoode, 1935) 176–7.

[25] DCB Online, Sam Hughes biography.

[26] Bridle, *The Masques of Ottawa*, 149.

[27] For press clippings, see LAC, Sam Hughes papers, v. 9, Scrapbook clippings, 1914.

[28] Nic Clarke, "'He was my best subaltern': The Life and Death of Lieutenant Herrick S. Duggan, 70th Field Company, Royal Engineers," *Canadian Military History* 17.2 (Spring 2008) 25.

[29] Nasmith, *On the Fringe of the Great Fight*, 35

[30] LAC, RG 24, v. 6931, file "canteens," narrative, 1. Quote from Sam H.S. Hughes, "Sir Sam Hughes and the Problem of Imperialism," *Report of Annual Meeting of the Canadian Historical Association* 29.1 (1950) 30.

[31] LAC, A.E. Kemp papers, MG 27 II-B-9, v. 118, file 8, despatch note; R.C. Fetherstonhaugh, *The 13th Battalion Royal Highlanders of Canada, 1914–1919* (Montreal, 1925) 22

[32] *Mail and Empire*, 21 October 1914.

[33] R.H.T., *Victor Gordon Tupper: A Brother's Tribute* (Oxford University Press, 1921) 11.

[34] Flick, *Just What Happened*, 31.

[35] Hansard, 6 February 1917, 537; and 26 April 1917, 809.

[36] John Allister Currie, *"The Red Watch": With the First Canadian Division in Flanders* (Toronto: McClelland, Goodchild & Stewart, 1916) 43.

[37] Urquhart, *Arthur Currie*, 50.

[38] MU, Urquhart papers, box 1, file 12, Betty to Urquhart, 18 September 1934. For training in England, see Andrew Iarocci, *Shoestring Soldiers: The 1st Canadian Division at War, 1914–1915* (Toronto: University of Toronto Press, 2008).

[39] Urquhart, *Arthur Currie*, 48–9.

[40] MU, Urquhart papers, 4027, box 1, file 12, Marshall to Urquhart, 16 November 1934.

[41] MU, Urquhart papers, 4027, box 1, file 12, Scudamore to Urquhart, 5 March 1934.

[42] Urquhart, *Arthur Currie*, 49.

[43] Urquhart, *Arthur Currie*, 50.

[44] LAC, Borden papers, Currie to Matson, 29 September 1914.

[45] MU, Urquhart papers, 4027, box 1, file 12, Ironside to Urquhart, handwritten, n.d [ca.1934].

[46] MU, Urquhart papers, 4027, box 1, file 13, Memo from General Sir Archibald Montgomery-Massingberd to Urquhart, ca. 1934.

[47] Dancocks, *Currie*, 43.

[48] Currie's diary, 27 February 1915.

[49] For the unleashing of gas at Second Ypres, see Tim Cook, *No Place to Run: The Canadian Corps and Gas Warfare in the First World War* (Vancouver: University of British Columbia Press, 1999).

[50] Anderson, *I, That's Me*, 76.

[51] For a narrative of Currie's headquarters actions, see WD, 2nd Brigade, April 1915, Narrative of Events, 22nd to 27th April, 1915.

[52] Brigadier-General Sir James E. Edmonds and Captain G.C. Wynne, *History of the Great War based on official documents by direction of the Historical Section of the Committee of Imperial Defence. Military Operations. France and Belgium, 1915*, volume I (London: Macmillan, 1927) 208.

[53] Allen, *Ordeal by Fire*, 83.

[54] See Hyatt, *General Sir Arthur Currie*, 39–40.

[55] See CWM, Sir Richard Turner papers, 19710147-001, diary, April–May 1915.

[56] WD, 2nd Brigade, April 1915, Narrative of Events, 22nd to 27th April, 1915, log of messages, 11:30 A.M.

[57] LAC, CP, v. 41, file 186, Comments on 2nd Draft, British Official History, n.d; Iarocci, *Shoestring Soldiers*, 159.

[58] George Cassar, *Beyond Courage: The Canadians at the Second Battle of Ypres* (Ottawa: Oberon, 1985) 141–2.

[59] Iarocci, *Shoestring Soldiers*, 154.

[60] LAC, CP, v. 41, file 186, Comments on 2nd Draft, British Official History, n.d.

[61] For the postwar acrimonious debate over this event between the British and Canadian official historians, see Timothy Travers, "Allies in Conflict: The British and Canadian Official Historians and the Real Story of Second Ypres (1915)," *Journal of Contemporary History* 24 (1989) 301–25.

[62] LAC, CP, v. 18, file 58, Lynn to Currie, (n.d., 6 April 1928).

[63] Iarocci, *Shoestring Soldiers*, 155.

[64] Urquhart, *Arthur Currie*, 92.

[65] See Tim Cook, *At the Sharp End: Canadians Fighting the Great War, Volume I: 1914–1916* (Toronto: Viking, 2007) 151–3.

[66] MU, Urquhart papers, box 1, file 15, Currie to Gregory, 22 October 1915.

[67] Urquhart, *Arthur Currie*, 98.

[68] Iarocci, *Shoestring Soldiers*, 172–5.

[69] Duguid, *Official History of the Canadian Forces in the Great War*, 421.

[70] LAC, Records of the Department of National Defence (RG 24), v. 2680, file HQC 4950 (pt. 1), Brown to MacBrien, 25 November 1925; Directorate of History and Heritage, A.F. Duguid Biography file, box 2, folder E, file 75, Relations between General Turner and General Alderson, 14 March 1934.

Chapter 6: A One-Man Army

[1] As recounted in Allen, *Ordeal by Fire*, 70. Also see, Capon, *His Faults Lie Gently*, 78; Leslie Frost, *Fighting Men* (Toronto: Clarke, Irwin, 1967) 97.

[2] For discounting the story, see Nicholson, *CEF*, 35; and Morton, *When Your Number's Up*, 25.

[3] Gwyn, *Tapestry of War*, 161.

[4] See the discussion in Ian Hugh Maclean Miller, *Our Glory and Our Grief: Torontonians and the Great War* (Toronto: University of Toronto Press, 2002); and Jeff Keshen, *Propaganda and Censorship during Canada's Great War* (Edmonton: University of Alberta Press, 1996).

[5] Borden papers, C-4238, Hughes to Borden, 3 May 1915, 22857.

[6] *CAR* 1915, 186.

[7] Haycock, *Sam Hughes*, 189.

[8] Robson Black, "General—The—Honorable—Sam: An Uncensored Character-Sketch of the Minister of Militia," *Maclean's* (January 1915) 38.

[9] Winter, *Lieutenant-General The Hon. Sir Sam Hughes*, 16.

[10] Haycock, *Sam Hughes*, 190.

[11] Borden, private diaries, 8 January 1915.

[12] *Ottawa Journal*, 26 April 1930.

[13] J.A. Corry, "The Growth of Government Activities in Canada, 1914–1921," *Canadian Historical Association Annual Report* 1940, 63–4.

[14] Robert Bothwell, Ian Drummond, and John English, *Canada, 1900–1945* (Toronto: University of Toronto Press, 1990), 142.

[15] Gwyn, *Tapestry of War*, 63.

[16] John English, *The Decline of Politics: The Conservatives and the Party System, 1901–20* (Toronto: University of Toronto Press, 1993) 96; Borden private diaries, 19, 23, 24, 26, 27 November 1914; Haycock, *Sam Hughes*, 192; Wallace, *The Memoirs of the Rt. Hon. Sir George Foster*, 177–8; for some of the letters, see Borden papers, C-4212, 12469–12796.

[17] Borden, *Memoirs*, II/566.

[18] Michael Bliss, "War Business as Usual: Canadian Munitions Production, 1914–18," in N.F. Dreisziger (ed.) *Mobilization for Total War: The Canadian, American and British Experience, 1914–1918, 1939–1945* (Waterloo, ON: Wilfrid Laurier Press, 1981) 46.

[19] Haycock, *Sam Hughes*, 235; but also see David Carnegie, *The History of Munitions Supply in Canada, 1914–1918* (London: Longmans, Green, 1925); Duguid, *Official History of the Canadian Forces in the Great War*, 112–3.

[20] Carnegie, *The History of Munitions*, 6.

[21] Sir Sam Hughes, "The War and Our Duty," *Address Delivered before the Canadian Clubs of Ottawa, 1915–1916* (Ottawa: The Davidson-Merrill Press, 1916) 50–1; for some of the challenges of the committee, and its internal workings, see LAC, Sam Hughes papers, v. 3, file 6, Minutes of the Shell Committee.

[22] MHRC, *Shell and Fuse Scandals: A Million Dollar Rake-off*, publication no. 49 (Ottawa: Central Liberal Information Office, n.d. [1916]) 4.

[23] Borden papers, White to Borden, 11 October 1915, 23663; Graham, *Meighen*, I/107; Borden, *Memoirs*, I/466.

[24] MHRC, War Contract Scandals, publication no. 44 (Ottawa: Central Liberal Information Office, n.d. [1915]) 37.

[25] Bliss, "War Business as Usual," 46.

[26] Haycock, *Sam Hughes*, 230; but also see Hansard, 1915, 1678, and Borden private diaries, 12 April 1915.

[27] Thomas White, *The Story of Canada's War Finances* (Montreal, 1921) 23 and 35.

[28] Borden papers, C-4214, Borden to Hughes, 15 June 1915, 12701; Hughes to Borden, 19 June 1915, 12703.

[29] Borden, *Memoirs*, I/468–9.

[30] Bliss, *A Canadian Millionaire*, 267.

[31] Capon, *His Faults Lie Gently*, 24.

[32] Bliss, *A Canadian Millionaire*, 245.

[33] Carnegie, *The History of Munitions*, 49–50.

[34] Robert Craig Brown and Donald Loveridge, "Unrequited Faith: Recruiting the CEF, 1914–1918," *Revue Internationale d'Histoire Militaire* No. 51 (1982) 54; *CAR* 1915, 186.

[35] Borden's diary, 8 April 1915.

[36] Borden, *Memoirs*, I/476.

[37] Bliss, *A Canadian Millionaire*, 255.

[38] DCB Online, Sam Hughes biography; Borden papers, C-4214, Claude MacDonell to Borden, 26 November 1914, 12597.

[39] Haycock, *Sam Hughes*, 230.

[40] Allen, *Ordeal by Fire*, 68.

[41] Allen, *Ordeal by Fire*, 71.

[42] Borden papers, Address, 18 December 1914, 34672.

[43] LAC, Sam Hughes papers, v. 1, file 14, speaking notes, no pagination.

[44] C.P. Stacey, *Canada and the Age of Conflict, 1867–1921* (Toronto: Macmillan of Canada, 1977) 178.

[45] On recruitment, see R.C. Brown and D. Loveridge, "Unrequited Faith: Recruiting the CEF 1914–1918," *Revue Internationale d'Historie Militaire* 51 (1982) 53–79.

[46] *CAR* 1915, 187–8; Borden, *Memoirs*, I/523.

[47] J.L. Granatstein and J.M. Hitsman, *Broken Promises: A History of Conscription in Canada* (Toronto: Oxford University Press, 1977) 36.

[48] LAC, MG 27 II-F-9, Harold Daly papers, v. 1, memoir notes.

[49] Granatstein and Hitsman, *Broken Promises*, 35.

[50] Desmond Morton, "French Canada and the War, 1868–1917," in J.L. Granatstein and R.D. Cuff, *War and Society in North America* (Toronto, 1971) 84–103; and Desmond Morton, "The Limits of Loyalty; French Canadian Officers and the First World War," in Edgar Denton (ed.) *The Limits of Loyalty* (Waterloo: Wilfrid Laurier Press, 1980).

[51] See Desmond Morton, *Fight or Pay: Soldiers' Families in the Great War* (Vancouver: UBC Press, 2004).

[52] G.R. Stevens, *A City Goes to War* (Brampton: Charters, 1964) 9–19.

[53] Duguid, *Official History of the Canadian Forces in the Great War*, 3.

[54] LAC, Sam Hughes papers, v. 1, file 8, Hughes to Borden, 17 October 1916; Ibid., v. 1, file 11, Address Delivered by Lieut-General Sir Sam Hughes … Victoria and Haliburton Counties, April 28th, 1917.

[55] Hansard, 30 January 1917, 263.

[56] Nicholson, *CEF,* 35.

[57] Haycock, *Sam Hughes*, 259; Borden papers, OC 190, Hughes to Borden, 16 September 1914, 15651.

[58] Gwyn, *Tapestry of War*, 158.

[59] LAC, Sir George Perley papers, MG 27 II D 12, v. 3, p 79, Perley to Borden, 9 May 1915.

[60] Borden private diaries, 9 July 1915.

[61] LAC, Sam Hughes papers, v. 3, file 7, Hughes to Kitchener, 7 April 1915; also see Robert Stewart, *Sam Steele: Lion of the Frontier* (Toronto: Doubleday Canada, 1979) 269–79.

[62] Bridle, *Sons of Canada*, 163.

[63] A.J.P. Taylor, *Beaverbrook* (New York: Simon and Schuster, 1972) 86.

[64] Willson, *From Quebec to Piccadilly*, 200.

[65] See Tim Cook, *Clio's Warriors: Canadian Historians and the Writing of the World Wars* (Vancouver: UBC Press, 1999) chapter 1.

[66] Willson, *From Quebec to Piccadilly*, 197.

[67] Urquhart, *Arthur Currie*, 136.

[68] LAC, RG 24, v. 1812, file GAQ 4-7, Duguid interview of Sir George Perley, 20 July 1929.

[69] Willson, *From Quebec to Piccadilly*, 206.

[70] Gwyn, *Tapestry of War*, 258.

[71] LAC, Lord Beaverbrook papers [hereafter LAC, BP], MG 27 II G 1, Series E, A-1764, Aitken to Borden, 3 December 1915; also see, Willson, *From Quebec to Piccadilly*, 205–6.

[72] Borden's diary, 10 June 1915.

[73] Willson, *From Quebec to Piccadilly*, 201.

[74] LAC, BP, A-1764, Aitken to Hughes, 6 October 1915.

[75] LAC, BP, A-1764, Aitken to Hughes, 26 September 1915.

[76] LAC, BP, A-1764, Hughes to Aitken, 2 November 1915.

[77] LAC, BP, A-1765, Alderson and Aitken, 25 [28?] September 1915; and Ibid., 16 October 1915.

[78] LAC, BP, A-1765, Aitken to Hughes, 5 June 1916; Ibid., 6 June 1916.

[79] LAC, BP, A-1764, Hughes to Aitken, 12 November 1915.

[80] LAC, BP, A-1765, Watson to Aitken, 12 October 1915.

[81] LAC, BP, A-1764, Aitken to Hughes, 10 May 1916; and Ibid., A-1765, Aitken to Watson, 10 August 1916.

[82] LAC, Sam Hughes papers, v. 3, file 7, Hughes to Kitchener, 22 May 1915 and Kitchener to Hughes, 23 May 1915.

[83] See Stephen Harris, "From Subordinate to Ally: The Canadian Corps and National Autonomy, 1914–1918," *Revue Internationale d'Historie Militaire* 51 (1982) 113–4.

[84] LAC, Borden papers, C-4314, Hughes to Aitken, 30 November 1915, 35582. For an equally outrageous missive to Kitchener, see the letter read into Hansard on 30 January 1917, 265.

[85] Urquhart, *Arthur Currie*, 118.

[86] Colonel William Wood, "Behind the Scenes of Canadian War History, The J. Clarence Webster Lectures for 1925–6," *The Argosy* 4.1 (Sackville, New Brunswick: June 1926) 39.

[87] LAC, BP, reel A-1764, Aitken to Hughes, 19 September 1915; Hughes to Aitken and back, 20 September 1915; Aitken to Hughes, 6 October 1915; 2 November 1915; reel A-1765, Aitken to Hughes, 5 June 1916.

[88] Robert Scott Demill, "The 1928 Cobourg Trial of Sir Arthur Currie and the Port Hope Evening Guide: The Rehabilitation of the Reputation of a Corps Commander," (University of Ottawa: MA thesis, 1989) 12.

[89] MU, Urquhart papers, box 1, file 12, Ironside to Urquhart, handwritten, n.d. [ca. 1934].

[90] Sir Sam Hughes, "Some Observations on the War," *Empire Club of Canada* (Toronto: The Bryant Press, 1917) 268.

[91] Canadian Letters and Images Project (hereafter CLIP), William R. Mitton, November 7, 1915.

[92] English, *The Decline of Politics*, 74–6.

[93] Gwyn, *Tapestry of War*, 198. For other reckless statements on German saboteurs in Canada, see Hughes, "Some Observations on the War," 267.

[94] J. Castell Hopkins, *Canada at War: A Record of Heroism and Achievement, 1914–1918* (Toronto: The Canadian Annual Review Limited, 1919) 64.

[95] Brown, *Borden*, II/54.

[96] Bliss, *Flavelle*, 274.

[97] Graham, *Meighen*, I/106.

Chapter 7: Divisional Commander

[1] MU, Urquhart papers, 4027, box 1, file 12, Lt-General Archibald Macdonell, n.d. (ca. 1934); LAC, MG 30 E 300, Victor Odlum, v. 3, file: Colonel A.F. Duguid, Duguid to Odlum, 16 February 1937.

[2] LAC, RG 24, v. 1504, HQ 683-1-30-5, G.W. Gordon-Hall to Duguid, 20 March 1937.

[3] Urquhart, *Arthur Currie*, 106.

[4] On Turner's protest, see RG 24, v. 1504, HQ 683-1-30-5, Turner to Duguid, 5 February 1937. On the British, see T.H.E. Travers, *The Killing Ground: The British Army, The Western Front, and the Emergence of Modern Warfare, 1900–1918* (London: Allen & Unwin, 1987), with the even more sympathetic study by Simon Robbins, *British Generalship on the Western Front, 1914–1918: Defeat into*

Victory (London: Frank Cass, 2005) 61, which argues that many officers and generals feared innovation or experimentation because they would be "removed if anything went well."

[5] LAC, Sam Hughes papers, v. 4, file 8, Currie to Hughes, 15 June 1916.

[6] LAC, Sam Hughes papers, v. 4, file 8, Currie to Hughes, 15 June 1916.

[7] MU, Urquhart papers, 4027, box 1, file 13, Romer to Urquhart, 15 August 1934.

[8] W.A. Griesbach, *I Remember* (Toronto: Ryerson Press, 1946) 348.

[9] For Currie's reports, see Duguid, *Official History of the Canadian Forces in the Great War*, appendix II, 86. Also see David Borys, "The Education of a Corps Commander: Arthur Currie's Leadership from 1915–1917," (University of Alberta: MA thesis, 2006) 23.

[10] LAC, A.E. Kemp papers, MG 27 II-D-9, v. 173, file 29, Order to the House of Commons from Sir Sam Hughes, 23–24 April 1919.

[11] LAC, Victor Odlum papers, MG 30 E 300, v. 15, R.C. Coops to Odlum, 31 July 1915.

[12] Willson, *From Quebec to Piccadilly*, 202–3.

[13] Currie was gazetted on September 14, 1915.

[14] Kenneth Radley, *We Lead, Others Follow: First Canadian Division 1914–1918* (St. Catharines: Vanwell, 2006) 134.

[15] Desmond Morton, *A Peculiar Kind of Politics: Canada's Overseas Ministry in the First World War* (Toronto: University of Toronto Press, 1982) 40.

[16] Daniel Dancocks, *Gallant Canadians: The Story of the Tenth Canadian Infantry Battalion, 1914–1919* (Calgary: Calgary Highlanders Regimental Funds Foundation, 1990) 62; Currie's diary, 18 and 19 October 1915; Hyatt, *General Sir Arthur Currie*, 52.

[17] W.L.M. King diaries, digitized, online at the Library and Archives Canada website, 30 May 1919.

[18] Morton, *A Peculiar Kind of Politics*, 46.

[19] MU, Urquhart papers, 4027, box 1, file 13, Frith to Urquhart, 8 January 1935.

[20] MU, Urquhart papers, 4027, box 1, file 12, Oliver to McMurray, 23 November 1934.

[21] Urquhart, *Arthur Currie*, 116.

[22] Urquhart, *Arthur Currie*, 116.

[23] MU, Urquhart papers, box 1, file 15, Currie to Gregory, 22 October 1915.

[24] Hyatt, *General Sir Arthur Currie*, 53.

[25] Dancocks, *Currie*, 60.

[26] John Harold Becker, *Silhouettes of the Great War: The Memoirs of John Harold Becker* (Ottawa: CEF Books, 2001) 155.

[27] Wilfred Kerr, *Arms and the Maple Leaf: Memories of Canada's Corps, 1918* (Seafroth, 1943) 28.

[28] Urquhart, *Arthur Currie*, xi.

[29] MU, Urquhart papers, 4027, box 1, file 12, Marshall to Urquhart, 16 November 1934.

[30] On raiding, see Cook, *At the Sharp End*, chapter 22; and Cook, *Shock Troops*, chapter 3.

[31] Currie's diary, 17 December 1915.

[32] On executions in the CEF, see A.B. Godefroy, *For Freedom and Honour: The story of the 25 Canadian Volunteers executed in the Great War* (CEF Books, 1998) and Teresa Iacobelli, "Arbitrary Justice?: A Comparative Analysis of Canadian Death Sentences Passed and Commuted during the First World War," *Canadian Military History* 16.1 (2007) 23–36.

[33] MU, Urquhart papers, 4027, box 1, file 13, Frith to Urquhart, n.d.

[34] MU, Urquhart papers, 4027, box 1, file 12, transcript of interview with General Kearsley, nd. [ca. 1934].

[35] *CAR* 1915, 190.

[36] Borden papers, OC 281, Hughes to Borden, 28 May 1915, 31777.

[37] Iarocci, *Shoestring Soldiers*, 224.

[38] For the story of the Ross, see A.F. Duguid, *A Question of Confidence: The Ross Rifle in the Trenches,* edited by Clive M. Law (Ottawa: Service Publications, 2000)

[39] DCB Online, Sir E.A.H. Alderson biography; Morton, *A Peculiar Kind of Politics*, 65.

[40] LAC, W.A. Griesbach papers, MG 30 E15, v. 1, file 4, Sam Hughes to Alderson, 7 March 1916.

[41] Willson, *From Quebec to Piccadilly*, 211.

[42] Willson, *From Quebec to Piccadilly*, 213–4.

[43] Borden papers, OC 183(2), Hughes to Borden, 24 March 1916, 14899-9030; and Borden, *Memoirs*, I/484–5.

[44] For the British component of the battle, see Jonathan Walker, "'An Unforgivable Sin': The Actions at St. Eloi Craters, 1916," *Journal of the Centre of the First World War Studies* 2.3 (November 2005).

[45] CWM, Sir Richard Turner papers, 19710147-001, diary, Narrative of St. Eloi Crater.

[46] For the battle, see Tim Cook, *At the Sharp End*, 323–42.

[47] LAC, BP, A-1764, Aitken to Hughes, 24 April 1916.

[48] LAC, Sir Richard Turner papers, MG 30 E49, folder 9, Alderson to Turner, 16 April 1916; DHH, Duguid Bio file, box 2, folder E, file 75—Relations between General Turner and General Alderson, 14 March 1934; WD, Sketches and Locations—Extracts and Flank (handwritten notes from A.F. Duguid, ca. 1938), G.271, II Army (AMS).

[49] LAC, BP, Hughes to Aitken, 21 April 1916; Aitken to Hughes, 21 April 1916.

[50] A.J.P. Taylor, *Beaverbrook* (New York: Simon and Schuster, 1972) 89–90; and Anne Chisholm and Michael Davie, *Beaverbrook: A Life* (London: Hutchinson, 1992) 132.

[51] LAC, RG 24, v. 1504, HQ 683-1-30-5, G.W. Gordon-Hall to Duguid, 20 March 1937.

[52] Robert Blake, *The Private Papers of Douglas Haig, 1914–1919* (London: Eyre and Spottiswoode, 1952) 140. LAC, RG 24, v. 20542, file 990.011 (D1), excerpt from Haig's diary, 21 April 1916.

[53] Nicholson, *CEF* 146, or Jeffrey Williams, *Byng of Vimy* (Toronto: University of Toronto Press, 1983, 1992) 117.

[54] LAC, BP, Aitken to Hughes, 24 April 1916. Haig received it on 27 April. See Beaverbrook papers, Hughes to Aitken, 27 April 1916.

[55] Capon, *His Faults Lie Gently*, 132.

[56] For Borden's poor view of Alderson, see Borden, *Memoirs*, II/696–7.

[57] Currie's diary, 28 May 1916.

[58] Willson, *From Quebec to Piccadilly*, 213–14.

[59] Williams, *Byng of Vimy,* 115.

[60] Gwyn, *Tapestry of War,* 282.

[61] See D.J. Goodspeed, "Prelude to the Somme: Mount Sorrel, June, 1916," in Michael Cross and Robert Bothwell (eds.), *Policy by Other Means: Essays in Honour of C.P. Stacey* (Toronto: University of Toronto Press, 1972).

[62] Charles Cameron, *War! What of It!* (self-published memoir, 2008) 47.

[63] Carman Miller, "Framing Canada's Great War: A Case for Including the Boer War," *Journal of Transatlantic Studies* 6.1 (April 2008) 12.

[64] MU, Urquhart papers, 4027, box 1, file 13, General Farmar, notes by Urquhart, n.d. [1934].

[65] Williams, *Byng of Vimy,* 130.

[66] MU, Urquhart papers, 4027, box 1, file 13, memo by Pat Hodgson on behalf of Lord Byng.

[67] LAC, RG 9, v. 3843, 44/4, extract from 1st Division's war diary, 6:20 P.M., 9 September 1916.

[68] Urquhart, *Arthur Currie,* 132–3.

Chapter 8: Endgame

[1] Borden, *Memoirs,* I/463.

[2] LAC, Sam Hughes papers, v. 1, file 8, Hughes to Borden, 1 September 1916.

[3] MHRC, *Shell and Fuse Scandals: A Million Dollar Rake-off,* publication no. 49 (Ottawa: Central Liberal Information Office, n.d. [1916]).

[4] Borden's diary, 16 April 1917.

[5] Borden, *Memoirs,* II/563-4.

[6] LAC, Borden papers, C-4314, extracts of Hughes's statements, 13 May 1916, 35646.

[7] LAC, Sam Hughes papers, v. 1, file 11, Address Delivered by Lieut-General Sir Sam Hughes …Victoria and Haliburton Counties, April 28th, 1917.

[8] On Hughes and his rumour campaign, see Bliss, *Flavelle,* 261–2, 267.

[9] LAC, Sam Hughes papers, v. 14, file 4, Sam Hughes to Garnet, 7 March 1917.

[10] J. Castell Hopkins, *Canada at War: A Record of Heroism and Achievement, 1914-1918* (Toronto: The Canadian Annual Review Limited, 1919) 65.

[11] Bliss, *A Canadian Millionaire*, 273.

[12] Borden's diary, 3 April 1916.

[13] Stacey, *Canada and the Age of Conflict, 1867–1921*, 178; Brown, *Borden*, II/27.

[14] Anderson, *I, That's Me*, 35.

[15] John Hughes (ed.), *The Unwanted: Great War Letters from the Field* (Edmonton: University of Alberta Press, 2005) 21.

[16] Hansard, 19 June 1917, 2448.

[17] Borden, *Memoirs*, I/448; Haycock, *Sam Hughes*, 149.

[18] Granatstein, *Canada's Army*, 75.

[19] Winter, *Lieutenant-General The Hon. Sir Sam Hughes*, 7.

[20] Morton, *When Your Number's Up*, 55.

[21] Borden, *Memoirs*, II/613.

[22] On forty divisions, see Sir Sam Hughes, "The War and Our Duty," *Address Delivered before the Canadian Clubs of Ottawa, 1915–1916* (Ottawa: The Davidson-Merrill Press, 1916) 56; Granatstein and Hitsman, *Broken Promises*, 37.

[23] LAC, Sam Hughes papers, v. 1, file 8, Hughes to Borden, 17 October 1916.

[24] Borden's diary, 15 August 1915.

[25] Willson, *From Quebec to Piccadilly*, 230.

[26] *Toronto Globe*, 24 August 1916.

[27] Allen, *Ordeal by Fire*, 68; also see LAC, A.E. Kemp papers, v. 157, file R-9, Rowell to Borden, 18 September 1916.

[28] George William Frost, *Sincerely Yours* (self-published, 1998) 17.

[29] CWM, Harry Kirkland papers, 2007171, letter, 8 August 1915.

[30] Leslie Frost, *The Record on Sir Sam Hughes Set Straight* (pamphlet, n.d.) 3.

[31] Brown, *Borden*, II/17.

[32] Desmond Morton and J.L. Granatstein, *Marching to Armageddon: Canadians and the Great War 1914–1919* (Toronto: Lester & Orpen Dennys, 1989) 8; Borden papers, v. 134, 7829-35, Hughes to MacArthur, 23 March 1911.

[33] Allen, *Ordeal by Fire*, 108.

[34] LAC, Borden papers, C-4314, Borden to Perley, 35604.

[35] LAC, reel A-1764, Hughes to Aitken, 14 October 1916.

[36] Borden, *Memoirs*, II/567.

[37] Winter, *Lieutenant-General The Hon. Sir Sam Hughes*, 29.

[38] Borden, *Memoirs*, II/567.

[39] On the council, see Morton, *A Peculiar Kind of Politics*, 78–83.

[40] LAC, Sam Hughes papers, v. 1, file 8, Borden to Hughes, 31 October 1916.

[41] DCB Online, Sam Hughes biography.

[42] Allen, *Ordeal by Fire*, 39.

[43] Borden, *Memoirs*, II/567; LAC, Sam Hughes papers, v. 1, file 8, Borden to Hughes, 18 October 1916.

[44] Borden, *Memoirs*, II/568.

[45] LAC, BP, A-1764, Hughes to Aitken, 26 October 1916.

[46] LAC, Sam Hughes papers, v. 1, file 8, Hughes to Borden, 26 October 1916.

[47] Borden papers, C-4214, G.H. Bradbury to Borden, 24 October 1916.

[48] Borden, *Memoirs*, II/568; also see the arguments in the letter from Hughes to Borden on 23 October 1916 in LAC, Sam Hughes papers, v. 1, file 8.

[49] LAC, Sam Hughes papers, v. 1, file 9, Borden to Hughes, 9 November 1916.

Chapter 9: Corps Commander

[1] Borden, *Memoirs*, II/681.

[2] MU, Urquhart papers, 4027, box 1, file 12, Turner to Currie, 26 November 1916.

[3] For a longer account of this, see Cook, *Shock Troops*, 42–54.

[4] Cited in Dancocks, *Currie*, 285.

[5] For this evolution in the platoon, see Bill Rawling, *Surviving Trench Warfare: Technology and the Canadian Corps, 1914–1918* (Toronto: University of Toronto Press, 1992).

[6] For the plan, see WD, Royal Artillery, Canadian Corps, April 1917, Canadian Corps, Artillery Instruction for the Capture of Vimy Ridge, (hereafter, Artillery Plan). The plan can also be found in RG 9, III, v. 3922, 8/3.

[7] Michael Boire, "Vimy Ridge: The Battlefield before the Canadians, 1914–1916," in Geoffrey Hayes et. al. (eds), *Vimy Ridge: A Canadian Reassessment* (Waterloo: Wilfrid Laurier University Press, 2007) 59.

[8] For the artillery battle, including the number of guns, see Tim Cook, "'We are hammering Fritz to pieces': The Gunners at Vimy," in Geoffrey Hayes et al. (eds.), *Vimy Ridge: A Canadian Reassessment* (Waterloo: Wilfrid Laurier University Press, 2007) 105–24.

[9] For casualties, see Currie's diary, 18–19 April 1917; for the 1st Division's battle, see Andrew Iarocci, "The 1st Canadian Division: An Operational Mosaic," in Geoffrey Hayes et al. (eds), *Vimy Ridge: A Canadian Reassessment* (Waterloo: Wilfrid Laurier University Press, 2007) 155–170.

[10] CWM, Sir Arthur Currie papers [hereafter CWM, CP], 19801226, 58A.1.59.4, Report of Operations carried out by the 1st Canadian Division, April 9th–May 5th, 1917.

[11] Currie's diary, 9 April 1917.

[12] CLIP, James Jones, diary, 9 April 1917.

[13] Currie's diary, 18–19 April 1917.

[14] Currie's diary, 3 May 1917.

[15] LAC, CP, v. 1, file 1, Currie to Brewster, 31 May 1917.

[16] MU, Urquhart papers, box 1, file 12, interview of Pat Hodgson, n.d. [ca. 1934].

[17] On the rumours, see LAC, Sam Hughes papers, v. 14, file 5, Currie to Garnet Hughes, 2 May 1917; LAC, W.A. Griesbach papers, MG 30 E15, v. 1, file 5, diary, 7 June 1917.

[18] LAC, Newton Rowell papers, MG 27 IID13, reel C-930, 1640, Currie to Rowell, 28 June 1917.

[19] Urquhart, *Arthur Currie*, 157–8.

[20] Urquhart, *Arthur Currie*, 158.

[21] MU, Urquhart papers, 4027, box 1, file 12, MacAlphine to Urquhart, 12 November 1934; Gary Sheffield and John Bourne, *Douglas Haig: War Diaries and Letters, 1914–1918* (London: Weidenfield and Nicolson, 2005) 186; Ian Malcolm Brown, "Lieutenant-General Sir Arthur Currie and the Canadian

Corps 1917–1918: The Evolution of a Style of Command and Attack" (University of Calgary: MA thesis, 1991) 22.

[22] Urquhart, *Arthur Currie*, 160–2.

[23] MU, Urquhart papers, 4027, box 1, file 13, Colonel Walter Gow, n.d. [ca. 1934].

[24] A.M.J. Hyatt, "Sir Arthur Currie and Conscription: A Soldier's View," *Canadian Historical Review* v. L.3 (1969) 290.

[25] Currie's diary, 10 June 1917.

[26] MU, Urquhart papers, 4027, box 1, file 12, Willis to Urquhart, n.d. [ca. 1934]; LAC, Borden papers, C-4430, Archie Macdonell to Borden, 14 December 1933, 150458; Wilfrid Bovey, "General Sir Arthur Currie: An Appreciation," *Canadian Defence Quarterly* XI.2 (January 1934) 146; On Batty Mac, see Ian McCulloch, "'Batty Mac': Portrait of a Brigade Commander of the Great War, 1915–1917," *Canadian Military History* 7.4 (Autumn 1998) 11–28; LAC, Sam Hughes papers, v. 14, file 5, Currie to Garnet Hughes, 8 May 1917; Urquhart, *Arthur Currie*, 69–74.

[27] LAC, Sam Hughes papers, v. 14, file 5, Currie to Garnet, 8 May 1917, and Garnet to Currie, 11 May 1917.

[28] LAC, Sam Hughes papers, v. 14, file 5, Currie to Garnet, 30 October 1917; also see MU, Urquhart papers, 4027, box 1, file 12, MacAlphine to Urquhart, 12 November 1934.

[29] LAC, CP, v. 1, file, 2, Garnet Hughes to Currie, 16 October 1916.

[30] MU, box 5, file 14, Embury to Urquhart, n.d. [1934]; MU, Urquhart papers, 4027, box 1, file 12, Colonel C.D.H. MacAlphine, a staff officer, to U, 12 November 1934; quote from Wilfrid Bovey, "General Sir Arthur Currie: An Appreciation," *Canadian Defence Quarterly* XI.2 (January 1934) 149.

[31] Urquhart, *Arthur Currie*, 164.

[32] LAC, Borden papers, C-4430, Archie Macdonell to Borden, 14 December 1933, 150458.

[33] LAC, CP, v. 27, file 7, Currie to McGillicuddy, n.d. (First page is missing.)

[34] LAC, CP, v. 18, file 64, Currie to R.H. Parmenter, 22 March 1928.

[35] Humphries, *The Selected Papers of Sir Arthur Currie*, 26.

[36] Dancocks, *Currie*, 202.

[37] Craig Brown and Desmond Morton, "The Embarrassing Apotheosis of a Great Canadian: Sir Arthur Currie's Personal Crisis in 1917," *Canadian Historical Review* (March 1979) 60.

[38] Borden papers, C-4430, Memorandum respecting the late Sir Arthur Currie, 13 August 1934, 150487.

[39] Borden papers, C-4430, Memorandum respecting the late Sir Arthur Currie, 13 August 1934, 150487; Sir Robert Borden, *Letters to Limbo* (Toronto: University of Toronto Press, 1971) 62.

[40] MU, Urquhart papers, box 1, file 12, Griesbach to Urquhart, 26 October 1934.

[41] F.A. McKenzie, *Canada's Day of Glory* (Toronto: William Briggs, 1918) 112.

[42] Extract from Henry Morgenthau's *All in a Life-Time* (1922) in RG 24, v. 1815, file 4-40.

[43] MU, Urquhart papers, box 1, file 12, Betty to Urquhart, 18 September 1934.

[44] T.G. Roberts, "I Remember Currie," *Ottawa Journal*, 9 April 1940.

[45] MU, Urquhart papers, 4027, box 1, file 12, Batty Macdonell to Hugh Cameron, 27 October 1934.

[46] T.G. Roberts, "I Remember Currie," *Ottawa Journal*, 6 April 1940.

[47] T.G. Roberts, "I Remember Currie," *Ottawa Journal*, 18 April 1940.

[48] "Gen. Currie, A Born Leader and Commander of Leaders," *Calgary Daily Herald*, 23 August 1919.

[49] MU, Urquhart papers, box 1, file 12, Ironside to Urquhart, handwritten, n.d. [ca. 1934].

[50] J.E.B. Seely, *Adventure* (London: Heinemann, 1931) 226.

[51] Editorial, *Canadian Defence Quarterly* XI.2 (January 1934) 128.

[52] MU, Urquhart papers, 4027, box 1, file 13, Impressions of A.C. by E.S. Hoare-Nairne.

[53] MU, Urquhart papers, 4027, box 1, file 12, Colonel C.D.H. MacAlpine to Urquhart, 12 November 1934.

[54] MU, Urquhart papers, 4027, box 1, file 12, Griesbach to Urquhart, 26 October 1934.

[55] Dancocks, *Currie*, 175.

[56] T.G. Roberts, "I Remember Currie," *Ottawa Journal*, 18 April 1940.

[57] LAC, Victor Odlum papers, MG 30 E 300, v. 3, file Currie, Odlum to Edward Kemp, 11 February 1919.

[58] See the correspondence by several of his former officers in the MU, H.M Urquhart papers, MG 4027, box 1, file 12 and file 13. For published sources, see A.G.L. McNaughton, "The Development of Artillery in the Great War," *Canadian Defence Quarterly* VI.2 (January 1929) 164; A.M.J. Hyatt, "The Military Leadership of Sir Arthur Currie," in Lieutenant-Colonel Bernd Horn and Stephen Harris (eds.) *Warrior Chiefs: Perspectives on Senior Canadian Military Leaders* (Toronto: Dundurn Press, 2001) 43–56.

[59] LAC, Victor Odlum papers, MG 30 E 300, v. 3, file Currie, Odlum to Edward Kemp, 11 Feb 1919.

[60] Bridle, *The Masques of Ottawa*, 158.

[61] Peter Simkins, "Haig and the Army Commanders," in Brian Bond and Nigel Cave (ed.), *Haig: A Reappraisal 70 Years On* (Barnsley: Pen and Sword, 1999) 92.

[62] MU, Urquhart papers, 4027, box 1, file 12, Personal Recollections of Currie by Brigadier-General Alexander Ross, ca. 1934.

[63] LAC, CP, v. 13, file 39, Currie to Ralston, 9 February 1928; and LAC, CP, v. 27, file 7, Currie to Frank Underhill, 17 September 1920; Currie's diary, 10 July 1917.

[64] William Stewart, "Attack Doctrine in the Canadian Corps, 1916–1918," (University of New Brunswick: MA Thesis, 1982) 106; LAC, RG 9, v. 3850, 61/2, First Army to Canadian Corps, 9 July 1917.

[65] LAC, CP, v. 2, file 4, Currie to Swayne, 23 January 1918.

[66] LAC, CP, v. 5, file 15, Currie to Rattray, 22 April 1920.

[67] Simon Robbins, "Henry Horne," in Ian F.W. Beckett and Steven Corvi, *Haig's Generals* (Barnsley: Pen and Sword, 2006) 112.

[68] LAC, RG 9, v. 3850, 61/4, Canadian Corps Artillery Order No. 63, 14 August 1917; G.W.L. Nicholson, *The Gunners of Canada: The History of the Royal Regiment of the Canadian Artillery, Vol. 1: 1534–1919* (Toronto: McClelland & Stewart, 1967), I/297.

[69] Christopher Pugsley, "Learning from the Canadian Corps on the Western Front," *Canadian Military History* 15.1 (Winter 2006) 24.

[70] WD, Canadian Corps, Appendix III-I-III/5, Summary of Operations, 9–16 August 1917.

[71] Currie's diary, 18 August 1917.

[72] Nicholson, *CEF*, 292; For differing views of the Hill 70 and Lens battles, see Cook, *Shock Troops*, 274–307; and the more critical Geoff Jackson, "'Anything but lovely': The Canadian Corps at Lens in the summer of 1917," *Canadian Military History* 17.1 (2007) 5–20.

[73] Nicholson, *CEF*, 295.

[74] LAC, CP, v. 27, file 7, Currie to Underhill, 17 September 1920.

[75] LAC, CP, v. 27, file 7, Currie to Underhill, 17 September 1920. Also see David Monger, "'No mere silent commander'? Sir Henry Horne and the Mentality of Command during the First World War," *Historical Research* 82.216 (May 2009) 341.

[76] LAC, RG 24, v. 1844, Battle Casualties—Hill 70 August 1917; Matthew Walthert, "Neglected Victory: The Canadian Corps at Hill 70," *Canadian Military History* 19.1 (Winter 2010) 36, note 82.

[77] LAC, CP, v. 13, file 39, Currie to Ralston, 9 February 1928; LAC, CP, v. 43, diary, 15–18 August 1917.

[78] Humphries, *The Selected Papers of Sir Arthur Currie*, 51.

[79] T.G. Roberts, "I Remember Currie," *Ottawa Journal,* 20 April 1940.

[80] LAC, CP, v. 5, file 15, Currie to Paterson, 8 March 1920.

[81] MU, Urquhart papers, box 1, file 12, Macdonell to Urquhart, 27 October 1934.

[82] Nicholson, *CEF*, 313.

[83] Currie's diary, 17 October 1917; also see LAC, CP, v. 27, file 7, Currie to Underhill, 17 September 1920.

[84] LAC, CP, v. 5, file 15, Currie to Rattray, 22 April 1920.

[85] LAC, CP, v. 27, file 7, Currie to Livesay, 26 January 1933.

[86] LAC, RG 9, v. 3859, 85/8, G.724/27-3, 20 November 1917.

[87] LAC, RG 24, v. 1810, file GAQ 1-6, Statement of Casualties at Passchendaele.

[88] F.A. McKenzie, *Canada's Day of Glory* (Toronto: William Briggs, 1918) 113.

[89] MU, Urquhart papers, 4027, box 1, file 13, Memo by Brig. General Embury.

[90] Hyatt, *General Sir Arthur Currie*, 90.

[91] LAC, CP, v. 1, file 2, Currie to Hearst, 14 November 1917.

[92] LAC, CP, v. 18, file 60, Currie to Harrington, 29 March 1928; also T.G. Roberts, "I Remember Currie," *Ottawa Journal*, 18 April 1940.

[93] Quote from MU, Urquhart papers, box 1, file 12, Macintyre to Urquhart, 20 November 1934.

[94] Dancocks, *Currie*, 123.

[95] For conscription, see J.L. Granatstein and J.M. Hitsman, *Broken Promises: A History of Conscription in Canada* (Toronto: Oxford University Press, 1977); and Carl Berger (ed.) *Conscription 1917* (Canadian Historical Readings, No. 8).

[96] Hansard, 18 May 1917, 1597.

[97] *Canadian Annual Review*, 1917, p. 520; J.L. Granatstein, "Conscription in the Great War," David Mackenzie (ed.), *Canada and the First World War* (Toronto: University of Toronto Press, 2005) 67.

[98] See Hyatt, "Sir Arthur Currie and Conscription," 287.

[99] MU, Urquhart papers, 4027, box 1, file 13, Oliver to Currie, 6 December 1917; also, Ibid., telegram from McInnes to Currie, 5 December 1917.

[100] LAC, Harold Daly papers, MG 27 II-F-9, v. 1, file 2, Currie to Daly, 10 December 1917.

[101] LAC, CP, v. 2, file "M-R," Currie to Perley, 10 December 1917.

[102] MU, Urquhart papers, 4027, box 1, file 13, Currie to Oliver, 9 December 1917.

[103] LAC, CP, v. 1, file 2, Currie to Sir William Hearst, 14 November 1917.

Chapter 10: "Once so powerful"

[1] Brown and Cook, *A Nation Transformed*, 217.

[2] Bliss, *A Canadian Millionaire*, 293.

[3] LAC, J.J. Creelman papers, MG 30 E8, file 1, diary, 19 November 1916.

[4] Marjorie Barron Norris (ed.), *Medicine and Duty: The World War I Memoir of Captain Harold W. McGill* (Calgary: University of Calgary Press, 2007) 242–3.

[5] Britton B. Cooke, "Major-General Sam Hughes," *Canadian Magazine* 45 (1915) 394.

[6] LAC, Borden papers, Hughes to Borden, 15 November 1916, 35894; House of Commons Debates, 29 September 1919, 624.

[7] Borden, *Memoirs*, II/571.

[8] *CAR* 1917, 554.

[9] Borden papers, C-4214, Casgrain to Borden, 15 November 1916, 12767.

[10] Ibid., Borden to Cassels, 24 November 1916, 12796.

[11] J.L. Granatstein, *Canada's Army: Waging War and Keeping the Peace* (Toronto: University of Toronto Press, 2002) 78.

[12] LAC, RG 24, v. 20541, file 990.009 (D2), Sam Hughes to Borden, Minute on Sir George Perley, 25 January 1917; also see, LAC, Kemp papers, v. 60, file 110, Hughes to Kemp, 30 March 1917.

[13] LAC, BP, A-1764, Hughes to Aitken, 8 December 1916.

[14] BP, A-1764, Hughes to Aitken, 8 December 1916.

[15] BP, A-1764, Hughes to Aitken, 8 December 1916.

[16] BP, A-1764, Hughes to Aitken, 5 February 1917.

[17] BP, A-1764, Hughes to Aitken, 8 December 1916.

[18] Borden, *Memoirs*, I/463.

[19] LAC, Sam Hughes papers, v. 14, file 4, Sam Hughes to Garnet, 7 March 1917.

[20] LAC, Sam Hughes papers, v. 14, file 4, Sam Hughes to Garnet, 7 March 1917; also see LAC, A.E. Kemp papers, v. 60, file 110, Hughes to Kemp, 29 March 1917.

[21] LAC, Sam Hughes papers, v. 14, file 4, Sam Hughes to Garnet, 7 March 1917.

[22] LAC, Sam Hughes papers, v. 14, file 4, Sam Hughes to Garnet, 7 March 1917.

[23] LAC, Sam Hughes papers, v. 14, file 4, Sam Hughes to Garnet, 7 March 1917; Ibid, 14-4, Bill (W. St. P. Hughes) to Garnet, 24 February 1917.

[24] Borden papers, C-4430, Borden to Macdonell, 14 December 1933, 150461.

[25] Borden, *Memoirs*, II/571.

[26] RG 24, v. 20541, file 990.009 (D2), Sir Sam Hughes to Garnet Hughes, 7 March 1917.

[27] Hansard, 30 January 1917, 253.

[28] Hansard, 30 January 1917, 254–5.

[29] Hansard, 30 January 1917, 268.

[30] Hansard, 30 January 1917, 266-7; Hansard, 2 February 1917, 419.

[31] LAC, Sam Hughes papers, v. 14, file 4, Sam Hughes to Garnet, 7 March 1917.

[32] See Norman Ward (ed.), *A Party Politician: The Memoirs of Chubby Power* (Toronto: Macmillan of Canada, 1966) 44.

[33] A few examples of his 'fact' books have survived and contain quotes, facts, and statements by himself and other members of Parliament. See LAC, Sam Hughes papers, v. 1.

[34] Capon, *His Faults Lie Gently*, 33.

[35] Winter, *Lieutenant-General The Hon. Sir Sam Hughes*, 171.

[36] W.A. Griesbach, *I Remember* (Toronto: Ryerson Press, 1946) 347.

[37] *CAR*, 1917, 466.

[38] Ward (ed.), *A Party Politician*, 46.

[39] Hansard, 19 June 1917, 2434; and *CAR*, 1917, 314-5; for an earlier reference, see Hansard, 30 January 1917, 267; LAC, Sam Hughes papers, v. 1, file 8, Hughes to Borden, 17 October 1916.

[40] For some of the largesse dispensed to Lindsay up to 1914, see *Lindsay Warder*, 28 April 1914; Brown, *Borden*, II/55.

[41] Capon, *His Faults Lie Gently*, 30.

[42] For his ideas on a new Commonwealth in the Empire, see Sam Hughes, "Canada's Future within the Empire," in E.A. Victor (ed.), *Canada's Future: What She Offers after the War* (Toronto: Macmillan Company, 1916) 10–11.

[43] This paragraph drawn from *CAR*, 1917, 314.

[44] Ian Hugh Maclean Miller, *Our Glory and Our Grief: Torontonians and the Great War* (Toronto: University of Toronto Press, 2002) 164.

[45] LAC, BP, A-1764, Hughes to Aitken, 20 August 1918; and A-1764, Aitken to Hughes, 9 Sepember 1918.

[46] Hansard, 23 February 1916, 1046.

[47] MU, Urquhart papers, 4027, box 1, file 12, Colonel C.D.H. MacAlpine to Urquhart, 12 November 1934.

[48] LAC, BP, A-1764, Hughes to Aitken, 17 August 1917.

[49] LAC, Sam Hughes papers, v. 1, file 8, Hughes to Borden, 14 January 1918.

[50] LAC, BP, A-1764, Hughes to Aitken, ca. March 1918.

[51] LAC, Sam Hughes papers, v. 1, file 8, Hughes to Borden, 1 October 1918.

[52] Hansard, 6 May 1918, 1488.

[53] LAC, Sam Hughes papers, v. 14, file 4, Sam Hughes to Garnet, 7 March 1917.

[54] Hansard, 6 May 1918.

Chapter 11: Costly Victory

[1] T.G. Roberts, "I remember Currie," *Ottawa Journal*, 6 April 1940.

[2] LAC, CP, v. 2, file 4, Currie to Swayne, 23 January 1918.

[3] Urquhart, *Arthur Currie*, 46.

[4] Chris McCarthy, "Queen of the Battlefield: The Development of Command Organisation and Tactics in the British Infantry Battalion during the Great War," in Gary Sheffield and Dan Todman (eds.), *Command and Control on the Western Front: The British Army's Experience 1914–1918* (Stroud: Spellmount, 2002) 185; also see Morton, *A Peculiar Kind of Politics*, 152–7.

[5] LAC, CP, v. 12, file 36, Currie to John Nelson, 9 December 1925; LAC, CP, v. 1, file 2, Currie to F.O. Loomis, 27 January 1918; Humphries, *The Selected Papers of Sir Arthur Currie*, 80–4.

[6] On using the 5th Division for reinforcements, see MU, Urquhart papers, 4027, box 1, file 12, Parsons, to Urquhart, 21 August 1934; LAC, CP, v. 27, file 7, Currie to McGillicuddy, n.d. (First page is missing.)

[7] Wilfrid Bovey, "General Sir Arthur Currie: An Appreciation," *Canadian Defence Quarterly* XI.2 (January 1934) 147.

[8] LAC, A.E. Kemp papers, v. 129, file B-3, Kemp to Borden, 24 February 1918.

[9] George Anderson Wells, *The Fighting Bishop* (Toronto: Cardwell House, 1971) 181.

[10] LAC, A.E. Kemp papers, v. 144, file H-4, Kemp to Borden, 25 February 1918.

[11] Hansard, 30 January 1917, 268; Hansard, 19 June 1917, 2447.

[12] MU, Urquhart papers, 4027, box 1, file 13, Currie to Swayne, 23 January 1918.

[13] MU, Urquhart papers, 4027, box 1, file 13, Currie to Loomis, 27 January 1918.

[14] LAC, CP, v. 1, file 1, Currie to Brewster, 27 January 1918.

[15] Radley, *We Lead, Others Follow*, 80. Also see Patrick Brennan, "'Completely Worn Out by Service in France': Combat Stress and Breakdown among Senior Officers in the Canadian Corps," *Canadian Military History* 18.2 (Spring 2009) 5–14.

[16] Urquhart, *Arthur Currie*, 205–6.

[17] LAC, Newton Rowell papers, MG 27 IID13, reel C-930, 1645, Currie to Rowell, 13 July 1918. I would like to thank Dr. Mark Humphries for sharing this reference with me.

[18] See Martin Kitchen, *The German Offensives of 1918* (Stroud: Tempus, 2005).

[19] *Canadian Corps Operations During the Year 1918—Interim Report* (Ottawa, 1919) 19–20; Currie's diary, 31 March 1918.

[20] Tim Travers, *How the War Was Won: Command and Technology in the British Army on the Western Front, 1917–1918* (London: Routledge, 1992) 32–7.

[21] Borden papers, C-4430, Memorandum in Connection with Sir Robert Borden's Letter respecting Sir Arthur Currie, 150503.

[22] Hew Strachan, *The First World War* (London: Simon & Schuster, 2003) 289.

[23] See Elizabeth Greenhalgh, *Victory through Coalition: Britain and France during the First World War* (Cambridge: Cambridge University Press, 2005).

[24] Stacey, *Canada and the Age of Conflict, 1867–1921*, 195.

[25] Harris, "From Subordinate to Ally," 122–3.

[26] Blake, *Haig's Papers*, 303–4.

[27] Brown, "Lieutenant-General Sir Arthur Currie and the Canadian Corps 1917–1918," 66.

[28] Currie's diary, 11 April 1918.

[29] C.B. Topp, *The 42nd Battalion, CEF, Royal Highlanders of Canada in the Great War* (Montreal: Privately printed, 1931) 186.

[30] For the angry reaction, see Cook, *Shock Troops*, 396–7.

[31] MU, Urquhart papers, 4027, box 1, file 12, Griesbach to Urquhart, 26 October 1934.

[32] MU, Urquhart papers, 4027, box 5, file 14, Hoarve-Nairne to Urqhuart, n.d. [ca. 1934]; Bridle, *The Masques of Ottawa*, 158.

[33] Urqhuart, *Arthur Currie* 223.

[34] Joseph Hayes, *The Eighty-Fifth Canadian Infantry Battalion: Nova Scotia Highlanders in France and Flanders* (Halifax: Royal Print & Litho, 1920) 103.

[35] Demill, "The 1928 Cobourg Trial," 28.

[36] Blake, *Haig's Papers*, 290.

[37] Tim Cook, "Documenting War & Forging Reputations: Sir Max Aitken and the Canadian War Records Office in the First World War," *War in History* 10(3) (2003), 265–95, and Maarten Gerritsen, "Corps Identity: The Letters, Diaries and Memoirs of Canada's Great War Soldiers" (Memorial University: Ph.D. dissertation, 2008).

[38] CWM, John McClung, 20030153-001, diary, 14 February 1917.

[39] LAC, Records of the CBC (RG 41), v. 9, H.W. Johnston, tape 1, page 14.

[40] LAC, CP, v. 1, file 1, Currie to Borden, 26 November 1918.

[41] MU, Urquhart papers, 4027, box 1, file 12, Currie to Macdonald, 5 March 1924.

[42] Currie's diary, 3 May 1918.

[43] LAC, RG 24, v. 1824, file GAQ, 5-42, The Growth and Control of the Overseas Military Forces of Canada, 2–16.

[44] Dancocks, *Currie*, 145.

[45] For Borden's hardening desire for greater autonomy, see Robert Craig Brown, "'Whither are we being shoved?' Political Leadership in Canada during World War I," in J.L. Granatstein and R.D. Cuff (eds.), *War and Society in North America* (Toronto: Thomas Nelson and Sons, 1971) 104–19.

[46] Borden, *Memoirs*, II/809–13; Currie's diary, 14 April 1918.

[47] Borden, *Letters to Limbo*, 59–61.

[48] Borden, *Memoirs*, II/809–13.

[49] Stacey, *Canada and the Age of Conflict, 1867–1921*, 220.

[50] Urquhart, *Arthur Currie*, 226–7; also, see David Lloyd George, *War Memoirs* (London, 1933) 3424.

[51] Dancocks, *Currie*, 141.

[52] A.M.J. Hyatt, "Sir Arthur Currie at Passchendaele," *Stand-To* (January–February 1965) 20.

[53] Willson, *From Quebec to Piccadilly*, 249–50.

[54] Martin Kitchen, *The German Offensives of 1918*; James McRandle and James Quirk, "The Blood Test Revisited: A New Look at German Casualty Counts in World War I," *Journal of Military History* 70 (July 2006) 686; Hew Strachan, "The Morale of the German Army," in Hugh Cecil and Peter Liddell, *Facing Armageddon: the First World War Experienced* (Barnsley: Pen and Sword, 1996) 390; LAC, RG 9, v. 4032, 1/11, Change in the Discipline and Morale of the German Army.

[55] Michael Neiberg, "'What True Misery Is': France's Crisis of Morale 1917," in Peter Dennis and Jeffrey Grey (eds.), *1917: Tactics, Training and Technology* (Canberra: The Chief of the Army's Military History Conference, 2007).

[56] E.S. Russenholt, *Six Thousand Canadian Men: Being the History of the 44th Battalion, Canadian Infantry, 1914–1919* (Winnipeg: Printed to the order of Forty-Fourth Battalion Association by the Montfort Press, 1932) 153.

[57] On logistics, see Michael P. Ryan, "Supplying the Materiel Battle: Combined Logistics in the Canadian Corps, 1915–1918," (Carleton University: MA thesis, 2005).

[58] J.F.B. Livesay, *Canada's Hundred Days: With the Canadian Corps from Amiens to Mons, Aug. 8–Nov. 11, 1918* (Toronto: T. Allen, 1919) 21.

[59] See for example, LAC, Online digitized War Diary (WD), 19th Battalion, Report of Capture of Marcelcave, 8 August 1918; F.W. Noyes, *Stretcher Bearers at the Double* (Toronto: Hunter Rose Company, 1937) 213–4; CWM, CP, 58A 1.60.3, Extract from G.H.Q. Summary of Information, 26 August 1918.

[60] *Canadian Corps Operations During the Year 1918—Interim Report* (Ottawa, 1919) 138.

[61] Nicholson, *CEF*, 407.

[62] Nicholson, *CEF*, 407.

[63] Nicholson, *CEF*, 414.

[64] "Gen. Currie on Disarmament," *The Legionary* VI.10 (March 1932) 5.

[65] MU, Urquhart papers, 4027, box 1, file 12, T. Stewart Lyon to Urquhart, 15 August 1934; for the letter, see RG 9, v. 3854, 73/5, Currie to Rawlinson, 13 August 1918.

[66] LAC, RG 24, v. 1844, 11-5, Amiens; on prisoners, see CWM, CP, 58A 1 60.3, Special Order [by Currie], 12 August 1918.

[67] LAC, RG 24, v. 1844, 11-5, Amiens.

[68] CWM, CP, 19801226-286, 58 A 1.62.1, [untitled speech by Currie], n.d. [ca. summer, 1919].

[69] Overseas Military Forces of Canada, *Report of the Ministry, Overseas Military Forces of Canada, 1918* (London, 1919) 144.

[70] Wilfrid Bovey, "General Sir Arthur Currie: An Appreciation," *Canadian Defence Quarterly* XI.2 (January 1934) 144.

[71] Currie's diary, 25 August 1918.

[72] MU, Urquhart papers, box 1, file 12, Harrington to Urquhart, 13 August 1934.

[73] LAC, CP, v. 18, file 60, Currie to Alistair, 7 December 1918.

[74] Schreiber, *Shock Army of the British Empire*, 76.

[75] Nicholson, *CEF*, 432.

[76] Currie's diary, 29 August 1918.

[77] Shane Schreiber, *Shock Army of the British Empire: The Canadian Corps in the Last 100 Days of the Great War* (Westport, Conn: Praeger, 1997) 81.

[78] LAC, Sir Arthur Currie papers, v. 2, file M-R, Currie to Morrison, 11 September 1918; WD, 4th Division, Report on the Scarpe Operations.

[79] LAC, CP, v. 1, file 1, Currie to Fraser, 7 December 1918.

[80] Daniel Dancocks, *Spearhead to Victory: Canada and the Great War* (Edmonton: Hurtig, 1987) 119.

[81] CWM, CP, 19801226, 58A 60.4, 1st Division Report of Operations, [Canal du Nord operation], Strength Return; MU, Urquhart papers, 4027, box 1, file 13, Major-General Griesbach, n.d; LAC, CP, v. 17 and 18, Cobourg trial transcripts, Currie vs. Wilson and Preston [hereafter Transcript], page 1151.

[82] Demill, "The 1928 Cobourg Trial," 35.

[83] Letters of George Hanes, 9 September 1918 and 16 September 1918. I would like to thank Ruth Thideman for generously sharing this letter from George Hanes.

[84] Sir James Edmonds, *Military Operations France and Belgium 1918*, volume IV (London: HMSO, 1947) 312.

[85] Overseas Military Forces of Canada, *Report of the Ministry,*157.

[86] Wilfrid Bovey, "General Sir Arthur Currie: An Appreciation," *Canadian Defence Quarterly* XI.2 (January 1934) 149.

[87] Transcript, 1809. Also see, LAC, CP, v. 27, file 7, Currie to Underhill, 17 September 1920. Also see Simon Robbins, "Henry Horne," in Ian F.W. Beckett and Steven Corvi, *Haig's Generals* (Barnsley: Pen and Sword, 2006) 108–9.

[88] On the role of the engineers, see Bill Rawling, *Technicians of Battle* (Toronto: Canadian Institute of Strategic Studies, 2001). For enemy defences, see Major-General Sir W. Hastings Anderson, "The Crossing of the Canal du Nord," *Canadian Defence Quarterly* 2.1 (October 1924) 65.

[89] Overseas Military Forces of Canada, *Report of the Ministry,* 162.

[90] LAC, Sir Arthur Currie papers, v. 1, file A to F, Currie to Borden, 26 November 1918.

[91] Morton, *When Your Number's Up*, 178.

[92] Currie's diary, 27 September 1918.

[93] MU, Urquhart papers, 4027, box 1, file 13, Gow to Urquhart, 15 October 1934.

[94] MU, Urquhart papers, 4027, box 1, file 13, Currie to Borden, 26 November 1918. Also see, LAC, RG 9 III-A-2, v. 353, file 106, Bristol to Embury, Press Censorship, 23 October 1918; LAC, Newton Rowell papers, MG 27 IID13, reel C-930, 1649, Currie to Rowell, 27 November 1918.

[95] MU, Urquhart papers, 4027, box 1, file 13, Currie to Borden, 26 November 1918.

[96] E.M. Andrews, *The Anzac Illusion: Anglo-Australian relations during World War I* (Cambridge University Press, 1993) 158; CWM, CP, 19801226, file 58A 1 61.4, Currie to Nelson, 5 February 1919; Daniel Dancocks, *Sir Arthur Currie: A Biography* (Toronto: Metheun, 1985) 174.

[97] LAC, CP, v. 1, file 2, Currie to Kemp, 1 November 1918.

[98] LAC, RG 24, v. 1844, file 11-5, Casualties, [Hundred Days]; Peter Simkins, "Building Blocks: Aspects of Command and Control at Brigade Level," in Dan Todman and Gary Sheffield (eds.), *Command and Control in the British Army on the Western Front* (Stroud: Spellmount, 2004) 165.

[99] J.E.B. Seely, *Adventure* (London: Heinemann, 1931) 226.

[100] MU, Urquhart papers, 4027, box 1, file 12, Macdonell to Urquhart, n.d. [ca. 1934].

[101] W.W. Murray, "General Currie and the Corps," *Canada* 9 December 1933.

[102] MU, Urquhart papers, 4027, box 1, file 12, Scudamore to Urquhart, 5 March 1935.

[103] LAC, CP, v. 2, File "M-R," Currie to Turner, 30 August 1918.

[104] Demill, "The 1928 Cobourg Trial," 36.

[105] LAC, CP, v. 2, File "M-R," Currie to Miller, 4 October 1918.

[106] For a revealing document into Currie's constant reappraisal, see CWM, CP, 19801226-286, 58A 1.62.1, Some Notes on the Recent Fighting, n.d. [ca. 13 or 14 October 1918].

[107] C.B. Topp, *The 42nd Battalion, CEF. Royal Highlanders of Canada in the Great War*, 282.

[108] Cook, *Shock Troops*, 573.

[109] LAC, CP, diary, 7 November 1918.

[110] Donn Farr, *The Silent General: Horne of the First Army* (Solihull: Helion and Company, 2007) 249.

[111] LAC, CP, v. 1, file 1, Currie to Borden, 26 November 1918.

[112] LAC, CP, v. 27, file 7, Currie to Frank Underhill, 17 September 1920.

[113] LAC, CP, v. 3, file 6, Birchall to Currie, 11 April 1919.

[114] LAC, CP, file 194, diary, 11 November 1918.

[115] Transcript, 1809.

[116] LAC, CP, v. 1, file, 2, Horne to Currie, 11 November 1918.

Chapter 12: Currie Accused, 1919

[1] For demobilization issues, see Desmond Morton and Glenn Wright, *Winning the Second Battle: Canadian Veterans and the Return to Civilian Life, 1915–1930* (Toronto: University of Toronto Press, 1987); Tim Cook, "From Destruction to Construction: The Khaki University of Canada, 1917–1919," *Journal of Canadian Studies* 37.1 (Spring 2002) 109–43.

[2] CWM, William David Bradley papers, 20090115, 26 February 1919.

[3] James Pedley, *Only This: A War Retrospect, 1917–1918* (Ottawa: The Graphic Publishers, 1927) 57.

[4] Currie's diary, 23 November 1919.

[5] Urqhuart, *Currie*, 275.

[6] MA, UP, circular, Alexander Godley to Urquhart.

[7] Currie's diary, 17 November 1918; LAC, CP, v. 15, file 44, Currie to Captain Alistair Fraser, 7 December 1918.

[8] LAC, Newton Rowell papers, MG 27 IID13, reel C-930, 1648, Currie to Rowell, 27 November 1918; Hyatt, *General Sir Arthur Currie*, 125.

[9] LAC, A.E. Kemp papers, v. 132, file C-20, Currie to Kemp, 16 March 1919.

[10] CWM, CP, 58A 1 61.4, Currie to Dobie, 9 February 1919.

[11] LAC, Sir Richard Turner papers, MG 30 E46, v. 7, file 39, Turner to Minister, OMFC, 3 April 1919.

[12] LAC, Victor Odlum papers, MG 30 E 300, v. 3, file Currie, Odlum to Edward Kemp, 11 February 1919.

[13] MU, Urquhart papers, MG 4027, box 1, file 12, Ross to Urquhart, n.d. [ca. 1934]. A.E. Kemp also investigated the rumours and found that they had been spread by Canadian soldiers coming back to France. Borden papers, 55845, Kemp to Borden, 5 March 1919.

[14] Demill, "The 1928 Cobourg Trial," 56; also see Bridle, *The Masques of Ottawa*, 163–4.

[15] LAC, CP, v. 10, file 32, Currie to General Bill Lindsay, 10 January 1920.

[16] LAC, CP, v. 15, file 44, Currie to Captain Alistair Fraser, 7 December 1918.

[17] LAC, W.A. Griesbach papers, MG 30 E15, v. 1, file 5, diary, 1914–1919, 8 December 1918.

[18] MU, Urquhart papers, box 11, file 3, Currie to Margerie Currie, 26 December 1918.

[19] LAC, CP, v. 15, file 44, Currie to Captain Alistair Fraser, 7 December 1918.

[20] MU, Urquhart papers, box 11, file 3, Currie to Margerie Currie, 26 December 1918.

[21] Hughes read this into Hansard on 4 March 1919 in his public attack on Currie. See Hansard, 4 March 1919, 207.

[22] LAC, BP, A-1764, Hughes to Aitken, 8 October 1918.

[23] LAC, BP, A-1764, Hughes to Aitken, 8 October 1918.

[24] CWM, CP, file 58A 1 61.4, Mewburn to Currie, 3 February 1919; Currie's diary, 11 March 1919.

[25] CWM, CP, file 58A 1 61.4, Hugh Dyer to Currie, 11 February 1919; MU, H.M Urquhart papers, MG 4027, box 1, file 12, Currie to Langley, 16 April 1919.

[26] W.L.M. King diaries, digitized, online at the Library and Archives Canada website, 30 May 1919.

[27] MU, Urquhart papers, 4027, box 1, file 12, Currie to Mr. Justice Gregory, 31 May 1919.

[28] LAC, CP, v. 15, file 44, Currie to Fraser, 7 December 1918.

[29] LAC, Borden papers, 55843, Currie to Kemp, 27 February 1919.

[30] Borden, *Memoirs*, II/550.

[31] Hansard, 4 March 1919, 199.

[32] LAC, Sam Hughes papers, v. 1, file 8, Hughes to Borden, 1 October 1918.

[33] House of Commons Debates, 4 March 1919, 207.

[34] CWM, CP, file 58A 1 61.7, Peck to Currie, 8 April 1919.

[35] LAC, CP, v. 18, file 64, Peck to Currie, 1 May 1928.

[36] For the confusion and hesitancy, see volume II of the Brown biography of Borden.

[37] CWM, CP, file 58A 1 61.7, Peck to Currie, 8 April 1919; CP, file 63, Peck to Currie, 2 May 1928.

[38] Urquhart, *Arthur Currie*, 277.

[39] Swettenham, *To Seize the Victory*, 4; also, see *CAR*, 1919, 34–5.

[40] *Toronto Globe*, 6 March 1919.

[41] Robert J. Sharpe, *The Last Day, The Last Hour: The Currie Libel Trial* (Toronto: Osgoode Society, 1988) 47.

[42] Cited in Dancocks, *Currie*, 195.

[43] Hansard, 14 March 1919, 467.

[44] Hansard, 14 March 1919, 468.

[45] Peck's defence made Canadian and international newspapers; see clippings in LAC, Kemp papers, v. 132, file C-20; House of Commons Debates, Session 1919, vol. 1, 14 March 1919, 468; CWM, CP, file 58A 1 61.7, Peck to Currie, 8 April 1919.

[46] CWM, CP, file 58A 1 61.5, Currie to Peck, 30 March 1919.

[47] Cited in Dancocks, *Currie*, 195.

[48] *Toronto Daily Star*, 6 March 1919.

[49] Brown and Morton, "The Embarrassing Apotheosis of a 'Great Canadian,'" 54; Urquhart, *Arthur Currie,* 31–2; Demill, "The 1928 Cobourg Trial," 12.

[50] LAC, Sam Hughes papers, file 14, file 4, Sam Hughes to Garnet Hughes, 2 May 1919.

Chapter 13: The War of Reputations

[1] *Halifax Chronicle*, 18 August 1919.

[2] MU, Urquhart papers, MG 4027, box 1, file 12, Brigadier H.H. Hertzberg to Urquhart, October 1934; Urquhart, *Arthur Currie,* 274–80.

[3] MU, Urquhart papers, box 1, file 12, Hertzberg to Urquhart, October 1934.

[4] Urquhart, *Arthur Currie,* 74.

[5] Dancocks, *Currie*, 200–1.

[6] Niall Barr and Gary Sheffield, "Douglas Haig, the Common Soldier, and the British Legion," in Brian Bond and Nigel Cave (ed.), *Haig: A Reappraisal 70 Years On* (Barnsley: Pen and Sword, 1999) 226.

[7] Borden papers, C-4430, Memorandum respecting the late Sir Arthur Currie, 13 August 1934, 150487; Borden, *Letters to Limbo*, 63.

[8] W.L.M. King diaries, digitized, online at the Library and Archives Canada website, 20 August 1919.

[9] LAC, CP, v. 5, file 15, Currie to Paterson, 8 March 1920.

[10] CWM, CP, file 58A 1 61.5, Currie to Mewburn, 17 March 1919.

[11] Demill, "The 1928 Cobourg Trial," 68.

[12] LAC, RG 9, III-B-1, v. 1033, file W-4-3, G.8/6-19, 30 December 1918; also see the correspondence in RG 24, v. 1733, file DHS-1-13.

[13] Overseas Military Forces of Canada, *Report of the Ministry*; also see the reprint in Humphries, *The Selected Papers of Sir Arthur Currie*, 211–314.

[14] *CAR*, 1919, 33; Overseas Military Forces of Canada, *Report of the Ministry*, 184.

[15] Swettenham, *To Seize the Victory*, vii.

[16] LAC, RG 24, v. 1812, file GAQ 4-5, Canadian Club Meeting No. 2, Château Laurier, 19 August 1919.

[17] LAC, RG 24, v. 1812, file GAQ 4-5, Canadian Club Meeting No. 2, Château Laurier, 19 August 1919.

[18] *CAR*, 1919, 42.

[19] *Toronto Globe*, 30 August 1919.

[20] W.L.M. King diaries, digitized, online at the Library and Archives Canada website, 30 May 1919.

[21] *Victoria Daily Colonist*, 7 October 1919; Dancocks, *Currie*, 312.

[22] Sharpe, *The Last Day*, 52.

[23] *Saturday Night*, 13 September 1919.

[24] W.L.M. King diaries, digitized, online at the Library and Archives Canada website, 30 May 1919.

[25] LAC, CP, v. 5, file 15, Currie to Radcliffe, 2 January 1920.

[26] LAC, CP, v. 3, file 8, Currie to G.P. Smith, 13 October 1919.

[27] LAC, CP, v. 5, file 15, Currie to Rattray, 19 January 1920; Ibid., Currie to Radcliffe, 6 July 1920.

[28] LAC, CP, v. 4, file 12, Currie to Lineham, 21 May 1920; LAC, Victor Odlum papers, MG 30 E300, v. 3, file Currie correspondence, Currie to Odlum, 10 March 1921.

[29] LAC, CP, v. 4, file 10, Currie to Clark, 21 May 1920.

[30] LAC, RG 24, v. 1812, GAQ 4-5, Address to the Women's Canadian Club, Montreal, 11.

[31] See Morton, *The Canadian General*, 354–7.

[32] A.M.J. Hyatt, "Sir Arthur Currie and Politicians: A Case Study of Civil-Military Relations in the First World War," in Richard Preston and Peter Dennis, *Swords and Covenants* (Croom Helm: Rowman and Littlefield, 1976) 158.

[33] Sir Arthur Currie, *Six Years at McGill* (n.d. [ca. 1926]) 2, in CWM, Currie papers, 19801226–287.

[34] See the search committee records in MU, RG 2, box 57, file 834.

[35] MU, Urquhart papers, box 1, file 16, Notes by Mr. W.M. Birks, 5 June 1936.

[36] LAC, CP, file 12, Currie to Lineham, 21 May 1920.

[37] LAC, CP, v. 5, file 15, Currie to General Percy 'P de B' Radcliffe, 6 July 1920.

[38] Dancocks, *Currie*, 207.

[39] LAC, CP, file 10, Currie to Clark, 21 May 1920.

[40] Hyatt, *General Sir Arthur Currie*, 133.

[41] Edgar Andrew Collard (ed.), *The McGill You Knew: An Anthology of Memories 1920–1960* (Don Mills: Longman, 1975) 224.

[42] LAC, Sam Hughes papers, v. 1, file 7, Hughes to Mad. Lavergne, 23 April 1918.

[43] LAC, Sam Hughes papers, v. 14, file 14-4, Sam to Garnet, 2 May 1919.

[44] LAC, Duke of Devonshire papers, MG 27 IIB4, diary extracts, microfilm A-653, 10 June 1919. I would like to thank Dr. Jeff Noakes for bringing this to my attention.

[45] Hansard, 29 September 1919.

[46] Sharpe, *The Last Day*, 52; Edward Peck, *Cy Peck, V. C.: A Biography of a Legendary Canadian* (Vancouver: Privately printed, 2006) 158–9.

[47] Hansard, 16 June 1920, 3763–4.

[48] Demill, "The 1928 Cobourg Trial," 73–4.

[49] *CAR*, 1919, 650.

[50] LAC, CP, v. 5, file 16, Currie to Scalter, 29 June 1920.

[51] LAC, Borden papers, reel C-4432, Borden to Hughes, 28 May 1921.

[52] Sam H.S. Hughes, "Sir Sam Hughes and the Problem of Imperialism," *Report of Annual Meeting of the Canadian Historical Association* 29.1 (1950) 30.

[53] Allen, *Ordeal by Fire*, 112.

[54] Capon, *His Faults Lie Gently*, 14.

[55] For the funeral, see Capon, *His Faults Lie Gently*, 13–7.

Chapter 14: Forging a New Legacy

[1] LAC, CP, v. 9, file 25, Currie to Givens, 17 November 1921.

[2] MU, Urquhart papers, box 1, file 16, Currie to Parmenter, 22 March 1928.

[3] *The Times*, London, 12 May 1920.

[4] *Ottawa Journal*, 15 May 1920.

[5] Frost, *McGill University*, 120.

[6] *CAR*, 1920, 654.

[7] Dorothy McMurray, *Four Principals of McGill: A Memoir* (Montreal: The Graduates' Society of McGill University, 1974) 16.

[8] *Montreal Herald*, 6 December 1933.

[9] Collard (ed.), *The McGill You Knew*, 228.

[10] LAC, CP, v. 12, file 37, Currie to Odlum, 12 July 1924.

[11] CWM, CP, 58 A 1.62.1, [untitled speech by Currie], n.d. [ca. summer, 1919].

[12] MU, Urquhart papers, box 1, file 16, Arts Undergraduate Banquet, 1930.

[13] Collard (ed.), *The McGill You Knew*, 21.

[14] LAC, CP, v. 5, file 14, Currie to Odlum, 10 March 1921.

[15] Dorothy McMurray, *Only Grandfathers Wore Beards* (unpublished memoir: held at the Canadian War Museum, Military History Research Centre, [n.d.]) 10.

[16] *Montreal Herald*, 6 December 1933.

[17] Sir Andrew Macphail, *McGill News* 15.1 (December 1933) 11.

[18] LAC, CP, v. 13, file 39, Currie to Richardson, 28 March 1924.

[19] MU, Urquhart papers, box 1, file 16, Urquhart notes on "leadership," Currie to Vinning, 2 April 1927.

[20] LAC, CP, v. 9, file 25, Currie to H.D. Lockhart Gordon, 22 September 1926.

[21] Sir Andrew Macphail, "Sir Arthur Currie: The Value of a Degree," *Queen's Quarterly* 41 (Spring 1934) 13.

[22] LAC, RG 24, v. 1812, file GAQ 4-5, The Canadians at Ypres, 1915, 3.

[23] LAC, CP, v. 12, file 37, Currie to Odlum, 12 July 1924.

[24] Graham, *Meighen*, I/265.

[25] LAC, CP, v. 10, file 31, Currie to Mackenzie King, 19 December 1921.

[26] W.L.M. King diaries, digitized, online at the Library and Archives Canada website, 10 April 1923; LAC, CP, v. 10, file 31, Currie to Mackenzie King, 1 September 1923; MU, Urquhart papers, box 1, file 16, The Civil Service, at Château Laurier, 25 November 1924.

[27] LAC, Victor Odlum papers, MG 30 E 300, v. 3, file Currie, Currie to Odlum, 12 July 1924.

[28] For Duguid and his challenges in writing the official history series, see Cook, *Clio's Warriors*, chapter 2.

[29] On Edmonds, see Andrew Green, *The Great War: Sir James Edmonds and the Official Histories 1915–1948* (London: Taylor & Francis, 2003).

[30] LAC, CP, v. 8, file 22, Currie to MacBrien, n.d. [ca. 1926]; also see, LAC, CP, v. 7, file 21, Currie to Crerar, 20 April 1925.

[31] LAC, RG 24, v. 1738, DHS 3-17 (vol. 2), Duguid to Edmonds, 9 December 1925; LAC, CP, v. 8, file 22, Currie to MacBrien, n.d. (ca. 1926).

[32] Quote from Tim Travers, "Allies in Conflict: The British and Canadian Official Historians and the Real Story of Second Ypres (1915)," *Journal of Contemporary History* 24 (1989) 308; Edmonds had similar problems with the Australians; see T.H.E. Travers, "From Surafend to Gough: Charles Bean, James Edmonds, and the making of the Australian Official History," *Journal of the Australian War Memorial* 27 (October 1995).

[33] RG 24, v. 1738, DHS 3-17 (vol. 3), Duguid to CGS, 13 March 1928.

[34] LAC, MG 26 K, R.B. Bennett papers (hereafter Bennett papers), Currie to Bennett, 24 March 1933.

[35] Sir Andrew Macphail, *Official History of the Canadian Forces in the Great War: The Medical Services* (Ottawa: King's Printer, 1925) 1, 12, 14, 17–24, 191–2.

[36] DHH, unprocessed registry files, box 58, file 10-4, pt. 1, MacBrien to Minister, 22 February 1922; and Macphail to MacBrien, 30 January 1923; Box 58, file 10-4, pt. 2, Macphail and Medical History, MacBrien to Private Secretary, Minister of National Defence, 18 January 1924.

[37] For this incident, see Bill Rawling, *Death Their Enemy: Canadian Medical Practitioners and War* (Ottawa: self-published, 2001) 66–8; Morton, *When Your Number's Up*, 203–4.

[38] LAC, CP, v. 10, file 29, Currie to Ross Hayter, 4 July 1922.

[39] Ian Ross Robertson, *Sir Andrew Macphail: The Life and Legacy of a Canadian Man of Letters* (Montreal-Kingston: McGill-Queen's University Press, 2008) 212.

[40] *Toronto Daily Star*, 11 July 1925.

[41] *Toronto Daily Star*, 28 July 1925.

[42] *Toronto Star*, 16 July 1925.

[43] *Toronto Telegram*, 14 July 1925.

[44] J. Boraston and G. Dewar, *Sir Douglas Haig's Command, 1915–1922* (London, 1922).

[45] See David French, "Sir Douglas Haig's Reputation, 1918–1928: A Note," *Historical Journal* 28.4 (1985) 953–60; Daniel Todman, "'Sans Peur et Sans Reproche': The Retirement, Death and Mourning of Sir Douglas Haig, 1918–1928," *The Journal of Military History* 67.4 (2003) 1083–1106; and Dan Todman, *The Great War: Myth and Memory* (London: Hambledon and London, 2005) chapter 3.

[46] LAC, CP, v. 10, file 32, Currie to Livesay, 11 January 1923.

[47] LAC, Victor Odlum papers, MG 30 E 300, v. 3, file Currie, Odlum to Currie, 6 April 1924.

[48] LAC, CP, v. 10, file 29, Haig to Currie, 30 March 1925; also see Currie to Haig, 27 April 1925. For Haig's visit, see John Scott, "'Three Cheers for Earl Haig'": Canadian Veterans and the Visit of Field Marshal Sir Douglas Haig to Canada in the Summer of 1925," *Canadian Military History* 5.1 (Summer 1996) 35–40.

[49] LAC, CP, v. 9, file 25, Currie to Gibson, 1 May 1926; also see LAC, CP, v. 10, file 29, Currie to Haig, 27 April 1925.

[50] LAC, CP, v. 9, file 25, Currie to Gibson, 29 November 1926.

[51] LAC, CP, v. 13, file 38, Currie to Pomphrey, 4 April 1925.

[52] Urquhart, *Arthur Currie*, 334.

[53] Serge M. Durflinger, *Lest We Forget: A History of the Last Post Fund, 1909–1999* (Montreal: The Last Post Fund, 2000) 71–5.

[54] For an overview, see Roger Graham, *The King–Byng Affair, 1926: A Question of Responsible Government* (Toronto: Copp Clark, 1967).

[55] LAC, CP, v. 9, file 28, Currie to Griesbach, 12 July 1926. Also see, LAC, CP, v. 15, file 44, Currie to Richardson, 16 September 1926.

ENDNOTES

Chapter 15: The Ghost of Sam Hughes, 1927–1928

[1] LAC, CP, v. 27, file 7, Walker to Currie, n.d. (ca. November 1927).

[2] "Who is the Greatest Living Canadian?" *Maclean's Magazine*, 15 May 1927, 10.

[3] Demill, "The 1928 Cobourg Trial," 83–4; S.J. R. Noel, *Patrons, Clients, Brokers: Ontario Society and Politics, 1791–1896* (Toronto: University of Toronto Press, 1990) 286. See William Thomas Rochester Preston, *My Generation of Politics and Politicians* (Toronto: D.A. Rose, 1927).

[4] Preston, *My Generation of Politics*, 370.

[5] Preston, *My Generation of Politics*, 391.

[6] *Port Hope Evening Guide*, 13 June 1927.

[7] LAC, CP, v. 18, file 60, Currie to Brothers, 30 March 1928.

[8] LAC, CP, v. 7, file 20, Currie to Campbell, 28 September 1927; John Sweetenham, *To Seize the Victory* (Toronto: Ryerson Press, 1965) 275.

[9] MU, Urquhart papers, box 1, file 16, Urquhart notes, "Byng–Currie," extract from Currie letter of 14 March 1922.

[10] LAC, Victor Odlum papers, MG 30 E 300, v. 3, file Currie, Odlum to Currie, 14 May 1928.

[11] LAC, CP, v. 18, file 60, Currie to Gow, 10 April 1928.

[12] LAC, CP, v. 18, file 60, Currie to Ralston, 22 June 1927.

[13] LAC, CP, v. 18, file 60, Currie to Anderson, 23 March 1928.

[14] MU, Urquhart papers, box 1, file 16, Currie to Parmenter, 22 March 1928.

[15] See Sharpe, *The Last Day*, 54–9, for a brilliant analysis of the Canadian legal system at the time of the trial.

[16] Transcript, 1026.

[17] Transcript, 1003.

[18] LAC, CP, v. 18, file 60, Currie to Duguid, 31 March 1928.

[19] Transcript, 954.

[20] Sharpe, *The Last Day*, 86.

[21] Sharpe, *The Last Day*, 87.

[22] *Toronto Telegram*, 17 March 1928.

[23] Sharpe, *The Last Day*, 89.

[24] Urquhart, *Arthur Currie*, 318.

[25] LAC, Victor Odlum papers, MG 30 E 300, v. 3, file Currie, Currie to Odlum, 5 April 1928; LAC, CP, v. 18, file 61, Currie to Winslow, 30 March 1928; LAC, CP, v. 18, file 64, Currie to Clark, 30 March 1928.

[26] LAC, CP, v. 18, file 59, Enemy's plan of battle, n.d.

[27] LAC, CP, v. 18, file 60, Currie to Hooper, 27 March 1928.

[28] LAC, CP, v. 18, file 61, Currie to Odlum, 5 April 1928.

Chapter 16: Trial of the Decade, April 1928

[1] LAC, CP, v. 18, file 60, Currie to Dyer, 5 April 1928.

[2] Sharpe, *The Last Day*, 99.

[3] Transcript, 47–51.

[4] Transcript, 148.

[5] Transcript, 295–299.

[6] Transcript, 26–27, 98–102.

[7] Transcript, 712.

[8] Transcript, 1028.

[9] *Toronto Telegram*, 24 April 1928.

[10] Transcript, 1207.

[11] Transcript, 1247.

[12] Transcript, 1328.

[13] Transcript, 2074.

[14] C.H.F. Carson, "Last Battle of Mons—in a Canadian Court," *Canadian Lawyer* 5.1 (February 1981) 8.

[15] Transcript, 1814.

[16] Transcript, 1820.

[17] Transcript, 1836.

[18] Transcript, 1837.

[19] Transcript, 1850.

[20] All quotes from Regan and Currie in Transcript, 1862–4.

[21] See Carson, "Last Battle of Mons," 10.

[22] Transcript, 1968.

[23] Transcript, 1970–1.

[24] Transcript, 1970–1.

[25] Transcript, 2004.

[26] Sharpe, *The Last Day*, 208–10; and "Counsel Finish Arguments in Currie Libel Suit," *Ottawa Citizen*, 1 May 1928.

[27] *Montreal Daily Star*, 1 May 1928.

[28] On the questions, see Carson, "Last Battle of Mons," 8.

[29] See Cook, *Shock Troops*, 578, for casualties on 11 November 1918.

[30] All closing remark quotations cited in Sharpe, *The Last Day*, 216–20 and *Montreal Daily Star*, 1 May 1928.

[31] For the judge's remarks, see Transcript, 2132–3.

[32] Transcript, 2152.

Chapter 17: Reputation Restored

[1] LAC, CP, v. 19, file 67, Goodland to Currie, 28 May 1928.

[2] *Ottawa Citizen*, 2 May 1928.

[3] Swettenham, *To Seize the Victory*, 19.

[4] LAC, CP, v. 18, file 61, Currie to Tait, 28 December 1928.

[5] *Montreal Daily Star*, 3 May 1928.

[6] Sharpe, *The Last Day*, 228.

[7] LAC, CP, v. 19, file 67, Currie to Dyer, 27 June 1928.

[8] LAC, CP, v. 19, file 67, Diespecher to Currie, 18 April 1928.

[9] LAC, CP, v. 19, file 65, Beattie to Currie, 3 May 1928.

[10] LAC, CP, v. 19, file 66, Caldwell to Currie, 2 May 1928.

[11] LAC, CP, v. 19, file 65, Currie to Anderson, 13 June 1928.

[12] LAC, CP, v. 19, file 65, Barclay to Currie, 11 May 1928.

[13] On weight loss and strain, see LAC, CP, v. 19, file 68, Currie to Norsworthy, 12 March 1928.

[14] LAC, CP, v. 19, file 70, George Kilpatrick, "Now it is Told: Recounting of Cobourg Trial," unpublished manuscript.

[15] LAC, CP, v. 9, file 25, Currie to Ada, 10 August 1931.

[16] LAC, Victor Odlum papers, MG 30 E 300, v. 3, file Currie, Odlum to Currie, 29 October 1928; LAC, CP, v. 8, file 24, Currie to Finley, 26 August 1929; LAC, CP, v. 11, file 33, Currie to Macdonell, 16 June 1928.

[17] LAC, CP, v. 18, file 64, Beatty to Currie, 6 June 1928.

[18] LAC, RG 24, v. 1813, file GAQ 4-15f, clipping, *Montreal Gazette*, 4 November 1942.

[19] Dancocks, *Currie*, 259.

[20] Dorothy McMurray, *Four Principals of McGill: A Memoir* (Montreal: The Graduates' Society of McGill University, 1974) 10.

[21] Dancocks, *Currie*, 261.

[22] For these pension boards, see Morton and Wright, *Winning the Second Battle*; and Rawling, *Death Their Enemy*, 105–8.

[23] For problematic wounds, see Cook, *No Place to Run*, 218–21.

[24] "Our Legion," *The Legionary* IX.5 (May 1934) 8.

[25] *Toronto Star*, 21 April 1927.

[26] Dancocks, *Currie*, 262.

[27] LAC, W.L.M. King diaries, 27 March 1930; Dancocks, *Currie*, 262–3.

[28] MU, Urquhart papers, 4027, box 1, file 12, Personal Recollections of Currie by Brigadier-General Alexander Ross, ca. 1934.

[29] For Currie's view of the problem, see "Sir Arthur Currie's Plan to Solve the Pension Tangle," *The Legionary* VI.6 (November 1931) 4–5, 28.

[30] LAC, CP, v. 9, file 25, Currie to Gibson, 29 November 1926.

[31] See Barbara Tunis, *In Caps and Gowns* (Montreal: McGill University Press, 1966) 53–6.

[32] Dancocks, *Currie*, 272–5.

[33] McMurray, *Four Principals of McGill*, 23.

[34] MU, Urquhart papers, box 1, file 12, Currie to Langley, 7 February 1927.

[35] Dancocks, *Currie*, 276.

[36] "Gen. Currie on Disarmament," *The Legionary* VI.10 (March 1932) 4.

[37] MU, Urquhart papers, box 1, file 16, radio address on Disarmament, 11 November 1931.

[38] LAC, Victor Odlum papers, MG 30 E 300, v. 3, file Currie, Currie to Odlum, 20 November 1931; LAC, CP, v. 15, file 44, Currie to Macdonell, 11 December 1931.

[39] "Gen. Currie on Disarmament," *The Legionary* VI.10 (March 1932) 4.

[40] *Montreal Gazette*, 13 December 1927.

[41] Sir Arthur Currie, "The Great Sacrifice—What has it served?" *The Legionary* Christmas Number (1933) 7.

[42] "Sir Arthur Currie's Plan to Solve the Pension Tangle, *The Legionary* VI.6 (November 1931) 4.

[43] For Currie's death, see Dancocks, *Currie*, 280.

[44] *Montreal Daily Herald*, 6 December 1933.

[45] *Montreal Daily Star*, 30 November 1933.

[46] For the funeral, see R.C. Fetherstonhaugh, "General Sir Arthur Currie: Tribute of the Graduates' Society of McGill University," *Canadian Defence Quarterly* XI.2 (January 1934) 152–5; and Ibid., "The Funeral of General Sir Arthur Currie," 156–8; and records in RG 24, v. 1815, GAQ 4-40, file: The Funeral of General Sir Arthur Currie.

[47] Garnet Hughes also assisted Hugh Urquhart in writing his biography of Currie.

[48] *Montreal Gazette*, 6 December 1933.

Conclusion: Revered and Reviled

[1] *Montreal Daily Star*, 30 November 1933.

[2] Sharpe, *The Last Day*, 246; Dancocks, *Currie*, 288.

[3] Borden papers, C-4430, Memorandum respecting the late Sir Arthur Currie, 13 August 1934, 150487.

[4] There is a third strand, and one largely confined to Quebec, which highlights the conscription crisis and how an English (imperial) majority imposed its will on a French (nationalist) minority.

[5] T.G. Roberts, "I Remember Currie," *Ottawa Journal,* 6 April 1940.

[6] Hyatt, *General Sir Arthur Currie,* preface.

[7] Swettenham, *To Seize the Victory,* viii.

[8] For the changing nature of the memory of the war in the English-speaking world, see Brian Bond, *The Unquiet Western Front: Britain's role in Literature and History* (New York: Cambridge University Press, 2002); and Dan Todman, *The Great War, Myth and Memory* (London: Hambledon, 2005).

[9] Demill, "The 1928 Cobourg Trial," 53.

[10] Dancocks, *Currie,* 285.

[11] Hyatt, "The Military Leadership of Sir Arthur Currie," 52.

[12] Capon, *His Faults Lie Gently,* 17.

[13] Leslie Frost, *The Record on Sir Sam Hughes,* 3; Capon, *His Faults Lie Gently,* introduction.

[14] Sam H.S. Hughes, "Sir Sam Hughes and the Problem of Imperialism," *Report of Annual Meeting of the Canadian Historical Association* 29.1 (1950) 30–1.

[15] Swettenham, *To Seize the Victory,* xi.

[16] Harold Sutton, "The Bookshelf," *Saturday Night,* 13 June 1931; clipping in LAC, RG 24, v. 1812, file GAQ 4–6.

[17] Pierre Berton, *Vimy* (Toronto: Random House, 1986) 41–2.

[18] Gwyn, *Tapestry of War,* 50; Dancocks, *Currie,* 255.

[19] Michael Bliss, *Right Honourable Men: The Descent of Canadian Politics from Macdonald to Chretien* (Toronto: HarperCollins, 2004) 81.

[20] "Trudeau Voted Worst Canadian in 'Unscientific' Online Poll," CBCNews.ca, 30 July 2007.

[21] J. Castell Hopkins, *Canadian Annual Review of Public Affairs, 1919* (Toronto: The Canadian Annual Review, Limited, 1920) 65–6.

[22] Sir Sam Hughes, "Some Observations on the War," *Empire Club of Canada* (Toronto: The Bryant Press, 1917) 271.

[23] Thomas White, *The Story of Canada's War Finances* (Montreal, 1921) 23.

[24] Borden papers, C-4214, see the correspondence in pages 12720–12726; Morton, *A Peculiar Kind of Politics,* 70.

ACKNOWLEDGMENTS

I have been the First World War historian at the Canadian War Museum since 2002, and the challenges of presenting the nation's complex past in a public history environment have made me a better historian. One could not hope for more enthusiastic colleagues, all of whom share a passion for museums, material culture, and military history. Although this book was written on my own time, I am grateful for the ongoing support of senior management at the Canadian War Museum, especially Dr. Dean Oliver and Mark O'Neal.

My association with Carleton University as an adjunct research professor is a happy one. I have benefited greatly from working up new courses, teaching upper-level students, and supervising graduate students. I look forward every week to seeing the dedicated students, and enjoy keeping in touch with those who have moved on to bigger and brighter futures.

Editor Tara Tovell worked painstakingly on *The Madman and the Butcher*. With her cheerfulness and skill at line and copy editing, Tara has made this a far better book, as she did for my two-volume history, *At the Sharp End* and *Shock Troops*.

I would like to thank my editor at Penguin Canada, Diane Turbide, whose expertise, professionalism, and encouragement made this a stronger book, even as she juggled many other projects as publishing director. The staff at Penguin Canada have worked diligently and I'm especially grateful to Justin Stoller, Debbie Gaudet, and David Ross.

I would also like to thank my agent, Rick Broadhead, who puts his considerable skills, expertise, and energy toward working on my behalf.

I would like to highlight the support of Terry Copp, Dr. Roger Sarty, and Michael Bechthold at the Laurier Centre for Military, Strategic and Disarmament Studies. I am especially grateful to Kathryn Rose, the Laurier Centre's archivist, who shared with me the transcripts of Sir Robert Borden's diary.

I was very lucky to be able to call upon colleagues to read and comment on the manuscript. Eric Brown, Dr. Doug Delaney, Dr. Mark Humphries, Dr. Andrew Iarocci, Dr. Peter MacLeod, and Dr. Ronald Haycock all offered insight through close readings of the manuscript. This small community of scholars is indicative of the larger one, which is generous with time and willing to share knowledge and give support.

My father, Dr. Terry Cook, read the manuscript and offered detailed edits of style and content. He, more than anyone in my life, has taught me how to write. My dad has chewed through more than a million published words over the last decade and I'm grateful for everything. The ongoing support of my mom, Dr. Sharon Cook, educator, professor, historian, and expert babysitter, is very gratifying. I want to thank both of my parents for their encouragement and love. My brother, Graham, who was wise enough to escape the clutches of history and become a successful lawyer, remains a source of inspiration.

While my head is sometimes in the past, my heart is in the present with my girls. My wife, Sarah Klotz, read the manuscript and offered expert commentary. Her unflagging support and love, along with that of our three daughters, Chloe, Emma, and Paige, allows me to do what I do. I could not write without them, and would not want to. This book is as much theirs as it is mine.

INDEX

CREDITS

Currie at Cobourg, 1928 (City of Toronto Archives, f1266 it 13157)

Death announcement of Currie, 1933 (*The Legionary,* December 1933, 6)

Soldiers of Canada poster, 1915–1916 ("Soldiers of Canada" 19790543-014 George Metcalf Archival Collection © Canadian War Museum)

Currie, 1915 (19920085-441 George Metcalf Archival Collection © Canadian War Museum)

Currie and the 50th Highlanders in prewar years, 1913–1914 (19801226-337#1 George Metcalf Archival Collection © Canadian War Museum)

Sam Hughes, 1905 (Library Archives Canada [LAC], PA-012223)

Hughes inspecting Vancouver, 1912–1913 (19810352-005 George Metcalf Archival Collection © Canadian War Museum)

Hughes on a vessel, 1915–1915 (WOD_2_01_22_2_2, University of Victoria, Brigadier General W.O.H. Dodds collection)

Currie and Haig, 1917 (LAC, PA-002497)

Beaverbrook, Hughes, and Garnet, 1916 (19930003-186 George Metcalf Archival Collection © Canadian War Museum)

"Can't even dent it," 1916 (LAC, Sir Robert Borden papers, 12737)

Currie issuing orders in the field, 1917 (19920085-826 George Metcalf Archival Collection © Canadian War Museum)

"Trouble with the deceased," 1917 (Archives and Collections Society [Capon fonds, Hughes])

Currie visiting graves, 1919 (19930065-983 George Metcalf Archival Collection © Canadian War Museum)

Entry into Mons, November 1918 (Inglis Sheldon-Williams, *The Return to Mons,* CWM 19710261-0813 Beaverbrook Collection of War Art © Canadian War Museum)

October 1918 calendar page (19680113-001 George Metcalf Archival Collection © Canadian War Museum)